Windows 8.1

Step by Step

Ciprian Adrian Rusen
Joli Ballew

ISBN: 978-0-7356-8130-9

Second Printing: April 2014

Printed and bound in the United States of America.

Microsoft Press books are available through booksellers and distributors worldwide. If you need support related to this book, email Microsoft Press Book Support at mspinput@microsoft.com. Please tell us what you think of this book at *http://www.microsoft.com/learning/booksurvey*.

Microsoft and the trademarks listed at *http://www.microsoft.com/about/legal/en/us/IntellectualProperty/Trademarks/EN-US.aspx* are trademarks of the Microsoft group of companies. All other marks are property of their respective owners.

The example companies, organizations, products, domain names, email addresses, logos, people, places, and events depicted herein are fictitious. No association with any real company, organization, product, domain name, email address, logo, person, place, or event is intended or should be inferred.

This book expresses the author's views and opinions. The information contained in this book is provided without any express, statutory, or implied warranties. Neither the authors, O'Reilly Media, Inc., Microsoft Corporation, nor its resellers, or distributors will be held liable for any damages caused or alleged to be caused either directly or indirectly by this book.

Acquisitions and Developmental Editor: Kenyon Brown

Production Editor: Melanie Yarbrough

Editorial Production: Octal Publishing Services

Technical Reviewer: Randall Galloway

Indexer: Potomac Indexing

Cover Design: Microsoft Press Brand Team

Cover Composition: Ellie Volkhausen

Illustrator: Rebecca Demarest

Contents

13   Sharing files and folders with my network   375

14   Keeping Windows 8.1 safe and secure   411

21   Troubleshooting problems   619

A   Using keyboard shortcuts and touch gestures   651

Introduction

Windows 8.1 is the latest operating system from Microsoft, and is an upgrade to Windows 8, which was released in October of 2012. Windows 8.1 brings many new features to the operating system, including but not limited to a new Start button, improved personalization options for both the Lock and Start screens, an enhanced PC Settings hub, the ability to snap up to four apps at once, improved apps with additional features, and more. Windows 8.1 is also made to run on a wider variety of devices and better incorporate multiple monitor setups. It can also be used successfully on tablets, computers with touch screens, and hybrids that combine the versatility of a laptop with the mobility of a tablet.

Although Windows 8 was groundbreaking and completely different from any other Windows operating system, Windows 8.1 is a re-imagination of even that. SkyDrive and Skype are completely integrated, there's a friendly Help + Tips app on the Start screen, and there are options available to boot directly to the Desktop. You can use the camera from the Lock screen. And there are subtle changes too, such as new apps not appearing on the Start screen, but instead only on in Apps view.

If you have read about Windows 8 or 8.1 or you have seen it in action, you know that there are many new things to learn, even if you are only moving from Windows 7. In this book, you'll learn not only which are the most important changes introduced by Windows 8.1 but also how to use its most important tools and features, so that you are productive and feel at ease as soon as possible.

Let's get started

Welcome to *Windows 8.1 Step by Step*. After reading this book, we hope you will agree that this book is the best guide for learning how to use Windows 8.1. We would love to hear what you think about our work. Also, your feedback will help us improve future books in the Windows Step by Step series.

Who this book is for

This book is for people new to Windows 8.1-based computers and Windows 8.1-based apps as well as for those upgrading from previous versions of Windows.

It's assumed that this book's readers are familiar with earlier Windows operating systems. Although the readers are new to Windows 8.1, they are not new computer users. They are familiar with the basics of using a computer, using a mouse and keyboard, opening, viewing, and saving files, switching between windows, finding content, and so forth.

What this book is about

This book is about Windows 8.1. It covers all the important things you need to learn about this operating system so that you can be productive when using it.

It starts with setting up Windows 8.1 for the first time and exploring the new Start screen. Each chapter covers more advanced information and considerations such as how to purchase and use Windows 8.1 apps browse the web with Internet Explorer 11, connect to a network, share files and folders, and prevent problems with your Windows 8.1 computer or device. This list is by no means complete; many other topics are also covered.

The book ends with a list of 20 useful tips and tricks that will improve the experience of Windows 8.1 and a few appendixes useful to people who like to do things by themselves such as installing or upgrading to Windows 8.1.

Acknowledgments

We would both like to thank Kenyon Brown and the team at Microsoft Press for making this book possible. It was a very interesting project with lots of work involved, but the result was worth it. We are proud of this book, and we hope all our readers will enjoy it and find it useful.

Ciprian would like to thank his teammate at 7 Tutorials—Marte Brengle—for patiently double-checking all his writing and pointing out mistakes he would not have noticed otherwise.

Joli would like to thank her agent, Neil Salkind (even though he is retired now), for all his hard work over the years, along with her family, Jennifer, Andrew, Allison, Dad, and Cosmo.

Conventions and features in this book

This book has been designed to lead you, step by step, through all the tasks you're most likely to want to perform in Windows 8.1. If you start at the beginning and work your way through all the exercises, you'll gain enough proficiency to use Windows. However, each topic is self-contained. If you have worked with a previous version of Windows, or if you completed all the exercises and later need help remembering how to perform a procedure, the following features of this book will help you locate specific information.

- **Detailed table of contents**   Search the listing of the topics and sidebars within each chapter.

- **Chapter thumb tabs**   Easily locate the beginning of the chapter you want.

- **Topic-specific running footers**   Within a chapter, quickly locate the topic you want by looking at the running footers at the bottom of odd-numbered pages.

- **Glossary**   Look up the meaning of a word or the definition of a concept.

- **Keyboard shortcuts**   If you prefer to work from the keyboard rather than with a mouse, find all the shortcuts in one place.

- **Detailed index**   Look up specific tasks and features in the index, which has been carefully crafted with the reader in mind.

You can save time when reading this book by understanding how the Step by Step series shows exercise instructions, keys to press, buttons to click, and other information.

Convention	Meaning
1	Numbered steps guide you through hands-on exercises in each topic.
→	The Set Up icon precedes a step-by-step exercise and indicates the practice files that you will use when working through the exercise. It also indicates any requirements you should attend to or actions you should take before beginning the exercise.

Convention	Meaning
	The Clean Up icon follows a step-by-step exercise and provides instructions for saving and closing open files or programs before moving on to another topic. It also suggests ways to reverse any changes you made to your computer while working through the exercise.
TIP	This section provides a helpful hint or shortcut that makes working through a task easier.
IMPORTANT	This section points out information that you need to know to complete the procedure.
TROUBLESHOOTING	This section shows you how to fix a common problem.
NOTE	These paragraphs provide a helpful hint or shortcut that makes working through a task easier.
Ctrl+C	A plus sign (+) between two key names means that you must press those keys at the same time. For example, "Press **Alt+Tab**" means that you hold down the Alt key while you press Tab.
Boldface type	Program features that you click or press are shown in boldface type.
Blue italic type	Terms that are explained in the glossary at the end of the book are shown in italic type within the chapter.
Blue boldface type	Text that you are supposed to type appears in color and bold in the procedures.
Italic type	Folder paths, URLs, and emphasized words appear in italic type.

Downloading and using the practice files

Before you can complete the exercises in this book, you need to copy the book's practice files to your computer. These practice files, and other information, can be downloaded from here:

http://aka.ms/Win8_1SbS/files

Display the detail page in your web browser and follow the instructions for downloading the files.

The following table lists the practice files for this book.

Chapter	File
Chapter 1: Introducing Windows 8.1	
Chapter 2: Personalize your Windows 8.1 device	
Chapter 3: Using apps on the Start screen	Carriage.jpg
	Farmhouse.jpg
	Sheep.JPG
	Trees.jpg
	Flying over the Hoover Dam.3GP
Chapter 4 Organizing files and folders	Hello from Joli and Ciprian.wma
	Notepad.txt
	Elevator.jpg
	Ferris Wheel.jpg
	Old Pub.jpg
	Take Off.3GPP
	The Stratosphere Ride in Las Vegas.3GPP
Chapter 5: Using Internet Explorer 11	None
Chapter 6: Using SkyDrive	Document1.docx
Chapter 7: Using the social apps	Document1.docx
Chapter 8: Shopping in the Windows Store	None
Chapter 9: Having fun with multimedia	None
Chapter 10: Playing games	None
Chapter 11: Connecting to a network and the Internet	None
Chapter 12: Allowing others to use the computer	PictureA.jpg
	PictureB.jpg
Chapter 13: Sharing files and folders with my network	None
Chapter 14: Keeping Windows 8.1 safe and secure	None
Chapter 15: Preventing problems	None
Chapter 16: Supervising a child's computer use	None
Chapter 17: Making my computer accessible	None

Chapter	File
Chapter 18: Using Windows 8.1 at work	None
Chapter 19: Using touch-compatible devices	None
Chapter 20: Tips for improving your computing experience	ForPrinting.pdf
	Lock - Switch User
	Restart
	Shut Down
	Sign out
	Sleep
	Stop Shut Down
Chapter 21: Troubleshooting problems	None
Appendix A: Using keyboard shortcuts and touch gestures	None
Appendix B: Enhancements for using multiple displays	None
Appendix C: Installing and upgrading to Windows 8.1	None
Appendix D: Moving your data and settings to Windows 8.1	None

Getting support and giving feedback

The following sections provide information on errata, book support, feedback, and contact information.

Errata

Every effort has been made to ensure the accuracy of this book and its companion content. If you do find an error, please report it on the Microsoft Press site:

1   Go to *http://microsoftpressstore.com*.

2   In the Search box, enter the book's ISBN or title.

3   Select your book from the search results.

4   On your book's catalog page, find the Errata & Update tab.

5   Click View/Submit Errata.

You'll find additional information and services for your book on its catalog page. If you need additional support, please send an email to Microsoft Press Book Support at *mspinput@microsoft.com*. Please note that product support for Microsoft software is not offered through the preceding addresses.

We want to hear from you

At Microsoft Press, your satisfaction is our top priority and your feedback is our most valuable asset. Please tell us what you think of this book at:

http://www.microsoft.com/learning/booksurvey

The survey is short, and we read every one of your comments and ideas. Thanks in advance for your input!

Stay in touch

Let's keep the conversation going! We're on Twitter at:

http://twitter.com/MicrosoftPress

Chapter at a glance

Navigate

Navigate the Start screen, page 14

Use

Use the new Start button, page 14

Search

Search for anything, page 25

Switch

Switch among open apps, page 40

Introducing Windows 8.1

IN THIS CHAPTER, YOU WILL LEARN HOW TO

- Set up Windows 8.1.

- Use Charms.

- Access the traditional desktop.

- Customize File Explorer.

- Work with windows and apps.

- Explore PC Settings and Control Panel.

- End a computing session.

Microsoft released Windows 8 in the fall of 2012, and this new and innovative operating system was very different from anything Microsoft had ever offered before for use with computers and tablets. For one, it supported touch natively—encouraged it in fact—and for another, it introduced the lock screen, Start screen, and apps like Mail and People. The operating system was also designed so that it could be used on virtually any device and by any type of user. At that same time Microsoft also unveiled the Windows Store, a virtual marketplace from which you could obtain more apps created by both Microsoft and third parties. It also included access to additional stores for music, video, TV, games, and so on. In addition, Windows 8 integrated the Microsoft account, a logon option that could sync settings and personalization options across multiple devices and offered free Microsoft SkyDrive space in the cloud. There was more to it of course, and this is only a brief overview of its capabilities.

Windows 8.1 is the latest update to this operating system. Windows 8.1 includes just about everything Windows 8 did and also offers many new features and personalization options. There is a Start button for one, and there are lots of new possibilities for customizing the Start and lock screens. Many of the apps have been updated, too, and there are fresh built-in apps like Calculator and Alarms. Beyond that, there are new Search features that incorporate the Bing search engine, the option to boot directly to the desktop (bypassing the

Start screen), and the capability to show four apps on the screen at once. The Camera app has been updated to include more photo and video taking and editing options. The Photos app offers new editing options, and there are hundreds of other new features in addition to these. All of these things, combined with what remains intact from Windows 8, makes Windows 8.1 easier to use and simpler to incorporate into your daily life than ever before.

Getting started with Windows 8.1

The first time you press the power button on a new computer, laptop, ultrabook, or tablet running Windows 8.1, you are prompted to perform a few setup tasks. After those tasks are complete, each time you press the power button or wake the computer from sleep, the Windows 8.1 lock screen appears. You can configure the lock screen to show various notifications (such as the number of new emails you've received) and customize it with your own photos in the form of a slide show. The lock screen makes it possible for you to see what is happening with some apps without having to log on and access the Start screen and the related apps. If no one is logged on, the lock screen still shows the time and date, information about a laptop's battery, and the network to which the computer is connected.

You bypass the lock screen to get to the logon options, where you select the desired user and enter a password, PIN, or picture password to gain access to the Windows 8.1 Start screen.

TIP There are several ways to bypass the lock screen, and you'll learn about these later in the chapter. If you're ready now though, click once on the lock screen.

In this chapter, you'll work through the primary setup tasks, and then you'll learn the ways to bypass the lock screen and get to the Start screen. Once there, you'll learn how to open apps, open desktop apps on the traditional desktop, use the new Start button, access Control Panel, use PC Settings, and safely end a computing session. Along the way, you'll begin to personalize the computer so that it's uniquely yours.

TIP Do you need a quick refresher on the topics in a chapter? See the key points at the end of each chapter.

PRACTICE FILES You do not need any practice files to complete this chapter. For more information about practice file requirements, see "Using the practice files" at the beginning of this book.

Setting up Windows 8.1

The first time you turn on a new computer running Windows 8.1, you are prompted to personalize the background color of the Start screen, name your device, and choose how you sign in to it, among other things. If a network is available, you can opt to connect to that, too.

TIP If you have already set up your computer running Windows 8.1, it is possible to make changes to the choices you made using Control Panel and PC Settings if you aren't pleased with them. You'll learn how to access Control Panel later in this chapter, and you'll learn about the PC Settings options here and throughout this book.

The Windows 8.1 personalization process prompts you to configure or input the following information (you might have already done this):

- **Background Color**   You choose the background color by using a slider provided for that purpose.

- **PC Name**   Your computer must have a name that is unique on your local area network. You can't have spaces or special characters in the name, such as !, @, +, and so on, but you are notified if you try to input a character that is prohibited.

- **Network**   If your computer detects a network, you are prompted to join it. If you want to join, and if it is a protected network, you must also input the password. You should connect to your local area network during setup. If you aren't prompted to join a network during the setup process or you are unable to, but you know one is available, make sure after setup completes that you've either connected an Ethernet cable or enabled the wireless feature on your computer and try to join the network then.

- **Settings**   These settings relate to how and when the computer installs updates; how Windows 8.1 protects the computer from unsafe content; whether apps can personalize the information offered through them based on your location, name, and account picture; how to share your data; and which keyboard settings to use. You can customize the available settings or use Express Settings. Often, choosing Express Settings is fine; you can always change the options later.

- **Microsoft account or Local User account**   You choose how you want to log on to your computer. If you have a Microsoft account and you want to access the data already associated with it, such as apps you've acquired from the Windows Store or photos you've saved to SkyDrive, or you want to sync settings (such as for Microsoft Internet Explorer Favorites and desktop backgrounds) across other computers running Windows 8.1, you should acquire and/or configure your Microsoft account during this step. You must have a Microsoft account to access and make purchases from the Windows Store, use SkyDrive, and use many of the other Windows 8.1 apps. If you do not have an account or do not want to sync with your existing Microsoft account, choose a local account instead.

> **IMPORTANT** In this book we assume you are using a Microsoft account. If you don't have one, get one the next time you are prompted. You will be prompted when you try to use an app that requires it.

- **Password**   This is the password you enter to unlock your computer. If you input a Microsoft account during setup, input the password already associated with that account. If you created a local account during setup, you can create a password for that account now. Although creating a password for a local user account is not mandatory, you should input one. Later, you can create other ways to unlock the computer, including using a picture password or a four-digit PIN (personal identification number).

  TROUBLESHOOTING You must be connected to the Internet during setup (which means you must have set up network access when prompted) to obtain a new Microsoft account. If you are having trouble with the related step, skip it and create an account after you are connected to a network. (You'll be prompted to do this when you open an app that requires it.)

- **Password Hint**   This comprises a few words that you type to remind you of your local account's password if you ever forget it. Input if prompted.

- **Set up your PC**   If applicable, you can choose an existing PC to sync your settings from, or, you can set your computer up as a new PC.

- **SkyDrive**   If you configured a Microsoft account during the personalization process, you will be prompted to make a choice whether to use SkyDrive.

After you've done these things, you'll need to wait a few minutes for Windows 8.1 to get your apps ready. The computer is ready to use when the Start screen appears.

Identifying your edition of Windows 8.1

There are three main editions of Windows 8.1 for consumers and small businesses: Windows 8.1, Windows 8.1 Pro, and Windows RT. (A Windows 8.1 Enterprise edition is available but only to customers with Enterprise licensing.) Consumers can purchase the first two from stores selling Windows 8.1. Windows RT is available on computers and tablets powered by ARM processors such as those used in today's smartphones and tablets; as a consumer, you can't purchase Windows RT separately and install it on your own computer or device.

Windows 8.1, Windows 8.1 Pro, and Windows 8.1 Enterprise are available in both 32-bit and 64-bit editions.

The key features (and this is a partial list) of each edition of Windows 8 are included in the following table.

Feature name	Windows 8.1	Windows 8.1 Pro	Windows RT
Upgrades from Windows 7 Starter, Home Basic, Home Premium, Windows 8	x	x	
Upgrades from Windows 7 Professional, Ultimate, Windows 8 Pro		x	
Start screen, Semantic Zoom, Live tiles	x	x	x
Windows Store	x	x	x
Apps (Mail, Calendar, People, Photos, SkyDrive, Music, Video, and so on)	x	x	x
Microsoft Office RT (Word, Excel, PowerPoint, OneNote, Outlook)			x
Internet Explorer 11	x	x	x
Device encryption	x	x	x
Connected standby	x	x	x
Microsoft account	x	x	x
Desktop	x	x	x
Installation of x86/64 desktop software	x	x	
File Explorer	x	x	x
Windows Defender	x	x	x
SmartScreen	x	x	x
Windows Update	x	x	x
Enhanced Task Manager	x	x	x

Feature name	Windows 8.1	Windows 8.1 Pro	Windows RT
Switch languages on the fly (Language Packs)	x	x	x
Better multiple monitor support	x	x	x
Storage Spaces	x	x	
Windows Media Player	x	x	
Exchange ActiveSync	x	x	x
File History	x	x	x
ISO / VHD mount	x	x	x
Mobile broadband features	x	x	x
Picture password	x	x	x
Play To	x	x	x
Remote desktop (client)	x	x	x
Reset and Refresh your computer or device	x	x	x
Snap	x	x	x
Touch and Thumb keyboard	x	x	x
Trusted boot	x	x	x
VPN client	x	x	x
BitLocker and BitLocker To Go		x	
Boot from VHD		x	
Client Hyper-V		x	
Domain Join		x	
Workplace Join	x	x	x
Group Policy		x	
Remote desktop (host)		x	

Windows 8.1 Enterprise provides all the features in Windows 8.1 Pro and additional features to assist with IT organization (Windows To Go, AppLocker, App Deployment, and so on). You might see this edition on a computer you use at work, but it's likely not the edition you have installed on your personal desktop computer or laptop.

Minimum system requirements

To run Windows 8.1, Microsoft recommends using a computer or device that has the following minimum requirements:

- 1 GHz or faster processor
- 1 GB RAM (32-bit) or 2 GB RAM (64-bit)
- 16 GB available hard disk space (32-bit) or 20 GB (64-bit)
- DirectX 9 graphics device with WDDM 10 or higher driver

However, this is the bare minimum required for Windows 8.1 to run, and there are a few caveats of which you need to be aware:

- Windows 8.1 apps have a minimum 1024 x 768 screen resolution. If you attempt to run the new Windows 8.1 apps with less than this resolution (for example, 800 x 600), you'll receive an error message.

- To show two Windows 8.1 apps on the screen at one time by using the Snap feature, you must have a minimum display resolution of 1366 x 768. To show three at once, you'll need a higher resolution than that. To show four apps at one time, you'll need a resolution of 2560 x 1440. If you have dual monitors, these statistics apply to both individually. So, with two monitors you might be able to show eight apps at one time!

- Using Windows 8.1 on a single-core processor running at 1 GHz is possible but won't be a great experience. Using at least a dual-core processor running at 1 GHz (processors that were sold from 2006 onward) is recommended. For the most part, the newer the processor, the smoother the experience.

- Using the 32-bit version of Windows 8.1 on a system with 1 GB of RAM will work, but the experience won't be great. For a smooth experience, you should have at least 2 GB of RAM, regardless of the Windows 8.1 version you are using, is recommended.

- The 16 GB or 20 GB (depending on the version) of space you must have available on your hard disk is the bare minimum for installing and using Windows 8.1. If you plan to install many apps and games, having at least 25 GB or more for the partition on which Windows 8.1 is installed is recommended.

- Using Windows 8.1 on solid state disks (SSDs) instead of traditional hard disks will provide a huge performance increase. You will enjoy the fastest start procedure ever experienced with a Windows operating system. Also, the apps and games will launch much faster than with traditional hard disks.

If you plan to install Windows 8.1 by yourself, read Appendix C, "Installing and upgrading to Windows 8.1." It provides clear, step-by-step instructions for installing and upgrading to Windows 8.1.

Windows RT

Windows RT often comes preinstalled on smaller, often less-powerful tablets, that run on ARM processors and offer touch navigation. Windows RT is a special case for the Windows operating system family, though. You can't buy Windows RT on a DVD and install it yourself, and Windows RT devices come with their own edition of Microsoft Office, called Microsoft Office RT, which now comes with Outlook RT. Windows RT is a sort of pared-down version of Windows 8.1.

That said, you can do almost anything with an RT device you can do with Windows 8.1 and Windows 8.1 Pro: You can access apps, SkyDrive, use device encryption, access the Internet, get more apps from the Windows Store, and so on. However, Windows RT does have its limitations. It is not a full-fledged operating system in the sense that you might be used to. One of the notable limitations is the ability to install apps that do not come from the Windows Store. You can't download a desktop app from the Internet or install it from a CD or DVD; all apps must come from the Windows Store. It is also limited in how you share media, and it does not come with Windows Media Player, among other things.

IMPORTANT This book was written with Windows 8.1 and Windows 8.1 Pro users in mind. You'll see references to Windows RT here, but this book is not specifically written for it.

Adapting exercise steps

The screen shots shown in this book were captured at a screen resolution of 1024 × 768, at 100 percent magnification, unless apps needed to be captured side by side. In these instances, we used 1366 x 768. (Most screen shots have been cropped to show the relevant parts, as well.) If your settings are different, what you see on your screen might not look the same as the one shown in this book.

If differences between your display settings and ours cause something to appear differently on your screen than what you see here, you might be able to locate a missing feature by maximizing a window (when working on the desktop), right-clicking inside an app to view charms we've called out; hovering the cursor over a relevant group, feature, or tab in a desktop app to see a tooltip; or expanding a menu or group by clicking the applicable down arrows. You can change your resolution in a worse-case scenario by right-clicking an empty area of the desktop and choosing Screen Resolution to get started.

Beyond that, in this book, we provide instructions based on traditional keyboard and mouse input methods. If you're using a touch-enabled device, you might give commands by tapping with your finger or tapping with a stylus. If so, substitute a tapping action any time we instruct you to click a user interface element. Use a double-tab when instructed to double-click the mouse. Also note that when we tell you to enter information, you can do so by typing on a keyboard, tapping in the entry box under discussion to display and use the On-Screen Keyboard, or even speaking aloud, depending on your computer or device. When we instruct you to click and drag, you touch, hold, and drag instead. Finally, for the most part, when we direct you to right-click the mouse, try a long tap on the computer screen.

SEE ALSO For more information about using a touch device, refer to Chapter 19, "Using touch-compatible devices."

Using the lock screen

The Windows 8.1 lock screen is much more functional than any lock screen you might have encountered in previous Microsoft operating systems, even Windows 8. Without unlocking your device you can view the time and date, and the lock screen shows whether you're connected to a network. If you are using a laptop, it also shows the status of the battery. You can also view small icons for your favorite apps here (if you are logged on) so that you can see the status of those apps without leaving the lock screen. You can even choose the photos you want to view there in a slide show. There are lots of ways to bypass the lock screen and unlock the computer. After you bypass this screen, you input your password.

TIP To access the camera (if one exists) while the lock screen is engaged, drag from the top to the bottom on the lock screen. (In contrast you can drag from bottom to top to access the log on screen.)

How you unlock the lock screen depends on the type of computer you're using.

- **Traditional desktop computer**   Press any key on the keyboard or click the mouse anywhere on the screen, or drag upward from the bottom of the screen. Type your password when prompted.

- **Traditional laptop computer**   Press any key on the keyboard or click the mouse (or appropriate trackpad button) anywhere on the screen. If applicable, type your password when prompted. You can also hold down the left trackpad button and drag your cursor upward.

- **Touch-compatible computer or tablet**   Place your finger anywhere near the middle or bottom of the screen and flick upward. If applicable, type your password when prompted.

Exploring the Start screen

After you've unlocked the computer, the Start screen appears, displaying tiles. If there are more tiles than there is space on the screen, you'll see a scroll bar across the bottom of the screen. When you move your cursor, a down arrow appears in the lower-left corner of the screen that offers access to apps that are not shown on this screen.

Tiles can serve many purposes. Many of the tiles open apps such as Mail, People, and Maps. All of the tiles you see in the preceding graphic are apps. Some of these tiles also offer up-to-date information for the app they represent; these are called *Live tiles*. You do not need to open the app to view the basic data a Live tile offers. For example, after you configure the Weather app, it can show up-to-date weather information for a city, and the Calendar app can show upcoming appointments and birthdays. This data appears on the Start screen so that you have access to it without opening the app itself. The information is dynamic and changes as the information it represents does. If you need to see more than a preview of the information, you can click the tile, and the app opens in a new screen from which you can access all its features. People, Calendar, Weather, Photos, Mail, and similar apps all do this. (You can get more apps from the Windows Store.)

SEE ALSO For more information about buying apps, read Chapter 8, "Shopping in the Windows Store."

Beyond offering access to the default apps that come with Windows 8.1 (and any you acquire from the Windows Store), the Start screen can also offer tiles for the majority of the desktop applications (desktop apps) you install yourself. You might see tiles for Microsoft Word, Microsoft Outlook, Microsoft PowerPoint, Adobe Photoshop, or other apps. Note that these are not apps like Mail and Weather. They're called desktop apps, and they are the traditional applications with which you are likely familiar. Often you obtain these by downloading them from a website or by installing them from a CD or DVD. (In contrast, you can get apps only from the Windows Store.)

To open an app from the Start screen or Apps view, you click its tile. To open a desktop app you either click its tile on the Start screen or Apps view, or you click its shortcut on the desktop. What you see after you do this depends on what you've clicked; an app will open in its own screen, which will take up the entire screen, whereas a desktop app will open on the desktop. It's important to note that you can also opt to open the traditional desktop from the Start screen. To do this, click the Desktop tile.

If you leave the Start screen and want to go back to it, tap the Windows key on your keyboard. Tablets often have a physical Windows button. Alternatively, you can position the cursor in the lower-left corner and click the Start button that appears there.

Moving around on the Start screen

It's likely that you will have more tiles on the Start screen than can be displayed on the viewable portion of it, so you need to know some techniques for getting to those tiles. To move around on the Start screen, you can use your mouse, keyboard, trackpad, or appropriate touch gesture. The method you choose depends on what kind of computer you have. Listed here are a few ways to move around on the Start screen (and there are others not listed here).

1

- **Scroll bar** Drag the scroll bar, which is at the bottom of the screen and appears when you move your cursor there. On a laptop with a trackpad, hold down the left mouse button while you drag across the trackpad, or position the cursor to the left or right of the scroll bar and click. On a tablet, you will see the scroll bar across the bottom when you flick left and right, but you don't need to have your finger on it to use it. Finally, using a mouse, click to the left or right of the scroll bar to navigate with it.

- **Flick left and right** Place your finger on an empty area of the screen and flick from left to right or right to left to scroll through the available tiles. You can also drag your finger slowly in lieu of flicking quickly. You must have touch-compatible hardware for this to work.

- **Auto scroll** Use your mouse's scroll wheel (in an up-and-down motion) to move through the tiles from left to right and right to left.

- **Pinch** Using touch, position two or more fingers apart from each other on the screen. Pinch inward to make all the tiles smaller, making it possible for you to see more tiles on the screen. Pinch outward for opposite results.

- **Click the down arrow** Move your mouse and in the lower-left quadrant of the screen click the down arrow that displays to access all of the available tiles.

TIP To make everything smaller on the Start screen without using the pinch technique, position your mouse in the lower-right corner and click the – sign that appears on the right end of the scroll bar. Click anywhere other than on a tile to return the tiles to their original size.

As noted in the previous bulleted list, clicking the down arrow that appears on the Start screen when you move the mouse cursor takes you to the Apps view (click the up arrow to return to the Start screen), as does flicking upward (click downward to return to the Start screen). This screen offers access to all of the available tiles.

As you might expect, if you click any tile on the Start screen or the Apps view, something opens. The desktop might open; a traditional window might open; an app might open in its own window without need of the desktop; or, a file, contact card, website, folder, or any other applicable window might open. Whatever happens, the Start screen disappears.

TIP If you move away from the Start screen, it's easy to return to it. Just press the Windows key on the keyboard, the Start button, or the Windows button on your tablet.

Moving tiles on the Start screen

You might already know that you'll use some apps regularly, such as Weather, Maps, SkyDrive, or Mail, simply by looking at the available tile names. You might also determine that there are some you won't use very much, if at all (perhaps Sports or Finance). If that is the case you could reposition the tiles on the Start screen to make your most-used tiles easily accessible (or you could wait and do it later when you have more experience with the apps). As an example, if you know that you'll use the Music app often, you might put that tile in the first position on the Start screen.

In this exercise, you'll move a tile from its current position on the Start screen to the first position. Repeat with other tiles as desired to personalize your Start screen.

 SET UP
Start your computer and unlock the lock screen. You need access to the Start screen for this exercise.

1 On the **Start** screen, locate the orange **Music** tile (it has headphones on it).

2 Click and hold the **Music** tile.

3 Drag the **Music** tile to the first position on the far-left side of the screen.

 **CLEAN UP**
The app is repositioned.

TIP If you move too many tiles now, what you see on your Start screen will be different from what you see in this chapter.

Customizing the Start screen with Live tiles

You know you can move tiles on the Start screen to another area of the screen to make those tiles more accessible. You can also personalize a few select tiles independently so that the information available on them suits your personal needs. For example, you can set your location for the Weather app (or give it permission to determine your location), and it will supply current weather information from the Start screen (provided it can get that information from the Internet). If you want to know more about the weather, you just click the app to open it. These interactive and customizable tiles are Live tiles, which mean that they are updated often with new information.

Customizing any interactive tile generally only requires you to open the app, access the customizable tools and features (called charms) with which you can change the settings, and input the desired information or make the desired choices. You might only need to click Allow, as well, to let the app learn your location.

In this exercise, you'll personalize the interactive Weather app located on the Start screen by letting the app determine your current location and adding a secondary favorite location.

 SET UP
You do not need any practice files to complete this exercise. If you aren't on the Start screen, position your mouse in the lower-left corner of the screen and click the Start button that appears. On a tablet, press the Windows button if available.

1   On the **Start** screen, click **Weather**. If prompted, click **Allow** to let this app learn your location.

2   Right-click the screen to access the available settings.

TIP Charms often appear after right-clicking inside an app.

3   Click **Places**.

4   In the Favorites section, click the + sign, and then type a city and state as applicable; if your city appears in a list, click it. Otherwise, click **Add** and make a selection from the results given. Repeat as desired.

⊗ CLEAN UP On the Places page, click the Back arrow to return to the main Weather app screen. To leave this app and return to the Start screen, position your cursor in the lower-left corner of the screen and click the Start button that appears.

TROUBLESHOOTING Live tiles and apps get their information from the Internet; thus, a working Internet connection must be available to retrieve information.

Using charms

Charms appear when you position your mouse in a specific area of the screen. Charms can also appear when you right-click inside an app. Software and hardware manufacturers can customize charms, so you won't always see the same charms for every app. In the previous section, you saw the charms available for the Weather app.

Windows 8.1 has some default charms that appear when you call on them, and their names do not change (although what you see when you click them can). To see these charms, position your mouse in the lower-right corner or upper-right corner of any screen. These are called *hot corners*. When you position your cursor here, the charms fly out from the right side. Charms include Settings, Devices, Start, Share, and Search.

TROUBLESHOOTING If you are using a device without a physical keyboard or mouse, swipe inward with your finger or thumb from the middle of the right side of the screen to see the default charms. Also, the background you see behind the charms depends on what you are doing when you access them, but the charms will always be the same.

KEYBOARD SHORTCUT Press Windows key+C to show the charms.

After the charms appear, their titles appear under them as you move your cursor toward them. You can show these charms while on the Start screen, the desktop, in apps, and in other windows and views. What you see when you click any charm depends on what is currently open and, if applicable, selected, when you access the charms.

When the charms are available, just click one to use it. When you click a charm (except for Start), a new pane opens and configuration options (or search or share options) appear. What you see depends on the charm you click.

The following list describes the five default charms available in Windows 8.1, from any screen, from the bottom-right or top-right hot corner.

- **Settings** Use this charm to access PC Settings, to get information about your network, to change sound levels, to set screen brightness, to turn notifications on or off, to turn off your computer, and more. If you access this charm while in an app (perhaps Calendar), you'll see different options at the top of the Settings pane. The following illustration shows what you see if you click the Settings charm while on the desktop.

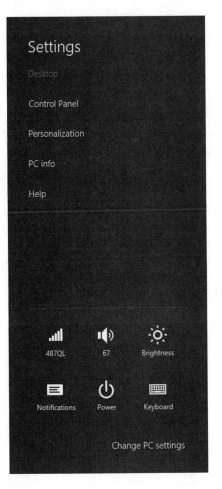

- **Devices**   Click this charm to access the devices that are available for use with the current app, screen, or window. For instance, you can use a second monitor if such a device is available, print, or play media.

- **Start**   Click this charm to access the Start screen.

- **Share**   Click this charm to access share options applicable to the current activity or open app. What you see here will differ depending on the app that's open. Sharing using the Photos app is a common way to use the Share charm.

- **Search**   Click this charm to open the Search pane. Use the Search window in the pane to search for anything on your computer, related settings, files, web images, and web videos. You'll learn how to search for something next.

TIP Try to get used to using the Windows key+C keyboard shortcut to access these charms if you prefer a keyboard over other options.

Searching for data, apps, files, and settings

Although there are many ways to search for something on a computer running Windows 8.1, one way is to simply start typing while you are on the Start screen. When you do, the Search pane opens and whatever you've typed appears in the Search window, with results underneath. The results might change as you continue to type. You can also invoke Search by using the Windows key+Q keyboard shortcut or by clicking Search from the charms. If you have a touch-only tablet, flick in from the right side and tap Search (at which point the On-Screen Keyboard appears, with which you can type what you're looking for). However you get there, when the Search pane is available and you type a few letters, results begin to appear.

You can click any option in the list of results if you see exactly what you want, perhaps an app or a file name. You can press Enter on the keyboard or click the magnifying glass to let Windows 8.1 and Bing decide what it thinks you're looking for. What appears in the results after allowing the search depends on that which you're searching. If it's a person, you'll probably get information from Wikipedia. If you've typed a place, you might get directions, reviews, and store hours. If you type the name of your favorite music album, you'll likely get results that include videos and music. In our example, pressing Enter on the keyboard causes the Finance app to open. With the results on the screen—no matter what kind of results they are—you can now scroll through the search view to see the information offered. You can click any item to see more information.

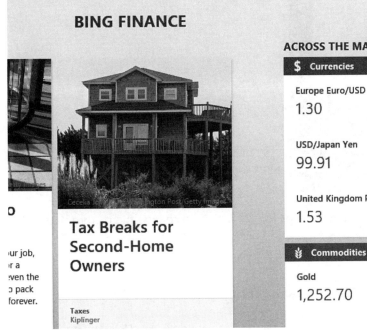

As you work with the Search feature, you'll learn that you can narrow your search by choosing from the available options in the Search pane. By default, Everywhere is the selected setting, which means that the results will come from all of the places Search can access. You can cull the results by clicking the down arrow adjacent to Everywhere and selecting Settings, Files, Web Images, or Web Videos.

In this exercise, you'll search Settings for the option to change the picture that appears on your computer's lock screen.

 SET UP
You do not need any practice files to complete this exercise.

1 Using any method, open the **Search** pane. Windows key+S is one option. Touch only users can swipe in from the right.

2 In the search window, type Lock Screen.

The Search pane shows results from everywhere.

3 Click the down arrow adjacent to **Everywhere** and then click Settings.

The Search pane shows results related to settings only.

4   Locate **Change the picture on your lock screen**.

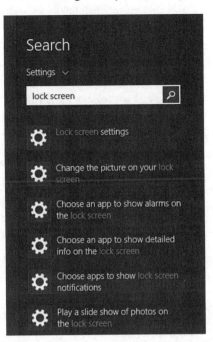

⊗ CLEAN UP

Click Change The Picture On Your Lock Screen if desired. Explore the options and click a new background if you'd like. Press the Windows key on the keyboard to return to the Start screen.

TIP When searching for documents, pictures, videos, and so on, in the Search pane, click Files.

Access the traditional desktop

If you've ever used a Windows-based computer, you are familiar with the traditional desktop. This is the screen on which you see the Recycle Bin and the taskbar, and it is where you accessed your personal folders, opened and worked with files, and used Windows Explorer (which was renamed File Explorer with the release of Windows 8) when using computers running Windows 7 or anything before it. The traditional desktop is still available, it's still called Desktop, and it's still where you'll do quite a bit of your work. You can access the desktop from the Start screen.

TIP When you open the Desktop for the first time, notice the new Start button. You can click this button to return to the Start screen, and you can right-click it to access options such as Shut Down or Sign Out, Task Manager, Power Options, and others.

You can open the desktop from the Start screen by clicking the Desktop tile. You can also use the Windows key+D shortcut. In addition, if you click a desktop app's tile or a related shortcut on the Start screen (one you might have saved there), perhaps for Word or File Explorer, the desktop will open on its own to house the app and make it available to you. After the desktop is open, you'll see familiar elements. Look for the taskbar, the notification area, the Recycle Bin, and other recognizable essentials in this graphic.

IMPORTANT It is possible to boot your computer directly to the desktop, but we'll suggest you don't do that yet. We want you to experience Windows 8.1 from the Start screen, at least for a while. However, if you decide later that's what you want, right-click the taskbar on the desktop and click Properties. You'll find the option on the Navigation tab.

Using the taskbar and Start button

Some applications, including Microsoft Paint, Microsoft WordPad, Microsoft Notepad, and others, open on the desktop. These aren't apps; they are desktop apps and thus need the desktop to work. When you find yourself at the desktop, by choice or necessity, you'll see features with which you are likely already familiar. The taskbar is one of them. The taskbar is the transparent bar that spans across the bottom of the screen when the desktop is active. You can also see the Start button. You'll learn about both here.

Let's look at the taskbar first. The taskbar is where you access running desktop apps, manage your open windows, and access the available touch keyboard, among other things. As with previous Windows editions, a notification area on the far right offers access to various system settings, including those that correspond with available networks, system sounds, the current state of the system, and the time and date. The lower-right corner is a hot corner that brings up the five default charms when you require them.

TROUBLESHOOTING If you don't see the taskbar, make sure you're on the desktop and not in an app. (Use Windows key+D to get there.) If you're sure you are on the desktop, position the cursor at the bottom of the screen; it could be that the taskbar is hidden. It will appear when you position your cursor there.

You can personalize the taskbar by pinning icons to it for desktop apps you use often. You'll learn to do this in an exercise later in this chapter. You can also move the taskbar by dragging it to another area of the screen (if it's unlocked), change the size of the icons that appear on it, and rearrange the icons by dragging them to different positions. You can right-click the taskbar to add or hide toolbars, too; you might like to enable the Address or Links toolbar. Toolbars appear next to the notification area when added.

SEE ALSO You can learn more about customizing your environment in Chapter 2, "Personalize your Windows 8.1 device."

The main purposes of the taskbar—beyond any its personalization options—are to offer immediate access to previously opened apps, files, folders, and windows; to make it easy to minimize, restore, and switch between open apps; and to navigate quickly to other areas of the computer through toolbars you add. You can click any icon on the taskbar to access the app, file, or folder it represents. For example, you can click the Internet Explorer icon to open the Internet Explorer on the desktop. You can click the Folder icon to open File Explorer.

TIP Some applications offer both an app version and a desktop version. Internet Explorer is one of these applications. When both options exist, use the app version. If you decide later that this doesn't offer what you need, try the desktop version.

Because you might not yet have much experience with files, folders, windows, and apps from which to draw, let's review some taskbar basics. The following list details what the icons on the taskbar do.

- **Touch keyboard** You can show or hide the icon for the touch keyboard. Just right-click the taskbar, point to Toolbars, and then click Touch keyboard. Repeat to undo this action.

- **Action Center flag** Click the Action Center icon (a flag) to see whether your computer requires your attention.

TROUBLESHOOTING If you don't see the icons called out here, click the up arrow.

- **Network** Click the Network icon to show the Networks pane. Click anywhere outside the pane to hide it. The Network icon sits to the left of the sound icon.

- **Sound** Click the sound icon and move the slider to raise or lower the volume.

- **Time and date** Click the time and date to show the calendar and to access the date and time settings.

    TIP You can reposition icons on the taskbar, (but not the items in the notification area) by dragging them with your mouse.

- **Open File Explorer** Click the folder icon to open File Explorer. From there, you can navigate to any area of your computer's hard disk.

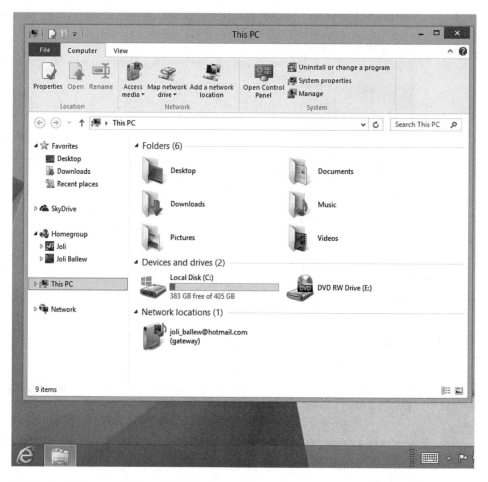

SEE ALSO Refer to the section "Understanding the Windows 8.1 file system" in Chapter 4, "Organizing files and folders."

As you know, you can personalize the taskbar. You'll learn quite a bit about that later in Chapter 2, but you can sample a taste of what's to come here.

In this exercise, you'll pin the Calculator app to the taskbar to personalize it.

➡ SET UP

There is no setup for this exercise. You do not need any practice files to complete this exercise. If you are not on the Start screen, click the Windows key or position the cursor in the lower-left corner of the screen and click or tap the Start button.

1   While on the Start screen, type **Calc**.

The results appear below the Search box.

2   Right-click the blue **Calculator**. (It is listed first here.)

3   Click **Pin To Taskbar**.

TIP The option above Pin To Taskbar in this exercise is Pin To Start. If you choose this option, a tile will appear on the Start screen.

❌ CLEAN UP
Click outside the Search pane to hide it. Open the Desktop to see the Calculator icon on the taskbar.

TIP If you work on the desktop regularly, pin your favorite desktop apps to the taskbar. To unpin something from the taskbar, right-click its icon on the taskbar and choose Unpin This Program From Taskbar. You can also unpin an item from the Start screen. To do so, right-click its tile and then click Unpin From Start.

Now, let's take a look at the Start button. The Start button offers a fast and easy way to return to the Start screen, no matter where you are. Simply click in the lower-left corner of the screen. Sometimes you'll see a simple button, whereas other times the word "Start" will display on it.

You can also right-click the Start button to access other areas of the computer and to change computer settings. You should be familiar with some of the items after reading this chapter: Search, Shut Down or Sign Out, and Desktop.

Programs and Features
Mobility Center
Power Options
Event Viewer
System
Device Manager
Network Connections
Disk Management
Computer Management
Command Prompt
Command Prompt (Admin)

Task Manager
Control Panel
File Explorer
Search
Run

Shut down or sign out ▶
Desktop

Working with multiple windows and apps

When you open a file such as a text document, the desktop appears, and a desktop app opens to make the file available. (WordPad is shown in the illustration that follows.) It might be Word, WordPad, Notepad, or something else. That app and the file are contained in a single window, and the app's features and data are available from it. You might have a document, a web browser, and File Explorer open, all of which are available from the desktop.

Likewise, you might also have opened several apps from the Start screen. You might have opened Maps, Mail, Weather, Music, and others. These apps aren't all available from one area such as the desktop; instead, you must switch among them by using keyboard and touch techniques. By default, only one app appears on the screen at any given time, although with the right hardware you can show up to four.

Because you'll often have multiple apps and desktop apps open at the same time, you need to know the traditional ways of managing multiple open windows on the desktop and then how to manage multiple open desktop apps and apps.

Let's start with the desktop. One way to manage multiple open windows on the desktop is to size them so that you can see all of them at one time. When positioned this way, you need to click only once in the window you want to use. The window you choose appears in the foreground and becomes the active window. This view isn't always effective, though, and you'll often need to maximize a window so that it takes up the entire screen.

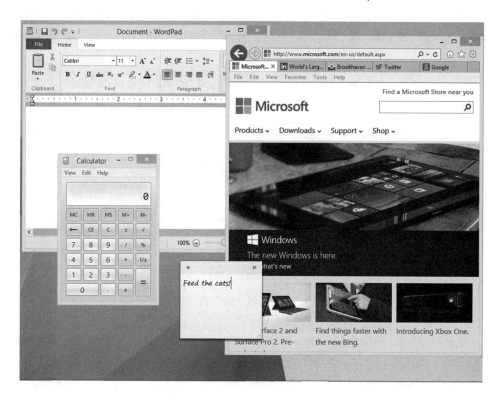

TROUBLESHOOTING If you can't access all the features in a window, maximize the window by clicking the square in the upper-right corner.

The problem with maximizing a window so that it takes up the entire screen is that you can no longer view or easily access the other open windows. They are now behind the active window. To get to those other windows requires knowing a few tricks.

Here are the most common ways to manage multiple open windows on the desktop:

- **Minimize to the taskbar**   You can minimize any maximized window to the task-bar. Doing so removes it from the desktop but does not close it. After it is removed (minimized), you can see the windows that were previously underneath it. One way to minimize a window is to click the respective icon on the taskbar (you may have to click it twice, once to make it the active window and the second time to minimize it); a more familiar way is to click the dash in the upper-right corner of the window. To restore the window, click its icon on the taskbar.

- **Close the window**   Click the "X" button to close the window and exit the app. You should save your work in the window before closing it.

- **Shake the window to keep**   To remove all but one window from the desktop and minimize the others to the taskbar, click, hold, and then shake the top of the window you'd like to keep. The other windows will fall to the taskbar.

- **Resize a window**   You can resize a maximized window by dragging the window downward by the upper-center part of the topmost toolbar. This causes the window to be in restore mode. When it's in restore mode, you can drag from the corners of the window to further manipulate its size.

  TROUBLESHOOTING You can't drag from a window's corner if the window is maximized. All desktop corners are hot corners by default, so when you position your cursor there, charms, the Start thumbnail, the last-used app, and so on appear. Even if you turn off the hot corners in PC Settings, you still can't do it.

- **Snap a window to take up half the screen**   You can drag from the top part of most windows to the left or right of the screen to snap it into place so that it takes up half the screen. You can also double-click when you have the double arrow at the top of a window to have the window fill to the height of the screen without changing the width.

- **Use Flip** The Alt+Tab keyboard shortcut displays thumbnails of open apps in the center of the screen. To use this shortcut, keep the Alt key depressed and press the Tab key to flip through the available apps. When the desired thumbnail is displayed, release the Alt key to ensure that the app is active. You can also flip to apps by using this method.

- **Use Peek** While at the desktop, position your cursor in the lower-right corner of the taskbar. The open windows become transparent, enabling you to see the desktop underneath. If nothing happens, right-click there and then, on the shortcut menu that appears, click Peek At Desktop. (You want Peek At Desktop to have a check beside it.) Peek is disabled by default.

These are all traditional ways to work with the desktop. Many are probably not new to you, such as resizing a window or minimizing a window to the taskbar. You might have even used Flip before. There are new, novel ways to move among apps and desktop apps, though. These involve positioning your mouse in a specific area of the screen and using touch gestures on compatible devices.

TIP It's okay to leave lots of apps open if you want. You don't have to open and close them continually. After they are in the background (not in use), they become inactive and use very few (if any) computer resources. They are designed so that you can leave them open and available without worrying about using too many of your computer's resources. Alternatively, it's best to close desktop apps when you are finished with them.

One way to move among the multiple open apps and the desktop is to use the Switch list. This list can be accessed by positioning the cursor in the upper-left corner of your computer screen and then slowly moving the cursor downward. You can also use the keyboard shortcut, Windows key+Tab. (Hold down the Windows key and press Tab as many times as needed to select the app to use.) After you have access to the list by using your mouse to access it, you can left-click, right-click, drag, and touch the thumbnail windows to perform other tasks.

If you simply click a thumbnail in the Switch list, it opens. You have other options, though. With a mouse, you can right-click to access options to close the app or to insert it to the left side or right side of the screen. When you opt to insert an app, you can show two of them on the screen at one time. You can choose the applicable Replace option to open the selected app and move away from the item currently open. You can also drag items from the list to a specific area of the screen if your display supports a high enough screen resolution.

TROUBLESHOOTING If you don't see the option to Insert Left or Insert Right when you right-click an app thumbnail, or if you can't drag and drop an app to snap it to the side of the screen when another app is open, you'll need to change the resolution of your computer screen to 1366 × 768 or higher. If you want four apps open at once, you'll have to set the resolution to 2560 × 1440.

In this exercise, you'll open three apps from the Start screen and switch among them by using various techniques involving a keyboard and mouse. You will then close one app and position another to take up a half of the screen.

➜ SET UP
There is no setup for this exercise. You do not need any practice files to complete this exercise.

1   Position your cursor in the lower-left corner of the screen and then, when the Start button appears, click it.

2   Click **Weather**.

3   Repeat to open **Music** and then **Maps**. If prompted to allow an app to use your location, click Allow.

4   With Maps active on the screen, on the keyboard, hold down the **Windows** key.

5   While holding down the **Windows** key, press **Tab** several times.

Different thumbnails are selected.

6   When the **Music** thumbnail is selected, release both keys.

The Music app opens.

7   Press and hold the **Windows** key and then tap the **Tab** key one time. Keep the Windows key depressed.

8   On the Switch list, right-click the **Maps** app. On the shortcut menu that opens, click **Close**.

9   With the **Music** app still active and the Switch list open, drag the **Weather** app inward from the left side.

It snaps into place.

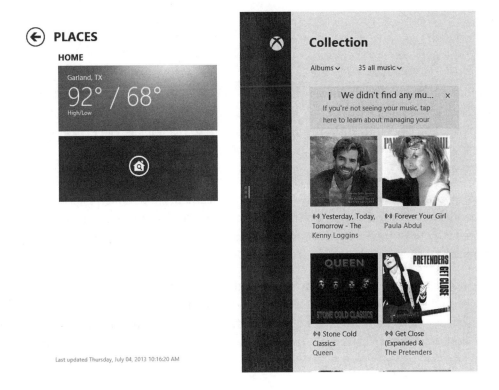

1

CLEAN UP
To return to the Start screen, on the keyboard, press the Windows key.

TIP After an app is snapped to one side of the screen, you can use the black bar that separates them both to move it. You can configure an app to take up less than half the screen. Just click and drag.

Remember, you can access the Switch list by using only the mouse. First, position the cursor in the upper-left corner. You'll see the last app used. You can click that to access it, or you can move the cursor down the left side, slowly, to show the entire Switch list.

TROUBLESHOOTING If you have so many windows and apps open that Flip or the Switch list are encumbered, close windows and apps you don't use.

If you have the option to use touch gestures, there's another option. You can just swipe your finger inward from the left side of the screen to move from app to app. You'll learn more about using touch in Chapter 19.

TIP You can close most apps by clicking at the top of the app and then dragging from the top of the screen to the bottom.

Customizing File Explorer

Before we move on to the final two topics in this chapter, using Control Panel and PC Settings and ending a computing session, let's take one last look at the desktop and File Explorer. You'll need to know the information here to manipulate File Explorer on your computer as you work through this book.

The goal of the Windows 8.1 File Explorer environment, available on the desktop, is to make finding, sharing, organizing, and working with documents, music files, pictures, videos, and other data as intuitive as possible. In addition, from File Explorer, you can easily access data stored in your HomeGroup, data on other storage devices connected to or part of your computer, and any data available to you on your network.

You access data in File Explorer by selecting the desired folder or location in the Navigation pane, on the left side of the File Explorer window, and then selecting the desired folders or file(s) in the content area on the right. With a folder or file selected, you can then use the ribbon to manage that data. The ribbon contains tabs and groups to help you perform tasks on the data you select.

Commands are organized on task-specific tabs of the ribbon and in feature-specific groups on each tab. Commands generally take the form of buttons and lists. Some appear in galleries. Some groups have related dialog boxes or task panes that contain additional commands.

Throughout this book, we discuss the commands and ribbon elements associated with the app feature being discussed. In this topic, we discuss the general appearance of the ribbon, things that affect its appearance, and ways of locating commands that aren't visible on compact views of the ribbon.

TIP Some older commands no longer appear on the ribbon but are still available elsewhere. You can make these commands available by adding them to the Quick Access toolbar, located just above the tabs on the ribbon by default, although it can be moved.

Dynamic ribbon elements

The ribbon you'll see in File Explorer is dynamic, meaning that the appearance of commands on the ribbon changes as the width of the ribbon changes. A command might be displayed on the ribbon in the form of a large button, a small button, a small labeled button, or a list entry. As the width of the ribbon decreases, the size, shape, and presence of buttons on the ribbon adapt to the available space.

For example, when sufficient horizontal space is available, the buttons on the View tab of the File Explorer window are spread out, and you can see all the commands available in each group.

If you decrease the width of the ribbon, small button labels disappear and entire groups of buttons hide under one button that represents the group. Click the group button to display a list of the commands available in that group. Depending on the content of the ribbon you're working with, you might also see small unlabeled buttons or a scroll arrow.

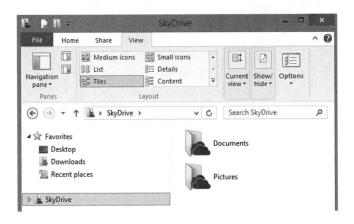

TROUBLESHOOTING If you don't see what is shown in any graphic in this book, maximize your File Explorer window and click the tab name if you can't see anything on the ribbon under it.

Changing the width of the ribbon

The width of the ribbon depends on the horizontal space available to it, which depends on the following three factors:

- **The width of the app window**   Maximizing the app window provides the most space for ribbon elements. You can resize the app window by clicking the button in its upper-right corner or by dragging the border of a window that isn't maximized.

TIP On a computer running Windows 8.1, you can maximize the app window by dragging its title bar to the top of the screen.

- **Your screen resolution**   Screen resolution is the size of your screen display expressed as pixels wide by pixels high. The greater the screen resolution, the greater the amount of information that will fit on one screen. Your screen resolution options depend on your monitor. At the time of this writing, the lowest possible screen resolution was 1024 x 768. The highest resolution depends on your monitor and your computer's display capabilities. In the case of the ribbon, the greater the number of pixels wide (the first number), the greater the number of buttons that can be shown on the ribbon and the larger those buttons can be. On a computer running Windows 8.1, you can change your screen resolution from the Screen Resolution window of Control Panel. You set the resolution by dragging the pointer on the slider.

Exploring PC Settings and Control Panel

If you used Control Panel in an earlier Microsoft operating system, note that it is still part of Windows 8.1. Control Panel (shown in the illustration that follows) is housed in a single window where you can make changes to your computer such as adding users, changing the desktop background, and managing your network, among other things. To navigate this, you click the links, make configuration changes, and use the Back button as desired.

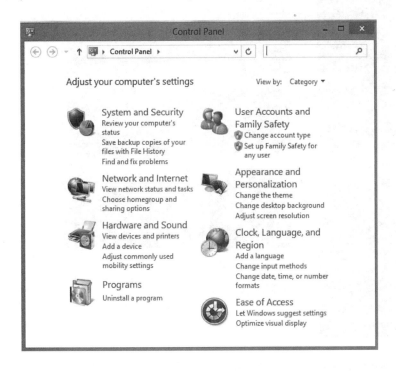

When Windows 8 was released in 2012, another option became available, the PC Settings hub, referred to as PC Settings. In Windows 8.1, it has been redesigned, as demonstrated in the illustration that follows. To navigate this, you click an item in the left pane and then click another entry in the results. From there you can make configuration changes. PC Settings has a back button to help you navigate it.

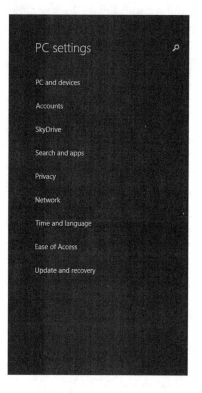

For the most part, we suggest that you make changes from PC Settings whenever you can. It's easy to navigate and even easier to make configuration changes. Control Panel is more robust and offers more features, and should be used when you can't find what you want in PC Settings.

TIP When you want to make a change to your computer, type what you'd like to do in the Search pane (just start typing on the Start screen and this will open). Select the option from the results. Depending on what you click and what is offered, either Control Panel or the PC Settings hub will open to the desired setting option. You won't have to know what setting is available where, or how to access it.

Understanding sleep

Your computer is likely configured to go to sleep after a specific period of time. While your computer is sleeping, it uses very little electricity. The hard disk(s) and monitor(s) power down and are quiet and dim. It's best to let your computer go to sleep when you can rather than turning it off. It causes less wear and tear, and the computer can be awakened much more quickly than it can be restarted. When a computer sleeps, your apps and windows remain open and ready. Your computer will go to sleep after a specific period of inactivity. You can change the defaults if desired.

In this exercise, you'll open PC Settings from the Start screen and change when your computer sleeps.

→ **SET UP**
There is no setup for this exercise. You don't need any practice files to complete this exercise.

1   Access the **Start** screen and then type Sleep.

2   Click **Change When The PC Sleeps** in the results. Note the settings icon shown here. Make sure you click the result that also includes this icon.

3   In the right pane, click the arrow under the **Sleep** option(s).

4   Use the drop-down lists in the right pane to make changes to when the computer
     sleeps.

(⊕) PC and devices   Screen

Lock screen   On battery power, turn off after

Display | 10 minutes   ⌄ |

Bluetooth   When plugged in, turn off after

Devices | 2 hours   ⌄ |

Mouse and touchpad
                                            Sleep
Typing
                                            On battery power, PC goes to sleep after
Corners and edges
                                            | 10 minutes   ⌄ |
Power and sleep
                                            When plugged in, PC goes to sleep after
AutoPlay
                                            | 4 hours   ⌄ |
PC info

     The sleep options are changed.

⊗ CLEAN UP

Position your mouse in the upper-left corner and click the Back arrow to return to the
main PC Settings hub page. Leave this open.

With a feel for how the PC Settings panes work, you can now explore the categories on the
left side. It's not important right now for you to understand every option; you'll return to
these settings many times as you work through this book. What's important now is to explore PC Settings and get an idea of what's available.

Here are a few category options to explore from the main PC Settings screen (the one that has PC Settings on the top). This is not a complete list, but you are encouraged to explore all of them. Click the Back arrow as applicable, when exploring.

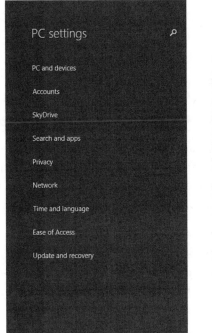

- **PC and Devices** Use this tab to change the lock screen background and to choose apps that appear on the lock screen with detailed status information. You can change the color of the Start screen's background and design here, too. Beyond that, you can enable or disable Bluetooth, change settings for the display, mouse, and touchpad, turn off hot corners, change power and sleep settings, and more. (If you click this, click the Back arrow to return to the PC And Devices screen.)

- **Accounts** Use this tab to change your account picture and manage your login options. You can add new users here, if you are logged on as an administrator.

- **SkyDrive** Use this tab to view your SkyDrive storage statistics, buy more storage, choose how to use SkyDrive to sync documents and camera photos, and more.

- **Search and Apps** Use this tab to clear your search history, choose how and when to be notified of updated information from apps such as Calendar and Mail, to set Quiet Hours (when you should not be disturbed), to see a list of apps and how much hard disk space they require, and to set the default apps for web browsers, email, music player, and so on.

- **Privacy** Use this tab to configure privacy options for apps, such as if they can use your camera or microphone, learn your location, and learn your name.

TIP Click every tab in the left pane of PC Settings now to see what's available, but don't make any changes beyond personalizing the lock screen, your User tile, and other nonessential areas. Click the Back arrow to return to the previous screen as applicable.

If you need access to more configuration options than those available in PC Settings, you can use Control Panel, which is just a different presentation of PC Settings with more options. You can open Control Panel from the Start screen. Just type Control Panel and then select it from the top of the list of results. (You can also right-click the Start button to access Control Panel.)

To use Control Panel, you choose the desired entry, access the areas you want to change, and make changes by selecting from the choices offered. As with PC Settings, you'll access these options often throughout this book when the required or desired options are necessary for instruction.

TIP If time allows, explore the options in both PC Settings and Control Panel, but don't make any major changes to the system yet.

Ending a computing session

When you are ready to end a computing session, you should, at the very least, secure your computer so that others can't access it. You can do this by locking it. You can access the Lock option from the Start screen by clicking your user name. When you lock your computer you must enter a password when you are ready to use it again. When you do, the computer will be just as you left it. Lock your computer anytime you leave it unattended.

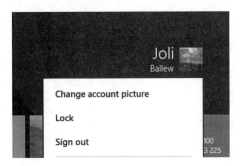

KEYBOARD SHORTCUT Press Windows key+L to lock your computer quickly.

From this same menu you can sign out of your computer. When you sign out, you'll be prompted to save any open files if applicable and you might be prompted to close open desktop apps. With that done, Windows 8.1 will close your computing session as if you were turning off the computer (but won't turn it off). When you log on again, you'll start a new computing session.

KEYBOARD SHORTCUT Press Windows key+I shortcut to access the Settings charm (and thus the Power setting).

> **IMPORTANT** If you lock your computer but don't have a password configured to unlock it, locking it doesn't do much good. Anyone can gain access.

Finally, you can completely shut down your computer. You should shut down your computer when you get on an airplane, reposition a desktop computer, or when you know you won't need your computer for some time. You can access the option to shut down the computer by right-clicking the Start button. You can also access this option by using the Settings charm, from the Power options. And finally, the option to shut down is available from the logon screen; you can shut down your computer without logging on.

TIP Shut down your computer when you want to move it to a new location, transport it in a car or bus, or know you won't be using it for at least two days.

In this exercise, you'll shut down your computer.

 SET UP
There is no setup for this exercise. You do not need any practice files to complete this exercise.

1   Position your cursor in the lower-left corner and screen.

2   Right-click **Start**.

3   Point to **Shut Down Or Sign Out**. In the submenu that opens, click **Shut Down**.

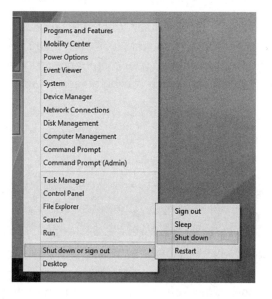

 CLEAN UP Leave the computer turned off until you are ready to use it again.

TROUBLESHOOTING If you see other options that prompt you to install updates before shutting down, choose that option.

Key points

■ When you set up Windows 8.1, you have to input some information, including your user name, computer name, a password, and more.

■ You click or flick upward to bypass the lock screen. You can click or flick downward to access the camera, if applicable.

■ The Start screen contains tiles that represent apps and desktop apps and offers access to various parts of the computer, including the desktop.

■ Charms offer access to additional, embedded settings, features, and configuration options.

■ Some tiles on the Start screen are configurable and will offer up-to-date information obtained from the Internet.

■ The traditional desktop is available from the Start screen and is still where you will do most of your work.

■ There are many ways to work with multiple open windows, including Flip, the Switch list, and hot corners.

■ Control Panel offers access to configuration options that you can apply, including adding users and configuring networks. PC Settings offers many of these settings in a more user-friendly environment.

■ You can end a computing session by locking the screen, logging off, letting the computer go to sleep, or shutting it down.

Chapter at a glance

Personalize

Personalize the Start screen with colors and designs, page 57

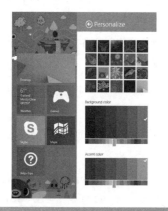

Name

Name a group of tiles on the Start screen, page 62

Boot

Boot to the desktop, page 77

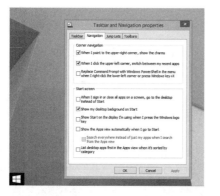

Use

Use the new Start button, page 78

Personalize your Windows 8.1 device

2

IN THIS CHAPTER, YOU WILL LEARN HOW TO

- Personalize your Start screen.

- Personalize your lock screen.

- Personalize the desktop and taskbar.

- Boot directly to the desktop or the Apps view.

- Access and explore advanced settings.

- Switch to a new power plan.

Now that you have Windows 8.1 set up and know your way around the lock screen, Start screen, and desktop, it's time to personalize the computer further so that it suits your exact wants and needs. In this chapter, you'll learn how to personalize the Start and lock screens to your own specifications. You'll also learn to personalize the desktop and associated elements, boot directly to the desktop or the Apps View, navigate Control Panel, and even switch to a different power plan. After you've worked through this chapter, your computer will be distinctively yours.

PRACTICE FILES   You do not need any practice files to complete this chapter.

Personalizing the Start screen

You learned quite a bit about the Start screen in Chapter 1, "Introducing Windows 8.1." You learned how to move tiles around and configure the Weather app to learn your location and to show up-to-date information from cities you select. There's probably quite a bit you'd still like to change, though. You might want to remove tiles for apps that you don't use and add tiles for those you do, configure how large or small a tile appears on the Start screen, and change the background and design on the Start screen, to name a few. You might also want to disable some of the Live tiles or name a group of tiles.

In this exercise, you'll personalize the Start screen with a new background color and design.

 SET UP
Start your computer and unlock the lock screen. You need to have access to the Start screen. You do not need any practice files for this exercise.

1   While on the **Start** screen, access the charms. A quick way to do this is to press Windows key+C.

2   Click **Settings.**

3   Click Personalize.

Settings

Start

Personalize

Tiles

Help

The Personalize options become available.

4   In the section at the top of the **Personalize** pane, click any design.

5   Click any **Background Color.**

6   Click any **Accent color.**

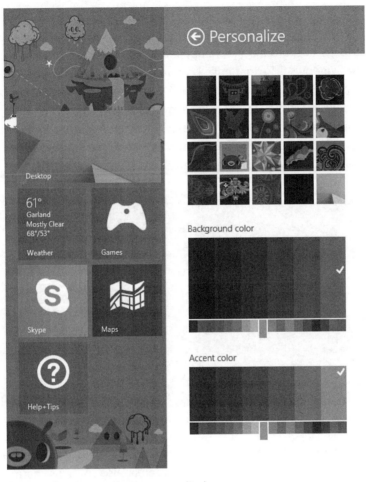

Personalization options are applied.

TIP If you are using a local user account, you should switch to a Microsoft account if you want the changes you make on the Start screen to follow you from computer to computer. This is possible only if those other computers can access the Internet to download your profile information, and only if you sign in on those computers by using your Microsoft account, though.

⊗ CLEAN UP
Click outside the Personalize pane to hide the pane and show the full Start screen.

TROUBLESHOOTING If, when you access the Settings charm you see Personalization instead of Personalize in the resulting pane, you aren't accessing the Settings charm from the Start screen. Try again, but this time, from the Start screen.

You can opt to use the background you've applied to your desktop to your Start screen. When you do, the Windows 8.1 experience is more unified and seamless. It makes the Start screen look like an overlay to your desktop, which is often a better way to become accustomed to Windows 8.1 if the Start screen seems confusing to you. To make this change select the last thumbnail that appears in the Personalize pane. Here, a background showing a sand dune is applied to both the desktop (not shown) and the Start screen (shown). Note the last thumbnail in the Personalize pane is selected.

Now you can personalize your Start screen to hold only the tiles you use often. To remove an unwanted app tile (or tiles), right-click it and then, on the toolbar that appears across the bottom of the screen, click Unpin From Start. This toolbar also contains charms to perform other tasks, as well. What else you see when you right-click an app depends on the tile or tiles you've selected. You might see Resize, Turn Live Tile On, or Turn Live Tile Off. If you right-click multiple tiles, you also see Clear Selection.

TIP Uninstall is an option on the toolbar that appears when you right-click a tile. Don't uninstall anything yet, though; you might decide later that you want to use the app.

A Live tile has information that changes often. You might have noticed that the News app scrolls through the latest headlines or that Mail scrolls through received emails. This information is dynamic, or live; thus the name "Live" tile. You might want to disable the live feature of some of those tiles if the constant flipping bothers you or if you don't need to view updated information when you access the Start screen. You might not want onlookers to see information you're acquiring, either. You can disable a Live tile by using the same technique you learned earlier to remove tiles you don't want: right-click the Live tile that you want to turn off and then click Turn Live Tile Off. The tile will remain, but updates will no longer appear.

TIP You might want to make a tile live, too. For instance, when Calendar is configured as live, appointments and events appear there as the day and time draws near.

Ideally, you should add tiles for apps that you use often if those tiles aren't already available on the Start screen. This requires a few more steps than removing a tile or repositioning one, but it's still easy.

TROUBLESHOOTING If you uninstall an app and decide that you want it back, check the Windows Store. You just might find it there.

In this exercise, you'll add a tile to the Start screen for Windows Media Player, Control Panel, and your favorite Windows desktop app.

 SET UP
Start your computer and unlock the lock screen. You need to have access to the Start screen. You do not need any practice files to complete this exercise.

1 On the **Start** screen, position the cursor in the lower-left quadrant of the screen, and then click the down arrow that appears.

2 Scroll right, right-click **Windows Media Player**, and then click **Pin To Start**.

3   Repeat Steps 1 and 2 to add Control Panel and your favorite desktop app.

 CLEAN UP
If applicable, return to the Start screen.

TROUBLESHOOTING If you can't find Windows Media Player in Step 2, click the down arrow next to Apps while in Apps view and click By Category. Then scroll to the Desktop category; it will be in there.

Although there are more things you can do to personalize the Start screen than what has been introduced here, one unique option is to name a group of tiles. Before you start though, drag a few app tiles so that some similar tiles are grouped together. You might put Mail, Internet Explorer, SkyDrive, Store, and People in a group, for example. These are all loosely related by their reliance on an Internet connection. It's up to you; you can group your tiles as desired.

In this exercise, you'll name a group of tiles on the Start screen.

 SET UP
Start your computer and unlock the lock screen. You need to have access to the Start screen. You do not need any practice files to complete this exercise.

1   Right-click an empty area of the **Start** screen and then click **Customize**.

2   Just above the group of tiles you want to name, click **Name Group**.

3 Type the desired name, press Enter on the keyboard to apply it, and then click an empty area of the **Start** screen to close the **Customize** options.

The new group name is applied.

CLEAN UP

No clean up is necessary.

SEE ALSO Chapter 3, "Using apps on the Start screen" shows you more personalization options, including how to resize app tiles, uninstall apps, and unpin app tiles from the Start screen.

Personalizing the lock screen

You learned a little about the lock screen in Chapter 1, including that it's more functional than any lock screen you might have encountered in previous Microsoft operating systems. You also learned that you can select a new background from PC Settings, and that the lock screen offers the time and date, and has tiles that represent some of your apps. You probably know that you can't click and engage those tiles, but you can get a quick glance at what's been updated since you last used your computer. For example, after you've set up Mail, its tile displays a number, notifying you of how many new email messages are currently unread. You might also see a Calendar tile, a People tile, and others, depending on how Windows 8.1 is currently configured.

In this exercise, you'll change the notifications that appear on the lock screen

SET UP

Start your computer and unlock the lock screen. You need to have access to the Start screen.

1   Access the charms and click **Settings**.

2   In the **Settings** pane, click **Change PC Settings**.

3   If a back arrow appears in the upper-left corner, click it, and then click **PC And Devices**.

The **PC And Devices** pane appears and lock screen is selected.

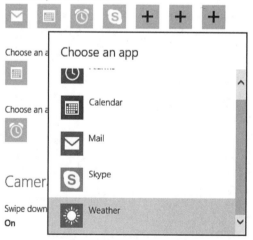

4   In the right pane, scroll to locate the **Lock Screen Apps** section. Click a + sign under **Choose Apps To Run In The Background And Show Quick Status And Notifications, Even When Your Screen Is Locked**. Click **Weather**.

5   To view detailed information for an app on the **Lock** screen, click the icon in the **Choose An App To Display Detailed Status** section, and then select the desired app. (You can only have one app at a time enabled.)

6   To view detailed information for an alarm on the **Lock** screen, click the icon in the **Choose an app to show alarms** section, and then select the desired app. You may only have one available, Alarms.

> **TIP** If you select an app to appear that is already showing on the lock screen, its placement on the screen will be altered.

7   Press **Windows key+L** to access the **Lock** screen and review your changes.

✖ CLEAN UP
Unlock the computer and return to the Start screen.

There is more to configure on the Start screen than just what notifications appear. You can also opt to display a slide show of photos on the lock screen and choose the folder from which the photos are selected. You can change the options so that the slide show will (or will not) run while a laptop is using its battery. (You won't be able to configure a slide show if you don't have any photos on your computer, though.) Beyond that, you can configure if you want to be able to use the camera from the lock screen (which you access by flicking downward), or, if you want to disable that feature. You configure the slide show and other lock screen features in PC Settings.

Play a slide show on the lock screen
On ![toggle on]

Use pictures from

![OneDrive icon] Pictures

![PC icon] Pictures

![Add icon] Add a folder

Include Camera Roll folders from this PC and SkyDrive
Off ![toggle off]

Only use the pictures that will fit best on my screen
On ![toggle on]

Play a slide show when using battery power
Off ![toggle off]

When my PC is inactive, show the lock screen instead of turning off the s
On ![toggle on]

Turn off screen after slide show has played for

Don't turn off   ⌄

⊗ CLEAN UP
Unlock the computer and return to the Start screen.

Changing your user account type

Your user account is associated with your specific user profile and is what defines you when you log on to your computer. This profile defines where your files are saved, what your Start screen design and color are, if you use SkyDrive, and how the tiles are arranged on the Start screen, among other things. You have several options for your user account, but the most common (and the one we suggest heartily) is the Microsoft account. The other most common type is the local account.

2

A local user account is an account that's available only from your own, personal computer. The settings you configure for your applications, apps, desktop and taskbar, backgrounds, Internet Explorer Favorites, app configuration on your Start screen, and other customizations are applied to and available from only your local computer. Your user profile is stored on your local computer and available only from there. If you use only one computer and you don't really care to use many apps, this should be fine. However, if you use multiple Windows 8–based computers (one at work, one at home, and perhaps a laptop when you're on the back porch) or use a Windows 8-based tablet or a Windows phone, you will want to consider using a Microsoft account instead. If you don't, you'll need to create a user name and account for each computer you use, you won't be able to download apps, and your settings won't be synchronized across the computers that you use. You also won't be able to access SkyDrive through the various built-in options either.

A Microsoft account is a global and roaming user account. Your profile is stored on the Internet in the cloud, and your user profile is accessible from the other computers, tablets, and devices running Windows 8–based operating systems. This means that all your settings, preferences, and configurations are available from any computer to which you can log on by using this account, provided that the particular computer is connected to the Internet and can access that profile. The purpose of storing your user profile on the Internet is so that you can move from computer to computer or device to device and have the same experience on one as you do on the other. In this scenario, any changes you make while logged on are saved to your profile, too, so if you make a change to say, your laptop's Start screen, that change will be applied when you next log on to your desktop computer, provided you've logged on to those devices with your Microsoft account and that you indeed do want to synchronize these types of settings. (You might notice a slight delay in loading your profile after logging on to a computer with your Microsoft account.)

TIP A Microsoft account is an email address such as your_name@hotmail.com or yourname@live.com, but it does not have to be from either of these domains. You might already have a Microsoft account. A Windows Live ID, an Outlook.com email address, a Live.com email address, or a Hotmail.com email address are Microsoft accounts. You can sign up for an account at www.live.com if you don't have one.

TROUBLESHOOTING A Microsoft account synchronizes only your personal settings and preferences. It's a user profile. You can't access apps you've installed on another computer running Windows 8 or 8.1, print to a remote computer's local printer, or use your home computer's webcam from another computer, for instance. You're not accessing your computer remotely with this feature; you're accessing only your user profile, which is stored on a server on the Internet.

You switch from a local account to a Microsoft account from PC Settings. You can access PC Settings by using the Settings charm. From the PC Settings screen, click Accounts. From the Your Account tab, click "Connect to a Microsoft account" and follow the prompts.

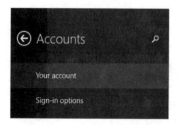

If you currently use a Microsoft account and want to switch to a local account, the option is in the same place (PC Settings, Accounts). However, to switch to a local account you'll need to first Disconnect from your current Microsoft account. Then, just follow the prompts to create a new, local account.

TIP By default, when you use a Microsoft account, certain settings are synchronized to the cloud. If you don't want a specific setting to synchronize among computers, you can turn off syncing for that one item. Some of the options include synchronizing desktop personalizations, app data, and web browser favorites, open tabs, home pages, and so on. In PC Settings, click SkyDrive and Sync Settings to make the changes.

Customizing your user account settings

After you've decided what type of account to use and applied the change if applicable, you can make other changes to your user account to customize it further. The changes will be saved to your user profile. One item to change is your user account picture. You'll need to have access to a picture you'd like to use to apply it, so if you don't yet have any pictures on your computer or network (or if your computer does not have a built-in camera or web cam you can use to take one), return here when you do.

2

In this exercise, you'll change the picture associated with your user account.

 SET UP
Start your computer and unlock the lock screen. You need to have access to the Start screen.

1   On the **Start** screen, in the upper-right corner, click your **User Name**.

2   Click **Change Account Picture**.

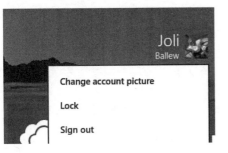

3   To take a new picture, click **Camera** (if applicable).

    a.   Click once on the screen to capture the photo.

    b.   Drag the box to crop the photo.

    c.   Click OK.

4   To use an existing picture, click **Browse**.

Account picture

Create an account picture

▢ Camera

▢ Backgrounds Wallpapers HD

▢ People

5   If you see an image you'd like to use, click it and select **Choose Image**.

6   If you don't see the picture you want to use, do the following:

   a.   Click **This PC** and then choose the folder or subfolder that contains the picture you want. SkyDrive is an option and has been selected as shown in the
illustration that follows.

   b.   Click **Go Up** and the **Files** down arrow as needed while navigating.

   c.   When you locate the image, click it and select **Choose Image**.

CLEAN UP

No clean up is required.

TIP After you have changed an existing account picture to a new one, you'll see the old picture next to the new one in PC Settings, in Accounts, from the Your Account tab. To apply that picture or any other that appears there at some later date, just click it to apply it.

Personalizing the desktop

You learned about the desktop in Chapter 1. There, you discovered that the desktop still exists in a form very similar to what you're likely already used to if you've spent any time with other Windows-based computers. You can personalize the desktop in the same ways, too. You can apply a new background and set a screen saver, for instance. You can have the background consist of a slide show of pictures you select. You can opt to apply a theme, which is a group of settings that, when combined, provide a motif. One theme, Flowers, combines backgrounds, screensavers, window colors, and sounds and is available from the Windows 8.1 desktop Personalization options. You can just choose a new background, too; there are many beautiful pictures from which you can choose or you can use one of your own.

SEE ALSO Learn how to boot your computer directly to the desktop later in the chapter in the section "Booting to the desktop."

In this section, you won't learn how to personalize every aspect of the desktop; that could fill an entire chapter, if not more! You will learn how to select a new background and apply a theme, and from there you can surmise how to make additional changes.

In this exercise, you'll apply the Flowers theme and customize which backgrounds you want to appear.

 SET UP
Access the Desktop. Use the Windows key+D keyboard shortcut to get there.

1   Right-click the **desktop** and then click **Personalize**.

2   In the **Windows Defaut Themes** section, click **Flowers**.

The Flowers theme is immediately applied, and new colors are associated with windows and the taskbar.

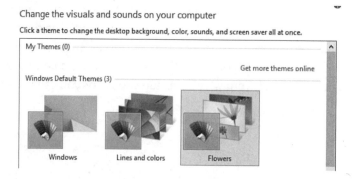

3   Click **Desktop Background** (not shown).

4   Clear a few images.

5   Use **Change Picture Every** to select an option.

6   Click **Save Changes**.

❌ CLEAN UP
If desired, explore Screen Saver, Color, and Sounds from the Personalization window.

SEE ALSO To learn more about tailoring settings to your liking, read the section "Advanced settings" later in this chapter.

Changing how the taskbar looks

The taskbar is the transparent bar that runs across the bottom of the screen when you're using the desktop. It can be almost any color if you've applied a theme. By default, it's locked and can't be moved. To unlock it, right-click the taskbar and then, on the shortcut menu that appears, click Lock The Taskbar (the option Lock The Taskbar should not have a check beside it) and now you can drag it to a different area on the screen. You might prefer the taskbar on the left side of the desktop, for instance (or across the top).

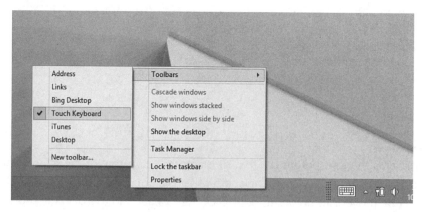

Beyond unlocking and then dragging the taskbar to a new place on the screen, you can also do the following:

- **Reposition buttons**   Drag icons from one area of the taskbar to another.
- **Pin icons**   Pin items to the taskbar, including icons for desktop apps, documents, folders, and more.
- **Auto-hide the taskbar**   Auto-hide the taskbar to keep it off the screen when it's not needed.
- **Change taskbar button size and grouping**   Use small or large taskbar buttons and choose to group or not group like icons when the taskbar is full.
- **Show or hide toolbars**   Show or hide toolbars, including the Address, Links, Touch Keyboard, and Desktop toolbars.

- **Enable Peek**   Enable or disable Peek, a feature outlined in Chapter 1 with which you can look at the desktop by temporarily making all open windows transparent. You use Peek by positioning your mouse in the lower-right corner of the screen. Peek is disabled by default. Click in the lower-right corner to access the option to enable it.

- **Customize the notification area**   Select which icons and notifications appear on the taskbar.

- **Use jump lists**   Configure how you want to use jump lists. Jump lists can show recently opened apps or recent items you've opened in an app.

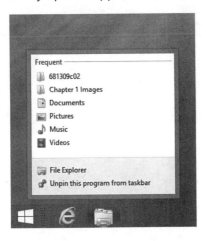

Try some of these features:

- **Reposition the taskbar**   Right-click the taskbar and then, on the shortcut menu that appears, clear the Lock The Taskbar check box, if applicable. Drag the taskbar to the left side of the screen. Repeat to position it again at the bottom.

- **Show hidden buttons**   Drag any slider, if possible, to view hidden taskbar buttons.

- **Test Peek**   Open any window or multiple windows. Position your mouse in the lower-right corner of the screen. If the windows turn transparent, Peek is turned on. If they do not, Peek is turned off.

In this exercise, you'll configure the taskbar by using the Taskbar Properties dialog box.

 SET UP
Access the desktop. If you're on the Start screen, press Windows key+D.

1   On the taskbar, right-click an empty area, and then click **Properties**.

2   In the **Taskbar And Navigation Properties** dialog box, on the **Taskbar** tab, select or clear the desired choices, and then click **Apply**.

> **TIP** From the Taskbar And Navigation Properties dialog box, on the Taskbar tab, next to the notification area, click Customize to change how you are notified of system events and to hide or show icons there. Refer to Chapter 14, "Keeping Windows 8.1 safe and secure," to learn more about this.

3   Click the **Navigation** tab, make the desired choices, and then click **Apply**.

4   Click the **Jump Lists** tab, make the desired choices, and then click **Apply**.

5   Click the **Toolbars** tab, make the desired choices, and then click **OK**.

✖ CLEAN UP
No cleanup is required.

Booting directly to the desktop or Apps view

If you looked closely at the Navigation tab in the previous exercise when you configured the taskbar's properties, you might have noticed the When I Sign In Or Close All Apps On A Screen, Go To The Desktop Instead Of Start option. By selecting this option, you can boot your computer directly to the desktop if you want to bypass the Start screen when you power on computer, unlock it, or wake it from sleep. It's okay to make this change if you want to; you'll still be able to access the Start screen anytime you like by clicking the new Windows Start button. The option to go directly to the desktop and the Start button are both shown here.

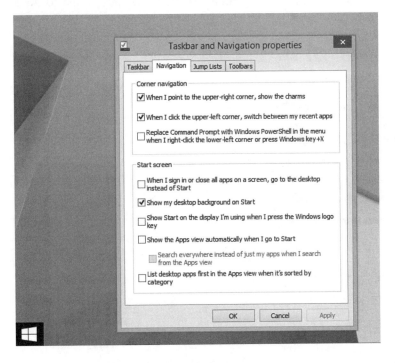

You can also boot your computer directly to the Apps view screen. This is the screen that appears when you click the down arrow while on the Start screen, showing all of the apps installed on your computer. The option to do this is also in the taskbar's Properties dialog box in the Navigation pane. The option that you want to select is Show The Apps View Automatically When I Go To Start.

Accessing and exploring advanced settings

There just isn't enough space in a single chapter to cover all the personalization options available in Windows 8.1. However, you can access all the options from a single location—Control Panel—and you can certainly explore and configure these settings to the extent you'd like. You can't harm your computer by changing these options, but you might make it look quite a bit different from what you'll see in this book.

In this exercise, you'll first view all the Appearance And Personalization options and then change the screen resolution.

 SET UP
Start your computer and unlock the lock screen. You need to have access to the Start screen.

1   Position the cursor in the lower-left corner of any screen.

2   Right-click the **Start** button and then click **Control Panel**.

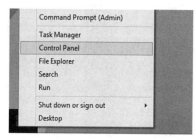

3   Verify that the **View By** is **Category** and then click **Appearance And Personalization**. All the personalization options appear.

4 In the **Display** list, click **Adjust Screen Resolution**.

5 Configure settings as desired and then click **Apply**.

Change the appearance of your display

	Detect
	Identify

Display: 1. Mobile PC Display ∨

Resolution: 1024 × 768 ∨

Orientation: Landscape ∨

Advanced settings

Project to a second screen (or press the Windows logo key ⊞ + P)

Make text and other items larger or smaller

What display settings should I choose?

| OK | Cancel | Apply |

CLEAN UP
Continue to explore the options as time allows, clicking the Back arrow as needed for navigation.

As you explore Control Panel, you'll see that clicking some options, such as Change The Theme or Change Desktop Background, open windows that you've already explored in this chapter. You'll also notice that you have access to the available fonts and to folder options with which you can view hidden files or state how you'd like to open icons. If you've used a Windows operating system before, these will look familiar. You'll also see a Back arrow and an Up arrow so that you can return quickly to the previous screen as you explore.

TIP In the Appearance And Personalization window, tapping a heading such as Taskbar results in a different dialog box than tapping an item under it, such as Customize Icons, on the taskbar.

Switching to a different power plan

A power plan is a group of settings that defines when your monitor goes to sleep and when the computer goes to sleep. Sleep occurs after a specific amount of idle time, and it protects your computer from prying eyes, from running down a laptop's battery, and from simply being "on" all the time. In the case of laptops and tablets, there are two sets of settings: one for when the computer is plugged in, and one for when it's running on battery power. One of the ways to get to these settings is from Control Panel, in the Hardware And Sound section, in Power Options.

Choose or customize a power plan

A power plan is a collection of hardware and system settings (like display brightness, sleep, etc.) that manages how your computer uses power. Tell me more about power plans

Plans shown on the battery meter

⦿ **Balanced (recommended)**   Change plan settings
Automatically balances performance with energy consumption on capable hardware.

○ Power saver   Change plan settings
Saves energy by reducing your computer's performance where possible.

Hide additional plans ⌃

○ High performance   Change plan settings
Favors performance, but may use more energy.

There are three power plans (but you can create your own quickly by editing any of them). On a desktop computer, the settings are as listed here. These same settings are applied to laptops that are plugged in to a wall outlet. However, laptops have a second set of settings for when the laptop is running on battery power.

- **Balanced**   This is the default plan. The display turns off after 10 minutes; the computer goes to sleep after 30 minutes.

- **Power Saver**   This plan is the best for minimizing power usage. The display turns off after five minutes; the computer goes to sleep after 15 minutes.

- **High Performance**   This plan is best when you need all the computing power you can obtain. The display turns off after 15 minutes; the computer never goes to sleep. To access this plan, you must click the arrow by Show Additional Plans.

You can change aspects of any plan. For instance, if you like the Balanced plan but would rather the display and computer go to sleep after 30 minutes instead of 10, you can easily make the change. You can restore the defaults for a plan with a single click, too. You can create your own power plan from scratch. However, the three default plans will likely suffice with a little tweaking.

From the same window where you switch or configure power plans, you can perform other power-related tasks. You can choose what a Power button does when you press it, for instance. If you have a laptop, you can configure what happens when you close its lid. If your computer has a Sleep button, you can configure what happens when you press it. The options for each of these include Do Nothing, Sleep, Hibernate, and Shut Down.

TIP On a laptop, you can switch power plans easily from the notification area on the taskbar. Just click the power icon one time to view the options.

In this exercise, you'll choose a power plan, and then you'll choose what happens when you press the Power button on your computer. This exercise requires that you use a laptop.

 SET UP
No setup is required for this exercise.

1   From any screen, right-click the **Start** button.

2   Click **Power Options**.

3   Select a plan to use or, leave **Balanced** (Recommended) selected.

4   In the left pane, click **Choose What The Power Buttons Do**.

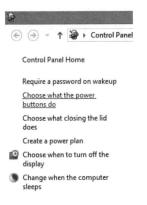

5   Make your choices as desired. Click the down arrows to access the options.

6   Click **Save Changes**.

7   Close the **Power Options** window.

 CLEAN UP
Close the Power Options window and return to the Start screen.

Key points

- You can personalize the Start screen by removing tiles you won't use, adding tiles you will use, and repositioning them as desired.

- The lock screen can offer up-to-date information about running apps.

- You can use a local user account or a Microsoft account when you log on to your Windows 8.1–based computer or tablet. With a Microsoft account, you can synchronize information among your devices, including backgrounds, Internet Explorer Favorites, and preferences, among others.

- You can personalize your user account with a picture.

- Using personalizations options, you can easily change the desktop, taskbar, and notification area when working on the desktop.

- You can configure your computer to boot directly to the desktop or Apps view.

- It's possible to set a new resolution, and perform other personalization tasks from Control Panel.

- Power plans are configurations that determine when your computer sleeps and when the display dims.

2

Chapter at a glance

View

View photos using the Photos app, page 90

Play

Play a song in the Music app, page 98

Watch

Watch a video with the Video app, page 102

Get

Get directions with the Maps app, page 108

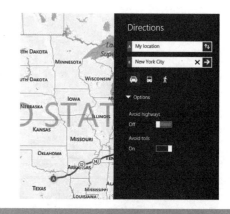

Using apps on the Start screen

3

IN THIS CHAPTER, YOU WILL LEARN HOW TO

- View and manage photos by using the Photos app.
- Edit photos by using the Photos app.
- View and manage music by using the Music app.
- View and manage video by using the Video app.
- Find a location by using the Maps app.
- Explore other default apps.
- Uninstall, remove, and edit apps.

You know about the apps available on the Start screen, and you've explored a few of them already. You've moved them, hidden them, and changed their sizes, and you know how to move among them when multiple apps are open. Now, you're ready to learn a little about what each of the most popular default apps offers.

In this chapter, you'll learn how to use the Photos, Music, Video, and Maps apps effectively (because these are the ones you'll likely use the most from the start), and then you'll learn what the other apps offer and where to learn more about them in this book.

PRACTICE FILES Before you can complete the exercises in this chapter, you need to copy the book's practice files to your computer. The practice files you'll use are in the Chapter03 practice files folder. You need to copy the contents of the Windows81Pictures folder to your Pictures folder, and the contents of the Windows81Videos folder to your Videos folder. There is a sidebar in this chapter to guide you through this process. A complete list of practice files is provided in the section "Using the practice files" at the beginning of this book.

Using the Photos app

You can use the Photos app, which is available on the Start screen, to browse and view the photos you've saved to the Pictures library and to Microsoft SkyDrive. You can also select photos which you can access from the Photos app to delete, copy, and cut and paste elsewhere. You can create new folders for organizing the photos you keep, too, and view details about the photos such as their size and date they were taken.

Beyond viewing and managing your photos, the Photos app offers a few editing tools, too. After selecting a photo to view in full screen, you can right-click the screen to open a menu on which you'll find options to rotate, crop, and edit (which includes applying auto fixes, and changing lighting, color, and adding effects). While in full-screen mode you can also set a photo for use on the lock screen or as a static image on the Photos tile. (By default that tile is Live, and photos will flip often.) Finally, you can start a slide show from any photo's options. Along the way, you can click the screen to see arrows for navigating the photos if you have them stored in multiple folders.

IMPORTANT In earlier versions of Windows, the Pictures library offered access to the Pictures folder and the Public Pictures folder. The same was true for the Music, Video, and Documents libraries too. That's changed. Now, a library only offers access to the related personal folder. So the Pictures library only offers access to the photos stored in the Pictures folder, and nowhere else. The same is true of the Music, Documents, and Videos libraries, too. However, it is possible to expand any library to include other folders, but you must do that using File Explorer on the desktop.

When you're in the Photos app, you can use the wheel on your mouse to scroll through what's there. What you see depends on the items you've saved or copied to the Pictures library. Scrolling with a mouse wheel moves the images and folders left and right. You can also use the scroll bar that appears at the bottom of the Photos app. When you enter a folder (even if you're simply accessing the main Photos app screen) and you see thumbnails of photos and any folders you've created, you're in Preview mode.

You won't see any pictures in the Photos app if you don't yet have any photos in your Pictures library. If this is the case (and if you want to follow the exercises in the chapter exactly), you will need to copy the files provided in the Practice Files folder for this book to your Pictures folder.

If you'd like to add your own pictures, you can do so by placing your pictures in the Pictures folder via one of various methods. One of the easiest ways is to choose Import from the Photos app charms. Another is to browse to the files to include (whether they are on a CD or DVD, on a network hard drive, or on a USB key or Secure Digital [SD] card), select the desired files, copy those files, and then paste them into the Pictures folder. If you're unsure how to browse to, copy, and paste files, refer to Chapter 4, "Organizing files and folders." Or, just use the practice files for now.

Copying practice files for the first time

The practice files you will use in this book are stored in the cloud, and you'll need to connect to the Internet to download them. You can find specific instructions for installing practice files at the beginning of this book and from the web page that holds the files. Those instructions tell you to do the following:

1   Navigate to the web page that holds the practice files, and click the download link.

2   Click Save As.

3   In the left pane of File Explorer, under Favorites, click Desktop.

4   After the files have downloaded, locate the folder on the desktop. Click Save.

5   Right-click and choose Extract All. Then, click Extract.

6   Either leave the new window open, or double-click the new folder that appears on the desktop. This is the folder that does not have a zipper on it.

7   Double-click Practice Files.

Now when prompted to copy files to your computer in any chapter of this book so that you can work through the exercies in it:

1   In the Practice Files folder you opened in the previous steps, double-click the folder that contains a chapter's files. In this case, Ch03.

2   Double-click the secondary folder that appears, in this case Chapter 3 Practice Files.

3   Double-click any subfolder that appears that contains the files you want to copy, in this case, Windows81Pictures.

4   Maximize the window, if applicable. Then, click the Home tab, and click Select All.

5   Click the Home tab again, and click Copy To.

6   In the resulting list, choose the folder to copy the files to, in this case, Pictures.

7   If there are more files to copy, click the Back arrow, which is under the ribbon the left side.

8   Double-click the desired subfolder, in this case, Windows81Videos.

9 Again, from the Home tab, click Select All.

10 Again, from the Home tab, click Copy To.

11 Finally, in the drop down list, choose the appropriate folder, in this case, Videos.

If you have trouble clicking Select All at any time, you are likely not working with the extracted files. If this happens, either click Extract All from the Extract tab, or open the folder you extracted in the first set of steps here.

Viewing and managing picture files and folders

3

After you have photos in your Pictures folder and can view them, you'll find that Photos also offers charms, just like all other apps you've explored. You can access these with a right-click with the mouse. The charms you see depend on which folder you're in or what picture you're viewing. For example, right-clicking a photo while it's in full-screen mode presents Delete, Open With, Set As, Slide Show, Rotate, Crop, and Edit. If you right-click that same picture when it is a thumbnail in a folder, you'll see Delete, Copy, Cut, Rename, Open With, Clear Selection, Select All, New Folder, and Import and Slide show.

TROUBLESHOOTING If you don't see any pictures in the Photos app, copy the practice files as detailed in the sidebar "Copying practice files for the first time," in the Introduction of this book, or from the website where the practice files are stored. Ensure that you've copied the pictures to the Pictures folder, too, and not somewhere else.

In this exercise, you'll use the Photos app to browse through photos in the Pictures library. You'll also review the available options in both Preview and full-screen mode.

➡ SET UP
You need to have copied the contents of the Windows81Pictures folder to the Pictures folder on your computer to complete this exercise. This folder is located in the Chapter03 practice file folder.

1 From the **Start** screen, click **Photos**.

2 If you've used the Photos app before, it might open with a photo or folder already selected. If so, click the screen and then click the **Back** arrow that appears in the upper-left corner until you are at the main screen. (If you copied the entire Windows81Pictures folder instead of only its contents, click the **Windows81Pictures** folder to open it.)

Pictures library

3   Right-click an empty area of the screen to display the **Select All**, **New Folder**, **Import**, and **Slide Show** charms in the bottom right corner of the screen. Click the Details charm in the top right-corner to access **Details** view (you might have to click it twice here). Click the charm again to revert to the previous view, if desired.

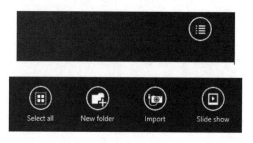

4   Right-click the Sheep.jpg picture to reveal more charms. Click **Open With** and then click **Paint**.

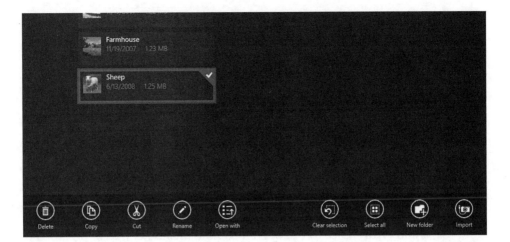

5 Click in the upper-left corner of the screen to return to the Photos app. Click **Clear Selection**.

6 Click the Sheep.jpg picture once to view it in full-screen mode. Click once on the screen to view the arrow located in the upper-left of the screen.

> **TIP** Hover the cursor over any photo thumbnail in the Photos app to see its name, file type, date modified, size, and more.

7 Click the upper-most **Back** arrow to return to the previous screen.

8 Click the Farmhouse.jpg file to view it in full screen mode. Right-click it to view the available charms.

✖ CLEAN UP
Leave the Photos app open to this screen.

Now that you've seen some of the charms—at least those that specifically apply when you are viewing pictures stored as thumbnails or while in full-screen mode—you can see how you could easily delete a single picture or view a slideshow of the images in a folder. You can select additional thumbnail photos by right-clicking them, too, although some of the charms will likely disappear when you do.

The options you can access by right-clicking a photo thumbnail while in the Pictures library include:

- **Delete** Click this to delete the selected photo(s).

- **Copy** Click this to copy the selected photo(s) and make them available for pasting elsewhere. The photos will remain where they are and will not be deleted.

- **Cut** Click this to cut the photos from the folder (remove them) so that you can use the Paste command to move the photo(s) somewhere else.

- **Rename** Click this to rename a single photo. You won't see this if you have more than one photo selected.

- **Open With** Click this to open the photo in another app or desktop app. You won't see this if you have more than one photo selected.

- **Clear Selection** Click this to clear the files you've previously selected. You can select files from only one folder at a time.

- **Select All** Click this to select all the pictures in a folder. With that done you can use other commands such as Delete, Copy, Cut, and Paste to manage the selected photos.

- **New Folder** Click this to create a new folder and name it. When a new folder is available, you can use Cut and Paste to move photos into it.

- **Import** Click this to import pictures that are stored on a device such as a camera or SD card, that is also connected to your computer.

- **Slide Show** Click to play a slide show of the images in the selected folder. Click any key to stop the slide show and the Back arrow to return to the folder that contains it.

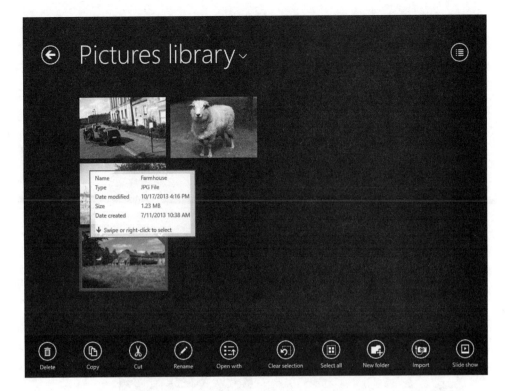

Importing photos by using the Photos app

Import is an option when you right-click the main Photos app screen. You use this charm to import (copy) pictures from a connected SD card, digital camera, SD card, and so on. You must connect the device that holds the pictures before you start. Once the device is connected, right-click as detailed in the previous section and click Import. Then, click the device that holds the pictures to import.

Next, click Select All or click the items to install manually (shown in the illustration that follows). Then, click Import. Wait while the importing process completes. Once the pictures are imported, you'll see them in a new folder in the Photos app.

DSCN0336			100_0025	
12/10/2009	2.22 MB		8/17/2006	876 KB
102_0032		✓	100_0024	
5/8/2008	758 KB		8/17/2006	782 KB
101_0001			100_0023	
12/24/2007	927 KB		7/29/2006	744 KB
100_0031		✓	100_0022	
9/23/2006	698 KB		7/29/2006	890 KB

Clear selection Select all Import Cancel

Editing photos by using the Photos app

There will be instances when you'll need to do some light editing on the photos in your Pictures folder. You might need to rotate or crop a photo, for instance, or you might want to apply some quick fixes to remove "red eye", adjust the lighting, or enhance the color. You can perform these types of edits (and more) from within the Photos app.

In this exercise, you'll use the Photos app to crop the Sheep.jpg picture you copied from the practice files earlier.

→ SET UP
You need to have copied the contents of the Windows81Pictures folder to the Pictures folder on your computer to complete this exercise. This folder is located in the Chapter03 practice file folder.

1   From the **Start** screen, click **Photos**.

2   If you've used the Photos app before, it might open with a photo or folder already selected. If so, click the screen and then click the **Back** arrow that appears in the upper-left corner until you are at the main screen. (If you copied the entire Windows81Pictures folder instead of only its contents, click the **Windows81Pictures** folder to open it.)

3   Click the Sheep.jpg picture.

4   Right-click the screen and then, from among the charms that appear, click **Crop**.

5   Drag from the corners of the crop box and drag the photo to position the Sheep in the center of the picture.

Apply   Cancel

6   Click **Apply**, and then click **Save A Copy**.

A copy is made and is automatically named Sheep (2).

CLEAN UP
Click the screen, and then click the Back arrow that appears in the top-left corner to return to the Photos app main screen. Leave the Photos app open to the screen that contains the cropped image.

Now that you have experienced the crop feature, you can right-click the edited Sheep.jpg photo and try some of the other editing options. Try using Rotate, and then give Edit a whirl. If time allows, click Edit and apply some of the available fixes, including Auto Fix, Basic Fixes, Light, Color, and Effects. If you decide not to apply any changes, right-click the image, and then click Cancel.

Using the Music app

The Music app offers access to your personal music collection; specifically the music that is stored on your computer in the Music library. You can add music by copying music files from CDs you own, by purchasing music online, by sharing from other devices you own, and in many other ways. You might not have any music on your computer yet, but that's okay. You can still work through this section.

SEE ALSO In Chapter 9, "Having fun with multimedia," you learn how to burn your music collection to CD.

The Music app also offers access to music you have stored in the cloud, specifically in Microsoft Xbox Music. When music is stored here, you can listen to it for free from all of the Windows 8–based devices you own. You'll need to select "match my music" when prompted by the Music app to enable this feature. You'll also be given the option to subscribe to an

Xbox Music Pass, with which you can get your music on your Xbox 360 and Windows Phone (for a fee), and download or stream as many songs as you like and listen to them for as long as your subscription is up to date.

Additionally, the Music app offers access to radio stations that are chosen based on songs you select, and the Xbox Music Store where you can purchase music, play samples, and more. After you've set music to play, you also have access to playback controls such as Previous, Pause, Next, Volume, and so on.

The first time you open the Music app, it will go through its own setup tasks. It will locate your music, offer Music Match, and pull in information as needed from the Internet, such as album cover art and song lists. When the Music app is ready and loaded, you'll have access to your personal music collection from the Collection tab. Depending on what you own and have access to, you might see various types of icons under the album covers. Click Go To Collection to get started.

View the music available in your collection, read any notifications about music in the cloud and on your computer, and then, note the icons associated with the music you find. If you do not see an icon under an album cover, it means that the music is stored and can be played on your computer. You own it. If you see a cloud icon, it means the music is on your device and in the cloud (which means you can listen to it from this device when you are not connected to the Internet and from other devices when you are). If you see what looks like a wireless signal, it means the music is available via streaming only (which means you must be connected to the Internet to play it).

Beyond the Collection tab, there are some other areas in the Music app to explore:

TIP Like the Photos app, you right-click a song or album to view the charms related to it (such as Add To, Play Selected, Buy Album, and Delete, among others).

- **Search**   Use this to search for any song that is available to you by using its song title, artist name, album title, and so on. You can also search the Xbox Music Store here.

- **Radio**   Use this to start new radio stations and access those you've already started. You pick a song or artist, and Xbox Music does the rest. You can create multiple radio stations.

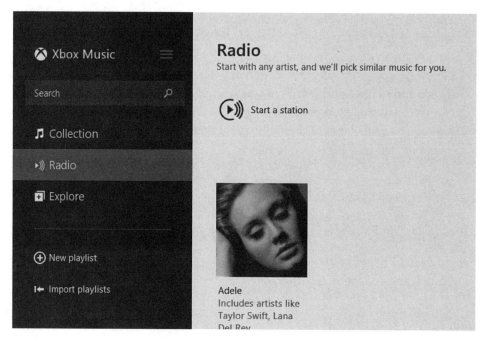

- **Explore**   Use this to browse, preview, and buy music. You can browse in various ways including New Albums or Top Albums, and remember, you can use the Search box to search for something specific.

- **New Playlist**   Use this to create a new playlist. After you create a playlist, you can add songs to it.

- **Import Playlists**   Use this to import existing playlists.

To view and play music you own and have saved to your computer, you choose the desired music from the Collection tab. You can sort the music by albums, artists, and songs, by date added, and by what music is on this computer or in the cloud. You can also sort by genre, alphabetically, or in other ways. The sorting options appear at the top of the Collection pane.

After you've decided on something to play and navigated your way to it, click the title and click the Play arrow. With that done, you can use the available controls.

Because every reader isn't going to have music on their computer, the best way to explore the Music app is by playing a sample of a song from the Xbox Music Store. You'll need to be online to do this.

In this exercise, you'll access the Xbox Music Store, view the track list for an album, play a sample of a song, and then pause the music.

 SET UP
From the Start screen, open the Music app. You do not need any practice files for this exercise, but you will need to be connected to the internet.

1　From the **Start** screen, click **Music**.

2　In the left pane, click **Explore**.

3　Click any album thumbnail and note the album list that appears.

4　Click any song one time, and then click the **Play** icon.

A sample of the song begins to play.

5　Using the controls, click **Pause**.

 CLEAN UP
Leave this screen open.

TIP While a song is playing, continue to browse available music and click the + sign adjacent to any song. Click Now Playing to add this song to the current music session.

As you would suspect, you can use media controls while playing a song or album to manage what's playing. You can shuffle the songs, too, which plays the songs in the playlist or on the album in random order. From the available charms, you can easily skip to the previous and next songs, and you can pause, play, and replay songs. The Back arrow takes you to the previous screen if you move away from it. To access the controls, right-click any music file. Note that ellipses offer additional controls.

3

5	Who Do We Think We Are (Album Version)	4:52
6	All Of Me (Album Version)	4:29
7	Hold On Longer (Album Version)	Repeat: off
8	Save The Night (Album Version)	Shuffle: off

0:16   3:06   ⏮   ▶   ⏭   🔊 80   ⋯

TIP There are many features to explore in Music. You can sort your music in various ways, you can create playlists, you can add music to the cloud, and you can explore the artist in more detail, among other things. There isn't enough room here to detail everything you can do, so spend some time exploring the Music app before moving on.

Using the Video app

The Video app offers access to your personal videos and the Xbox Video Store. When you first open the Video app, scroll to the left to locate the area named Personal Videos to access the videos stored in the Videos library on your computer. If you copied the practice files for this chapter as instructed earlier in the sidebar, you'll see a video there.

Next to the Personal Videos section is any media you've purchased including movies and TV shows, or media you have rented. You may see headings including my tv or my movies. Following that is Home, where selected videos appear including anything that's currently playing and paused, and that is followed by Recommendations, New Movies, Featured Movies, New TV Shows, and Featured TV Shows. You can obtain media here and browse to media by using specific categories. Much of the time, you can either buy or rent the media, and you can watch it on your Xbox if you have one.

In this exercise, you'll play the video Flying over the Hoover Dam.

 SET UP
To complete this exercise, you need to have copied the contents of the Windows 81Videos folder to the Videos folder on your computer according to the instructions in the sidebar "Copying practice files for the first time." This folder is located in the Chapter03 practice file folder.

1   From the **Start** screen, click **Video**.

2   Scroll left and click the thumbnail for **Flying Over The Hoover Dam**.

3   Right-click the screen, click the **Volume** icon, and then use the slider to adjust the volume. Note the other options.

4   If the video finishes, click either of the **Play** icons to restart it.

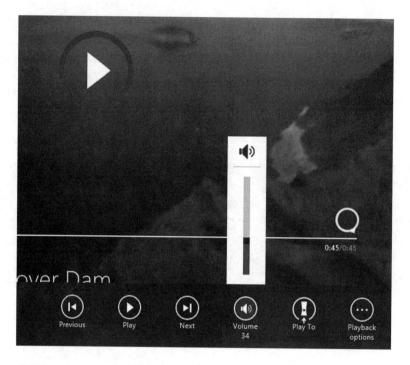

5   If the controls disappear from the screen, click once. Drag the circular icon to move to a new position in the video.

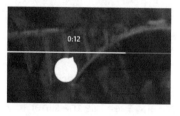

 CLEAN UP
Position the cursor at the top of the screen, wait until it becomes a hand, and then drag downward to close the Video app.

Using the Maps app

The last app you'll explore in depth is Maps. As with any other app, you click its tile on the Start screen to open it. If you are prompted, be sure to turn on location services so that Maps can determine your location.

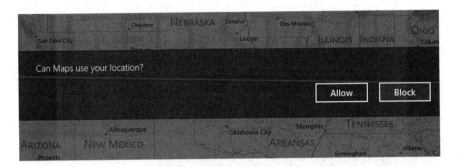

After Maps is open, right-click the screen to see the available charms.

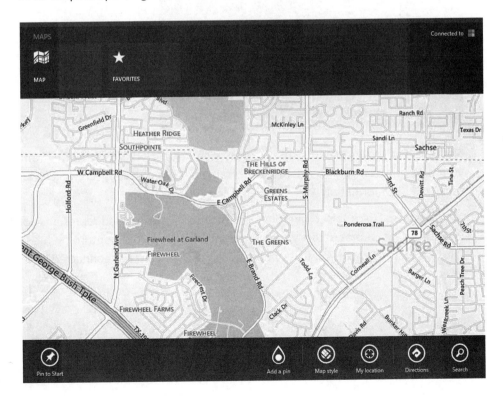

The features available in Maps are:

- **Map** To return to the map if you've navigated away from it, perhaps to view your list of favorite places.

- **Favorites** Use this to add places to a Favorites list. One option for Favorites is Home. Once you've configured favorites you can return here to click them and locate them on the map quickly.

- **Pin To Start** Use this to create a pin on the Start screen that will open Maps to a specific location you define.

- **Add A Pin** Use this to mark a location on a map with an icon called a pin.

- **Map Style** Click this to change the style of the map from Road View to Aerial View.

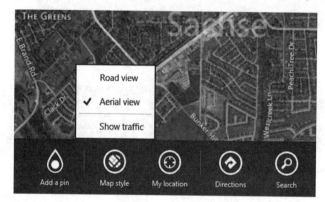

- **Show Traffic** Available from the Map Style charm, click this to show the traffic in your area or on a route you've mapped. Traffic is represented by red, yellow, and green. Traffic information won't be available in all areas.

- **My Location** Click this to pinpoint your location. The diamond represents your location. Maps cannot detect your current location if you did not turn on the required location services when you first opened Maps or if you are not connected to the Internet.

TIP Click the diamond that represents your location for more information about it and/or to add information of your own.

- **Directions** Click this to get directions from one place to another. By default, your current location will be used as one of the entries (provided location services is turned on). Type an address and click the right-facing arrow to get directions, or choose from any option in the available list.

  - **Reverse Route** Click the two arrows located next to your starting location when Directions is selected to reverse the route offered.

  - **Go arrow** Click the blue, right-facing Go arrow after inputting the required information to get directions to a place.

  - **Options** Choose from car, bus, or walking icons for specific directions using these means of transportation, and click Options to instruct Maps to avoid highways and/or tolls.

  - **Search** Click to open the Search pane, which you can use to type the name or address of the place you'd like to go.

In this exercise, you'll get directions from your current location to New York City by way of a car and avoid tolls.

SET UP
From the Start screen, open Maps. You do not need any practice files to work through this exercise.

1   In the **Maps** app, right-click and then, from among the charms that display, click **Directions**.

2   If you don't see **My Location** in one of the boxes, type your current address.

3   In the empty box, type New York City. Click **New York City** in the results.

4   Click the **Car** icon and then, in the **Options** section, move the **Avoid Tolls** slider from **Off** to **On**.

5   To the right of **New York City**, click the blue **Go** arrow.

The route appears with turn-by-turn directions.

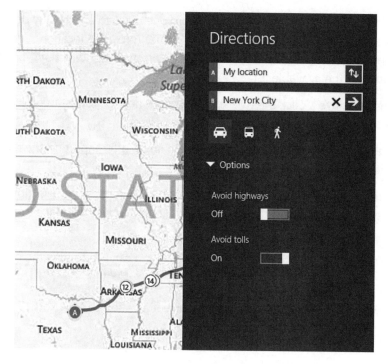

6   Right-click and then, on the shortcut menu that appears, click **Clear Map**.

TIP You can zoom in and out by using the scroll wheel of your mouse or the icons on the screen. If you have a compatible touch screen device, you can also pinch in and out by using your fingers.

⊗ CLEAN UP
Leave this app open.

Continue as time allows and explore some of the other options, such as Favorites. It's easy to create a favorite for your home: Right-click the map, click Favorites, click Add Home, and then type your home address. (If you are at home you can click the Location button, shown here.) On the keyboard, press Enter.

You can add additional favorites by right-clicking the Favorites screen, clicking the + sign that appears, and then repeating the previous steps. If at any time you see multiple results, pick the result you want from the list and then click the Add Favorite icon in the black box that appears.

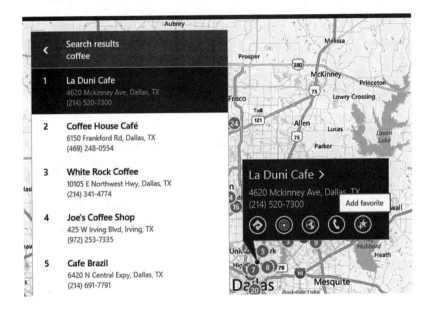

Exploring the other apps

There are many other apps on the Start screen besides Photos, Music, Video, and Maps, but they all open similarly, most offer right-click options to access the charms, you can scroll when there's more data than will fit on the screen, and you can often click screen elements to cause something to happen or a new app page to open. In this section, you'll learn a little about those other apps and where to learn more about them in this book.

Additional apps available from the Home screen include the following:

- **Mail**   Use this app to set up, obtain, and manage email. You'll learn about the Mail app in Chapter 7, "Using the social apps."

- **People**   Use this app to access information about your contacts. Here, you link the app to your Microsoft account, Facebook, Twitter, Skype, and others. With this app, you can see what your contacts are up to from a single app. You'll learn about the People app in Chapter 7.

- **SkyDrive**   Use this app to access your personal SkyDrive folders, in which you can store pictures, documents, music, and other data on Internet servers. You can then access your SkyDrive data from anywhere. You'll learn about SkyDrive in Chapter 6, "Using SkyDrive."

- **Desktop**   Use this app to open the desktop from which you run desktop apps such as Paint and use system tools such as Control Panel.

- **Calendar**   Use this app to access your calendar, on which you can input appointments, events, birthdays, and other data. As with other apps, you can click to change the view, input information, and more. You'll learn about Calendar in Chapter 7.

- **Finance**   Use this app to follow stock prices and access stock report information. You can personalize this app with your own information or just browse the latest financial news.

- **Weather**   Use this app to obtain up-to-date weather information from your current location and other locations you configure. You learned about the Weather app in Chapter 1, "Introducing Windows 8.1."

- **Internet Explorer**   Use this app to access the Internet. You'll learn about this app in Chapter 5, "Using Internet Explorer 11."

- **Sports**   Use this app to open Bing Sports, in which you can read top sports stories, sports news, schedules, and more.

3

- **Store**   Use this app to access the Windows Store, where you can get apps (classified in many categories, including Travel, Productivity, Games, and the like). You'll learn about the Windows Store in various chapters, including Chapter 8, "Shopping in the Windows Store."

- **Games**   Use this app to access, manage, and view your games and game activity. You can also access the Marketplace, where you can purchase new games. If you have an Xbox and have configured an avatar, you'll see it here. You'll learn about games in Chapter 10, "Playing games."

- **Help + Tips**   Use this app to get information, help, and tips for using Windows 8.1. You'll learn more about this in Chapter 21, "Troubleshooting problems."

- **Camera**   Use this to access the camera available on your computer, as applicable, and to view camera options. You'll use your camera, if you have one, to hold video chats. You'll learn more about the Camera app in Chapter 7.

- **News**   Use this app to get the latest news from *msnbc.com* and other sources. News is an easy app to use; just scroll through the headlines and click to read more.

- **Food & Drink**   Use this to read articles about food and drink, review and add recipes, create a shopping list, plan a meal, and more.

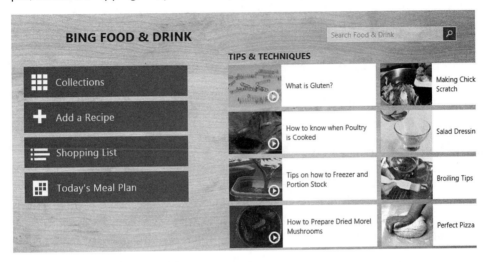

- **Travel**   Use this app to open Bing Travel, in which you can view featured destinations and panoramas, read articles, and more.

- **Reading List**   Use this app to read articles and other items you've saved from other apps for reading later.

- **Skype**   Use Skype to communicate via text, phone, and video. You'll learn about Skype in Chapter 7, Using the social apps.

- **Health & Fitness**   Use this app to read articles, track a diet, calculate calories, manage an exercise program, access information about drugs and conditions, and more.

   TIP There are other apps available from the Apps view, including Scan, Sound Recorder, and more, as well as apps you've obtained from the Windows Store.

Managing apps for the long term

You learned quite a bit about apps in Chapter 1 and Chapter 2, "Personalize your Windows 8.1 device," including how to move apps, use Live tiles, and how to customize those tiles. You learned here how to use many of the apps, including Photos, Music, Video, and Maps, and where to learn more about the rest of the apps on the Start screen. There are a few more things to know, including how to manage apps for the long term.

Here are a few things you can do with apps to make the Start screen more user friendly, to hide apps you won't use, to make app tiles larger or smaller on the Start screen, and more.

- **Show Apps view**   Click the down arrow in the lower-left quadrant of the Start screen to access the Apps view. If you like this view, you can configure it as the default by right-clicking the desktop's taskbar, clicking Properties, and making the appropriate choice from the Navigation tab.

- **Filter Apps view**   Click the arrow beside Apps in Apps view to sort what is there by name, date installed, most used, or category.

- **Unpin an app from the Start screen** Right-click any app and click Unpin From Start to remove it from the Start screen.

- **Uninstall an app** Right-click any app and click Uninstall to remove it completely from your computer.

- **Make an app tile larger or smaller** Right-click any tile to access options to resize it.

- **Make an app tile stop flipping through information or showing personal information on the Start screen (or to allow it to do this)** Right-click an app with a Live tile and choose Turn Live Tile Off (or Turn Live Tile On).

- **Clear multiple selections** Click Clear Selection. (You can select multiple apps on the Start screen by right-clicking them.)

- **Run as an administrator**   Right-click any compatible desktop app to run it with administrator privileges. You can also open the file location, uninstall the app, and more.

Exploring accessories and tools

Finally, the Start screen offers access to the Windows 8.1 accessories and system tools. There are quite a few of each—too many to detail here. However, most of the accessory names are intuitive, as are the Windows system tools names. To access the available accessories and system tools, go to the Apps view. To open one of these, just click it one time.

As just mentioned, not every accessory or tool is covered in this book. However, a few are worth noting and exploring here.

- **Paint**   Use this to draw your own artwork by using paint brushes and tools such as the Pencil, Paint Bucket, and Text. You can use this app to create a flyer, for example.

- **Snipping Tool**   Use the snipping tool and drag the cursor around an area of the screen to capture that potion of it. You can use the captured portion as an illustration.

- **Control Panel** Use this to open Control Panel, which opens on the desktop and offers access to more personalization, networking, and security options.

↑ 🖳 ▸ Control Panel ▸   ∨ | ↻

Adjust your computer's settings   View by: Category ▾

System and Security
Review your computer's status
Save backup copies of your files with File History
Find and fix problems

Network and Internet
View network status and tasks
Choose homegroup and sharing options

Hardware and Sound
View devices and printers
Add a device
Adjust commonly used mobility settings

Programs
Uninstall a program

User Accounts and Family Safety
Change account type
Set up Family Safety for any user

Appearance and Personalization
Change the theme
Change desktop background
Adjust screen resolution

Clock, Language, and Region
Add a language
Change input methods
Change date, time, or number formats

Ease of Access
Let Windows suggest settings
Optimize visual display

In this exercise, you'll access the Help And Support option from the Windows System category when viewing All Apps on the Start screen.

→ SET UP
Start your computer and unlock the lock screen. You need to have access to the Start screen.

1   On the **Start** screen, type Help and Support.

2   Click **Help And Support** from the results. It will have a blue question mark beside it.

3   Maximize the window if applicable.

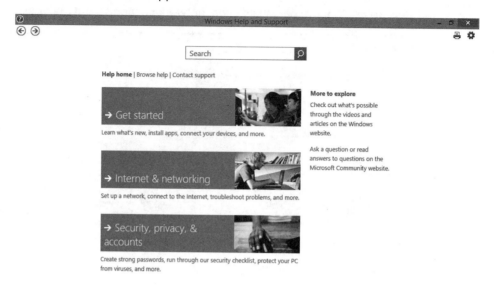

4   Browse the **Help And Support** pages as you would any webpage.

✖ CLEAN UP
No cleanup is required.

Key points

- Windows 8.1 comes with many default apps that are available from the Start screen.

- You use the Photos app to manage and view photos stored on your hard disk, and to manage and edit them.

- You use the Music app to access and play your own music and to buy music from the Xbox Music Store.

- You use the Videos app to access movies, TV shows, and compatible videos that are stored on your computer and to buy movies and TV shows from the applicable Xbox stores.

- You use the Maps app to find places and businesses, and to get turn-by-turn directions to places you've mapped.

- There are lots of other apps to explore, including People, Calendar, and others, many of which are outlined in this book in various chapters.

- The Apps view offers access to apps that don't appear on the Start screen, accessories, and system tools. You can also access third-party apps and apps you've acquired from the Windows Store.

3

Chapter at a glance

Use
Use subfolders to organize data, page 123

Access
Access SkyDrive from File Explorer, page 127

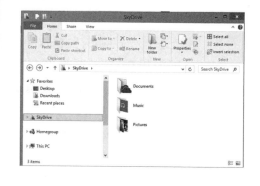

Copy
Copy files to a new location, page 138

Personalize
Personalize your File Explorer view, page 150

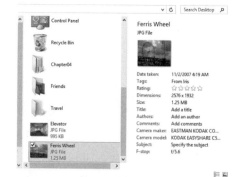

Organizing files and folders

4

IN THIS CHAPTER, YOU WILL LEARN HOW TO

- Understand the Windows 8.1 file system.

- Describe the most common file types.

- Acquire and save files effectively.

- Navigate the File Explorer ribbon interface.

- Organize and share files and folders.

- Customize and search File Explorer.

You acquire all kinds of data files, including but not limited to documents, spreadsheets, pictures, presentations, videos, and executable apps. You save those files with recognizable file names in appropriate folders. For instance, you save the personal documents you create in the Documents folder. If you want to share documents, you can save them to the Public Documents folder. There are other folders beyond those related to documents, including Pictures and Public Pictures, Music and Public Music, Videos and Public Videos, and so on. As you acquire more data, you should create your own subfolders within these to expand this built-in folder system.

TIP Always store data in related default folders, at least for now. When you run most backup apps, the default folders and the subfolders in them will be included automatically.

Although there are multiple ways to access the data you acquire (including from within apps), File Explorer is the most comprehensive, and is available from the desktop's taskbar. File Explorer always opens on the desktop. By using File Explorer, you can access your data, view it in various ways, search for files and folders, and even burn files to CDs and DVDs, all from a single window.

Understanding the Windows 8.1 file system

The first step to understanding how best to save, browse to, and organize data is to learn the differences among files, folders, and subfolders, and what types of folders Windows 8.1 already includes. With that knowledge, you can save data better and use File Explorer more effectively to locate and manage your data in the future.

TIP File Explorer offers a ribbon for performing common tasks and a Navigation pane for locating the data you save.

The main differences among files, folders, and subfolders are as follows:

- **File** Any unique, stand-alone piece of data such as a single document, spreadsheet, or presentation; an executable file; a picture or video; a screen shot of a map; or an itinerary. You save files in folders.

- **Folder** A mechanism for grouping data, generally data that is alike in some way. Windows 8.1 has several preinstalled folders ready for you to use, including Documents, Music, Videos, Downloads, and Desktop, among others. You can create your own folders, too.

- **Subfolder** Folders within other folders. You create subfolders to organize your data and then you move data into those folders.

Windows 8.1 offers the following folders from File Explorer when This PC is selected; no files are stored there by default when you install Windows 8.1:

- **Desktop**   A folder that holds the items you've saved to the desktop.

- **Documents**   A folder that holds items you've saved here, usually documents, text files, PDFs, spreadsheets, presentations, and so on.

- **Downloads**   A folder that holds the items that you've downloaded from the Internet, such as executable files.

- **Music**   A folder in which you can save your music audio files as well as any items media apps have saved here by default. When you purchase music from the Internet, it will likely be saved here, too.

- **Pictures**   A folder that holds your photos, preferably pictures you've imported from a digital camera or memory card as well as pictures you've acquired from the Internet, email, or other means. You will see a subfolder here named Camera Roll if your device has a built-in camera and you've taken at least one picture with it.

- **Videos**   A folder in which you save primarily your video files videos. Media you acquire online might be saved here by default, as well.

TIP There are public counterparts to Documents, Downloads, Music, Pictures, and Videos. You save data to these related Public folders when you want to share it with others who can access your computer directly or via a network. These folders are located on the computer's hard disk, under C:\Users, in the Public folder.

In this exercise, you'll explore the folders already on your own computer by using File Explorer. What you see when you click a folder in the Navigation pane (the left pane in the File Explorer window) might include data you've already acquired, or you might see only the practice files that you've copied here while working through this book.

→ SET UP

Copy the practice files that are located in the Chapter04 folder to your computer. Specifically, copy the file in the PracticeMusic subfolder to your Music folder; copy the files in the PracticePictures folder to your Pictures folder; copy the files in the PracticeVideos folder to your Videos folder; copy the file in the PracticeDocuments folder to your Documents folder.

SEE ALSO To learn how to install the practice files, refer to the section "Using the practice files" in the Introduction of this book. Also, refer to the sidebar "Copying practice files for the first time" in Chapter 3, "Using apps on the Start screen," for additional instructions.

1   On the **Start** screen, type explorer. In the results, click **File Explorer**.

    KEYBOARD SHORTCUT Use the Windows key+E keyboard shortcut to open File Explorer from anywhere, even from the Start screen.

2   Maximize the window if necessary. In the **Navigation** pane, click **This PC**.

    The default folders are available from the Content pane.

    TROUBLESHOOTING If you do not see the Navigation pane, on the ribbon, click View, choose Navigation Pane, and then select it. (You'll learn more about the ribbon in the section "Navigating the File Explorer ribbon interface" later in the chapter.)

3   Double-click **Documents**.

    The Documents folder opens.

4   Click the **Back** arrow and then double-click **Pictures**.

⊙ ⊙ ▾ ↑ 🖳 ▸ This PC ▸   ⌄

☆ Favorites   ◢ Folders (6)
　🗀 Cloud Drive
　🖥 Desktop   🗀 Desktop   🗀 Documents
　📥 Downloads
　📋 Recent places   🗀 Downloads   🗀 Music

☁ SkyDrive
                         🗀 ☑ Pictures   🗀 Videos
🖳 Homegroup
　🖥 Joli   ◢ Devices and drives (2)
　🖥 Joli Ballew
                         🖴 Acer (C:)   💿 DVD RW Drive (D:)
🖳 This PC   380 GB free of 449 GB

                         ◢ Network locations (1)

5   Click the **Back** arrow and then double-click **Music**.

6   Click the **Back** arrow and then double-click **Videos**.

This PC ▸ Videos

Flying over the   Take off   The Stratosphere
Hoover Dam   Ride in Las Vegas

 CLEAN UP
Click the Back arrow to return to the This PC screen.

TIP Notice the Favorites option in the left pane of File Explorer. You can click anything in this list to go there quickly.

There are other options available in the Navigation pane of File Explorer beyond what's available from This PC. Microsoft SkyDrive is one of them. You'll learn about SkyDrive in Chapter 6, "Using SkyDrive," but we'll briefly introduce it here. You'll also see Homegroup and related options if you've joined a homegroup (see Chapter 13, "Sharing files and folders by using my network") and Network and resulting options if you have a network already configured (see Chapter 11, "Connecting to a network and the Internet"). Because you might not yet have either, we'll skip those for now.

Anyone who logs on to a Windows 8–based computer with a Microsoft account has the ability to save files to SkyDrive. SkyDrive is a folder in the Navigation pane of File Explorer that offers a place to save your files on the Internet. You'll get 7 GB of free space there, and you can use that space to back up important files or to make files accessible from any computer you can log on to that can access the Internet. On Windows 8–based computers, you can access the files you store there from the SkyDrive app; from other computers you can visit *https://skydrive.live.com/* and log on to access your files.

To get a glimpse of what SkyDrive offers, in the Navigation pane, click SkyDrive to see what appears in the Content pane. What you see will depend on whether you've set up and/or used SkyDrive, and what configuration changes, if any, you've performed.

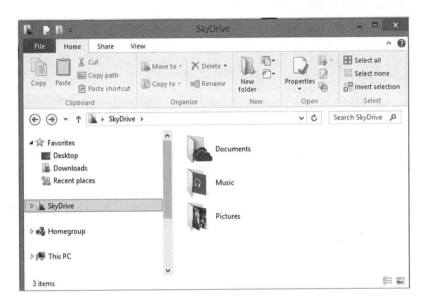

Now, while reading the rest of this chapter, think about the things you might want to save to SkyDrive. As an example, if you work on specific files from various computers, you might want to save those files to SkyDrive so that you can always access the latest version. You might want to let Windows 8.1 back up all of the photos you take with your camera here, too. You might want to save to SkyDrive by default. You can configure these options for SkyDrive from PC Settings as well as others. For now though, simply take notice that you can save files there, and consider doing so. Here are SkyDrive options from PC Settings.

SkyDrive storage

6.99 GB available of 7.00 GB

Buy more storage

When you save files to SkyDrive, you can get to them from any device, even if something happens to this PC.

Save documents to SkyDrive by default

On

See my files on SkyDrive

Regarding libraries

Libraries were a prevalent part of Windows 7 and Windows 8. Libraries were available in the Navigation pane of File Explorer and offered access to both the personal and public folders related to the library selected. As an example, the Documents Library offered easy access to what was in both the (My) Documents folder and the Public Documents folder. You could separate the data if you wanted to, but it was not separated by default. You could also add other folders to libraries to include them. However, libraries were mostly misunderstood by users and rarely used effectively.

Libraries are still available in Windows 8.1, but they are different now. A library, by default, only offers access to the related personal folder. So, the Documents library only offers access to what is in the Documents folder (and no longer offers access to what's also in the Public Documents folder). This is true of the other libraries (Music, Pictures, Videos).

If you still want to show a Libraries section in the Navigation pane, you can do so on the View tab, under the Navigation pane option. Just select Show libraries so that a check mark appears by it. The updated default libraries will then reappear in the Navigation pane. For more information on this, refer to the section "Customizing File Explorer by using the View tab" later in this chapter.

Another way to enable and incorporate libraries is to create a new folder (perhaps on the desktop) and name it (we'll create a folder named Travel), right-click that folder and then, on the shortcut menu that appears, click Include In Library. Then, click Create New Library. After you do this, the traditional libraries will appear in the Navigation pane, as will your new library. You can continue to expand on this structure as desired.

If you upgraded to Windows 8.1 from Windows 7, you will still see the old format for libraries, meaning you'll have access to both the personal and public folders if you opt to show Libraries in the Navigation pane. However, if you upgraded from Windows 8, or if you installed Windows 8.1 clean, you won't.

TIP You can open multiple File Explorer windows. To do so, right-click the File Explorer icon on the taskbar and then, on the shortcut menu that appears, click File Explorer to open a new window.

Explaining the most common file types

You can open and view hundreds of kinds of files on your Windows 8–based computer. The most common sorts of files are documents, spreadsheets, presentations, music, pictures, videos, and executable files. You might occasionally work with recorded TV or specialized files from third-party apps, but for the most part, the types of files you encounter will be common ones.

You save each of these files as a specific *file type*. You choose the file type during the save process. (If you copy a file from another source, it already has a file type.) For example, when you save a document you've created by using Microsoft Word, you name the file, choose a place to save it, and select the desired file type from a list. The file type gives the file a specific extension, generally three or four letters that appear at the end of the file name (but don't necessarily appear in the list of options). The name, place, and file type you select defines the file so that Windows 8.1 can distinguish it from other files, locate it, and offer it for viewing.

To save files effectively, you need to know a little about the choices available in apps you'll use to create them. The list that follows shows the types of files you'll encounter most often and their file name extensions. You have the option to select a file type when you save a file. The illustration shows the options when saving a picture file in Paint.

TIP To show file extensions in File Explorer, on the ribbon, click the View tab, and then select File Name Extensions.

- Microsoft Office files

  - Microsoft Word (.doc and .docx)

  - Microsoft Excel (.xls and .xlsx)

  - Microsoft PowerPoint (.ppt and .pptx)

  - Microsoft Publisher (.pub and .pubx)

- Music files

  - Windows Media audio files (.asx, .wm, .wma, and .wmx)

  - Windows audio files (.wav)

- MP3 audio files (.mp3 and .m3u)

- AAC files (.aac)

- Picture files

    - JPEG files (.jpg and .jpeg)

    - TIFF files (.tif and .tiff)

    - RAW files (.raw)

    - GIF files (.gif)

    - Bitmap files (.bmp)

    - PNG files (.png)

- Video files

    - Windows Media files (.wm, .wmv, and .asf)

    - Apple QuickTime files (.mov and .qt)

    - AVI files (.avi)

    - Windows Recorded TV Show files (.wtv and .dvr-ms)

    - MPEG Movie files (.mp4, .mov, .m4v, .mpeg, .mpg, .mpe, .m1v, .mp2, .mpv2, .mod, .vob, and .m1v)

    - Motion JPEG files (.avi and .mov)

    TIP If you can't determine the file type from the file name, you can determine it from the file's Properties page, as detailed in the next set of steps.

- Miscellaneous

    - Executable files (.exe)

    - Microsoft Notepad (.txt)

    - PDF Reader (.pdf)

    - OpenOffice and LibreOffice (.odt, .ott, .oth, and .odm)

By default, file extensions are not shown in the lists you'll peruse while searching for a file to open using File Explorer. This is true of most other methods, as well, such as opening a file from the File menu of an app like Paint or WordPad. If you are interested in knowing the file type, you can do this by viewing the file's Properties page. The Properties page for any file offers its file extension and other information. You can open the Properties page by right-clicking the file and then, on the shortcut menu that appears choosing Properties. The Properties dialog box for any file also offers the name of the app with which the file is configured to open, the option to open the folder that contains the file, and other data and options.

TIP The list of options you see when you right-click a file will depend on the type of file you've chosen. For example, if you right-click a compatible image file, the option to Set As Desktop Background is available. This option is not available when you right-click a text document or a video.

In this exercise you'll open the Properties page for a file on your own computer and learn its file type.

 SET UP
You need to have copied the practice files located in the Chapter04 folder to complete this exercise.

1   Open the **File Explorer** window by using the **Windows key+E** keyboard shortcut.

2   Click **This PC** and then double-click the Documents folder.

3   Right-click **Notepad**.

A shortcut menu appears.

▸ This PC ▸ Documents

Open
Print
Edit
Open with   ▸
Share with   ▸
Send to   ▸
Cut
Copy
Create shortcut
Delete
Rename
Properties

4   Click **Properties**.

The Properties dialog box opens.

TIP By default, extensions for files aren't shown.

5   On the **General** tab, note what's listed beside **Type Of File**.

In this example, Text Document (.txt) is the type.

TIP To change how a specific type of file will open by default. In the Properties dialog box, click the General tab, click Change, and then select a new app.

CLEAN UP
Click Cancel to close the Properties dialog box.

Acquiring and saving files effectively

You acquire files in many ways. You might obtain picture files from a webpage or from an email. You can copy photos from a digital camera or memory card that you own. You can copy documents from a flash drive, external drive, or corporate server. Of course, you also create your own files by using word processing, spreadsheet, and presentation apps, to name a few. There are thousands of ways to acquire data.

When you get or create data, you must save it. When you save a file, you name the file, choose a place to save it, and select a file type. You will probably want to name the files descriptively, but even if you don't (or you forget to) you can still sort files by various *metadata*—which is the data that describes data—that is added to them automatically, such as the date a file was created, among other things. Additionally, at least at first, you should strive to save data files in their respective default folders, too. Save personal documents to the Documents folder, personal pictures the Pictures folder, personal audio files to the Music folder, and so on. Alternatively, you could save your files to the related folder on SkyDrive. All of these options for saving are available from File Explorer.

Similarly, you should opt to save data that you'd like to share with others or access from networked devices (such as media centers) to their Public folder counterparts. For instance, you might consider saving your music files to the Public Music folder, your vacation videos to the Public Videos folder, and your favorite pictures to the Public Pictures folder, because when you do, you make those files easily accessible from any device on your network. You have to choose this option specifically, though; no data is saved to the Public folders by default. (It is possible to create a homegroup for sharing data, as is detailed in Chapter 13.)

TIP Public folders aren't as easy to get to as personal folders. Consider creating a shortcut for the Public folders on your desktop if you find you use those folders often.

In this exercise, you'll create a file in WordPad, save it to your personal Documents folder, and then to the Public Documents folder.

Return to the Start screen. No other setup is required for this exercise.

1   On the **Start** screen, start typing **WordPad**.

2   Click **WordPad** in the results; it should be the first entry.

3   Type I will save this file as a rich text document.

4   Click **File** and then click **Save As**. (Do not simply point to Save As; you must click it.)

5   In the **Save As** dialog box, in the **File Name** box, type My WordPad Document.

6   Verify that **Rich Text Format (RTF)** is selected in the **Save As Type** box. If necessary, click the arrow in that window to select it.

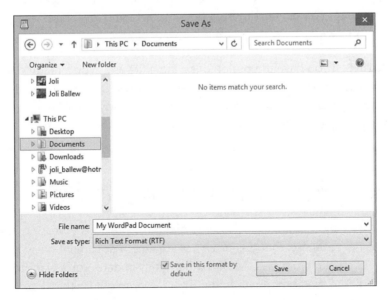

7   In the **Navigation** pane, click **This PC** and then double-click **Documents**.

8   Click **Save**.

9   Repeat Steps 4 and 5.

10   In the **Navigation** pane, click **This PC**. Scroll if necessary to the **Devices and Drives** section. Double-click the entry that represents your computer's hard drive, which is generally C, double-click **Users**, double-click **Public**, and then double-click **Public Documents**.

11   Click **Save**.

 CLEAN UP

In WordPad, in the upper-right corner of the window, click the Close button (the red X) to close it.

SEE ALSO The section "The most common file types" explained earlier in this chapter.

It is important to understand that the options you see in the Save As Type list depend on the app you're using to save the file. In Notepad, if you click the arrow to open the list, you can see that you have only one option, Text Documents (*.txt). WordPad offers more, including but not limited to Open Document Text and Office Open XML Document. As you saw earlier, Paint offers completely different options, including .jpg, .bmp, and .gif. You'll see additional options as you work with different software apps.

TROUBLESHOOTING If you have the option of saving a file as a type already called out in this chapter (such as a .doc, .jpeg, or .gif) versus something you've never heard of (such as .ged), save the file by using the most universal format. That way you'll be able to open the file in other apps, not just in the app in which you created or saved it.

Copy photos from an external drive

You can acquire data by creating it, such as you did in the previous exercise by using WordPad. In this next exercise, though, instead of creating a document file, you'll acquire a different type of data: picture files. As with other types of data, you'll want to save the pictures you acquire to the appropriate folder. That folder might be the Pictures folder on SkyDrive, the Pictures folder from This PC, or the Public Pictures folder, available from the root drive, under Users and Public. When you use File Explorer to copy photos, you can be sure you know exactly where they are saved. (Some apps save by default in a folder that you might not prefer, for example.)

To work through the following exercise, you'll need to connect a camera, camera card, or flash drive that contains pictures. You might also have a backup drive with pictures. If you don't have this at hand, you can return here when you do. This exercise lets you see what might happen by default, and then you use File Explorer to copy the photos to the Pictures folder manually.

TROUBLESHOOTING Most often, when you connect a device that contains photos, a message appears in the upper-right corner of the screen that prompts you to select a default action to take when such media is connected (such as opening a folder to view the files or automatically importing photos). It may also be that nothing happens, other than the device appearing in the Navigation pane in File Explorer. Sometimes, however, certain actions might occur automatically, such as an app opening offering to do things with your photos. If this happens, and you want to copy the files manually using File Explorer, close the app or opt not to choose any default action when prompted.

In this exercise, you'll access pictures from a digital camera, memory card, or USB flash drive by using File Explorer and copy those photos to the Pictures folder on your computer.

 SET UP
Cameras must be installed before they can be used to import files. To install a camera, connect it and see if it will install on its own. If it does not, run the installation file from the included CD or DVD, or get the required files from the manufacturer's website. USB flash drives and memory cards don't require any special setup.

1   Connect the device that contains the pictures to copy.

2   In **File Explorer**, in the **Navigation** pane, click **This PC**.

3   Double-click the external drive or device. Here, this is **PICBACKUP (H:)**.

4   Hold down the **Ctrl** key and click each item to import (copy). You can select folders.

5   On the ribbon, click the **Home** tab, and then click **Copy To**.

6   Click **Pictures**.

❌ CLEAN UP

When the copy process has ended, disconnect the external device. In the Navigation pane, click This PC and then double-click Pictures to see the newly copied photos.

Navigating the File Explorer ribbon interface

File Explorer uses a graphical user interface feature called the *ribbon* that is becoming the defacto standard for navigation. The ribbon runs across the top of the window and is made up of several tabs. You've already used the ribbon to copy files and have probably noted that it presents a lot of elements. You click any tab to access the groups of related options and tools. Each time you click a new tab, the ribbon displays a different group of tools, depending on which tab you clicked. The names of the tabs are mostly intuitive and share attributes with other ribbon-enabled windows and apps.

The ribbon is a highly contextual interface. The tabs and options on the ribbon change depending on what you have selected in the Navigation pane. For example, if you click SkyDrive in the Navigation pane, you see a specific set of tabs on the ribbon that includes File, Home, Share, and View. You can see what's on each tab by clicking it. If you click a specific item in a folder, perhaps a photo, the tabs change again. In the case of a selected photo, a new tab appears (Picture Tools Manage). If you select a video file, you will see File, Home, Share, View, and Video Tools (Play).

TIP If you click an option under Favorites you'll likely see only File, Home, Share, and View.

To understand how to use the ribbon, you must know which tabs will appear most often and what is available under these tabs. When working with folders, the following are the most common tabs you'll encounter:

- **File**   You use this tab to open a new File Explorer window or a command prompt, to clear history, to get help, or to access your most frequent places for storing data. For the most part, what you see under the File menu is the same no matter what you have selected in the Navigation pane.

- **Home**   This tab presents tools to cut, copy, and paste compatible, selected data available in the window. You can also copy the file path, move or copy data, delete data, rename data, create a new folder, and select data, among other things. Options you see here will change depending on what's selected in the folder window.

  TROUBLESHOOTING If you don't see a ribbon, but instead see only menu titles, in the upper-right corner, below the Close button (the red X), click the arrow located to the left of the Help button.

- **Share**   Use the tools on this tab to send files in an email message, compress (zip) files, burn selected files to a CD or DVD, print, fax, and share with users in your homegroup, among other things and as applicable. (You can't print a video you've selected, for instance, so Print will be dimmed in that case.)

  TIP Additional "contextual tabs" might appear, such as Picture Tools, if you select certain types of items in the open folder or library.

  KEYBOARD SHORTCUT Use the shortcut Windows key+P to quickly print an open file.

Use the Share tab to choose with whom to share the data, among other things.

- **View** Tools on the View tab make it possible for you to change how the files appear in the window (Extra Large Icons, Large Icons, Medium Icons, and so on). You might also be able to hide or show the Navigation pane, Preview pane, and Details pane; choose how to sort the data in the window; and show or hide file name extensions; among other things.

> **TROUBLESHOOTING** If you can't see all the tabs, or if the items on the tabs seem condensed, maximize the File Explorer window. If you don't see the ribbon, but instead see only tab names, at the top of the window, on the Quick Access toolbar, click the arrow, and then clear the Minimize Ribbon check box.

- **Manage** In varying instances a Manage tab appears, such as when you select a photo. From that tab, you can often rotate an image, set it as background, or show a slide show.

> **TIP** Rarely, an unexpected tab will appear or a common tab will be missing. For instance, if you click This PC in the Navigation pane, you'll see only three tabs: File, Computer, and View. If you select a drive in the Content pane, though, another tab will appear, Drive Tools, Manage.

In this exercise, you'll explore various tabs on the File Explorer ribbon and use the ribbon to delete the My WordPad Document file you created earlier in this chapter. Later, you'll learn how to use more of the commands you see on these tabs.

➡️ SET UP
You need to have previously created the My WordPad Document file, as described earlier in this chapter, and saved it to the Documents folder.

1   Open **File Explorer** by using any method desired.

2   In the **Navigation** pane, click **This PC**, and then double-click **Documents**.

3   Click the **Home** tab (if applicable).

4   Click the **My Wordpad Document** file (click it just once; do not double-click it).

5   On the **Home** tab, click **Delete**.

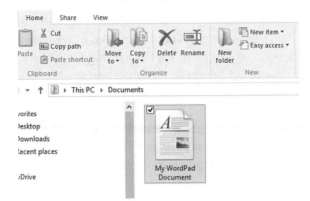

SEE ALSO For more information on deleting files, see the section "Working with deleted files and the Recycle Bin" later in this chapter.

✖ CLEAN UP
Leave this window open.

To summarize, the ribbon offers the tools you need to perform tasks when working with files, folders, and subfolders, and the tabs are named so that you can easily determine what should be available on them. For instance, if you want to share a file by printing it, sending it by email, burning it to a CD, or even faxing it, the Share tab offers this functionality. If you want to change how you view files in File Explorer or if you'd like to sort your files, group them, or hide or view specific parts of File Explorer, the View tab offers this functionality. Don't worry if this is all new to you; it's pretty intuitive, and you'll catch on quickly.

TIP In the next few sections, you'll learn how to use the tools available under other tabs, including Share and View.

Organizing files and folders

There are many ways to organize your files and folders beyond saving them in the appropriate folders and with recognizable names. One way to organize your files for the long term is to create subfolders within the existing default folders and move data into those subfolders. By using subfolders, you can easily expand the existing file system. This makes navigating your data more intuitive when using File Explorer. Windows 8.1 makes it easy to create a subfolder, and you'll learn how to do it in the next exercise.

TIP The best way to keep your data organized is to create folders with descriptive names and move corresponding data into them as you acquire it (as opposed to later, after the data has become a problem). Consider creating folders named Travel, Taxes, Health, Pets, and so on.

Either before or after you create subfolders and begin to move data into them, you can give those folders more recognizable names than they have now. Names such as Tax Summary 2013, Jennifer's Wedding, or My Las Vegas Vacation 2011 are certainly understandable and better than something less descriptive (such as Taxes, Pictures, or Vacation). You can delete files you no longer need, too. Finally, if you decide to archive data that you no longer want to store on your computer, you can burn those files to a CD or DVD.

In this exercise, you'll create a subfolder within the Pictures folder.

 SET UP
You do not need any practice files for this exercise.

1   Open **File Explorer** by using any method desired.

2   In the **Navigation** pane, click **This PC**, and then double-click **Pictures**.

3   On the **Home** tab, click the **New Folder** icon.

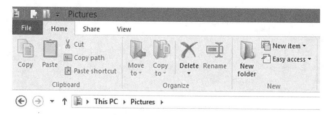

A new folder appears, waiting to be named.

4   Type a name for the folder and then press the **Enter** key.

Taxes 2013

TROUBLESHOOTING If you accidentally press Enter before you've typed a name and end up with a folder named New Folder, click it once and then, on the ribbon, click Rename. Alternatively, you can right-click the folder and click Rename.

✖ CLEAN UP
Leave File Explorer open for the next exercise.

After you create a subfolder, it's easy to move data into it. You can just drag files from the window to the newly created folder. This works great if the new folder and the data you want to move into it are both in the same window. However, if dragging isn't so straightforward, you can use the Move To command on the Home tab of the ribbon.

TIP You can select multiple, noncontiguous files by holding down the Ctrl key while you select them. To select contiguous files, hold down the Shift key, click the first of the series of files, click the last in the series to select those and all of the files in between.

In this exercise, you'll move two files at one time from one folder to another by using the Move To command in File Explorer.

→ SET UP
You need the practice files located in the Chapter04 folder, as outlined in the section "Using the Practice Files" in the Introduction of this book.

1   Open **File Explorer** by using any method desired.

2   In the **Navigation** pane, click **This PC**, and then double-click **Pictures**.

3   Click the **Elevator** file to select it (do not double-click it).

4   Hold down **Ctrl** and click **Ferris Wheel** (again, do not double-click it).

      TIP   If you are using a touch screen you'll see a check mark appear beside the selected files.

5   On the **Home** tab, click **Move To**.

6   Click **Choose location**.

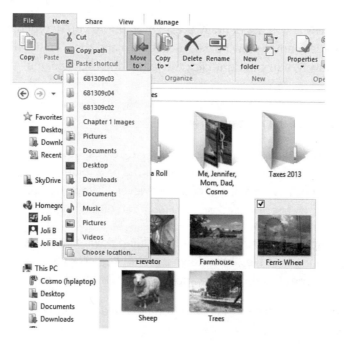

      TIP   If you see the folder to which you'd like to move the files, you can select it. If you do not see the folder, click Choose Folder and browse to it.

7   In the **Move Items** dialog box that opens, click **Desktop**. (Desktop is listed under This PC in the Move Items dialog box.)

8   Click **Move**.

After you click Move, the dialog box closes, and the two files you selected are now available on the desktop

 CLEAN UP
Leave File Explorer open for the next exercise.

TIP Use Copy To if you want to copy the files instead of move them. The process is the same.

Renaming files

When you import pictures from a digital camera by using any of the available built-in tools, your camera software, or a photo-editing app, those imported pictures are given names. Every file must have its own name. The names given aren't very descriptive, though. The file names applied might be a cryptic form of the date on which the photos were imported, or they might be partial names created by using tags you applied during the process, but usually they are not the names you'd apply to them, given the opportunity.

TIP Take time to name files effectively when you acquire them so that renaming files doesn't take you all day when you decide that it needs to be done.

Other types of files are also often named inappropriately, generally because you're in a hurry to save them. File names such as Dad, Summary, Presentation, Taxes, and so on don't give much information about their contents. If you find yourself opening the file to figure out what it is, the name is not descriptive enough.

TIP The Home tab on the File Explorer ribbon offers the Rename button, which becomes available only after you select a file.

In this exercise, you'll rename a file by using the Rename command in File Explorer.

 SET UP
You need the practice files located in the Chapter04 folder.

1   Open **File Explorer** by using any method desired.

2   In the **Navigation** pane, click **This PC**. Double-click **Videos**.

3   Click the **Take Off** file to select it (do not double-click it).

4   On the **Home** tab, click **Rename**.

5   Type Helicopter Ride

6   Press **Enter**.

CLEAN UP
Leave File Explorer open for the next exercise.

TIP You can rename a file, delete it, and perform other tasks by right-clicking the file and choosing the appropriate option from the shortcut menu that appears.

Sharing files by using the Share tab

Now that you have some experience with File Explorer, the ribbon, and working with files, you can use that knowledge to explore other tools that are available on the ribbon and to use those tools with less guidance. For instance, you can likely figure out how to burn a file to a CD or DVD because Burn To Disc is a command on the Share tab, provided your computer or laptop offers the required drive. Likewise, you can deduce how to print the Sheep.jpg photo by using the Print command that's located on that same tab. In both instances, you select the desired file, click the desired command, and follow any instructions provided; for instance, you might have to insert a disc or put paper in the printer.

Some commands are less intuitive than, for example, Print. The Zip command is one of those. When you zip a file (or files), you *compress* it. When you compress a group of files or a single large file, it takes up less space on your hard disk. People often zip large files or groups of files before they send them as attachments to email messages to reduce the amount of time it will take the files to arrive at their destination. In the past, people zipped files because of a lack of hard disk space. (The practice files you downloaded for use with this book were zipped.)

Fax is another intuitive but odd command. It's a little different from the others because you need access to a fax server or telephone line to actually send a fax, and most home users don't have that access. If you already have something in place with which you can send faxes from your computer, though, the process is intuitive. If you'd like to be able to send faxes from your computer, you'll have to perform the setup tasks that appear when you click the Fax command.

There are some tools you can now explore on your own from the Share tab. (Remember that not all options appear for all data.)

- **Email**   Select any file (or multiple files) in a File Explorer window to activate this option. Click Email. If you've chosen a picture (or multiple pictures) to send in email, you'll be prompted to choose a picture size first. After you click Email, your default email app will open, and the file(s) will be attached.

    TROUBLESHOOTING If you do not have a dedicated email client installed and configured on your computer this command won't work and will appear dimmed. The command can't use a web-based email solution.

- **Zip**   Select multiple files to compress them. After they are compressed, you can send the compressed folder (which contains the files) as an attachment to an email message. To decompress, double-click the compressed files. You can see that a file is zipped because a zipper appears on it. (The practice files you downloaded to your desktop for use with this book were in a folder that had a zipper on it.)

- **Burn To Disc**   Select the file or files to burn (copy) to a CD or DVD. Click Burn To Disc. Insert a disc when prompted and follow any instructions to complete the copy process.

- **Print**   Select the file or files to print and then click Print. You might be prompted to choose a printer, set printer properties, or perform other tasks, depending on your printer and current computer setup. The document might just begin to print with no other input from you. The Print command will appear dimmed if you have selected something that can't be printed, such as a song in the Music library.

- **Fax**   Select a file to fax. Click the Fax command. Follow any prompts to complete the fax process.

SEE ALSO To share data with others on your network, which can involve using the various homegroup and share commands on the Share tab of File Explorer, refer to Chapter 13.

Customizing File Explorer by using the View tab

On the View tab in File Explorer, you can change how the window displays on the screen. You can hide or show the Navigation pane, change how the files appear (for example, as a detailed list or as icons), and hide files and folders you don't use very often. You can show panes that do not currently appear, including the Preview pane and the Details pane. You can also group files in various ways, show file name extensions, and more. The best way to learn your way around these options is to show and hide these panes, show and hide files, and change how the files and folders appear in the File Explorer window.

TIP You might not want to customize File Explorer too much right now, especially anything having to do with hiding files, folders, or the Navigation pane. If you change it too much, it won't look like what you see in the screen shots in this book.

Here are the options you can safely explore on the View tab.

- **Navigation Pane**   The Navigation pane is the one on the left of the File Explorer window that contains the folder list, and sections including Favorites, SkyDrive, Homegroup, This PC, and Network. To hide this pane, click an item in the Navigation Pane that also shows the Home tab (like desktop). Then, on the View tab click Navigation pane. On the list that appears, click Navigation Pane again. This hides the pane. Repeat to show the pane. Note that this is also where you show the Libraries in the Navigation pane.

- **Preview Pane**   The Preview pane generally offers a preview of the selected file, without having to open it. Click Preview Pane to show this pane; click it again to hide it.

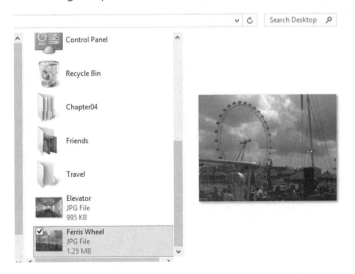

- **Details Pane** The Details pane offers comprehensive information about a file. The information offered is similar to what you'd see if you viewed the file's Properties page. Click Details Pane to show this pane; click it again to hide it.

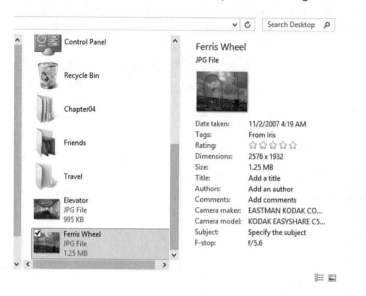

- **Layout Group Options** The options in the Layout group include Extra Large Icons, Large Icons, Medium Icons, Small Icons, List, Details, Tiles, and Content. Click each to view it and see the effect.

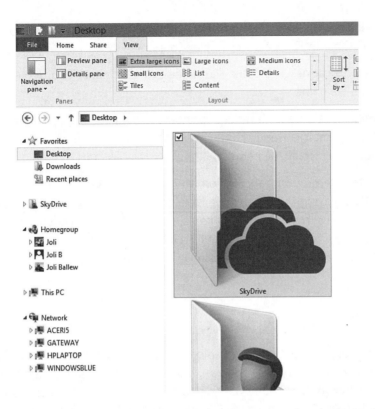

- **Sort By** You use the Sort By option to arrange data by Date, Size, Rating, and other attributes. Click Sort By and select an option, such as Date Taken, to group data differently.

- **Group By** By default, files and folders are listed alphabetically and in ascending order in File Explorer, but you can change that by using the Group By options. Click Group By and select any option to group by that criterion.

- **Item Check Boxes**   Select the Item check boxes to show the check mark when items are selected. Clear the check boxes to hide these marks.

- **File Name Extensions**   Select the File Name Extensions check box to see the extension after the file name.

- **Hidden Items**   Select this check box to show the data you've previously hidden. The data you'll see (that is currently hidden) will appear dimmed, and you can use Hide Selected Items to display the items.

- **Hide Selected Items**   With this option, you hide items you don't need to access regularly while leaving those items available on your computer. To hide any item, select it, and then click Hide Selected Items. The items will be hidden. To reveal them, select the Hidden Items check box (detailed in the previous bullet), select the item to reveal, and then click Hide Selected Items to display the item.

Searching in File Explorer

You know how to share files by using File Explorer and how to change the way you view files there. As you acquire more data, however, it will become increasingly difficult to sift through it to find what you want. One way to deal with large amounts of data is to customize what's shown in a File Explorer window by searching for the files you want. When you do this, only the files that match criteria you set appear in the window. This is a good way to cull information when you've stored a lot of data.

In this exercise, you'll search for a specific file in File Explorer.

 SET UP
You need the practice files located in the Chapter04 folder.

1   Open **File Explorer** by using any method desired.

2   In the **Navigation** pane, click **This PC**.

3   In the upper-right corner of the screen, in the **Search This PC** window, type Old Pub.

4   Note the results.

CLEAN UP
Leave File Explorer open for the next exercise.

TIP If you have so many files that you need to use this method to find them, do some housecleaning. Create subfolders and move data into them and delete files you no longer need.

Working with deleted files and the Recycle Bin

You learned earlier in this chapter how to delete a file (or other item) in File Explorer; you just select the item and then, on the Home tab of the ribbon, click Delete. You can select multiple items by holding down Shift or Ctrl. You might know other ways to delete a file, including right-clicking the item and then choosing Delete from the resulting contextual menu or selecting the item and pressing the Delete key. However you do it, files and folders you delete are sent to the *Recycle Bin* and are removed from their current positions in the folder. The Recycle Bin holds deleted files and data until you manually empty it.

In this last exercise, you'll restore a file by using the Recycle Bin.

 SET UP
You need to have completed the previous exercises in the chapter, namely creating the My WordPad Document file and then deleting it.

1   On the desktop, double-click the **Recycle Bin** to open it.

2   Locate the deleted file, **My WordPad Document**, and click it to select it (do not double-click it).

3   On the ribbon's **Recycle Bin Tools Manage** tab, click **Restore The Selected Item**.

4   Return to the **Documents** folder to verify that the file is restored.

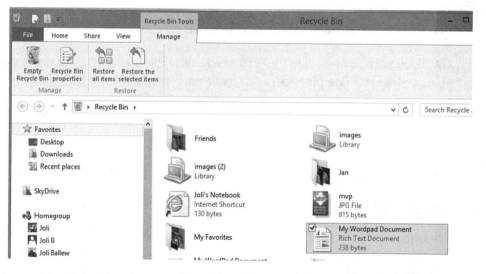

There are a few other things you can do while in the Recycle Bin, including emptying it. You can also restore every item that's in there. You should make it a habit to empty the Recycle Bin two or three times a year. You do this on the Manage tab. To access this screen, on the desktop, double-click the Recycle Bin. (Note that when you empty the Recycle Bin, you will no longer be able to restore anything previously in it.)

The Recycle Bin has other tabs to explore, too. When you explore them, you'll find familiar tools on each. For instance, on the Recycle Bin Home tab, you can delete specific files permanently, move files somewhere else, and even view the properties for a file. Likewise, on the Share tab, you can send email and burn files to a disc. On the View tab, you can change how items in the Recycle Bin appear in the window.

Key points

- You save data as files, save files in folders and subfolders, and access folders from This PC in File Explorer.

- Windows 8.1 comes with its own file system that includes various default folders to which you should save data, including but not limited to Documents, Public Documents, Pictures, Public Pictures, Music, Public Music, Videos, Public Videos, Downloads, and others.

- File Explorer is the best way to navigate to the data you keep and offers the ribbon to help you navigate it.

- You can use SkyDrive from File Explorer to save data to your SkyDrive folder in the cloud.

- The tabs that you'll use most often on the File Explore ribbon are Home, Share, and View. You use these tabs to work with the data you collect, including renaming, deleting, sending email, printing, moving, and so on.

- It's possible to customize File Explorer by hiding and showing data or culling data by searching for something specific.

- You can restore deleted files from the Recycle Bin, provided that you haven't yet emptied it since deleting the desired file.

4

Chapter at a glance

Learn

Learn about the new full screen interface of Internet Explorer, page 162

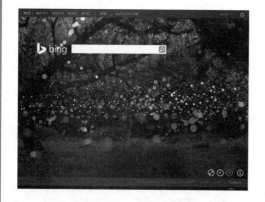

Pin

Pin websites to the Start screen, page 174

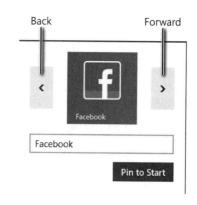

Browse

Browse the Web privately, page 176

Choose

Choose the Internet Explorer version you want as the default, page 181

Using Internet Explorer 11

5

IN THIS CHAPTER, YOU WILL LEARN HOW TO

- Start the different versions of Internet Explorer.

- Use the Internet Explorer 11 interface.

- Pin websites to the Start screen.

- Browse the web by using the InPrivate mode.

- Manage the files you download from the web.

- Set the default Internet Explorer version that you want to use regularly.

Internet Explorer 11 in Windows 8.1 has two incarnations that can be used to browse the web: a minimalistic full-screen version, and the desktop version you know from earlier Windows operating systems. The new browser also brings several improvements versus previous versions, including faster page load times, side-by-side browsing of websites, enhanced pinned site notifications and apps settings, and other improvements.

Because the browsing experiences are very different, this chapter focuses mostly on the new full-screen version of the browser. In this chapter, you'll review the new interface and learn how to use it to browse the web. Next, you'll see how to create favorites and pin websites on the Start screen, how to browse the web without leaving any traces in your browser, and how to download files. You'll understand one of the most important security features in Internet Explorer and Windows 8.1— the SmartScreen filter—and its role in securing your system. In addition, you'll learn how to set either of the two Internet Explorer versions as the default.

PRACTICE FILES You don't need any practice files to complete the exercises in this chapter. For more information about practice file requirements, see the section "Using the practice files" in the Introduction of this book.

What is new about Internet Explorer 11

Internet Explorer 11 in Windows 8.1 incorporates two important changes from earlier versions found in Windows 7 or Windows Vista.

The first and most important change is that in Windows 8 and Windows 8.1 there are two versions of Internet Explorer. One is available directly from the Start screen, with which it shares the same full-screen interface. It is referred to as the *Internet Explorer Windows 8.1* app. The other version is available on the desktop and uses the traditional desktop look to which you are accustomed from Internet Explorer 9 and previous versions of Windows. It is referred to as the *desktop Internet Explorer*.

They are the same app, and the same engine used for browsing the web. However, their looks are very different and so is the experience of browsing the web.

The Internet Explorer Windows 8.1 app runs in full-screen mode, providing you with all the screen space you need for viewing webpages and browsing the web. Its interface elements are minimalistic and optimized for touch. This mode of browsing the web doesn't offer any support for add-ons or plug-ins except Adobe Flash Player, which is built in to the browser. According to benchmarks published by different sources, the Internet Explorer app offers slightly less performance than its desktop counterpart. However, the performance differences are very small (up to a maximum of five percent in some tests), and most people will not notice the difference when browsing the web. It is great if you are using tablets or computers with touch and you want a web-browsing experience without clutter, toolbars, and add-ons. Even though it is optimized for touch, you can use the Internet Explorer app just as easily with a mouse and keyboard. It might seem scary at first because it is new and different, but if you read the rest of this chapter, you should have no problem getting acquainted with it and using it comfortably.

The Internet Explorer desktop version uses an interface with which you are familiar, optimized for use on desktop computers or laptops, using a mouse and keyboard. The web-browsing performance it offers is slightly better than the Internet Explorer app. It also offers full support for add-ons and plug-ins (something that's not available in Internet Explorer app).

The second important change you will find in Internet Explorer 11 is its noticeably better web-browsing performance. First, it has excellent support for open web standards such HTML5 or Cascading Style Sheet (CSS3), and the speed with which it loads websites has improved considerably. This means that, compared with earlier versions of Internet Explorer, you enjoy a much better browsing experience. Also, you achieve longer battery life on a laptop or tablet when browsing the web with the new Internet Explorer than with other browsers. This is because it includes power-saving features that balance the resources used while browsing the web and the amount of energy required for them. Last but not least, Internet Explorer 11 sends the Do Not Track signal to websites to help protect your privacy. Therefore, websites that provide support for this signal will not track your visits and cannot store detailed information about the pages you visited.

Internet Explorer 11 is integrated with Microsoft SkyDrive and it can synchronize your active tabs, favorites, home pages, history, and settings.

TIP To learn how to set Windows to synchronize your settings, read Chapter 6, "Using SkyDrive."

It also introduces a download manager in the Windows 8.1 app, a feature which was not present in Internet Explorer 10. Last but not least, both versions of Internet Explorer now support the same touch navigation features, which makes the transition between versions smoother when used on touch devices.

Starting Internet Explorer 11

You can start Internet Explorer by using the default shortcuts Windows 8.1 provides. However, which of the two versions you start depends on where the shortcut is placed.

On the Start screen is a tile named Internet Explorer. If you want to start the Internet Explorer app, click this tile.

If you want to start the Internet Explorer desktop app, you must go to the desktop and then, on the lower-left side of the taskbar, click the Internet Explorer icon.

The desktop Internet Explorer

You can also start Internet Explorer by using the search function on the Start screen. Just type the word *Internet*, and its shortcut appears instantly. This shortcut starts the version of Internet Explorer that you set as the default. If you have made no configuration changes to Windows 8.1, it will start the Internet Explorer app.

Using the Internet Explorer app

The new Internet Explorer app, even though simple in structure, can be confusing at first, especially to those who have not used mobile browsers such as the one found on smart-phones powered by Windows Phone.

When you open it, you see the homepage that is set and a small toolbar at the bottom of the window with a few buttons and options. The toolbar is minimized as soon as you click where websites are loaded.

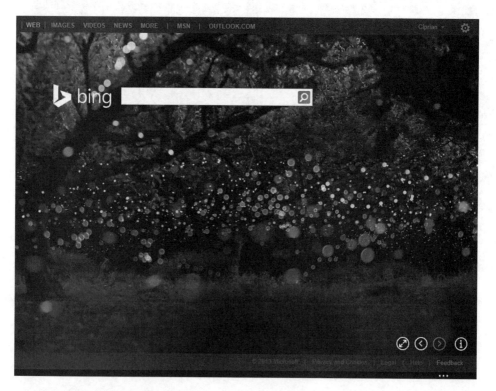

If you want to bring the toolbar back, swipe upward from the bottom edge of the window toward the middle. You can also right-click with a mouse.

Let's look at the buttons one by one, from left to right, and see what they do:

- The Back button takes you to the previous page you visited. The button is active after you visit more than one webpage. The same effect can be achieved by flicking right if you are using a touch-enabled screen. A transparent version of this button appears if you move the mouse to the left side of the browsing window.

- Next to the Back button is an icon that always changes. This is the icon that represents the website you are currently viewing. If no icon is detected for that website, the default Internet Explorer icon appears.

- The Address bar is where you type the address of the website you want to visit. This bar can also be used as a search box. You can type a search term and press the Enter key or click the adjacent Go button. Internet Explorer displays the search results relevant to your search term by using the default search engine you have set. If you have not changed its default configuration, search results will be displayed by using Microsoft Bing.

- Next to the Address bar is the Refresh button with which you can reload the webpage you are viewing so that you can see the updates that have been made to it, if any, since you arrived on the page.

- The Tabs button displays a list of the tabs that are currently open.

- The Favorites button opens the list of Internet Explorer favorites and options for adding the current website as a favorite, pinning it to the Start screen, or sharing it with others using the Share charm.

- The Page Tools button gives access to a small contextual menu that can be used to search on the current webpage, view the same page on the Internet Explorer desktop app, view downloads or access the Windows Store app for the loaded website when one is available.

- The Forward button takes you to the next page if you previously used the Back button. Click it and it will take you forward. The same effect can be achieved by flicking left if you are using a touch-enabled screen. A transparent version of this button appears if you move the mouse to the right side of the browsing window.

5

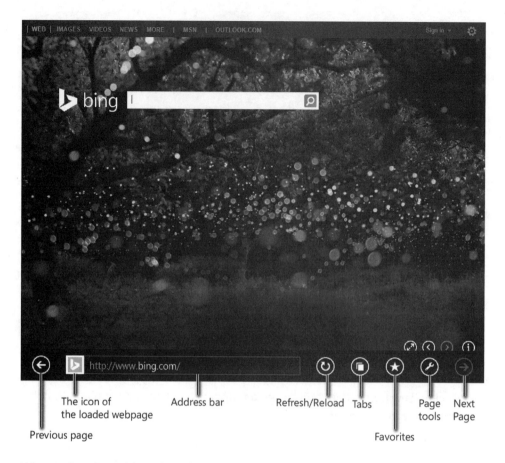

The icon of the loaded webpage

Address bar

Refresh/Reload

Tabs

Page tools

Next Page

Previous page

Favorites

When using the Address bar, the Internet Explorer window changes to help you find what you want as quickly as possible. It displays the websites you visit frequently, the Go, Favorites, and Tabs buttons. The Favorites button can be used to quickly access your favorite websites, whereas with the Tabs button, you can quickly access all opened tabs.

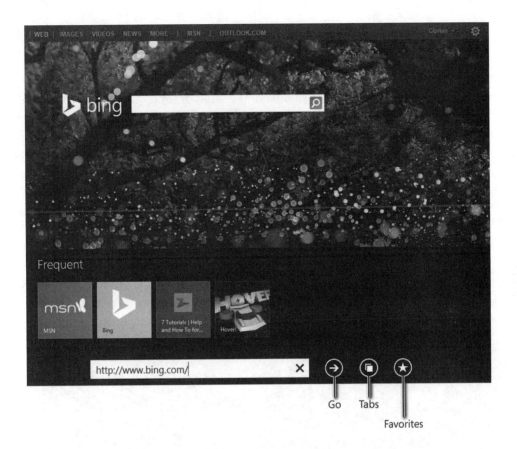

Go   Tabs

Favorites

As you type (it doesn't matter whether it is the address of a website, the name of a website, or a search term), Internet Explorer begins searching your most frequently visited websites, the websites you pinned to the Start screen, and your browsing history. It also displays search suggestions from Microsoft. If it finds entries that match what you have typed so far, it will display the appropriate results. Then, you can just click the result that matches where you want to go.

If you want to search the web for something that you have not yet visited, finish typing the search term and click the Go button adjacent to the Address bar or press Enter on your keyboard. This triggers a web search, using the search engine that you set as default.

If you right-click somewhere in the middle of the Internet Explorer window, you will see the Tabs pane. It shows the tabs you opened and the websites loaded in each tab. The active tab displays a blue border, whereas the tabs open in the background have no visible border. Each tab has a Close button (the X in the lower-right corner) that dismisses that tab. To switch between tabs, click the one that you want to view. If you want to create a new tab, in the upper-right of the Tabs pane, click the + button.

Near the new tab button is the Tab Tools button (the ellipsis character). This button offers two options: start a new InPrivate tab, and reopen the recently closed tab.

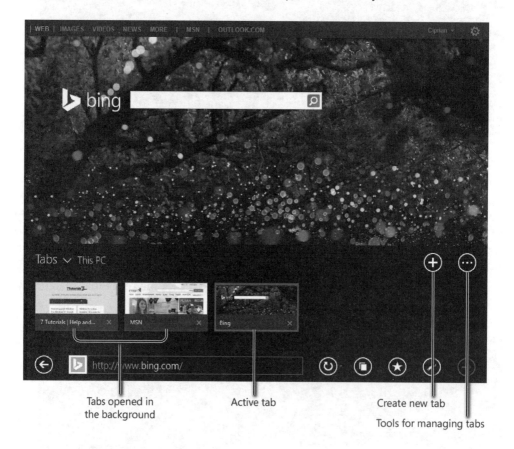

Tabs opened in the background   Active tab   Create new tab

Tools for managing tabs

When browsing the web, notice that the Page Tools button on the bottom toolbar can have a slightly different icon, depending on the websites you are visiting. On most websites, it shows a wrench icon. On some websites, however (Wikipedia, for example), it will also present a small plus sign below the wrench.

 No app available

 App available

When this sign is displayed, it means the website you are visiting has a Windows 8.1 app available in the Windows Store. If you click or tap it, the Page Tools menu appears. This time, the menu will have an option named Get App For This Site. A click takes you to the Windows Store, from which you can install the app specific to that website. Another small but useful feature is the new Reading view. When you open an article on a website, in the address bar, a book icon appears adjacent to the URL. Click this icon to reload the current page in Reading view, which strips out all the advertisements and clutter on the page, displaying only the essential content. With this view, you can enjoy a better reading experience while browsing the web.

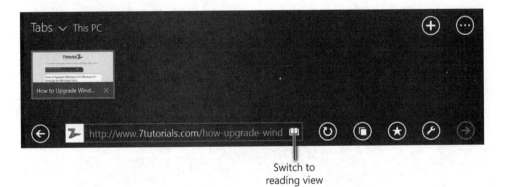

Switch to
reading view

If you have copied a link to a webpage, you can paste it into the Address bar to view that page. You might appreciate the Paste And Go option, which automatically pastes the link and loads it into the browser. To access it, right-click the Address bar.

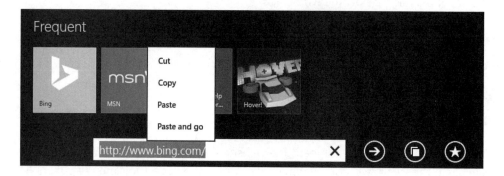

When you right-click a webpage, a shortcut menu appears, offering options with which you can copy content and links and open links in a new tab, a new window or the same tab, and save pictures directly to your picture folders.

To make navigation easier if you're using the desktop, the Internet Explorer app gives you the ability to navigate backward and forward without having to bring up the toolbar on the bottom of the app window. Hovering the mouse on the left or right side of the window displays a transparent Back or Forward button, depending on where you placed the button. Clicking it takes you to the previous or next webpage you visited in the active tab.

The Internet Explorer app includes a new Flip Ahead feature so that you can navigate your favorite sites just as you would read a magazine. It replaces the need to click or tap links with a more natural forward-swipe gesture on touch-centric devices (and forward button with the mouse).

As you can see from this section, the new Internet Explorer app is not difficult to use. If you take some time to experiment, visit a few websites, and do searches on the web, you'll become comfortable using it and start to enjoy this new way of browsing the web. That's true whether you use a classic desktop computer or a computer with touch or a tablet.

Using the Internet Explorer desktop app

The Internet Explorer desktop app has a more complex interface than its Windows 8.1 full-screen counterpart. At the top of its window are several buttons and fields for managing the way you navigate the web. At the upper-right are three buttons that give you access to different configuration menus.

On the bottom and right side are scroll bars that you can use to move through the content of a webpage when the content is bigger than your Internet Explorer window.

Buttons for navigating to
and between websites.

Buttons that give access to
different configuration menus.

Scroll bars

The middle of the window, taking up most of the space, is where websites are loaded and viewed.

Let's see in more detail what each button does. Moving from left to right are the following buttons:

- **The Back and Forward buttons**   These become active as soon as you browse to more than one page on the Internet. You can use them to navigate back and forth between the different pages you visited.

- **The Address bar**   This is where you type the address of the website that you want to visit. You can also use this bar as a search box. You can type a search term and press Enter or click the Search button in the Address bar. Internet Explorer displays the search results relevant to your search term by using the default search engine that you set. If you have not changed its default configuration, search results will be displayed by using Bing.

- **Down arrow in the Address bar**   This reveals Autocomplete suggestions, based on what you have typed in the Address bar.

- **The Refresh button**   Use this to reload the current webpage so that you can see the updates that have been made to it, if any, since you opened the page.

- **Active tabs**   Next to the Address bar are the tabs you have opened. The tab that is active always has a lighter color, whereas those in the background are a slightly darker tone. When you open a webpage, its name becomes the title of the tab. To change between tabs, just click them. If you want to close the active tab, click the Close button to the right of the name.

- **Square, unlabeled button**   Use this button to open a new tab. Click it, type the address of the website that you want to visit in the Address bar, and then press Enter. The website is now loaded in its own tab.

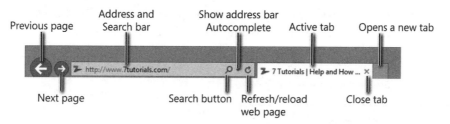

In the upper-right corner of the Internet Explorer window are three buttons. Let's see what they do:

- The first button (the one that looks like a small house) takes you to the homepage you have set for Internet Explorer on the desktop. By default, this is the *MSN.com* website, but it can be changed to something else.

- The second button (the star) opens a menu for managing your favorite websites, the feeds to which you have subscribed, and the history of your browsing.

- The third button (the gear icon) opens the Tools menu that you can use to configure many aspects of how Internet Explorer works.

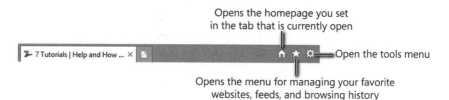

If you are familiar with Internet Explorer 9, which was available in Windows 7 and Windows Vista, you'll notice that not much has changed in terms of the interface. If you are comfortable using Internet Explorer 9, you will have no problems using the Internet Explorer 11 desktop app.

Adding favorites in Internet Explorer

Unlike Internet Explorer 10, in Internet Explorer 11 you can add favorites from the full-screen app, as well. The process is quite simple. When adding a new favorite, you can set its name and change its location by adding a new folder or selecting a specific Favorites folder from the ones that already exist. Also, you can change its icon. To change the icon, click the Forward arrow near the website's icon. As you might expect, when you pressed Forward, a Back button becomes available for navigating backward through the available icons. However, some websites do not provide multiple icons to choose from. If you want to add those to your favorites, the Forward and Back buttons will not be available.

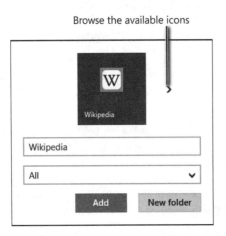

Browse the available icons

In this exercise, you'll learn how to add a website to your Favorites in Internet Explorer.

➡ SET UP
Go to the Start screen and start Internet Explorer. Navigate to the Wikipedia website (*www.wikipedia.org*). If you don't use Wikipedia, you can go to any other website you use frequently.

1   To the right of the **Address** bar, click the **Favorites** button.

2   Click the **Add To Favorites** button.

3　Set the name, icon, and location for this website's entry in your list of favorites.

Wikipedia

Wikipedia	
All	⌄

| Add | New folder |

4　When done, click **Add**.

❌ CLEAN UP
Close Internet Explorer.

Wikipedia is now added to your list of Favorites in Internet Explorer, and you can easily access it from the Favorites menu.

Pinning websites to the Start screen

Pinned websites appear as shortcuts on the Start screen. Each shortcut includes the icon of the website (if any) plus the name of the website. Websites that provide specific support for this feature can display custom icons, backgrounds, and the latest updates. When you click the shortcut, the website opens in Internet Explorer.

When pinning a website to the Start screen, you can select its icon from the list of available icons, by pressing the Back and Forward buttons. You can also type a custom name for the website.

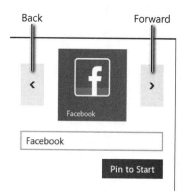

In this exercise, you'll learn how to pin a website to the Start screen.

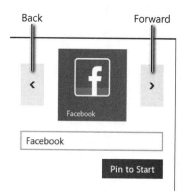 SET UP

Go to the Start screen and start Internet Explorer. Navigate to the Facebook website (*www.facebook.com*). If you don't use Facebook, you can go to any other website you use frequently.

1   Click the **Favorites** button near the **Address** bar. If the Address bar is minimized, first right-click to bring up the tabs and then click Favorites.

2   Click the **Pin Site** button.

3. Type the name that you want to use for the website and, if you want, select another icon, by browsing through the available icons.

4. When done, click **Pin To Start**.

CLEAN UP
Close Internet Explorer.

Facebook is now pinned to the Start screen, and you can use the shortcut that was created to quickly access it whenever you want.

Where can I set my homepage?

Internet Explorer 11 will open either the homepage you have set (the msn.com page is the default) or the tabs opened in the last browsing session. You can change this behavior by using the Settings charm and going to Options or in the desktop Internet Explorer, by going to Internet Options in the Tools menu.

Browsing the web by using the InPrivate mode

InPrivate mode is a way of browsing the web without leaving traces in the browser. When you open an InPrivate tab, all the websites you visit in that tab, the passwords you enter, the cookies that are created, and the temporary files that are downloaded are deleted as soon as you close the tab or you close Internet Explorer. An InPrivate tab is marked by the blue InPrivate icon. This icon does not appear on a normal tab.

InPrivate is turned on

InPrivate Browsing helps prevent Internet Explorer from storing data about your browsing session. This includes cookies, temporary Internet files, history and other data.

To turn off InPrivate Browsing, close this browser tab.

Read the Internet Explorer privacy statement online

This way of browsing is useful when you don't want to be tracked or when you're using someone else's computer and you don't want to leave traces of the sites you visited. This browsing mode is highly recommended when using public computers to browse the web.

In this exercise, you'll learn how to visit a website by using the InPrivate mode.

SET UP

From the Start screen, start Internet Explorer.

1 Right-click somewhere in the middle of the Internet Explorer window to bring up the **Tabs** view.

2 Click the **Tab Tools** button (the ellipsis character).

3 Click **New InPrivate tab** so that a new tab is opened in the InPrivate mode.

4 Type the address of the website that you want to visit and then click the **Go** button.

✖ CLEAN UP

Close Internet Explorer when you have finished browsing the web.

The website is now loaded in InPrivate mode. As soon as you close this tab, any traces of your visit to this website are deleted.

Downloading files from the Internet and managing them

The process for downloading files is similar to other browsers with which you are accustomed. You are first asked whether you want to run or open the file you are about to download (depending on its type) or save it on your computer.

When you click Save, the file is automatically downloaded to the Downloads folder. You are not asked whether you want to save the file to another location. The default Downloads folder can be changed only for the desktop version of Internet Explorer.

A progress bar appears. If you are downloading multiple files at the same time, the information is aggregated, and you are shown how many downloads are in progress and how much time remains until all of them are finished. You can close this notification or cancel the download altogether.

After a file is downloaded, you are given options relevant to its file type. You can run executable files, whereas you can open other files.

As mentioned earlier in this chapter, the Internet Explorer 11 app for Windows 8.1 now includes a manager for your downloads. In the Downloads window, you can view all the recent files that were downloaded, run or open them, open their location, delete them, or clear items individually or the entire list.

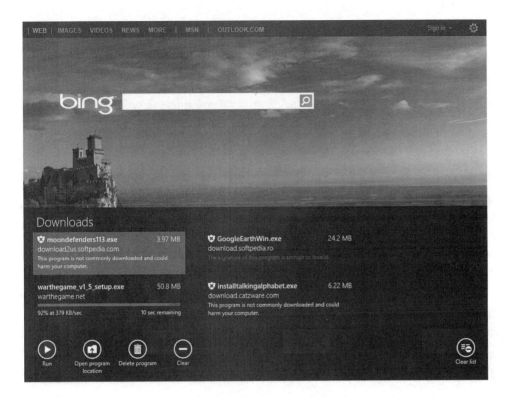

In this exercise, you will learn how to access the Downloads window in the Internet Explorer 11 app.

 SET UP
Go to the Start screen and start Internet Explorer.

1   Right-click somewhere in the middle of the window to bring up the **Tabs**.

2   Click the **Page Tools** button to access its menu.

3   Click **View Downloads**.

4   Manage the list of Downloads as you see fit.

⊗ CLEAN UP
Close Internet Explorer when you have finished browsing the web.

Understanding the SmartScreen filter in Internet Explorer

Sometimes when you try to download files, Internet Explorer doesn't allow you to do so, issuing a warning that the file has been reported as unsafe and it was blocked by SmartScreen filter. The same can happen when you try to view certain websites to which your access is blocked, and you see a similar message.

SmartScreen filter is a security feature Microsoft introduced after Internet Explorer 8. It tracks what websites Internet Explorer users visit and, when a dangerous file or website has been detected, it blocks access to it to protect you. Files that are reported and confirmed as malware won't download to your computer thanks to this security feature. Also, websites that are reported and confirmed as distributing malware or trying to steal personal information from visitors are automatically blocked. Therefore, don't be upset if SmartScreen has prevented you from downloading a file or visiting a webpage; you just have avoided harm to yourself or to your system.

SmartScreen filter also looks at how commonly files are downloaded. If you are trying to download a file that is rarely downloaded by other Internet Explorer users, you are warned that the file "is not commonly downloaded and could harm your computer."

If you know what that file is supposed to do and you trust the source from which you download it, you can go ahead and run it. If not, it is best either to delete it or to scan it for malware by using Windows Defender or any other security solution before trying to run it. This way, you make sure that you stay away from viruses and other forms of malware.

File Explorer uses the same technology, and you are warned before running files that are marked as infected by SmartScreen filter.

Setting the default Internet Explorer version

In Windows 8.1, you can set one of two versions of Internet Explorer as your default. Having both available and starting in different scenarios can be confusing. It is best to give both a try, decide which you like best, and set that one as your default.

You set the default version in the Internet Options window, on the Programs tab. There, you are asked to choose how you open links. The default is to let Internet Explorer decide. If you choose Always In Internet Explorer, the Internet Explorer app will always be used to open links on your Start screen or in the apps you use.

However, the Internet Explorer shortcut on the desktop will continue to open the Internet Explorer desktop app. All the other shortcuts and links will open the Internet Explorer app.

Setting the Internet Explorer desktop app as your default involves a bit more configuration. In this exercise, you'll learn the steps for setting up this option.

SET UP

Go to the desktop and start Internet Explorer.

1   In the upper-right corner of the Internet Explorer window, click the **Tools** button.

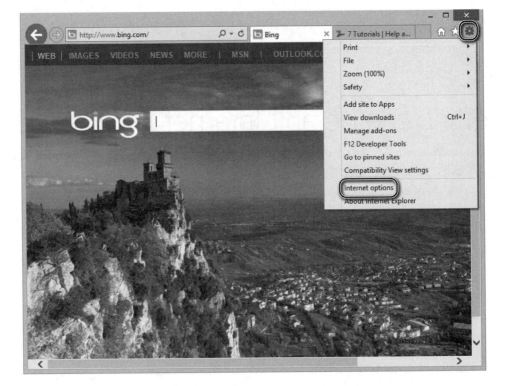

2   In the **Tools** menu, click **Internet Options** to open the Internet Options window.

3   Click the **Programs** tab to find the options for configuring how Internet Explorer is opened.

Internet Options   ? ☒

| General | Security | Privacy | Content | Connections | Programs | Advanced |

Opening Internet Explorer

Choose how you open links.

| Let Internet Explorer decide ▾ |

☐ Open Internet Explorer tiles on the desktop

Manage add-ons

Enable or disable browser add-ons installed in your system.   [Manage add-ons]

HTML editing

Choose the program that you want Internet Explorer to use for editing HTML files.

HTML editor: [▾]

Internet programs

Choose the programs you want to use for other Internet services, such as e-mail.   [Set programs]

File associations

Choose the file types that you want Internet Explorer to open by default.   [Set associations]

[OK]   [Cancel]   [Apply]

4   In the **Opening Internet Explorer** section, in the Choose how you open links list, select **Always In Internet Explorer On The Desktop**.

Opening Internet Explorer

Choose how you open links.

| Let Internet Explorer decide ▾ |

Let Internet Explorer decide
Always in Internet Explorer
Always in Internet Explorer on the desktop

5

5   Beneath the list box, select the **Open Internet Explorer Tiles On The Desktop** check box.

6   Click **OK**.

✖ CLEAN UP
Close Internet Explorer.

Now, all the Internet Explorer shortcuts in Windows will open only the desktop Internet Explorer version. Also, when you click a link to a website in any app or on the Start screen, it will be opened by using the same version.

TIP If you want the Internet Explorer app to be used as the default, follow the same procedure but select Always In Internet Explorer at step 4 and clear the Open Internet Explorer Tiles On The Desktop check box.

Key points

- Internet Explorer 11 brings with it many changes and improvements to the browsing experience.

- Pinning websites is a way of storing your favorite websites on the Start screen so that you can access them from there.

- When browsing the web from a public computer, it is best to browse by using the InPrivate mode. This way, you leave no traces, and Internet Explorer does not store your personal data.

- SmartScreen filter is a Microsoft technology that protects you from downloading and running infected files and from accessing malicious websites.

- After you decide which Internet Explorer version you like best, it is good to set it as your default.

5

Chapter at a glance

Browse

Browse SkyDrive from the SkyDrive app, page 190

Upload

Upload files to SkyDrive, page 192

Download

Download files from SkyDrive, page 196

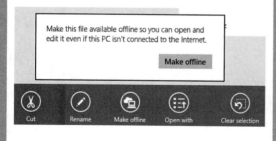

Synchronize

Synchronize your Windows 8.1 settings, page 205

Using SkyDrive

6

IN THIS CHAPTER, YOU WILL LEARN HOW TO

- Work with Microsoft SkyDrive and learn about its features and limitations.

- Upload files to SkyDrive.

- Download files from SkyDrive.

- Synchronize your Windows 8.1 settings.

Microsoft SkyDrive is a service by which you can store your files on the Microsoft servers in the cloud. You can upload documents, pictures, and other types of files and access them from anywhere: your web browser (Internet Explorer 11, for instance), your Windows Phone, your Microsoft Xbox One and all kinds of computers and devices. By using SkyDrive, you can synchronize files among multiple devices or share some of your stored files and folders with other people. It's useful for sharing big files with friends and family and for doing collaborative work on Microsoft Office documents. Further, synchronizing important files across devices frees you to use them whenever you need them from almost any device or computer with an Internet connection.

Windows 8.1 uses SkyDrive to synchronize your settings across the computers and devices with which you log on to your Microsoft account, so you can configure your Windows 8.1 settings on one computer and have them replicate automatically on all others that use the same Microsoft account.

The basic SkyDrive service is free to all users with a Microsoft account and includes 7 GB of space. However, paid plans are also available for people who want more storage space. The features are the same in all plans, and so is the functionality.

In this chapter, you'll learn how to access SkyDrive, upload files to it, download files from it, access it from a web browser, configure it and synchronize your Windows 8.1 settings across multiple computers and devices.

PRACTICE FILES The practice files you will use to complete the exercises in this chapter are in the Chapter06 practice file folder. Before you can complete the exercises in this chapter, you need to install the practice files specified in the section "Using the practice files" in the Introduction of this book to their default location.

Using SkyDrive

The first time you log on to Windows 8.1 with a Microsoft account, you are asked whether you want to turn on SkyDrive and its synchronization settings.

It is best to choose to use it, since this service is at the core of the Windows 8.1 computing experience. However, if you do not want to turn it on it right away, you can click Turn off These SkyDrive Settings and turn it on later, from PC Settings.

To use SkyDrive in Windows 8.1, you need a Microsoft account instead of a local account. If you try to access SkyDrive from a local account, Windows will ask you to change your account settings and add a Microsoft account.

SEE ALSO If you want to learn more about user accounts in Windows 8.1 and how to use a Microsoft account, read Chapter 12, "Allowing others to use the computer."

To access SkyDrive, upload, download, or synchronize files and settings, you must have a working Internet connection.

After you satisfy all the prerequisites, you will see in Windows 8.1 both a SkyDrive app on the Start screen and a SkyDrive section in File Explorer. Both give you access to your SkyDrive. Any changes made in one of these locations are reflected in the other. For example, if you upload a file using the SkyDrive app, you will see that file available in the SkyDrive section in File Explorer, in the exact same folder into which you uploaded it.

SEE ALSO If you want to learn more about File Explorer and how you can use it to browse and organize your files, read Chapter 4, "Organizing files and folders."

In Windows 8.1, you will find the SkyDrive folder in your User folder. This folder is placed on the disk drive where Windows is installed, in the Users folder, followed by your account name. For example, if your user account is named Ciprian and Windows 8.1 is installed on the C drive, the SkyDrive folder is at: C:\Users\Ciprian\SkyDrive. If the default location does not suit your needs and setup, you can change it in File Explorer.

SEE ALSO If you want to learn more about how to change the location of the SkyDrive folder, read Chapter 20, "Tips for improving your computing experience."

Browsing SkyDrive from the SkyDrive app

You open the SkyDrive app from the Start screen by clicking its tile.

You can also search for the word *SkyDrive* and click the appropriate search result.

When you open SkyDrive, the app takes a few seconds to load information about the folders and files you have uploaded. For each folder, you see its name and for each file, you see an icon representative of its type, and the name of the file. For pictures, you see a preview of the file instead of an icon. In the lower-right corner of a folder or file, you might see a small icon, comprising a computer and a cloud. That icon displays only for files and folders that are physically available on your computer. It also means that you can use them when you're offline. If you do not see this icon, it means that the folder or file is available online on your SkyDrive, and you can download it to your computer for offline access.

If you right-click a file, a contextual menu opens at the bottom of the SkyDrive app window, the file is selected, and a check mark appears in its upper-right corner.

To open a folder or a file, click it. When you open a file, SkyDrive opens it with the app that is set as the default on your computer for opening that file type. For example, Portable Document Format (PDF) files are opened by default with Reader.

If you want to browse through different areas of SkyDrive, click SkyDrive to open a menu with the standard locations: your SkyDrive and This PC. In the upper-right of the app window are two buttons: the first is for switching to the Details View and back to the Thumbnails View (the default view for the SkyDrive app); you use the second for searching through the SkyDrive.

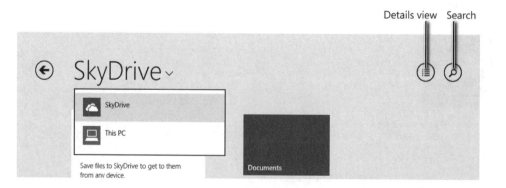

SkyDrive displays the files and folders available on your Skydrive, whereas This PC displays your user's libraries, the Desktop, the Downloads folder, and devices and drives.

On the left side of the name of your SkyDrive is the Back button, which you use to go back to the previous location. When you open SkyDrive, because you haven't opened anything, the Back button is not visible.

When you open the folders existing on the SkyDrive, you will see their names listed on the top, like a breadcrumb. There, you will always see the current folder and its parent. Clicking on its parent takes you to that location, without having to click the Back button.

The contextual menu shown at the bottom of the SkyDrive window displays useful buttons. What buttons are displayed depends on where you are in SkyDrive and what was selected. To view this menu, right click an item on your SkyDrive.

On the left side of the menu, you will see the following buttons:

- **Delete**   This appears only if at least one file or folder is selected. A click deletes the item(s) you have selected.

- **Copy**   This appears only if at least one file or folder is selected. A click copies the item(s) you have selected to the clipboard.

- **Cut**   Again, this appears only if at least one file or folder is selected. A click cuts the item(s) you have selected, so that they can be moved to a different location.

- **Rename**   This displays only when one file or folder is selected. Use this button to rename the selected file or folder.

- **Make Offline**   This button is available only when one or more files are selected. You use this button to download the selected file(s) or folder(s) to your computer. If the selected item is available for offline use, this button appears as Make Online-Only. By pressing it, SkyDrive will no longer store the selected item on your computer and make it available for offline use.

- **Open With**   Use this button to select the app with which to open the selected file. This button is not shown when selecting folders.

On the right side of the menu, there are a few global options available:

- **Clear Selection**   This appears only if at least one file or folder is selected. Its purpose is to clear the current selection of files or folders.
- **Select All**   Use this to select all the items found in the current folder.
- **New Folder**   Use this to create a new folder on the SkyDrive at the current location.
- **Add Files**   Click this to upload new items to SkyDrive.

Using your mouse or finger to point to an item from SkyDrive reveals more information about it, including its name, type, and the date on which it was last modified, its size, and the people with whom it is shared.

Name	Ciprian Rusen Bio.pptx
Type	Microsoft PowerPoint Presentation
Date modified	11/12/2012 2:56 AM
Size	361 KB
Date created	11/12/2012 2:56 AM

You can see that SkyDrive is relatively easy to use. To become proficient with it, go through the next sections and exercises.

Uploading a file by using the SkyDrive app

Uploading files to SkyDrive is a simple task. You can upload one or more files at one time. With the SkyDrive app, you can browse through multiple folders and select only the ones that you want uploaded. When selected, the files are shown on the bottom half of the window, in the SkyDrive list. To remove a file from that list, click or tap it.

| kamus_2.04 | moondefen... | warthegam... | Copy to SkyDrive | Cancel |

After you select the files, click Copy To SkyDrive and wait for the upload to finish.

On SkyDrive, you can upload any type of files. However, official support is only provided for the following file types.

- Documents saved as PDF files, text files, Office files of any kind, and files saved with the Open Document Format (ODF) such as those created by using LibreOffice or OpenOffice

- Photos saved as JPG, JPEG, GIF, BMP, PNG, TIF, and TIFF file types

- Videos saved as AVI or WMV file types

- Audio files saved as WAV or MP3 file types

During the upload process, progress information is displayed in the upper-right corner of the SkyDrive app window. If you click or tap it, more information about the process appears. In this exercise, you'll learn how to upload a file to SkyDrive by using the SkyDrive app.

➜ SET UP

To complete this exercise, you need the Document1.docx file in the Chapter06 folder in your practice files. When this file is available, open the SkyDrive app and browse to the folder to which you want to upload the file.

1   Right-click somewhere in the empty space of the **SkyDrive** app window to open the contextual menu.

2   Click the **Add files** button to open the upload window.

3   Browse to where you saved the Document1.docx practice file.

4   Click the **Document1.docx** file to select it.

5   Click the **Copy to SkyDrive** button to start the upload procedure.

6   Wait for the upload procedure to end. It should not take more than a few seconds.

 CLEAN UP
When the upload is complete, close the SkyDrive app.

The Document1.docx practice file is now uploaded to your SkyDrive.

Downloading a file by using the SkyDrive app

Downloading files with the SkyDrive app is as easy as uploading them. During the download process, the progress displays in the upper-right corner of the SkyDrive app window.

Downloading 58 items...

If you click the progress line, more information about the process appears. Like the upload process, you can download one file at a time or select multiple files and download them to the same location on your computer. You can also download folders.

There's one very important thing to keep in mind, though. If you set the SkyDrive app to access all files offline via the Settings charm, there won't be any need to download files to your computer or device. All of the files on your SkyDrive will be downloaded automatically to your Windows 8.1 computer or device and they will be available for use even if you don't have an Internet connection available. However, to save bandwidth, by default, the SkyDrive app is set to not access all files offline.

In this exercise, you'll learn how to download a file from SkyDrive by using the SkyDrive app. The procedure for downloading folders works the same way.

 SET UP
Open the SkyDrive app and browse to the folder that contains the file that you want to download.

6

1   Right-click the file that you want to download.

    The contextual menu opens at the bottom of the SkyDrive app window.

2   Click the **Make Offline** button.

    A confirmation message appears by SkyDrive.

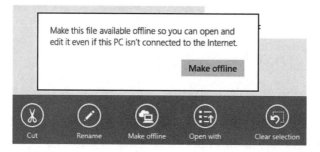

3   Confirm that you want to download the file by clicking **Make Offline**.

4   Wait for the download to finish.

![CLEAN UP icon] CLEAN UP
When the download is complete, close the SkyDrive app.

The file you selected is now saved on your computer in the SkyDrive folder. If you open File Explorer, click SkyDrive, and go to the folder where the file was located, you will find the file there. It is now available for you to work on it, even when an Internet connection is not available.

Accessing SkyDrive from a web browser

You can access SkyDrive from a web browser at any time. Go to *https://skydrive.live.com* and log on with your Microsoft account details. You now have complete access to all your files and folders stored on SkyDrive. If you logged on with your Microsoft account in Windows 8.1, and you're using Internet Explorer as your browser, you won't need to log on to the SkyDrive service. You are automatically logged on by Windows.

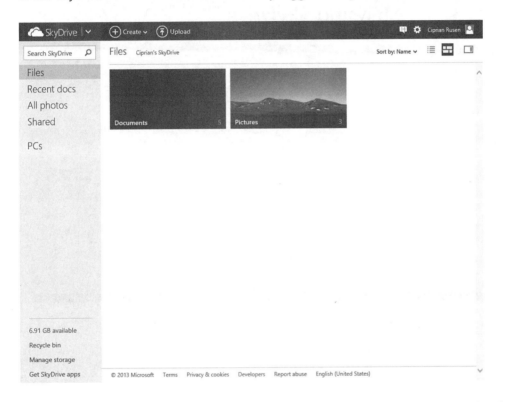

With the help of your web browser, you can download files from SkyDrive, organize them in folders and subfolders, or add new files. You can also share files and folders with others.

Last, you can view the pictures uploaded to SkyDrive and edit Office documents by using Microsoft Office Web Apps. They are simplified versions of Office apps with which you can view documents and perform some basic editing. They are free to use and work very well.

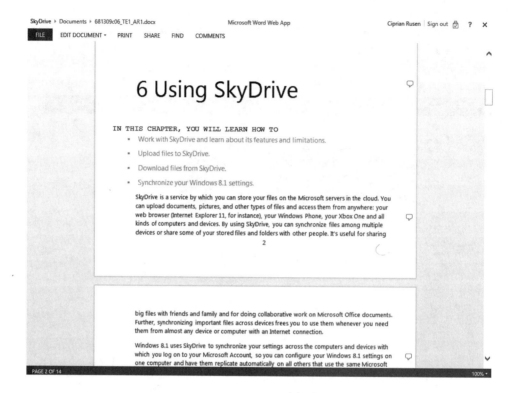

Accessing SkyDrive from File Explorer

You can also access your SkyDrive from the Desktop. If you open File Explorer, you will find the SkyDrive section in the left pane. Double-click to open it and you can see the folders stored on your account.

You can add or remove files as you would normally when working with local files or folders. All the changes you make in the SkyDrive folder are automatically synchronized with Microsoft's servers and available on other devices and computers via the SkyDrive service If you want to make a file available only online, right click it and select Make Available Online-Only. If there's an online file you want to download to your computer, right click it and select Make Available Offline. If you want to set SkyDrive to store all your files on your PC so they are available also when offline, don't forget to start the SkyDrive app, go to the Settings charm and then to Options. There you will find a switch for turning this feature On or Off.

Sharing a SkyDrive folder

You can share both files and folders from your SkyDrive via email, social networks such as Facebook, Twitter, and LinkedIn, and via direct links that you can copy and paste into documents and other items. You can give editing permissions to others or you can only let them view what you are sharing. You can also require everyone who accesses the shared item to sign in to be able to view it or edit it. You can find all of these settings in the Share window.

Share	Send a link to "Camera Roll" in email
Send email	To
Post to 🇫 🐦 in	
Get a link	Include a personal message (optional)
Help me choose	
Permissions	
This folder is not shared	

☑ Recipients can edit
☐ Require everyone who accesses this to sign in

Share   Close

You can share in several ways, the quickest being directly from File Explorer.

In this exercise, you'll learn how to share a folder via SkyDrive from File Explorer.

 SET UP
Ensure that you have a working Internet connection available and then open File Explorer.

1   Click the **SkyDrive** section.

2   Browse to the SkyDrive folder you want to share and then click it.

3   On the ribbon, double-click the **Share** tab.

4   In the **Share With** section, click **SkyDrive**. Your default browser is opened and you are asked if you are sure that you want to share this folder.

Are you sure you want to share this folder?

Sharing this folder is not recommended because some apps automatically add files to it. If you share the folder, people might see files you don't want them to.

If that's okay, you may continue and share this folder.

Don't share this folder   **Share this folder**

5   Click **Share This Folder**.

The Share window opens in your browser.

6   Leave the **Send Email** section selected and then, in the **To** field, type the email address of the person with whom you want to share the folder.

7   In the box below the **To** field, type a message for that person.

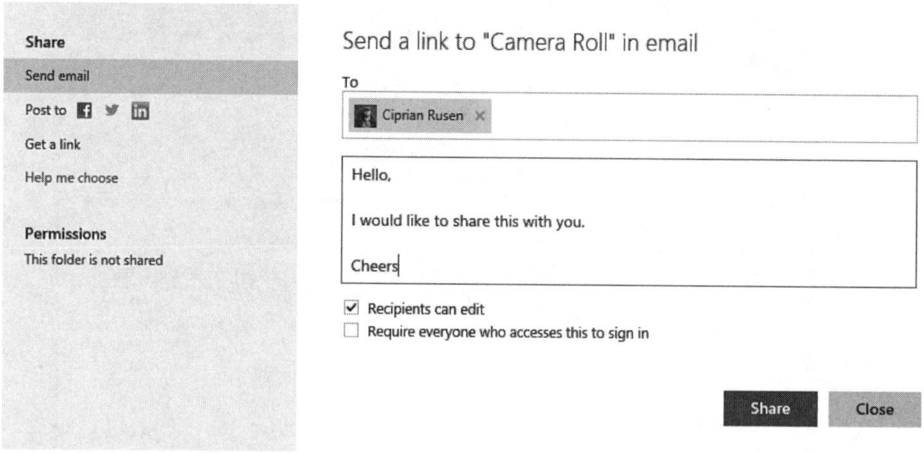

Share

Send email

Post to [facebook icon] [twitter icon] [linkedin icon]

Get a link

Help me choose

Permissions

This folder is not shared

Send a link to "Camera Roll" in email

To

[icon] Ciprian Rusen ✕

Hello,

I would like to share this with you.

Cheers

☑ Recipients can edit
☐ Require everyone who accesses this to sign in

[Share] [Close]

---

8   Set whether you will allow the recipient to edit the folder and whether you will
    require the recipient to sign in prior to accessing the folder.

9   When you're done configuring all the settings, click **Share**.

    You are informed that folder is shared with the person you specified.

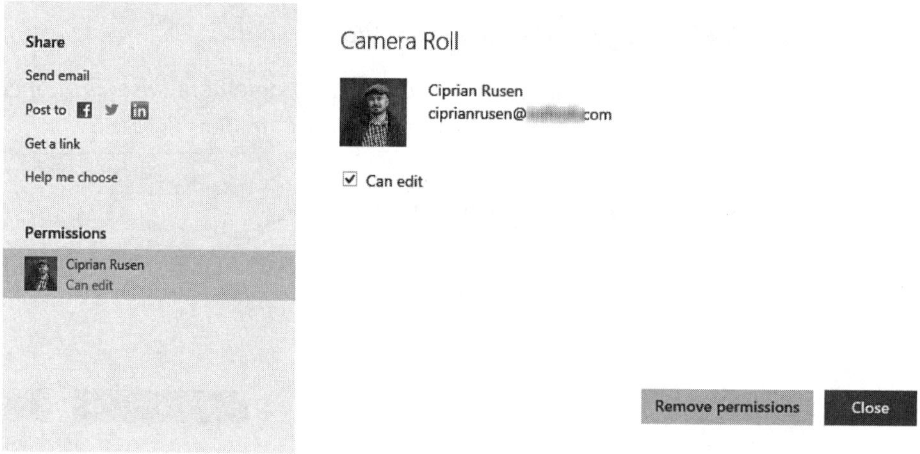

Share

Send email

Post to [facebook icon] [twitter icon] [linkedin icon]

Get a link

Help me choose

Permissions

[icon] Ciprian Rusen
      Can edit

Camera Roll

[photo] Ciprian Rusen
        ciprianrusen@████com

☑ Can edit

[Remove permissions] [Close]

---

10 Click **Close**.

[✕] CLEAN UP
Close your Internet browser.

The procedure for sharing a file is the same. The only exception is that you won't be asked
whether you are sure that you want to share this folder, after step 4.

Accessing SkyDrive's settings

You can configure the way SkyDrive works in Windows 8.1 by using PC Settings. The SkyDrive section in PC Settings is split into four areas:

- **File Storage** You can view the storage space available on your SkyDrive and buy more storage when needed. You can also set whether Windows 8.1 will use SkyDrive as the default save location for your documents.

- **Camera Roll** Use this if you want SkyDrive to automatically upload your photos and videos from the Camera Roll folder. You can choose the quality of your uploaded photos and also you can turn on and off the option to automatically upload your videos to SkyDrive. These settings apply only to the Camera Roll folder found in your Pictures library. Other pictures and videos are not impacted by the settings found in this section. The Camera Roll folder is used by the Camera app and other similar apps from the Windows Store. Desktop apps that are capable of taking pictures or recording video do not use this folder.

6

- **Sync Settings**   Here, you can set which Windows settings are synchronized auto-matically via SkyDrive. To learn more on this subject, read the next section.

- **Metered Connections**   Use this to set whether SkyDrive is allowed to use metered connections to synchronize your files and settings.

Synchronizing your Windows settings

One of the greatest features of SkyDrive is that Windows 8.1 can use it to synchronize your user account settings across the computers on which your Microsoft account is used. If you make a change on one computer, it will be reflected on other computers the next time you log on.

However, not all Windows 8.1 settings are synchronized, even though most of them will be. The settings that are synchronized, if you set them to be, are the following:

- Your Start screen tiles and tile layout

- Your desktop background, desktop colors, the lock screen, and your user account picture

- The active desktop theme, high contrast, and taskbar settings

- The list of Windows 8.1 apps installed on your computers and devices

- Your settings and purchases within Windows Store apps

- Internet Explorer Favorites, open tabs, home pages, history, and settings

- The sign-in information for the homegroup, network access, some of your apps, and websites (if you are using Internet Explorer as your browser)

- Your language preferences: keyboard, input methods, personal dictionary, and the display language

- Ease of access settings: the narrator and the magnifier

- Your printers settings, mouse and mouse cursor settings and those of File Explorer

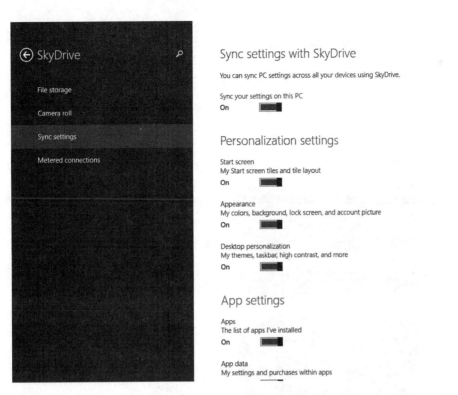

Another great aspect of the synchronization feature is that the SkyDrive space used for storing your settings is not counted against your SkyDrive space allocation. That space is reserved for uploading the files you want.

As with other SkyDrive features, you need a Microsoft account to synchronize your settings. SkyDrive doesn't work on local user accounts.

Also, after you log on to your computer or device by using your Microsoft account, you need to set it as trusted for your passwords to be synchronized. If you haven't done this, you can do so from the SkyDrive section, in the Sync Settings area found in PC Settings. Just click the Verify link and follow the instructions.

To view or change these settings, you need to verify your identity.
Verify

In this exercise, you'll learn how to turn on the synchronization of your Windows 8.1 settings and select what is being synced.

 SET UP
Open PC Settings.

1   Click the **SkyDrive** section.

2   Click the **Sync Settings** area to view the available synchronization settings.

（←）SkyDrive   🔍

File storage

Camera roll

Sync settings

Metered connections

Sync settings with SkyDrive

You can sync PC settings across all your devices using SkyDrive.

Sync your settings on this PC
On

Personalization settings

Start screen
My Start screen tiles and tile layout
Off

Appearance
My colors, background, lock screen, and account picture
Off

Desktop personalization
My themes, taskbar, high contrast, and more
On

App settings

Apps
The list of apps I've installed
On

App data
My settings and purchases within apps

3   Change the switch for the items that you want to synchronize from **Off** to **On** and the other way around for those you don't want to synchronize.

✖ CLEAN UP
Close PC Settings and then repeat this procedure on all the computers that use the same Microsoft account and on which you want settings to be synchronized.

From now on, each change you make in the Windows 8.1 settings will be synchronized on all the computers on which synchronization was set up.

Key points

- Using SkyDrive requires a Microsoft account and an Internet connection.

- Use the SkyDrive app to browse the content of your SkyDrive and to upload, download, and view files.

- You can upload or download multiple files at once to and from SkyDrive.

- SkyDrive can also synchronize your settings across computers and devices with Windows 8.1.

6

Chapter at a glance

Add

Add a Microsoft email account to the Mail app, page 216

Add your Outlook account 📧

Enter the information below to connect to your Outlook account.

Email address
> seventutorials@live.com

Password
> •••••••••

Show more details

`Connect` `Cancel`

Connect

Connect to your Facebook account by using the People app, page 227

← Stay in touch with your Facebook friends **f**

See your Facebook friends and their updates here, and in other apps and websites where you use this Microsoft account. Just connect **Facebook** to **seventutorials@live.com**.

What else happens when I connect? ⌄

`Connect` `Cancel`

Manage

Manage your schedule by using the Calendar app, page 233

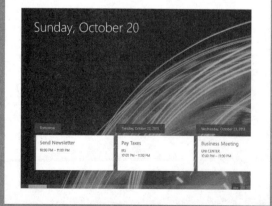

Record

Record video and take pictures by using the Camera app, page 242

Using the social apps

IN THIS CHAPTER, YOU WILL LEARN HOW TO

- ☒ Use the Mail app and send an email with a Microsoft SkyDrive attachment.
- ☒ Use the People app and add your Facebook account.
- ☒ Use the Calendar app.
- ☒ Use the Camera app.

Being social is a key component of nearly everyone's computing life. Windows 8.1 tries to meet the need for interaction with our friends, family, and coworkers by offering a few well-integrated apps: Mail, Calendar, and People. These apps are built into the operating system but are also available in the Windows Store. To complete the social experience, you can also use the Skype app so that you have all the important social tools available at your fingertips.

The tiles of these apps are found on the Start screen. At first, they are static and don't display any data. When you start using the apps, their tiles automatically display live data such as updates from your friend on Facebook whose birthday is today or the schedule of your next meeting.

These apps are well integrated and, after you add an account to one of them, it can be accessed from all the others. For example, you can add your Outlook.com account to the Mail app. Then, you can view your Outlook.com calendar in the Calendar app and your Outlook.com contacts in the People app.

You can use the Camera app when you need to take pictures or record video via your webcam. With it, you can also change your Microsoft account profile picture or take a picture that is later on used as the wallpaper for the Windows 8.1 lock screen.

In this chapter, you'll learn the basics about using the social apps included in Windows 8.1 (Mail, People, Calendar), the basics about using the Camera app and a bit about Skype and its main features.

PRACTICE FILES The practice files you will use to complete the exercises in this chapter are in the Chapter07 practice file folder. Before you can complete the exercises in this chapter, you need to install the practice files specified in the section "Using the Practice Files" in the Introduction of this book to their default location.

Using the Mail app

The Mail app runs in full-screen mode, just like all Windows 8.1 apps. Its interface is minimalistic and focuses on browsing and reading your email messages. Unfortunately for users who are accustomed to the Desktop, it might not be easy to find your way at first, so learning the basics of navigating this app is the place to start. As you'll see in this section and the ones that follow it, Mail is a simple app that is easy to learn.

When you open the Mail app for the first time and no email accounts exist, you are asked to add them. You can add many types of email accounts: Outlook (which works with @live.com, @hotmail.com and @outlook.com email addresses), Google (if you are using a @gmail.com email address), AOL, Yahoo and other accounts, including business email accounts that use Exchange ActiveSync or IMAP for sending and receiving email messages.

Add an account ✉

Outlook.com		
Outlook.com, Hotmail.com, Live.com		
Exchange		
Exchange and Office 365		
Google		
Connect		
Other account		
Connect		
AOL		
Connect		
Yahoo!		
Connect		

As soon as you have added email accounts, things change. The app window is then split into three columns.

☒ In the column on the left are useful shortcuts for your Inbox, newsletters, social updates, email folders, favorites, and flagged messages. If you have set up multiple email accounts in the Mail app, on the bottom of this column you will also see the Accounts icon. Click this to switch between your email accounts. On screens with resolutions of 1366×768 or higher, the Accounts icon is replaced by the name of each email account added to the Mail app. Click the account you want to use in order to access it.

☒ In the middle is the Inbox column, displaying the inbox folder for the selected email account. The name of the sender, the date or time of receipt, and the subject are all displayed for each message. This column can also display messages from folders other than your Inbox (Sent Items, for instance) depending on what you select in the first column.

☒ On the right, the messages you select are displayed in their entirety.

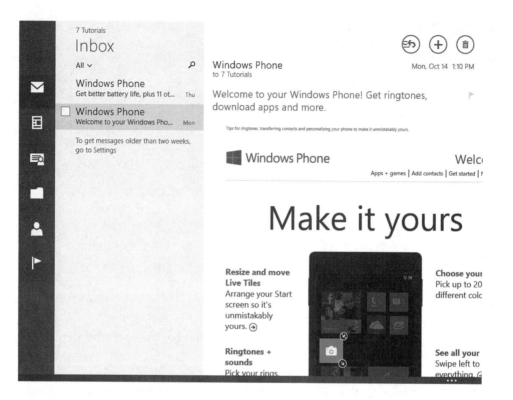

To display a contextual menu, right-click or swipe upward from the bottom edge. This menu includes the following buttons:

- ☒ **Manage Folders** Opens a menu that contains options for emptying the current folder, marking the emails as read, creating a new folder, or creating a new subfolder and pinning to Start the current folder.

- ☒ **Select** When you use this button, the current message is selected and check boxes appear for the other messages in the current folder. You can choose other messages simply by selecting the corresponding check box.

- ☒ **Move** Use this button to move the selected message(s) to another folder.

- ☒ **Sweep** Use this button to delete the selected message plus other messages from the same sender. Your sweeping rules can also be enabled so that they are applied automatically to future messages from the same sender.

- ☒ **Junk** Marks the selected message as junk or spam and moves it to the Junk folder. If you are browsing the Junk folder, the button is changed to Not Junk. When pressing it, the selected message is no longer marked as junk and it is moved to the Inbox.

⊠ **Flag**   Use this button to flag the selected message, so that you can easily find it in the future. Flagged messages are also displayed in the Flagged folder. When selecting a flagged message, the button is renamed to Remove Flag and does what its name implies.

⊠ **Mark Unread**   Use this button to mark the email message that is currently open as unread.

⊠ **Delete**   Use this button to delete selected message(s).

⊠ **Open Window**   Opens the selected message in a new Mail app window.

⊠ **More**   Pressing this button displays a small menu with options for synchronizing your mail and printing the selected message.

The three buttons in the upper-right corner of the window do the following:

⊠ Open a small menu with options to reply to the message or forward it to other people.

⊠ Create a new email message.

⊠ Delete the email message.

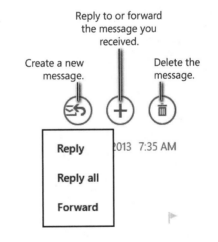

Create a new
message.

Reply to or forward
the message you
received.

Delete the
message.

Ciprian Rusen
to Ciprian Rusen

Reply

Reply all

Forward

2013 7:35 AM

test email

Hello,

Just like with any other Windows 8.1 app, you can change the settings of the Mail app by using the Settings charm. There, you have options for grouping messages by conversation, when to mark unread messages as having been read, and lots of options for configuring each email account, how it gets synchronized, how often, and which items are synchronized, etc.

Adding a Microsoft email account to the Mail app

You can add any number of email accounts from different email services to the Mail app. By default, it is well integrated with the popular Outlook service from Microsoft and Gmail from Google. You can also add business email accounts that use Exchange ActiveSync or IMAP for sending and receiving email messages.

The integration with Outlook.com is very good and you can add multiple email accounts to the Mail app. Outlook.com has been integrated with the older Hotmail.com and Live.com services and it is the current email service provided by Microsoft. If you have a @live.com, @hotmail.com or @outlook.com email address, when you set up the Mail app, you should choose Outlook as the type of account you want to add.

In this exercise, you'll learn how to add a Microsoft email account to the Mail app. To demonstrate the integration with older email services from Microsoft, I will be using a sample @live.com email address.

➡ SET UP

Ensure that your Windows 8.1 device is connected to the Internet. Then, open the Mail app and have your account details at hand (the correct email address and password).

1   Press **Windows key+C** or swipe from the right side of the screen and then select the **Settings** charm.

2   Click **Accounts** to open the list of accounts already added to the Mail app.

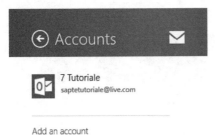

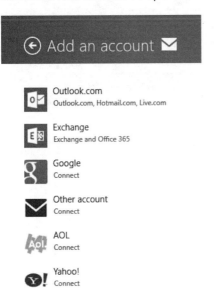

3   Click **Add An Account** to open the list of types of accounts that you can add.

4   Click **Outlook** to open the **Add Your Outlook Account** window.

5   Type the email address and password in the appropriate boxes.

Add your Outlook account

Enter the information below to connect to your Outlook account.

Email address

seventutorials@live.com

Password

•••••••••

Show more details

[Connect]   [Cancel]

6   Click **Connect.** Wait a few seconds for the Mail app to connect to your email account and display the messages in your inbox.

 CLEAN UP
Close the Mail app.

The email account you specified is now added to the Mail app and can be accessed each time you use the app.

Adding a Google account to the Mail app

You add a Google email account to the Mail app the same way you add an Outlook account except that you click Google instead of Outlook.

Many Google users use a two-step verification process that enhances the security of their email accounts and lowers the chances of unwanted people gaining access to the accounts. If this process is enabled for your Google account, you cannot use your standard Google password to add your account to the Mail app. First, you need to generate a new app-specific password just for the Mail app and use that instead of your password at step 5 in the preceding exercise.

You can generate app-specific passwords by going to your Google account, choosing Security, and then clicking Manage Your App Specific Passwords link, in the 2-Step Verification section. Choose an appropriate name for the new app-specific password and then click Generate Password.

Application-specific passwords

Some applications that work outside a browser aren't yet compatible with 2-step verification and cannot ask for verification codes, for example:

- Email programs including Outlook, Apple Mail, or Thunderbird
- Older Android smartphones

To use these applications, you first need to **generate an application-specific password**. Next, **enter** that in the password field of your application instead of your regular password. You can create a new application-specific password for each application that needs one. Learn more

▶ Watch the video on application-specific passwords

┌─ **Step 1 of 2: Generate new application-specific password** ──────────────┐
│ Enter a name to help you remember what application this is for: │
│   │
│ **Name:** │ Mail App in Windows 8.1 │   │ Generate password │   │
│   │
│   ex: "Bob's Android", "Gmail on my iPhone", "GoogleTalk", "Outlook - home computer", "Thunderbird" │
└──┘

Google generates a random password that you can type in the Mail app instead of your Google mail password to access the messages in your Google account.

7

Sending an email with a SkyDrive attachment

When sending files as email attachments, you use both inbox space and some bandwidth when uploading the file. The recipient will also use space and bandwidth.

By using the SkyDrive app, you upload a file once to your SkyDrive and then share it by email, using the Mail app, with as many people as you want. You don't need to upload the file each time you want to send it to someone.

The people to whom you send the file can access it through a direct link that is automatically included in the message. It doesn't fill up their inbox space, and they can download the file if and when they want.

You can share files with anyone; it doesn't matter whether the person uses the SkyDrive service. Also, you can type the email address of the people to whom you want to send it or select them from your list of contacts stored in the People app.

In this exercise, you'll learn how to send an email message that shares a file uploaded to your SkyDrive.

 SET UP
Ensure that your Windows 8.1 device is connected to the Internet. To complete this exercise, you need the Document1.docx file in the Chapter07 folder in your practice files. When this file is available, open the SkyDrive app and upload this file. After the file is uploaded to SkyDrive, follow the steps in this exercise.

1   In the SkyDrive app, right click the Document1.docx file; a check mark appears in the upper-right corner of its icon.

2   Press **Windows key+C** or swipe inward from the right side of the screen and then click **Share**.

3   Click **Mail** to display the Mail app on the right side of the screen.

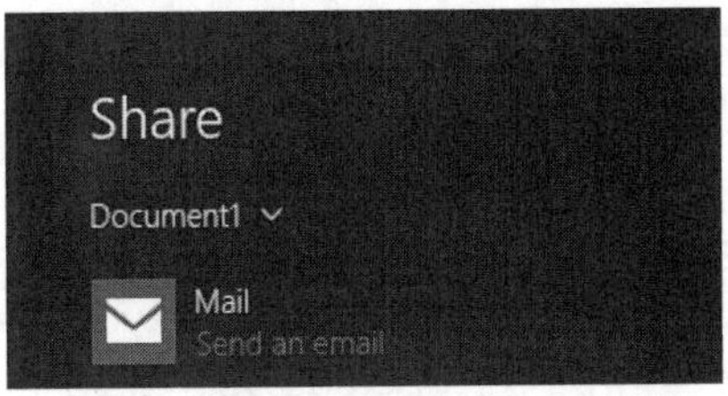

Share

Document1 ∨

✉ Mail
Send an email

4   In the **To** field, type the email address of the person to whom you want to send the
message.

5   In the body of the message, type the message that you want to send.

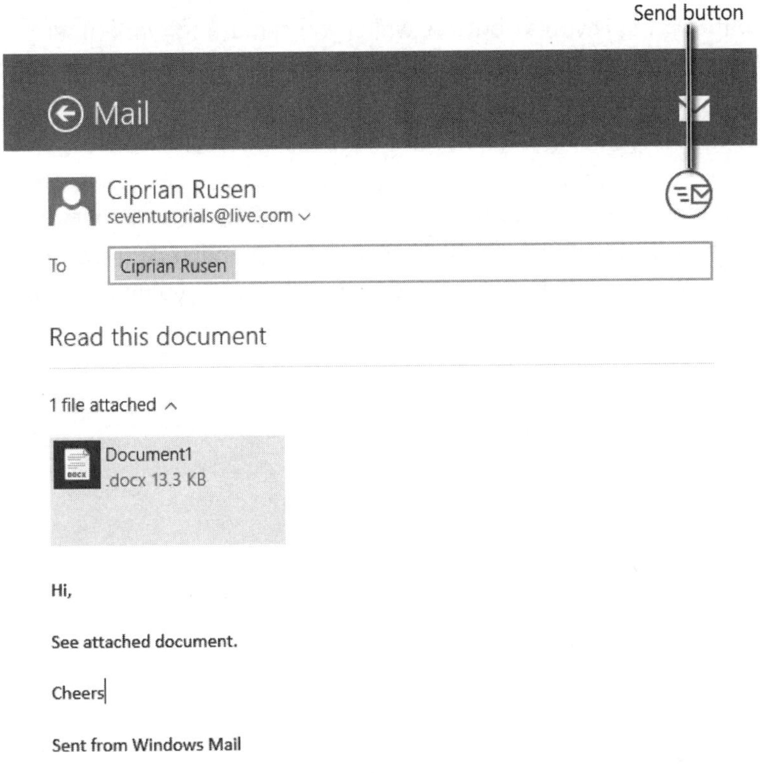

Send button

← Mail   ✉

👤 Ciprian Rusen
    seventutorials@live.com ∨   ✉

To   Ciprian Rusen

Read this document

1 file attached ∧

📄 Document1
    .docx 13.3 KB

Hi,

See attached document.

Cheers

Sent from Windows Mail

6   In the upper-right corner of the Mail app window, click the **Send** button.

❌ CLEAN UP
Close the SkyDrive app.

The email message has been sent, and the recipient can access the SkyDrive file from the
direct link included in the message.

Using the People app

The People app displays all the contacts you have for all the email accounts and services you have added in the Mail app and, through your Microsoft account, it can access social networking services such as Facebook, Twitter, and LinkedIn, as soon as you authorize your Microsoft account to access these services. You can also add your Skype account. The People app downloads all your friends and contacts and share their latest updates.

When you open the People app, you are presented with plenty of information. A column on the left named Me is for viewing notifications, including the most recent one. Next, you can view contacts you have set as favorites and their pictures. A click opens their contact details. Below that is the Favorites button, which you can use to mark other people as your Favorites. When you do that, their pictures are added next to the others, and you will be able to quickly access their contact details and their latest updates. Below the Favorites button is the What's new section for viewing the latest posts and updates on the social networks to which you are connected. On the right, your contacts are listed, grouped in alphabetical order. In the lower-right corner, in the Connected To section, there is a list of icons that represent the accounts to which the People app is connected. In the upper-right corner is the Search box. You can use this to quickly find contacts by typing their name.

Go to notifications

Search Box

You list of contacts
organized in
alphabetical order

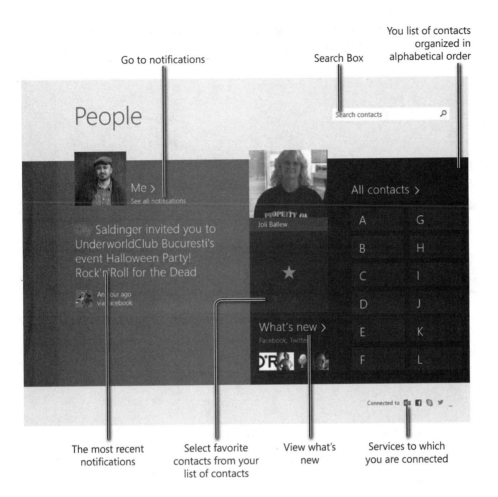

People

Search contacts

Me >
See all notifications

Saldinger invited you to
UnderworldClub Bucuresti's
event Halloween Party!
Rock'n'Roll for the Dead

An hour ago
via Facebook

PROPERTY OF
Joli Ballew

★

What's new >
Facebook, Twitter

All contacts >

A   G

B   H

C   I

D   J

E   K

F   L

Connected to

The most recent
notifications

Select favorite
contacts from your
list of contacts

View what's
new

Services to which
you are connected

7

You access a contact by clicking the letter it starts with. The People app shows the contacts whose names start with that letter. Click the person you are interested in.

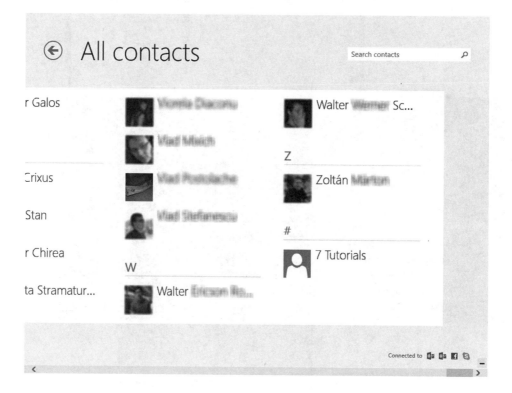

When opening a contact, you can see the contact details that have been stored and, if available, any updates from that person on the social networks to which you are connected.

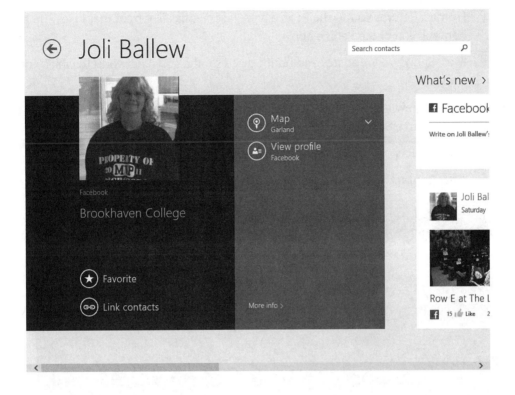

To show the menu with contextual options, right-click or swipe upward from the bottom edge of the screen to display the following buttons:

- ⊠ **Home** Returns you to the People area. It serves as a shortcut that takes you to the home screen of the People app.

- ⊠ **Me** Shows your updates and notifications on the social networks to which you're connected.

- ⊠ **What's New** Shows updates from all your contacts on all the social networks to which you're connected.

- ⊠ **All Contacts** Opens a list with all your contacts, listed in alphabetical order.

- ⊠ **New Contact** Click this to create a new contact.

As you can see, using the People app is relatively easy. If you integrate it with the social networks you are using, it can be a great tool for managing your connections with other people.

To configure the People app, use the Settings charm. From there, you can add new accounts, manage existing accounts, and set options like how your contacts are sorted and whether you would like to hide contacts from a specific list of accounts.

Connecting to your Facebook account by using the People app

You can easily integrate the People app with Facebook. After you add your Facebook account, your Microsoft account is also connected to it, so your contacts will be synchronized with Facebook.

If your Microsoft account (Formerly Windows Live ID) is already connected to your Facebook account, your Facebook friends will show up in the People app, and you won't need to add the Facebook account again.

When you connect the People app to your Facebook account, Facebook asks whether to remember the browser used to access it. Because the People app will access your Facebook account often, in order to deliver the latest updates, it is best to choose Save Browser.

Last but not least, you will be asked whether you want to let Windows remember your Facebook sign-in name and password. Choosing Yes allows the People app to get the latest updates automatically, without asking for your Facebook password, each time it tries to connects to this social network to the latest data.

In this exercise, you'll learn how to add your Facebook account to the People app.

 SET UP
Ensure that your Windows 8.1 device is connected to the Internet and then open the People app.

1   Press **Windows key+C** or swipe inward from the right side of the screen and select **Settings**.

2   In the **Settings** pane, click **Accounts**.

Settings

People
By Microsoft Corporation

Accounts

Options

Help

About

Feedback

Permissions

Rate and review

3   At the bottom of the Accounts window that opens, click **Add An Account**.

← Accounts

7 Tutorials
seventutorials@live.com

Skype
live:seventutorials

Add an account

4   Click **Facebook** and then wait for a few seconds.

The Stay In Touch With Your Facebook Friends window opens.

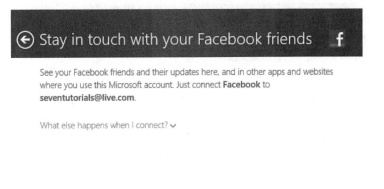

5   Click **Connect**. At the prompt, type your Facebook login details.

6 Type your email address and your password and select the **Keep Me Logged In** check box.

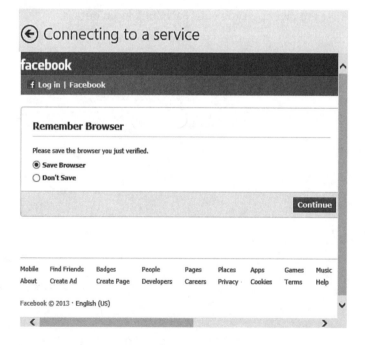

7 Click **Log In**.

You are asked whether you want to remember the browser you are using.

8   Select **Save Browser** and then click **Continue**.

After a few seconds, you receive the announcement that you're ready to go.

We're setting things up now, so it might take a few minutes until you see any changes.

 Add more accounts in settings
You can add more accounts or change these connection settings at any time in the settings for this app.

9   Click **Done.** You are then asked whether you want to let Windows remember your sign-in name and password.

Let Windows remember your sign-in name and password so you don't have to.

Stored sign-in info can be used with other apps as well (so you won't need to enter it again), and it's automatically synced to all your PCs.

10 Click **Yes** and then wait for the People app to download and synchronize your Facebook data.

CLEAN UP
When you are done using the People app, close it.

The People app needs some time to synchronize with your Facebook account. Don't be surprised if it takes minutes instead of seconds, especially if you have a slow Internet connection or many friends and updates that need to be synchronized.

Adding a new contact to the People app

You can add new contacts from the People app to all your email accounts. However, the People app cannot add contacts to the social networks to which you are connected. You have to do that by accessing the individual social networks themselves in a web browser such as Internet Explorer.

In this exercise, you'll learn how to add a new contact to the People app.

SET UP

Ensure that your Windows 8.1 device is connected to the Internet and then open the People app.

1   Right-click to open a contextual menu at the bottom of the window.

2   Click **New Contact** to open the **New Contact** window.

3   In the **Account** list, select the account in which you want to store this contact.

4   Complete the contact details that you want to store.

New contact

Account	Email	Address
7 Tutorials	Personal ⌄	⊕ Address
	seventutorials@live.com	
	⊕ Email	Other info
Name		⊕ Other info
First name		
7	Phone	
	Mobile ⌄	
Last name		
Tutorials		
	⊕ Phone	
Company		
⊕ Name		

5   In the upper-right corner, click the **Save** button (the diskette icon).

The new contact's page appears, complete with the data you just added.

CLEAN UP

Close the People app.

The contact you created is saved and automatically synchronized with the account you selected.

Editing or deleting a contact from the People app

When you access a contact in the People app, you can view information about it, edit it, add to it, remove information from it, or delete the contact. You can also pin the contact to the Start screen, set it as a Favorite, or link it with another contact from another account. All these activities are initiated from the contact's page or the contextual menu. To access that menu, first, open the contact that you want to edit and then right-click the screen or swipe upward from the lower edge of the screen.

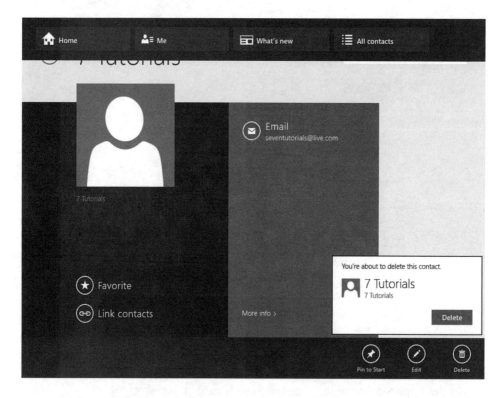

You can delete only contacts that are stored with your email accounts. To delete contacts from the social networks to which you are connected, you must access those social networks in a web browser.

Using the Calendar app

The Calendar app is very simple. It automatically takes your calendar data from all the email accounts you added in the Mail app and shows all events from all accounts. When you open it, it displays the What's Next view that shows upcoming events in your calendar.

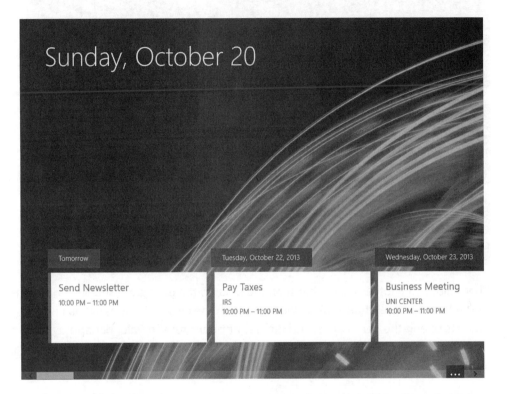

To change how you view the calendar, right-click the screen or swipe upward from the bottom edge of the screen. A contextual menu appears, presenting several options. On the top are buttons for changing how you view your calendar: by day, by week, or by month. On the bottom is a button for synchronizing your calendar, one for changing the background of the What's Next View and one for adding a new event to your calendar.

When selecting another view other than the default, the events are shown in different colors, each color representing the account to which the event was added. You can add new accounts or edit the permissions and different options for the Calendar app by using the Settings charm. Also, each time you add an email account to the Mail app, its calendar is synchronized automatically by the Calendar app.

To open an event, click it. When you open a recurring event, you are asked whether you want to Open One or Open Series. If you click Open One, only the current event opens, and any changes you make effect only that specific event. If you click Open Series, you open the series of recurring events, and any changes you make will be applied to the entire series.

When you open the event, you can add details to it or remove details from it. To save your changes, in the upper-right corner, click the Save button (the diskette icon). To delete the event, click the Delete button (the trash-can icon).

To close the event without saving the changes you made, in the upper-left corner, click the Back button. You are asked whether you want to save your changes. Choose Discard Changes.

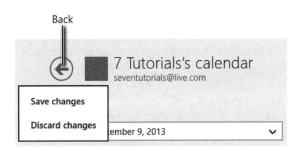

As you can see, the Calendar app is not complex, and you will likely become familiar with the way it works, with little effort .

Adding an event to your Calendar

Adding an event to any of your calendars is an easy task, too. However, you need to complete some information for the event to be created and saved. The Calendar app asks you to complete the following fields:

⊠ **Calendar**   Select the calendar on which you want this event to be saved.

⊠ **When**   You must fill in the date when the event is taking place.

⊠ **Start**   You must fill in the hour when the event starts.

⊠ **How Long**   Fill in the duration of the event. The default value is one hour, but if your event doesn't last that long, it is best to change the duration to the length of time you expect it to last.

☒ **Location**   In this field, you specify information about where the event takes place, but you do not have to fill in this field.

☒ **Who**   Use this box to invite others to the event and share the event details. You can type the email addresses of the people you want to invite.

☒ **How Often**   You can set the frequency of the event. It can be set to once or every day, every weekday, and many other values.

☒ **Reminder**   Set this to specify when you want to receive a reminder about the event and for how long in advance of it you want to be reminded. You can choose one of the following values: none, at start time, 5 minutes, 15 minutes, 30 minutes, 1 hour, 18 hours, 1 day, or 1 week.

☒ **Status**   Use this box to set your status during the event to show others who have access to your calendar data. The default value is Busy. Other choices include Free, Tentative, and Out Of Office.

☒ **Private**   This option is useful when your calendar is shared with others. If you set the event as private, other people can't view the details of this event.

☒ **Add A Subject**   Use this box to add a name for the event.

☒ **Add A Message**   Use this field to add a message to share with the people you will invite or to add any information that is useful to you or others.

7 Tutorials's calendar ⌄
seventutorials@live.com

Add a subject

Add a message

When

Tuesday, October 22, 2013   ⌄

Start

9   ⌄   00   ⌄   AM   ⌄

How long

1 hour   ⌄

Location

Who

Invite people

How often

Once   ⌄

Reminder

15 minutes   ⌄

Status

Busy   ⌄

☐ Private

7

To save the event, in the upper-right corner of the window, click the Save button. If you have invited other people to the event, the Save button will change to a Send Invite button. Clicking it saves the event in your calendar and sends invitations to the people you specified in the Who field.

In this exercise, you'll learn how to add a new event to your calendar.

 SET UP
Open the Calendar app.

1   Right-click or swipe upward from the lower edge to open a contextual menu at the bottom of the window.

2   Click the **New** button to open the window for creating the event.

3   At the top of left column, click the name of the current calendar or the arrow adjacent to its name.

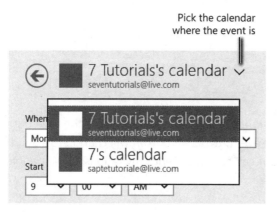

4   Select the calendar in which you want this event stored.

5   Complete all the important fields with the relevant information: When, Start, How Long, Where, and enter any people you want to invite.

7 Tutorials's calendar ⌄
seventutorials@live.com

When

| Sunday, October 20, 2013 | ⌄ |

Start

| 6 | ⌄ | | 30 | ⌄ | | PM | ⌄ |

How long

| 1 hour | ⌄ |

Location

| School of Fine Art |

Who

| Invite people |

Show more

6   Click **Show More** to reveal additional details to complete.

7   Complete any of the additional information that is useful to you.

8   On the right side of the window, type a name for the event and any other important details that you'd like to add.

Business Meeting   (🖫)

We need to discuss the latest developments on our project.|

9   Click the **Save** or **Send Invite** button, depending on whether you invited people to the event.

 CLEAN UP
Close the Calendar app.

The event you have created is added to your calendar and you will be reminded about it, depending on how you set the reminder. If you invited other people they will automatically receive the invite to this event, via email.

Using the Camera app to take pictures or record videos

You can use the Camera app if you have a webcam installed on your Windows 8.1–based computer or device. You can record videos, take quick pictures, or use it to change the picture of your Microsoft account.

When you start it for the first time, you are asked whether you want to allow this app to use your location. This decision is entirely up yo you, but you can still use the app even if you select Block. If you allow it to use your location, this data will be stored in the metadata of the pictures and videos taken with this app.

Can Camera use your location?

Allow   Block

The Camera app is very simple. When you open it, it automatically turns on your camera and it displays whatever is in front of the camera. On the right are two buttons: the top button is for taking recording video and the other is for taking a picture.

The app offers some customization options. To display them, right-click in the app screen or swipe upward from the bottom edge of it. On the menu that appears, there are only two buttons: Timer and Exposure. After taking several pictures or recording videos with the Camera app, a third button the Camera Roll appears. It can be used to access the pictures and videos that you took with this app.

You use the Timer button to set a time when you want to take a picture or make a recording. You use the Exposure button to set a custom exposure level for your camera. Other cameras with more advanced support for Windows 8.1 might provide more configuration options. For most cameras though, only these two buttons are available.

To take a picture, click the Picture button on the right. To start recording video, click the Video button above it. When you start recording video, the Video button turns into a Stop button.

7

Click it to discontinue recording. All of the pictures and videos made with the Camera app are stored in your Pictures library, in a folder named Camera Roll. You can browse the files within that folder by using File Explorer or the Camera app itself.

As soon as you have taken your first picture or made a video recording, you will see a Back arrow on the left side of the Camera app window. Click it to display the latest recording or picture you have taken. Then, the Forward arrow appears on the right. Use these arrows to browse through the files recorded by the Camera app.

Back   Forward

Although it might not be obvious at first, the Camera offers app also some basic editing tools. When you view the pictures taken with this app, right-click to bring up a contextual menu that presents these tools.

You have plenty of options from which to choose:

 Camera   This button takes you to the main screen of the Camera app.

 Delete   Click this to delete the current picture.

- ⊠ **Open With**   Use this to specify another app or program with which to open the current image.

- ⊠ **Set As Lock Screen**   Sets the current picture as the wallpaper for the lock screen.

- ⊠ **Slide Show**   This starts a slideshow with all the pictures and videos recorded by the Camera app. To stop a running slideshow, on your keyboard, press the Esc key.

- ⊠ **Rotate**   Use this button to rotate the pictures 90 degrees clockwise.

- ⊠ **Crop**   Use this tool to trim the picture to a smaller size.

- ⊠ **Edit**   This button displays additional editing options, such as: Auto Fix, Basic Fixes, Light, Color, and Effects.

When you view the videos recorded with the Camera app, right-click to bring up a contextual menu that presents tools specific to editing video. There are fewer tools available for video, as compared to the tools for editing picture, but they are useful nonetheless:

- ⊠ **Camera**   This button takes you to the main screen of the Camera app.

- ⊠ **Delete**   Click this to delete the current video.

- ⊠ **Open With**   Use this to specify another app or program with which to open the current image.

- ⊠ **Slide Show**   Starts a slideshow with all the pictures and videos recorded by the Camera app. To stop the slideshow, on your keyboard, press the Esc key.

- ⊠ **Trim**   Use this to cut the video's length.

In this exercise, you'll learn how to record a video with the Camera app and view it.

 SET UP

Ensure that your webcam is installed correctly and then open the Camera app.

1   Click the **Video** button on the right to start recording.

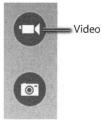
Video

2   After you have recorded what you want, click the **Stop** button on the right. The Back button appears on the left side of the screen.

3   Click the **Back** button.

4   Wait for the video you just recorded to play back to you.

5   When the video has ended, on the right side of the screen, click the **Forward** button.

✖ CLEAN UP

When you are done using the Camera app, close it.

I'm sure you'd agree that the Camera app is really easy to use.

Using the Skype app

Windows 8 bundled a Messaging app that could be used to chat with your friends in the People app. In Windows 8.1 this app has been phased out and replaced by Skype. You can use it with your old Skype account or with your Microsoft account. By default, Skype signs in with your Microsoft account. If you also have a Skype account you can merge both of them and get access to your credit and all your contacts.

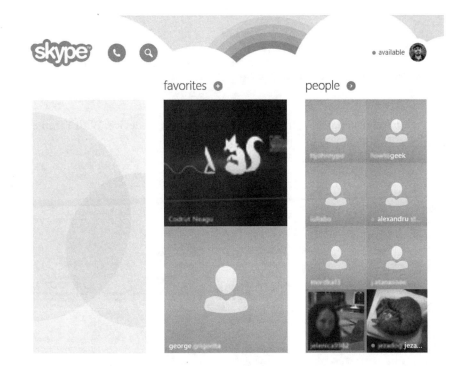

When compared to the former Messaging app, Skype is more complex and delivers more features, including video conversations and the ability to exchange attachments with the people to whom you're conversing. You can also use Skype to call phones internationally, by using your Skype Credit or active subscription. To chat with a person, simply click on his or her name. In the chat window, you can type a message or call that person using the call button.

During a call, you can also add more participants to your voice or video conversation.

Using the Yammer app

If your company is using Yammer, you can find the Yammer app in the Windows Store, for free.

Search for it and install it on your Windows 8.1 computer or device. With Yammer you can keep in touch with your company's social network.

You can easily access the updates posted by your colleagues at work, "like" or respond to messages, post your own updates, preview documents and images, as well as share content with your coworkers.

Key points

☒ The Mail, Calendar, and People apps are well integrated and easy to use, even with a mouse and keyboard.

☒ When you add an account in the Mail app, you can access it from the other apps.

☒ You can lower your inbox space usage by using SkyDrive to share email attachments.

☒ You can access the latest updates from your Facebook friends by using the People app.

☒ Using the Camera app, you can quickly record videos, take pictures, and perform basic editing tasks.

7

Chapter at a glance

Search
Search for an app by category, page 251

Install
Install an app, page 257

Maps		Photos
Microsoft Solitair... **NEW**		Reader
Music		Reading List

Use
Use an app, page 258

Rate
Rate an app, page 262

Write a review

Fresh Paint

Rating
★ ★ ★ ★ ★

Review – optional
Title

Comments

0/1000

Note: The name and picture for the Microsoft account you use with the Store will be posted with your review.

Submit   Cancel

Shopping in the Windows Store

8

IN THIS CHAPTER, YOU WILL LEARN HOW TO

- Browse and search the Windows Store.

- Explore an app's listing page.

- Obtain, install, and use an app.

- Update and reacquire apps.

- Write a review for an app you own.

- Understand subscriptions and in-app purchases.

You know about apps. You've explored the apps on the Start screen that come as part of Windows 8.1 , including Music, People, Internet Explorer, and others. You can easily obtain more apps from the Windows Store.

In this chapter, you'll learn how to access the Windows Store, browse and install apps, search for an app by name, automatically update the apps you obtain, and more. Note that as the Windows Store evolves, more categories, apps, and other items will likely be added. What you see here is what was available as of this writing.

TIP Microsoft has complete control over the apps that are available in the Windows Store and requires developers to write apps to certain criteria. This helps to ensure that they are safe and functional and do not contain adware or spyware, among other things.

PRACTICE FILES You do not need any practice files to complete this chapter. For more information about practice file requirements, see the section "Using the practice files" in the Introduction of this book.

Exploring the landing page and categories

To enter the Windows Store, you simply click its tile on the Start screen. If you're connected to the Internet and have logged on with a Microsoft account, you'll be taken to the landing page of the Windows Store. This is also referred to as the Windows Store's "Home," and you can access it at any time by right-clicking the screen and then, from the charms that appear, clicking Home.

TIP Any time you see a number on a tile on the Start screen, it means new data that affects you is available. A number on the Windows Store tile means updates for apps you own are available. If you've configured the Windows Store to install updates automatically, you might never see this.

After you enter the Windows Store, you can explore what's shown initially, which includes the categories, Picks For You, Trending, New & Rising, Top Paid, and Top Free. You might also see a category that represents your computer manufacturer that lists apps you might enjoy based on your specific machine. Use your mouse and the scroll bar that appears across the bottom of the screen to navigate. There is also a Search box in the upper-right corner.

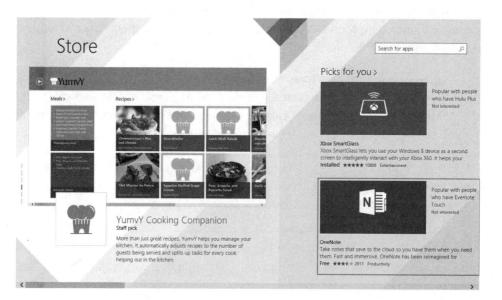

To see more apps, scroll to the right to access Top Paid or Top Free, among other options. These apps have been purchased and/or downloaded many times by other users and offer ratings under the app title. You can also click Top Free to see everything in that category. Note the Back arrow that appears when you are in the Top Free view.

However you navigate to an app you'd like to explore, if you click its tile you're taken to the app's listings page, which you'll learn about later in this chapter. The listings page offers more information about an app. When exploring apps in this way, you can use the Back arrow that appears in the upper-left corner to return to the previous screen.

You can also right-click the screen to sort the available apps by category. You'll see the five categories listed earlier on the far left, but to the right of that are categories that you can explore by type. Some of the categories are listed here:

- **Games** This category offers games for kids (and adults) of all ages.

  TROUBLESHOOTING If you don't see the app you want on the landing page of the Windows Store, right-click to choose a category or, in the Search box, type the name of the app.

- **Social** This category offers apps for social networking websites.

- **Entertainment** This category presents apps that are related to entertainment (such as Netflix and YouTube).

- **Photo** This category offers apps for photo-sharing sites, apps that work with a built-in webcam, and apps with which you can fix your photos by removing red-eye, cropping, and so on.

- **Music & Video** This category offers apps for listening to Internet radio, learning song lyrics, listening to podcasts, and more. This isn't the Xbox Music store; what you'll find here are music-related apps.

- **Sports**   This category offers apps for keeping up with your favorite sports teams and learning more about the sports you play or watch.

- **Books & Reference**   This category offers apps such as third-party eReaders and dictionaries, bibles, and similar reference books.

- **News & Weather**   This category offers apps that involve news and weather, often from well-known national entities.

- **Health & Fitness**   This category offers apps that can help you stay or get fit, lose weight, keep track of diet and exercise, and so on.

- **Food & Dining**   This category offers apps for cookbooks and finding restaurants, reading restaurant reviews, and more.

- **Lifestyle**   This category offers apps that help you to sell a car, keep a journal, participate in an auction, and so on. If you don't see Lifestyle, click the right-facing arrow that appears next to News & Weather to access this and other categories.

- **Shopping**   This category offers apps that make it easy to shop by using an app. Look for apps from popular auction sites, phone directories, and shopping sites.

- **Travel**   This category offers apps about travel, including hotel locations, maps, and more.

- **Finance**   This category offers apps to help you manage your finances, review stock prices, and so on.

- **Productivity**   This category offers apps to help you be more productive. Here you'll find online storage solutions, note-taking apps, among others.

- **Tools**   This category presents apps that you can use to compress files, connect your cell phone, manage computer resources, and more.

- **Security**   This category presents apps with which you can protect your computer or device and keep your data secure.

- **Business**   This category presents business apps, including apps that help you to look for a job, create presentations, and so on.

- **Education**   This category offers apps related to education, including those to help you learn about planets, learn to spell words, and so on.

- **Government**   This category offers apps related to governing and government entities.

Searching the Windows Store

Browsing the Windows Store by scrolling and clicking the default titles such as Top Free might work fine for you, at least for now, but as more apps become available, browsing by what's trending or by a specific category will become cumbersome. It won't be long before there are hundreds of thousands of apps to navigate! With this in mind, note that there is an option to search the Windows Store for a specific app. You can also sort results you find by category, price, or rating, among other options.

To use the Search window from the landing page, type something about the app for which you're looking. Then, in the results, use the sorting options to refine the results. If you see an app you want, click it; if you don't see it, click the Back arrow and try again.

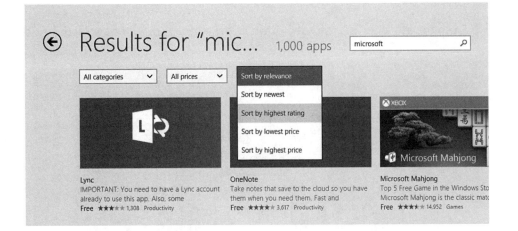

TIP If you don't know what kind of app you might want or the name of any specific app, you can type the name of a publisher or other criteria.

In this exercise, you'll use the built-in Search box to find the Microsoft Solitaire app in the Windows Store.

 SET UP
If you are not on the Start screen, position your mouse in the lower-left corner of the screen and then click the Start button that appears. You do not need any practice files to complete this exercise.

1 On the **Start** screen, click **Store**.

2 If necessary, click any **Back** arrows(s) to return to the landing page.

3   In the **Search For Apps** box, type Microsoft Solitaire, and then, on the keyboard, press **Enter**.

Search results and culling options appear.

TROUBLESHOOTING You must have a working connection to the Internet to use the Windows Store.

4   From the available lists, click the down arrow adjacent to **All Prices**, and then click **Free**.

5   Click **Microsoft Solitaire Collection** to go to its listing page.

⊗ CLEAN UP
Leave this screen open until you've read the next section.

TROUBLESHOOTING Many of the apps you'll acquire get the information that they present to you from the Internet (such as those that give you up-to-date weather and news); thus, for many apps, a working Internet connection must be available to retrieve accurate information after installation.

Exploring an App's listing page

Because Microsoft requires all new apps to pass its certification process successfully before they can be listed in the Windows Store, you probably won't run across apps that don't work or that cause your Windows 8–based computer or tablet to freeze or fail. However, it never hurts to read the reviews of apps, just in case. You might find that the app is not all that you expected it to be, or that to access all features of an app, you must purchase the full version of it.

There are many other types of information on an app's listing page beyond reviews. You can also get an overview and details about the app and learn what permissions it needs to work properly. For example, a weather app will certainly need permission to access your location. Other apps might want to access your Pictures library or other areas of your computer. You can use all this information to decide whether the app is right for you.

TIP If you ever become lost in the Windows Store, right-click the screen and then click Home.

You can access this information and more on every listing page. Here's some of what you will find from each of the available tabs on an app's listing page:

- **Description**   The first items listed for an app are its full description, a list of features, and the content rating.

- **Ratings And Reviews**   Scroll right on the listings page to access user reviews and ratings; click Ratings And Reviews to sort those reviews by Newest, Oldest, Highest Rated, Lowest Rated, and Most Helpful or by how many stars the rating was given. If you move away from the listings page and want to return to it, simply click the Back arrow to return to it.

- **Details**   From the app's listings page, scroll right to access the details of the app. Here, you can view the release notes, supported processors (x86, x64, ARM), supported languages, and more.

- **Related Apps**   Scroll to the far right of the listings page to see related apps.

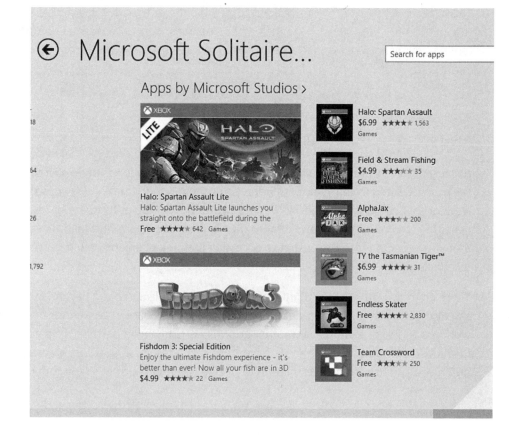

TIP The developers who read the reviews will take note of your suggestions. If you get an app and have a suggestion, write a review and then add your suggestion to the end of it.

Obtaining and installing an app

Many of the apps from the Windows Store are free. However, paid apps start at $1.49 and run to $999.99. Apps can also have a trial window ranging anywhere from 24 hours to 30 days.

In this exercise, you'll obtain a free app.

 SET UP
If you are not on the Start screen, position your mouse in the lower-left corner of the screen and then click the Start button that appears. You do not need any practice files to complete this exercise.

1   On the **Start** screen, click **Store**.

    TROUBLESHOOTING If you leave the Windows Store app and return to it, you'll return to the location from which you left it. Therefore, if you left the app while viewing an app's listings page, the Windows Store will open there. To get back to the Home screen, click the appropriate Back button(s).

2   Locate an app to install by using any method introduced so far. Click the app name to access its listing page.

3   On the listing page, click **Install**.

    You can follow the progress in the upper-right corner of the screen.

4   When the installation is complete, return to the Start screen, and then click the down arrow to open the Apps view.

    TIP Newly installed apps appear on the Apps view screen. Right-click it there to pin it to the Start screen, if desired.

5   Click the app to open it.

    TROUBLESHOOTING An app must complete the installation process before you can use it.

❌ CLEAN UP
Leave the app open and available while you read through the next section.

Using apps

The first time you open an app, you might be prompted to do something. You might need to log on with an existing user name and password, click Play to start a game, or click an icon to view the various app options. You might be prompted to let the app access personal information such as your Microsoft Xbox LIVE information. Whatever the case, when the app is ready, you'll have access to its features.

An app might ask for something that makes you uneasy, such as access to your location. If you want to use the app appropriately you might need to grant that permission. For instance, if you want a new weather app to offer information regarding the town in which you live, you'll be best served by allowing it to learn your location. At times, though, you might encounter an app that asks for permissions you feel are unnecessary, and you might want to block permissions for such an app.

After you've worked past any logon screens, granted permissions, or otherwise reviewed information about an app, you're ready to use it. It's up to you to learn how to use a specific app, and many come with instructions. If you don't see what you need, try right-clicking the app's landing page. If that doesn't work, with the app open, click the Settings charm. You might see items there such as About, Options, Credits, Permissions, Rate And Review, and so on.

TIP To add an app tile to the Start screen, right-click it while in Apps view and then, on the toolbar that appears, click Pin to Start. To uninstall it from your computer, choose Uninstall.

Updating apps

App developers are constantly creating apps and updating the apps they've already released. App updates might fix bugs, add new features, and offer additional data or options.
By default, apps update themselves when updates become available. You can also turn this
feature off and check for updates manually, if you like.

In this exercise, you'll review the app updates options and check for updates and install
them if necessary.

 SET UP

If you are not on the Start screen, position your mouse in the lower-left corner of the
screen and then click the Start screen button that appears. You do not need any practice
files to complete this exercise.

1   On the **Start** screen, click **Store**.

2   Click any **Back** buttons to return to the landing page of the Windows Store.

3   Position the cursor in the lower-right corner of the screen to display the charms, and
     then click the **Settings** charm.

     The Settings options appear.

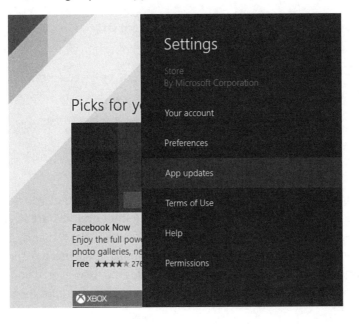

4   Click **App Updates**. Note the default options.

Automatically update my apps
Yes

Automatic app updates aren't available when using a metered Internet connection.

Check for updates

App licenses

If you're not seeing up-to-date info for the apps you own, try syncing app licenses.

Sync licenses

5   To check for updates manually, in the **Automatically Update My Apps** section, move the slider from Yes to No, and then click **Check For Updates**.

❌ CLEAN UP
Move the slider for **Automatically Update My Apps** from Off to On. Click the Back arrow to return to the previous screen.

TROUBLESHOOTING If apps aren't working correctly or you've received errors about licensing issues, from the Settings charms and App Updates, click Sync Licenses.

Reacquiring apps

You can uninstall apps that come with Windows 8.1 as well as apps that you acquire from the Windows Store directly. You just right-click the app (either on the Start screen or in the Apps view) and then, on the menu that appears, click Uninstall. You can also unpin the app if it's on the Start screen, which is a better choice if you think you'll use the app again at a later date. By using this option, you can pin it again, if desired. However, if you've actually uninstalled apps and now decide you want them back, you can reacquire them from the Windows Store.

To reacquire an app, use any search method to locate it in the Windows Store. From the app's listing page, choose Install. If you think you uninstalled an app but really didn't, you won't see the Install option. Instead, you'll see the date the app was last updated.

TIP Right-click in any window in the Windows Store and then, on the menu that appears, click Your Apps to see what apps you own. You can sort the list by what's installed and what isn't on your PC, and by the apps that are installed on other devices you own.

Write a review

You can write reviews for apps you own. You'll see the option on the app's listing page. You can also rate and review an app by using the Settings charm while in an app. One of the easiest ways to find an app and write the review is to do it from within the Windows Store.

In this exercise, you'll write a review for an app you own.

 SET UP
No setup is required for this exercise.

1   On the **Start** screen, click **Store**.

2   From any location within the Windows Store, right-click the screen, and then, on the menu that appears, click **Your apps**.

3   Click the tile for an app you own; locate the options to **Rate This App** and **Write A Review**.

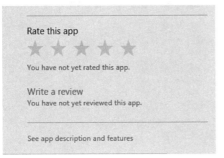

TROUBLESHOOTING You won't see Write A Review if you don't own the app.

4   Click the applicable number of **stars** to apply a rating.

5   Click **Write A Review**.

6   In the **Title** box, give your review a name, and then, in the **Comments** box, write your review. Click **Submit**.

Write a review

Fresh Paint

Rating

★ ★ ★ ★ ★

Review – optional

| Title |

| Comments |
| |
| |

0/1000

Note: The name and picture for the Microsoft account you use with the Store will be posted with your review.

Submit   Cancel

TIP After you click Submit, you'll have to wait for your review to become available.

 CLEAN UP
No cleanup is required. However, if you changed your mind about writing a review, click Cancel.

Understanding subscriptions and in-app purchases

Some apps include options that offer in-app purchasing and subscriptions. In-app purchases are those you make while using an app. For instance, consider a game for which you might need to purchase fruit or farm animals to reach the next level or to beat an opponent. You can also subscribe to a particular app; for example, a newspaper or magazine. Be careful with subscriptions, though; many will self-renew monthly or yearly.

Key points

- The Windows Store offers apps that are sorted by what is popular and by category, such as Games and Music & Videos.

- You can browse for apps in the Windows Store based on their categories or by the top free apps, or you can search for an app by name.

- You can sort apps in a category in many ways, including by ratings and release date.

- The listing page for an app offers information, reviews, and the option to install the app, among other things.

- You can reinstall apps you've previously uninstalled.

- You can update apps you own and write reviews, as applicable.

8

Chapter at a glance

Burn

Burn a CD, page 270

Access

Access videos, page 272

Create

Create a playlist, page 275

Install

Install Media Center, page 280

Having fun with multimedia

9

IN THIS CHAPTER, YOU WILL LEARN HOW TO

- Explore Windows Media Player.

- Use Windows Media Player to rip your CD collection.

- Create playlists and burn them to CDs.

- Configure streaming options.

- Obtain Windows Media Center.

- Learn about Windows Media Center features.

Windows 8.1 offers many options for viewing and managing your media. This includes photos, videos, music, television, and more. You already learned quite a bit about accessing media from the various media apps on the Start screen, including the Photos, Music, and Video apps; these were covered in Chapter 3, "Using apps on the Start screen." In this chapter, we'll look at two desktop apps with which you can view and manage media: Windows Media Player and Windows Media Center. Both open on the desktop in their own windows.

TIP Windows Media Center does not ship with Windows 8.1; it's an add-on. You'll learn how to obtain Windows Media Center later in this chapter.

By using both Windows Media Player and Windows Media Center, you can access the media stored on your computer and on computers configured to share media on your home network, and browse, play, and view music, photos, and videos. You can create playlists of music and view photos in various ways. However, these two desktop apps are different in many ways.

Windows Media Player was created to give users a way to easily synchronize portable music devices, burn and rip music CDs, listen to music, and create music playlists. Windows Media Center offers many more options, including the ability to create slide shows of pictures, watch and record live TV, and browse and play media with a compatible remote control. Windows Media Player is just that—a player—whereas Windows Media Center is in essence an entertainment center. Usually, Windows Media Player requires less setup and is easier to use because you generally use it only to listen to and manage music. Windows Media Center requires more setup but offers more features and configuration options, including the ability to watch and record live TV provided you have the required hardware for doing so.

In this chapter, you'll learn how to use Windows Media Player and how to obtain Windows Media Center and a little about the features it offers. Remember, however, that the Music, Photos, and Video apps are available on the Start screen, and those are much easier to use and more streamlined than Windows Media Player and Windows Media Center. You should try out all the apps along with Windows Media Player and then decide what you prefer to use (or need to use) for managing and playing specific types of media in varying circumstances.

PRACTICE FILES You don't need any practice files to complete the exercises in this chapter. For more information about practice file requirements, see the section "Using the practice files" in the Introduction of this book.

Exploring the Windows Media Player interface

You open Windows Media Player just as you open any app or desktop app: You just start typing its name on the Start screen. You'll see Windows Media Player in the results and can click the result once to open the app.

After Windows Media Player opens, if you're prompted to choose a setup option, choose the Recommended Settings; you can always go back and customize them if desired. Depending on the options you choose, the types of media already on your Windows 8–based computer, music shared by other computers on your network, and other factors (such as other media apps you've installed and the type of media you've collected with them), you might see that some media (but perhaps not all of it) is already available. By default, Media Player populates itself automatically with compatible music from the Music library and will do the same with media from the Pictures library and Videos library. You'll also see an entry in the Navigation pane if there's a CD in the CD/DVD drive. The Navigation pane is shown here:

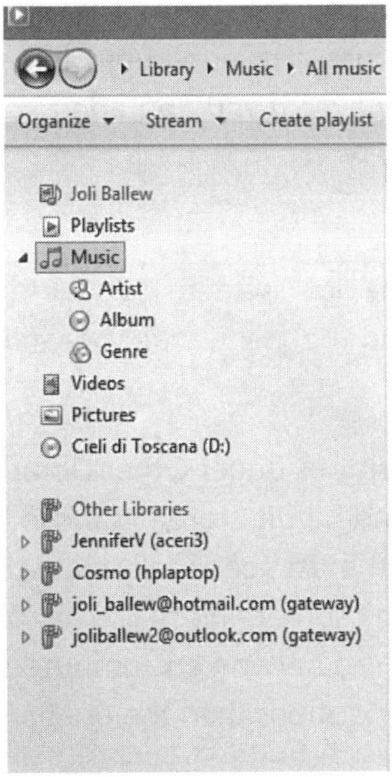

Understanding libraries

A library is a virtual storage area that offers access to the data stored in related personal folders and any other folders you manually add. For example, by default the Music library offers access to data saved on your computer in your personal Music folder. There is also a Pictures library and a Videos library, and you can create your own libraries, as well. Libraries played a large part in data management in Windows 7, and offered access to both the related personal and private folders. Now, libraries only offer access to the private folders by default.

However, If you upgraded to Windows 8.1 from Windows 7, you will still see the old format for libraries, meaning you'll have access to both the personal and public folders if you opt to show Libraries in the Navigation pane. However, if you upgraded from Windows 8, or if you installed Windows 8.1 clean, you won't.

TIP To pin Windows Media Player to the Start screen, on the Start screen, type **Media**, right-click Windows Media Player in the results, and then, on the menu that appears, click Pin To Start. You can also choose the option Pin To Taskbar.

While using Windows Media Player, you might also notice entries under Other Libraries. If you do, media sharing is already set up on your network, and media stored in those libraries is available to you on your Windows 8–based computer. You must specifically state that you want to share media with other networked computers; it isn't something that is enabled by default. To do that, open Windows Media Player at the desired networked computers and click the Stream list to configure sharing. You may see other options than the ones shown here.

TIP If you store all your music, pictures, or videos somewhere other than in the default libraries, you'll have to instruct Windows Media Player where to look for them. You can do that by using the Organize, Manage Libraries list.

When you look closely at Windows Media Player, you'll see that several items run across the top of the interface. There are Back and Forward buttons, a Search window, and an icon to change the view. These probably look familiar to you if you've read other chapters in this book.

The titles you see (such as the name of your media library, the library that is currently selected, and how the data in that library is currently sorted) might differ from what you see here, though. You can click the arrow beside any title name to change the library you are in or the media you are browsing. What you see when you click a right-facing arrow depends on which arrow you click. To change from the current library (for example, Music) to another (for example, Recorded TV), you click the arrow just before Music. (Depending on the type of media you own, you might see an option for Other Media.)

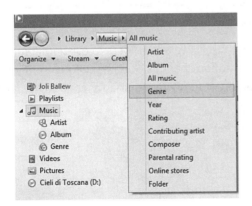

TROUBLESHOOTING If you do not see the library titles across the top of the Windows Media Player interface, you have something other than a default library selected in the Navigation pane. You might have a CD selected, for instance. To rectify this, select Music in the Navigation pane.

To narrow down what's shown in any selected library, such as Music, click the arrow that appears directly after the name of the selected library. For example, you could show only music from a specific genre rather than all your music.

Beyond the lists for Organize, Stream, and Create Playlist detailed later in this chapter, there are tabs for Play, Burn, and Sync.

- **Play**   Click this tab and drag songs to the resulting area, create a playlist of songs, and save it. You can play any song by clicking it once, and songs in a playlist will continue to play in order unless Shuffle is enabled.

- **Burn**   Click this tab and use this area to drag songs and create a list of songs to burn to an audio CD that you can play in most CD players (such as the one in your car).

- **Sync**   Click this tab and use this area to drag songs and sync them to a compatible portable music device.

   You can use the commands that run across the interface under the previously discussed titles to perform tasks on the media in your library, configure preferences, share your media, change the Windows Media Player layout, and even customize the Navigation pane, among other actions.

- **Organize**   Click the arrow for the Organize list to add folders to existing libraries (to expand your library), apply media information changes, sort the data currently visible, customize the Navigation pane by adding or removing elements, change the layout, and configure options.

- **Stream** Click the arrow for the Stream list to allow devices on your network to access the media stored on your Windows 8–based computer and play it. You can also let those devices control Windows Media Player, and you can make your media accessible via the Internet. You'll learn more about this later in this chapter.

- **Create Playlist** Click the arrow for the Create Playlist list to create a playlist or an auto playlist. You'll learn about this later in this chapter.

- **Rip CD** You'll only see the Rip CD option if you have inserted a CD in the CD/DVD drive and if that CD has not already been copied (ripped) to your computer.

- **View Options** Click the Views list arrow to change how media is displayed on the screen. The choices include Icon, Tile, and Details.

Finally, Windows Media Player has several items in the Navigation pane.

- **Playlists** Offers access to the playlists you've created, copied, or synced. A playlist is a group of songs that you group together. You might have a workout playlist, a sleep playlist, and a dinner playlist, for example. Click any playlist to begin playing it.

- **Music** Offers access to music that is stored on your local computer. Click any song or album to access and play it.

- **Videos**   Offers access to videos that are stored on your local computer. Click any video to play it.

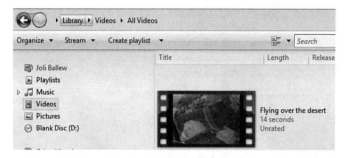

- **Pictures**   Offers access to pictures that are stored on your local computer. Click any picture to view it.

- **CD or DVD (the name appears) or Blank Disk**   Only offers access if you have a CD or DVD in the CD/DVD drive.

- **Other Libraries**   Offers access to media that's been shared on your local network through other computers and compatible devices.

Ripping your CD collection

There are many ways to populate your Windows 8–based computer with music. You can buy music from the Xbox Music Store. You can copy the media from another computer, you can access the media from a shared drive on your home network, and you can copy music from a portable music player. You can also copy the music from CDs you currently own in a process known as *ripping*.

When you rip a CD, there are several settings you can configure prior to copying the songs; you'll use these options to change the default settings if you need to. You might need to change settings when you rip a CD if you plan to copy the songs to an older MP3 player that doesn't support the default Windows Media Audio format. You might also want to increase or decrease the Audio Quality settings. Lower quality takes up less storage space, but higher quality sounds better. You might also opt to eject the CD automatically after the rip has completed, which is a good option if you plan to sit down and rip your entire music collection. As you might have guessed, there are even more options from which to choose.

TIP See Chapter 8, "Shopping in the Windows Store," and Chapter 4, "Organizing files and folders."

In this exercise, you'll rip a CD, use the highest quality setting, and opt to eject the CD after the rip is complete.

 SET UP
Open Windows Media Player. Get a music CD that you own. You do not need any practice files for this exercise.

1 Place the music CD in the CD/DVD drive.

2 In the Navigation pane, if the CD is not selected, select it.

3 Clear the check boxes for any songs that you do not want to copy.

4 Click **Rip Settings** located to the right of **Rip CD**. You might need to click a right-facing arrow to access this.

5   Click **Audio Quality** and then choose **192 Kbps (Best Quality)**.

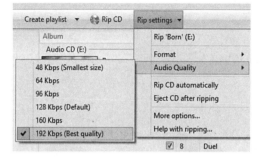

6   Repeat step 4, but this time click **Eject CD After Ripping**.

7   Click **Rip CD**.

The ripping process starts.

 CLEAN UP
Repeat the process as desired.

Creating and burning playlists

You are likely to already be familiar with playlists: A list of songs on a CD or album is a playlist. The older mixed tapes with which you might be familiar were playlists, too. So it's probably no surprise to you that you can create playlists that consist of your own music in Windows Media Player. You can create playlists for almost any occasion, including parties, workout routines, or even meditation sessions. After a playlist is created, you can synchronize it to other devices, burn it to a CD, and share it across your home network.

Creating a playlist is simple, if you haven't created one yet. In the Navigation pane, click Playlists, and you will see the Click Here prompt to create your first one. After you've done that, you name the playlist, locate the songs to add to it, and drag them into it. You'll use a similar dragging process to create a playlist to burn to a CD, detailed later in this section; read that section if you aren't sure how to drag the files to the new playlist.

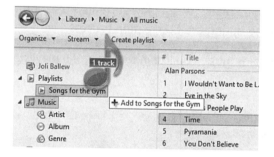

If you already have playlists, the option to Click Here to create one will not display. In that case, you can either add songs to an existing playlist or create a new one by clicking Create Playlist on the menu bar at the top of the window.

To add songs to an existing playlist or a new playlist you just created, locate the song to add, and then drag it on top of the playlist's name. Note that songs you drag to playlists aren't moved there; only the titles are added to the list. The music files remain in whatever folders they normally reside in on the hard disk.

TIP If you aren't sure how to drag songs to create a playlist, work through the upcoming exercise to burn songs to a CD. The process is similar.

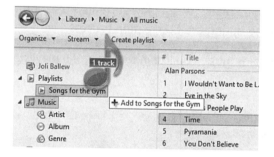

TIP To select multiple, noncontiguous songs at one time, hold down the Ctrl key while selecting.

You can also create another kind of playlist—an *auto playlist*. When you create an auto playlist, you name it and then set criteria. Criteria can be almost anything; Windows Media Player will use the criteria you set to create a playlist automatically. For instance, you can create an auto playlist that contains only songs added to your library before or after a specific date or songs that you've played the most in the past year. After criteria are set, your playlist will be created and automatically managed. To start an auto playlist, on the menu bar, click Create Playlist, and then click Auto Playlist.

9

You can burn any playlist you create to a CD, provided it will fit and you have the required rights to copy the music. A typical CD holds about 80 minutes of music. If your playlist won't fit on one CD, you'll be prompted to span it over several (which is often the case with audio books and auto playlists). If you don't already have a playlist created that you want to copy to a CD, you can create one on the go during the CD creation process.

In this exercise, you'll burn a CD that contains music you like in the form of a playlist.

→ SET UP
You will need a computer that includes a CD-recordable drive, a blank CD, and music that you own available in Windows Media Player.

1 Open **Windows Media Player**.

2 Insert a blank, recordable CD into the CD/DVD drive.

3 Back in **Windows Media Player**, click the **Burn** tab.

4 Browse to the songs to add and then drag them to the **Burn List**.

5 Rearrange the order the songs in the list by dragging them up or down to a new position.

TROUBLESHOOTING If you drag a song to the Burn List and see a red circle with a line through it, you can't add that song to the burn list. There are many reasons this can happen, but it is usually because you don't have the proper permissions or haven't purchased the song.

6   When the list is complete, click **Start Burn**.

CLEAN UP
Remove the CD from the CD/DVD drive and test it in a CD player.

Now that you understand the interface, how to navigate to various music tracks, and how to create playlists, spend some time playing the music you have on your computer. Playing music here is quite similar to playing music in the Music app you've already explored; you just select the song to play and use the controls to manage playback.

Sharing media across a network

You can share the media you've acquired on your Windows 8–based computer with compatible computers and devices on your network. Devices can include tablets, media centers, smart phones, and Microsoft Xbox sets. For these other devices to gain access, however, you must enable streaming options in Windows Media Player. To do this, on the menu bar, click Stream.

There are varying options on the Stream menu, and what you see depends on how your computer and network are configured. You must click the desired option to access their features and settings.

- **Allow Internet Access To Home Media**   Select this option to stream music, pictures, and videos from your home computer to a computer outside your home (such as one at a vacation home). You can configure this computer to send your media over the Internet. After you configure this option on your home computer, you must configure the same option on the outside computer so that it can receive the media.

- **Allow Remote Control Of My Player**   Select this option to allow other computers and devices on your home network to push music, pictures, and videos to Windows Media Player and to remotely control Windows Media Player.

- **Automatically Allow Devices To Play My Media**   Select the available option so that other computers and devices on your home network can access the media you store on this computer. This is most likely the first option you'll want to choose.

- **More Streaming Options**   Use this option to choose media-streaming options for specific computers and devices on your network. For example, you might allow access to your Xbox 360 but prevent access from your child's computer.

After it is configured, your media library will appear on allowed network devices.

Obtaining Windows Media Center

So far, you've learned about Windows Media Player. As you learned in the introduction of this chapter, Windows Media Center is another media option that offers access to, management of, and the ability to play and watch any media that are available to you. It offers more features than Media Player, including the ability to record live TV, provided that your computer is equipped with the proper hardware. You can use Windows Media Center instead of your current Digital Video Recorder (DVR) if you decide you like it.

You have to get Windows Media Center yourself; it's an available add-on feature and is not included with Windows 8.1 by default. There are two options for obtaining Windows Media Center. One is to add the Windows 8.1 Pro Pack, which is what you'll do if you are running Windows 8.1; it costs $99. The other option is to add the Windows 8.1 Media Center Pack, which is what you'll do if you are running Windows 8.1 Pro; it costs $9.99. Don't worry, when you click I Want To Buy A Product Key Online in Step 2, you'll be prompted as to which is suitable for your computer system.

1   On the **Start** screen, type add features and then, from the results in **Settings**, click **Add Features To Windows 8.1**. (If prompted, click Yes to allow access.)

2   Click **I Want To Buy A Product Key Online** or **I Already Have A Product Key**, as applicable.

3   Work through the resulting process, which might involve purchasing the add-on and/or inputting a product key.

4   Accept the license terms and click **Add Features**.

5   Wait while the add-on installs.

When you start Windows Media Center, the setup process begins. You can choose Express or Custom. Because there are so many choices, it's generally best to choose Custom. When you choose Custom, you'll set up Windows Media Center by walking through each step of the configuration process.

During setup, you might be prompted to do the following:

- Connect to the Internet.

- Allow Media Center to download album cover art, music and movie information, and TV Program Guide listings automatically and periodically.

- Optimize how Windows Media Center looks on your specific display.

- Set up or configure speakers.

- Set up or configure media libraries.

- Configure advanced settings for your specific setup.

- Configure your live TV signal.

You'll see the main screen when Windows Media Center is ready.

Exploring Windows Media Center features

You can navigate the Windows Media Center interface by using touch (if you have a compatible monitor), by using the arrow keys, by using a mouse, and even by using a compatible remote. At the main landing page, move up and down and left and right to see everything that's offered. You'll see various categories in which you can view and manage all of your media libraries.

With Windows Media Center you can do the following (with the required hardware):

- Access all the pictures available to you, including shared pictures; add folders that contain media; and create slideshows, tag and rate pictures, and sort pictures in various ways.

- Access and watch videos available to you, including shared videos. You can add additional video folders and sort videos in various ways, too.

- Access your music library, sort music, create playlists, add other music folders, and view album art, among other things.

- Automatically play music that you've configured as your favorites.

- Listen to FM radio and configure presets. You must have the proper hardware configured for this to work.

- Search for specific music.

- Access movies in your Video library. You can sort movies by genre, year, parental ratings, and more.

- Access the movie guide. If a TV tuner is configured and Live TV has been set up, you'll see the movies that are currently playing.

- Play a DVD by using the CD/DVD drive.

- Access the TV guide and schedule recordings. One way to record TV is to right-click the show that you want to record. There are myriad settings to explore.

9

- View TV programs you've recorded. You can sort by date recorded, title, and original air date, and you can access shared recordings.

- Watch Live TV and access playback controls, record what's on, and browse the guide. You can also pause Live TV. If you haven't set up Live TV, the option will be named Live TV Setup.

  TROUBLESHOOTING If, after setting up your TV tuner, Live TV doesn't appear, restart your computer. Often this resolves the problem.

- View sports events, see scores, follow players, and more.

- Access all Windows Media Center settings. If you want to change something about Windows Media Center, you do it here.

- Synchronize Windows Media Center content to a compatible portable device.

- Add a media extender so that you can view your media on other devices on your home network.

Key points

- Windows Media Player is most often used for playing music, but you can also use it to view pictures, videos, and other compatible media.

- You can rip and burn CDs by using Windows Media Player.

- With Windows Media Player, you can share media across your home network and access media shared by other computers on the network.

- Windows Media Center is most often used for watching and recording television, although you can also use it to view and listen to other media, including pictures, videos, and music.

- Windows Media Center takes longer to set up, start, and find media than Windows Media Player does, but it offers more features than Windows Media Player.

- With Windows Media Center, you can watch, pause, and record Live TV, and then play back those recordings.

9

Chapter at a glance

Find

Find games in the Windows Store, page 289

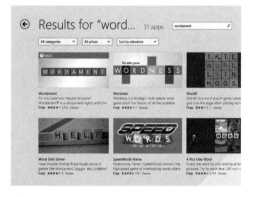

Learn

Learn a game's system requirements, page 290

Explore

Explore Xbox games from Windows 8.1, page 294

Connect

Connect Windows 8.1 to your Xbox, page 295

Playing games

10

IN THIS CHAPTER, YOU WILL LEARN HOW TO

- Find and purchase, download, and install games from the Windows Store.

- Determine whether you can play a specific game on your Windows 8.1 computer or device.

- Use the Games app to find games that work in Windows.

- Connect Windows 8.1 to your Xbox console.

We use computers, gadgets, and devices to be productive and do our work, but we also like to use them to have fun. Playing games can be an entertaining activity, and with Windows 8.1, you can play more games than ever. With the introduction of the Windows Store and the Games app for Windows, you have even more platforms and ways to find and purchase games, both for your computer and for your Xbox console. You can play not only desktop games but also touch-enabled games that use the interface of Windows 8.1.

With Windows 8.1, you can also connect to your Xbox console so that you can find, purchase, and download games and media to your console more quickly than by using your Xbox controller.

In this chapter, you'll learn how to find games by using the Windows Store and Games apps, determine a game's system requirements, and learn how to connect your Windows 8.1 computer or tablet to your Xbox console.

PRACTICE FILES You don't need any practice files to complete the exercises in this chapter. For more information about practice file requirements, see the section "Using the practice files" in the Introduction.

How to find games in the Windows Store

The Windows Store has a section dedicated to games where you can find diverse titles for computers and other devices running Windows 8.1. For each game, you are shown its price, average user rating, a brief description, its content rating and its main features.

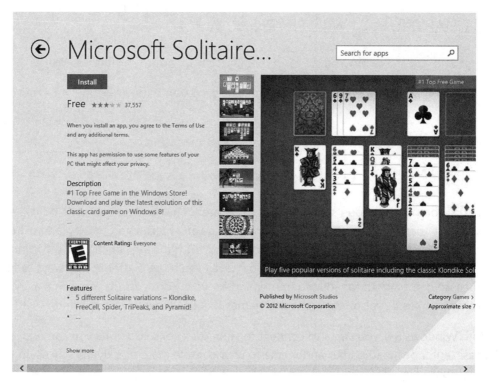

On the right side of a game's page, you can view several screen shots from that game and, if you scroll further to the right, you can access its user reviews and ratings, view more details about what's required to play the game, view a list of related apps (meaning similar games) and view a list with other games from the same publisher.

When browsing the Games section in the Windows Store, you are first presented with games that are in the spotlight. Scroll to the right, and you can view the games that are popular right now, then the latest releases and, finally the top paid and top free games.

In this exercise, you'll learn how to find games in the Windows Store and how to install them on your Windows 8.1 computer or device.

 SET UP
Open the Windows Store.

1 Right-click anywhere within the Windows Store screen.

The contextual menu opens on the top.

Home	Your apps	Your account
Picks for you	Games	Sports
Top paid	Social	Books & Reference
Top free	Entertainment	News & Weather
New & Rising	Photo	Health & Fitness
Trending	Music & Video	Food & Dining

2 In the second column of categories, click the **Games** entry.

The Games category is now shown.

10

3   In the upper-right corner, in the Search box, type wordament, and then click the search icon on the right.

The list of search results appears.

4   Click the **Wordament** search result.

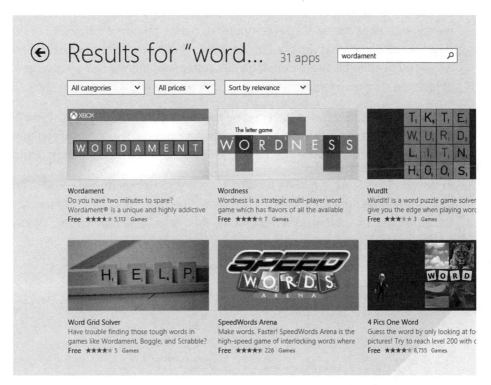

The game's Windows Store page displays.

5   Read the information that interests you about the game and click **Install**.

❌ CLEAN UP
Wait for the game to be downloaded and installed. Then, close the Windows Store.

The Wordament game is now installed, and you can find its shortcut in the Apps view, which is, accessible using the arrow on the bottom-left side of the Start screen.

What's required for playing games

With the introductions of Windows 8 and Windows 8.1, the world of gaming became much richer. In addition to the desktop games you know and love, you can also enjoy new types of games designed for touch devices (for instance, tablets).

Just like operating systems that have a very clear set of system requirements that must be met for them to work, games have individual system requirements depending on their size, complexity, and other criteria. If your computer or device can run Windows 8.1, it doesn't mean it can run all games that work on Windows 8.1. That's why before purchasing and installing a game you need to be aware of that game's system requirements. If your system doesn't meet at least the minimum requirements, you won't be able to play the game without problems.

Those requirements are always shared by the developers of each game. If you bought a game from a store, the requirements will be on the back or side of its cover. If you purchase a game online, the requirements are listed with the description of the game on its dedicated page.

In the Windows Store, a game's requirements are shown on its page. Open a game's page and scroll to the right until you find the Details section. There, you will see notes shared by the developer, the permissions required by the game, its recommended hardware, and supported processors.

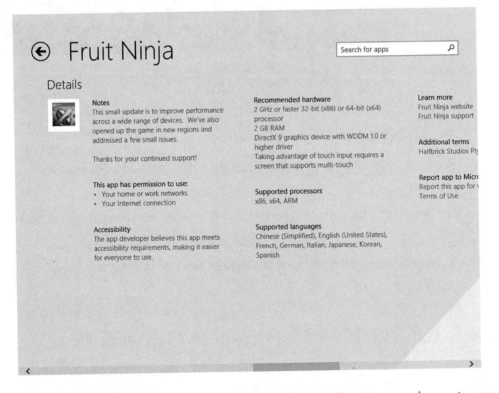

If your Windows 8.1 computer or device meets the game's system requirements, you will be able to play it.

More so than other types of software, gaming performance is closely tied to the configuration of your device. As such, having the latest drivers installed for your system's most important hardware components is paramount. If you want to play three-dimensional games with advanced graphics, it is important to update your video card's drivers regularly. In such scenarios, using the latest video card driver offered through Windows Update is not enough to ensure smooth game performance in all games. Therefore, you must download the latest drivers from the website of your video card's manufacturer for your specific video card model.

Using the Games app

With the help of the Games app, you can find, purchase, and install Xbox games from Windows 8.1. You can also find Xbox games that works on Windows and install them on your Windows 8.1 computer or device.

When you open it, you see information about the latest games and offers available.

If you scroll to the right, you can view games from the Windows Store that work on your Windows 8.1 computer or device.

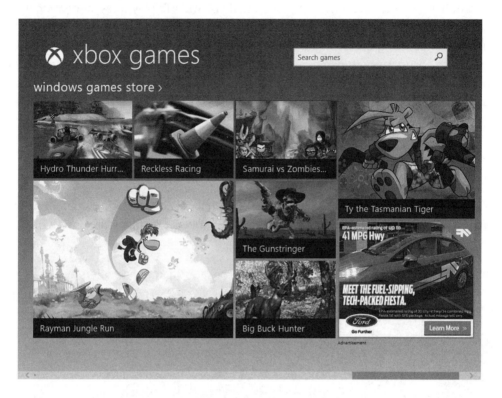

If you scroll to the left, you can see your recent game activity, what your Xbox friends are doing, and you can edit your Xbox profile.

Clicking a game, opens the game's page. You are shown information about the game and given options to play it, view more details about the game, or play its trailer. Some titles might offer more information and options, whereas others less.

If you want to play a game, click Play to go to its page in the Windows Store, where you can purchase and install it, as shown earlier in this chapter.

Connecting Windows 8.1 to your Xbox

You can connect to your Xbox console from any Windows 8.1 computer or device connected to the same network and using the same Microsoft account. You do this with the help of the Xbox SmartGlass app, which you need to download and install from the Windows Store.

SEE ALSO To learn more about the Windows Store and how to download and install apps, read Chapter 8, "Shopping in the Windows Store."

The Xbox SmartGlass app automatically connects to your Xbox and displays your ongoing activity on the console, in the Now Playing section. For example, if you are playing a game, its name and a screen shot are displayed; if you are using the Xbox Dashboard, its name and logo are displayed.

Below the Now Playing section, there is a button labeled Remote. If you click it, you can use the Xbox SmartGlass app to control your Xbox remotely. For example, you can type text directly to your Xbox or you can simulate the use of a controller and send commands to the console.

If you scroll to the right, you can view the recent activity on your Xbox and access the Spotlight section. Here, you can view movies and games that are currently in the spotlight. If you click any of them, you can view more information, and you are given the option to play them on your Xbox console.

10

XBOX 360.

Halo 4
2013, Microsoft Studios, Shooter
Xbox 360

Set Beacon

The Games on Demand version supports English. The Master Chief returns to battle an ancient evil bent on vengeance and annihilation. Shipwrecked on a mysterious world, faced with new enemies and deadly technology, the universe will never be the same. Enlist aboard the Infinity to experience Halo's original multiplayer and Spartan Ops - innovative episodic fiction-based co-op missions.

⊜ Explore game

(⬆) Play on Xbox 360

In this exercise, you'll learn how to connect your Xbox to your Windows 8.1 computer or device through the Xbox SmartGlass app.

➜ SET UP

First, install the Xbox SmartGlass app from the Windows Store, if you don't have it installed yet. Start your Xbox console and log on by using your Microsoft account. The Xbox LIVE gamer tag must use the same Microsoft account as the Windows 8.1 computer or device to which you want to connect it.

1   On your Xbox, click **Settings**, and then choose **System**.

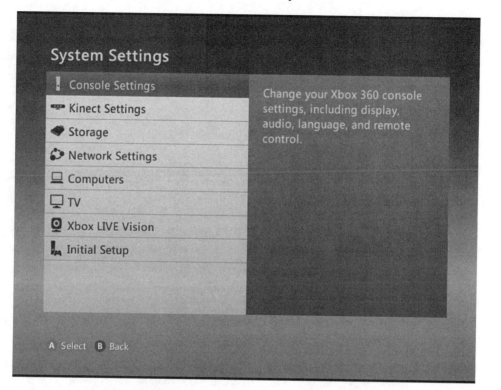

10

2   In the System Settings window, click **Console Settings**, and then choose **Connected Devices**.

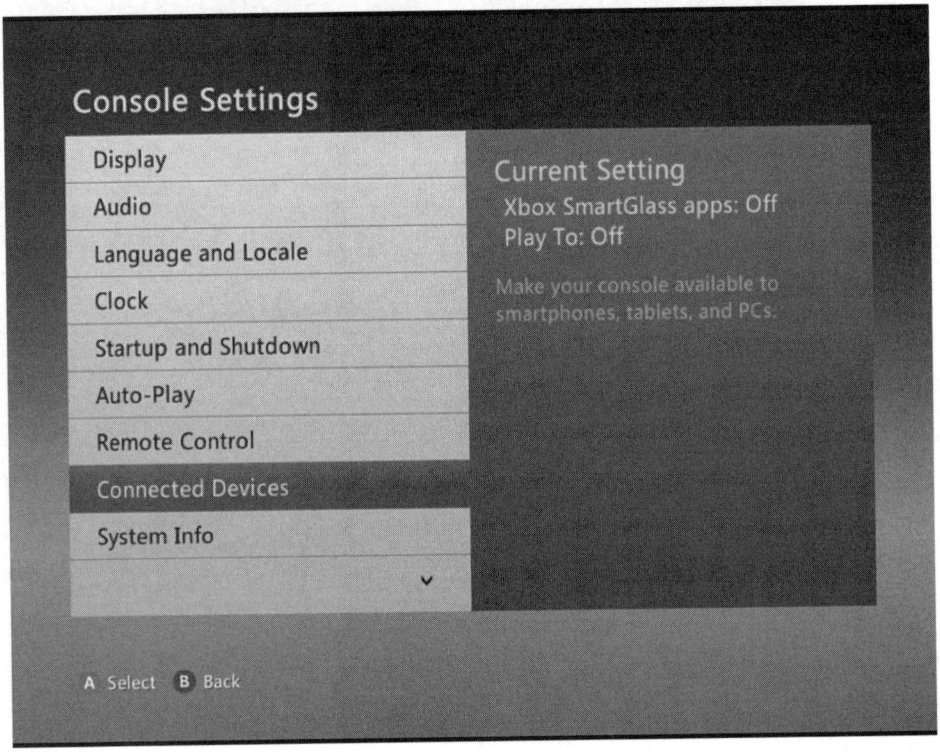

Console Settings

	Current Setting
Display	Xbox SmartGlass apps: Off
Audio	Play To: Off
Language and Locale	
Clock	Make your console available to
Startup and Shutdown	smartphones, tablets, and PCs.
Auto-Play	
Remote Control	
Connected Devices	
System Info	

A Select   B Back

3   In the Connected Devices window, select **On** for both Xbox SmartGlass Apps and Play To.

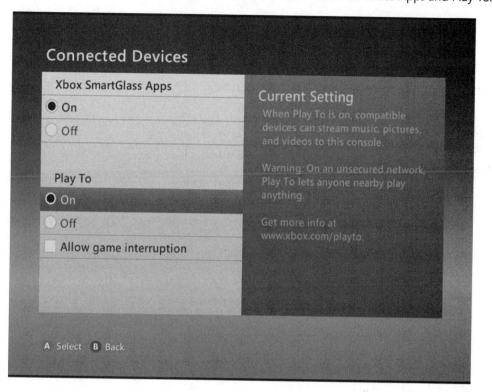

4   Set whether you want to allow game interruption or not when the Xbox is controlled remotely.

5   On your Windows 8.1 computer or device, launch the Xbox SmartGlass app while your Xbox console is still turned on.

6   Wait for the app to connect automatically to your Xbox. A confirmation of the connection is displayed both in the Xbox SmartGlass app and on your Xbox console.

CLEAN UP
When you are done using Xbox SmartGlass, close the app and your console.

Now, you can start using the Xbox SmartGlass app. Each time you run Xbox SmartGlass, it searches for your Xbox console. If it finds it online, you can use the app and all its features. If it doesn't find the console, you are informed and given advice on how to fix the problem.

Key points

- You can find games in the Windows Store, not just apps.

- Prior to purchasing and installing a game, check its system requirements to learn whether you can play it on your Windows 8.1 computer or device.

- With the Games app, you can find Xbox games that also work on your Windows devices.

- You can connect your Windows 8.1 computer or device to your Xbox console through the Xbox SmartGlass app.

10

Chapter at a glance

Use

Use the Network And Sharing Center,
page 306

Connect

Connect to a wireless network, page 310

Work

Work with a hidden wireless network,
page 317

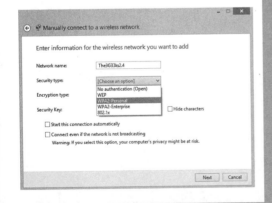

Manage

Manage network connections from PC
Settings, page 324

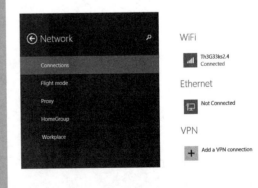

Connecting to a network and the Internet

11

IN THIS CHAPTER, YOU WILL LEARN HOW TO

- Open the Network And Sharing Center.

- Connect to a wireless network.

- Connect to a hidden wireless network.

- Update the profile of your active network connection.

In this chapter, you'll first learn the jargon used when working with network connections. As you will see, it isn't as scary as it sounds, and the basic concepts can be understood by anyone with a little computing experience. Then, you'll learn about the Network And Sharing Center and its importance in managing network connections and settings. Finally, you'll learn how to access different configuration panels that you'll find in the Network And Sharing Center and how to change the active network profile, depending on the type of the network to which you are connected.

You'll also learn how to connect to wireless networks, including those that are hidden and cannot be detected automatically by Windows 8.1.

PRACTICE FILES You don't need any practice files to complete the exercises in this chapter. For more information about practice file requirements, see the section "Using the practice files" in the Introduction of this book.

Understanding the jargon: router, ISP, network adapter, and other terminology

Before connecting to the Internet and your home network, you need to learn a little bit of computer networking jargon. Don't worry! It isn't as difficult as it might seem when you hear it the first time.

First and foremost, you need a working Internet connection provided by an *Internet Service Provider* (ISP). The ISP connects its Internet service either to a single computer in a home or to a home networking device, such as a router, that shares the Internet connection with computers and devices in your home.

The router is a device that handles the data being sent between the computers in your network and between those computers and the Internet. You will need a router if you want to create your own home network, even if you have only one computer or wireless device to connect to it. If you have a router, you need to be sure it's correctly configured so that your computers can connect with one another and access the Internet. Instructions for doing this are provided in the router's manual and by your ISP.

For a computer to connect to the network and the Internet, it needs a network adapter or network card. In tech-talk, this is also called a *Network Interface Card* (NIC). Desktop computers generally have a network card that is connected to the router through a standard network cable, which you can buy at any computer shop. You plug one end into your computer and the other end into the router. The router does all the settings, and before you know it, you are connected.

However, mobile computers such as laptops, netbooks, or tablets need a wireless network adapter (wireless network card) that detects and works with wireless network signals.

The trouble with network adapters (both wired and wireless) is that they need appropriate Windows 8.1 drivers installed. A driver is a computer program that makes it possible for other programs to interact with the particular device for which it was created. For example, the driver for your computer's video card is the means by which games can interact with it and generate the advanced graphics shown on your screen. Windows 8.1 interacts with your network card via the card's driver and uses it to connect to a network and the Internet.

If you bought your computer with Windows 8.1 preinstalled, you won't need to worry about drivers. They are already installed and working. However, if that is not the case, you need to use another computer that is connected to the Internet. Search for the latest network drivers developed for your specific computer model and network card. When you find them, download and install them on your Windows 8.1–based computer. Only then can you connect to your home network and the Internet.

One last item you should learn about is the security of wireless networks. Wireless networks can be either secured or unsecured. A secured network transmits data by using advanced encryption algorithms and, to connect to it, you need to know its security key or password. There are many types of wireless network security, with names that are a veritable alphabet soup, such as WPA2-PSK, WPA-PSK, or WEP. If you know the appropriate password, you should be able to connect to it no matter the type of security it uses. Unsecured networks don't have any encryption and do not require passwords to connect to them. However, you should be wary about connecting to such networks, especially those found in public places. Other, less-savory individuals can use these networks to access data on your computer.

Now that you know the basics, it is time to get practical and learn how to get connected to the Internet in Windows 8.1.

TIP If you want to know more about creating and securing home networks, read my book *Network Your Computers & Devices Step by Step* (2010, Microsoft Press).

Using the Networking And Sharing Center

All the important network and sharing configuration settings are done by using a tool named the Network And Sharing Center. It was first introduced in Windows Vista, and subsequently it was fine-tuned in Windows 7 and then in Windows 8.

The Network And Sharing Center window is split in two areas: a central area and a column on the left (or sidebar) that presents links to access and configure specific settings).

11

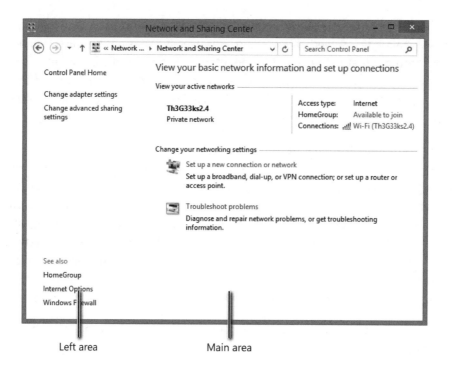

Left area   Main area

In the main area, you can see information about your active network connection (if any), such as the name of the network to which you are connected, the network profile (Private or Public) assigned to it, and the access type (Internet access, limited access, and so on). You can also learn whether a HomeGroup is available in your network and whether your computer has joined it. Below that, there are shortcuts for setting up a new connection or another network and for starting troubleshooting wizards, which help you fix all kinds of networking problems.

As mentioned a moment ago, in the area on the left side, there are shortcuts for changing the settings of your network adapter or network card, changing your network sharing settings, and accessing the configuration of the HomeGroup, Internet Options, and Windows Firewall.

In this exercise, you'll learn how to open the Network And Sharing Center.

 SET UP
Open Control Panel.

1   Ensure that you are viewing **Control Panel** by category and not by large or small icons. To change the view, in the upper-right corner, click the **View** list, and then select **Category**.

2   Click the **Network and Internet** section to open the window of the same name.

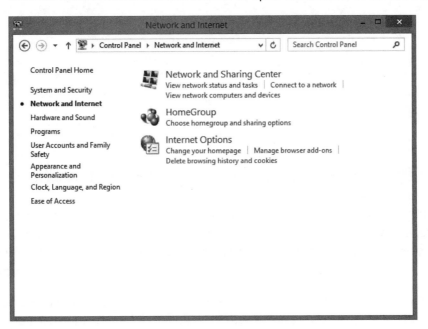

3   Click **Network and Sharing Center**.

The Network And Sharing Center window opens, in which you can configure different networking aspects.

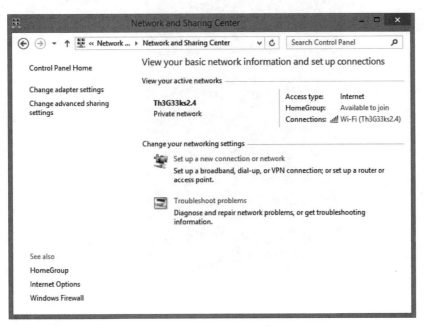

CLEAN UP

When you finish working with the Network And Sharing Center, in the upper-right corner, click the Close button (the red X) to dismiss the window.

TIP You can open the Network And Sharing Center in many other ways. You can also go to the Desktop, right-click the network icon in the notification area, and then select Open Network And Sharing Center.

Connecting to a wireless network

In today's world, a growing number of people use laptops, netbooks, or tablets instead of traditional desktop computers. As a result of this trend—plus the growing number of devices such as smartphones—more people use wireless networks on a regular basis. Windows 8.1 offers all you need to connect to wireless networks as easily as possible.

You can view and access available wireless networks in the Networks panel. The panel lists the name of each network, the strength of its signal, and whether it is secured. All unsecured wireless networks display an exclamation mark above the signal-strength icon.

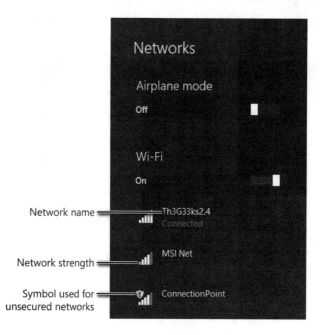

Before you try to connect, be aware that you can connect only to networks for which you have the appropriate connection details: the name of the network and the security key, if the network is secured against unauthorized access. This means that you can connect only to the following types of wireless networks:

- Your home's wireless network, if you have one set up correctly, for which you should know the connection details

- The wireless networks of friends and neighbors who have shared their network connection details with you

- The wireless network of your workplace, for which the connection details are available from the network administrator or the IT support department

- Public wireless networks (that are generally unprotected), which are typically in locations such as airports, libraries, bars, cafes, and so on

After you are connected to a network for the first time, the Network Connection Wizard asks whether you want to enable sharing and connect to devices such as printers and TVs on that network. If you are connecting to a public, unsecured network, you should always be cautious and choose No.

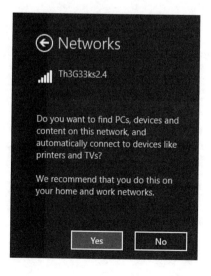

Furthermore, you must have a security solution active and running on your system to ensure that your computer is protected from attacks and unauthorized access. Windows Defender and Windows Firewall, included with Windows 8.1, should provide a good level of protection. You should keep them turned on if you have not installed security solutions provided by companies other than Microsoft.

TROUBLESHOOTING If Windows 8.1 has not detected any connections, and you know that there is at least one wireless network available in your area, you should check whether your wireless network card has the appropriate drivers installed and whether the network card is turned on.

When connecting to a wireless network, the Connect Automatically check box appears. If you select it, the next time you log on to Windows and the same network is detected, Windows 8.1 automatically connects to it by using the same details you provided the first time you connected.

If the connection is successful, The word "Connected" appears below the name of the network in the Networks list. Available networks to which you have not connected don't display status. Networks to which you connected but for which Windows 8.1 identifies issues will display "Limited" below their names.

On the Desktop, similar icons appear in the taskbar. If there are network connectivity issues, they are signified by a yellow exclamation mark. Also, when the wireless network card on your laptop or tablet is disabled, an X in a red circle appears on its icon.

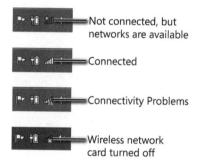

You can open the Networks panel by using several methods. If you are on the Desktop, the simplest way is to click the network icon in the notification area on the taskbar. If you're using a tablet or a computer with a touch-enabled monitor, use the Settings charm.

11

In this exercise, you'll learn how to open the Networks panel, view all the available wireless networks in your area, and then connect to one of them.

 SET UP
First, ensure that a wireless network is available for which you know the connection details (network name and security password) and then go to the Start screen.

1   Swipe inward from the right side of the screen or press **Windows key+C** to open the charms.

2   Click **Settings** to open the contextual settings for the Start screen.

3   Click the wireless network icon (the first of the six icons at the bottom of the Settings pane).

The Networks panel opens.

4   Click the network to which you want to connect.

5   Select the **Connect Automatically** check box.

6   Click **Connect**.

You are prompted to type the security key.

TIP If the network to which you are connecting is not secured, you are not asked for a password. If this is the case, skip the next step.

7   Type the security key and then click **Next**.

You are asked whether you want to turn on sharing and find PCs, devices, and content on this network.

> **TIP** If you typed an incorrect password, Windows 8.1 informs you that it cannot connect to the network. If this happens, repeat the procedure, starting with step 1, retyping the correct password.

8   Click **Yes**.

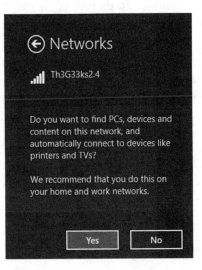

Windows takes a few seconds to connect to the network you selected.

⊗ CLEAN UP
If the Networks panel doesn't disappear, click anywhere in the empty space on the Start screen.

Connecting to a hidden wireless network

Hidden wireless networks are networks that do not broadcast their names, called *Network ID* or *Service Set Identifier* (SSID) in tech-talk. Although few people use such networks, some people feel a bit more secure if they have their home wireless network hidden from unwanted guests.

If you've set your wireless network this way, be aware that, according to the Microsoft TechNet community and other reputable websites, hidden wireless networks are not actually undetectable or more secure. On the contrary, computers and devices configured to connect to such networks are constantly disclosing the Network ID of those networks, even when they are not in range. As a result, using such a network actually compromises the privacy of the computers connected to it. If you still want to use and connect to such networks, this section shows how it is done, but you should know where to get the important technical details you need.

First and foremost, you need to know all the identification and connection details of the hidden wireless network to which you want to connect. To do this, open your router's configuration page and then the Wireless Configuration menu. Write down the values for the Network ID (SSID) and Security fields. Routers love to use intimidating tech talk, so prepare to encounter some weird-sounding acronyms. Routers have very different interfaces, depending on their model and manufacturer. There is no standard way to access this information. If you don't know how to find it, check the user manual that came with your router for help and instructions.

Depending on what type of security your wireless network employs, you need to write down the value of the following important fields.

- For WEP security, note the value of the WEP Key field.
- For WPA2-PSK(AES) security, note the value of the Preshare Key field.

These key fields store the password for connecting to the wireless network.

If the security for your router is not turned on, you need to know only the network name (the value of the Network ID (SSID) field).

When completing all the required details to connect to the hidden wireless network, consider the following aspects.

- When asked about the security type of the network, you must make the correct selection; otherwise, the connection won't work. You must select WEP for WEP security, or WPA2-Personal for WPA2-PSK(AES) security. If security for the hidden network is not turned on, select No authentication (Open).

Manually connect to a wireless network

Enter information for the wireless network you want to add

Network name: The3G33ks2.4

Security type: [Choose an option]
    No authentication (Open)
    WEP
    WPA2-Personal
    WPA2-Enterprise
    802.1x

Encryption type:

Security Key: ☐ Hide characters

☐ Start this connection automatically
☐ Connect even if the network is not broadcasting
    Warning: If you select this option, your computer's privacy might be at risk.

Next   Cancel

- For the encryption type, Windows 8.1 gives you a default value you cannot change.

Encryption type: AES

Security Key:

- Because Windows cannot detect hidden networks, select Start This Connection Automatically and Connect Even If The Network Is Not Broadcasting. Windows cannot detect a hidden network to connect to it.

☑ Start this connection automatically
☑ Connect even if the network is not broadcasting
    Warning: If you select this option, your computer's privacy might be at risk.

TIP WPA2-Enterprise and 802.1x are not covered in this book because they are specific to business networks. If you need to connect to a hidden business network, contact the network administrator or the IT help desk team for guidance.

In this exercise, you'll learn how to connect to hidden wireless networks.

 SET UP
Ensure that you have a hidden wireless network available for which you know the connection details (network name, security password, and so on). Open the Network And Sharing Center.

11

1   Click **Set Up A New Connection Or Network**.

The Set Up A Connection Or Network window opens.

2   Select **Manually Connect To A Wireless Network** and then click **Next**.

3   In the **Network Name** box, type the name of the wireless network to which you want to connect.

4   In the **Security Type** box, choose the type of security your wireless network uses.

5   In the **Encryption Type** box, you are shown the type of encryption Windows 8.1 will
     use for your network connection.

6   In the **Security Key** field, type the password used to connect to the wireless network.

7   Select the **Start This Connection Automatically** check box

8   Select the **Connect Even If The Network Is Not Broadcasting** check box and then
     click **Next**.

11

A message appears, indicating that you have successfully added the wireless network to your computer.

9   Click **Close**.

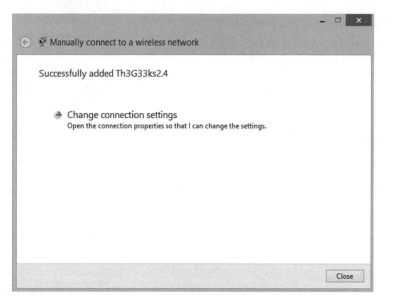

 CLEAN UP
Close the Network And Sharing Center.

If the network is in range, Windows 8.1 will automatically connect to it.

Compatibility with older routers and networking equipment

Just like Windows 8, Windows 8.1 provides support for the newest network protocols and network devices. For examples, it is able to connect to modern wireless networks that use the 802.11n and 802.11ac networking standards. If you have bought a laptop, tablet or a hybrid computer with Windows 8.1, you should not have any issues connecting to such networks.

If you cannot connect to a wireless network from your Windows 8.1–based computer, but all your computers with earlier operating systems can connect, you might need to upgrade the firmware on your wireless router. Consult the webpage for your router to see whether any upgrades are available. If there are upgrades, download and install the latest version of firmware. Unfortunately, some older router models do not work very well with computers that use newer versions of Windows unless you perform a firmware upgrade. Others might not work at all with newer Windows versions, and you will need to replace it altogether with a new router.

To learn whether you will have issues, it is best to check the compatibility with Windows 8.1 for your specific router and networking equipment. To help you out, Microsoft has created the Compatibility Center website (*http://bit.ly/17Mvosr*). There, you'll find a very long list of devices for which Microsoft provides information regarding their compatibility with Windows 8.1.

Connecting to the Internet through a mobile modem

Another option for connecting to the Internet, for example, when you are on a trip, is to use a mobile Internet modem that you plug into your laptop or netbook. If you are using a tablet with Windows 8.1, connecting is even easier because the operating system offers support for inserting a SIM card from your mobile operator, so you can use it to stay connected through its network. Although most tablets can use SIM cards, some models don't offer hardware support for them and can only connect to the Internet through wireless networks. You should be aware of the connectivity options offered by the tablet you purchase.

Even though the steps for connecting to the Internet through a mobile modem are different, depending on the modem model and your mobile operator, the principles are always the same.

- You need a mobile Internet modem that you can plug into your computer.

- After it's plugged in, you need to install the drivers for the modem and the software that will connect to the Internet. These are provided by your mobile operator, in the package with the modem itself or on the manufacturer's website.

- Major mobile operators, such as AT&T, Verizon, and Vodafone, are likely to offer a Windows 8.1 app through the Windows Store, so check there to see if one is available.

11

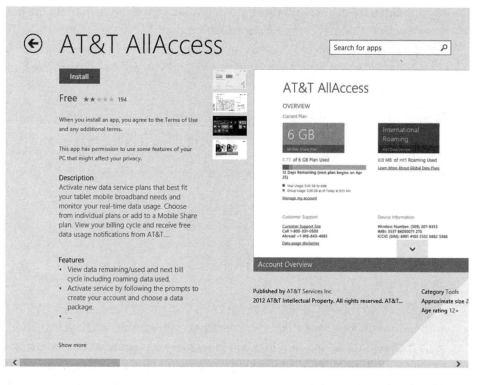

- To connect to the Internet, you need to use the app provided by your mobile operator, which is specifically designed for this task. The app will ask for the PIN of the SIM card used with your modem and then connect to the Internet.

- The quality and speed of the connection can vary depending on where you are and the quality of the infrastructure your mobile operator has in that area.

If an app is not available, don't worry. Your mobile operator probably offers a desktop app that you can use to connect to the Internet.

Connecting to the Internet through MiFi wireless routers

MiFi is a technical term used for wireless routers that act as mobile Wi-Fi hotspots. MiFi stands for "My Wi-Fi".

Such devices can can be connected to a mobile phone (cellular) carrier and provide internet access for up to ten devices. They work at a distance up to 30 ft (10 m) and can provide internet or network access to any wireless device, from your laptop to your tablet or smartphone.

Managing network connections using PC Settings

Another place where you can manage network connections and configurations is PC Settings. Among the list of sections, you will find the Network section, which has settings related to your connections, the wireless devices installed on your computer or tablet, the proxy settings, HomeGroup, and workplace settings, for those on business networks that provide special services like business apps and services for Windows 8.1.

In this section, we will focus on the part that deals with managing your network connections. In the Network section, click Connections. There you can see the status of your Wi-Fi connection (if a wireless network card is installed on your computer) and Ethernet connection (if a network card is installed on your computer).

11

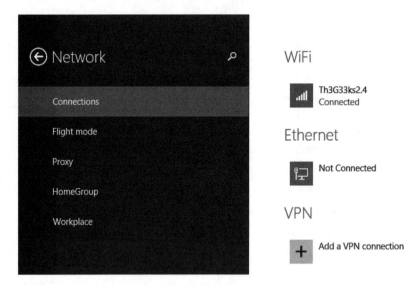

From here, you can also add your own Virtual Private Network (VPN) connection, so that you can connect to your workplace environment.

SEE ALSO If you want to learn more about setting up a VPN connection to your workplace, read Chapter 18, "Using Windows 8.1 at work."

When you click the available wireless network connection, you can set whether you want to find computers, devices, and content available on that network and automatically connect to devices like network printers and TVs.

Th3G33ks2.4

Find devices and content

Find PCs, devices and content on this network and automatically connect to devices like printers and TVs. Turn this off for public networks to help keep your stuff safe.

On

Data usage

Show my estimated data use in the Networks list

Off

Set as a metered connection

Off

Properties

SSID:	Th3G33ks2.4
Protocol:	802.11g
Security type:	WPA2-Personal
IPv4 address:	192.168.1.146
IPv4 DNS Servers:	192.168.1.1
Manufacturer:	Intel Corporation

Then, you can set whether you want Windows 8.1 to show your estimated data use in the Networks list. By default, this data use is shown only for mobile data connections (3G or 4G). Next, you can set whether you want to set the active connection as a metered connection.

Last but not least, you will see the properties of the active network connection. This includes the network name (or SSID), the protocol being used, the type of encryption, the IP address, the model of the network card you are using and its manufacturer, the driver version and the MAC address (physical address). At the bottom of the Properties section, there is a Copy button. You can use this to copy all the data listed in the Properties section to the Windows clipboard, which you can then paste into a document or text file.

11

If you access the properties of an Ethernet (wired) connection, fewer buttons are displayed. Obviously, there will be no switch for setting it as a metered connection, or any switch for showing your estimated data use.

(←) Network

Find devices and content

Find PCs, devices and content on this network and automatically connect to devices like printers and TVs. Turn this off for public networks to help keep your stuff safe.

On

Properties

IPv4 address:	192.168.1.5
IPv4 DNS Servers:	192.168.1.1
Manufacturer:	Intel Corporation
Description:	Intel(R) 82574L Gigabit Network Connection
Driver version:	12.6.47.1
Physical address:	00-0C-29-72-82-22

Copy

In the Properties section you will also see less information. Because wired connections don't have a network name (SSID) being broadcast, this field will be missing as well as those related to the protocol and security type.

In this exercise, you will learn how to access the Network section in PC Settings and view the properties of your active network connection.

→ SET UP
Ensure that you are connected to a network. Then, go to the Start screen.

1   Swipe inward from the right side of the screen or press **Windows key+C** to open the charms.

2   Click **Settings** to open the contextual settings for the Start screen.

3   At the bottom of the Settings charm, click **Change PC Settings**.
     The PC Settings pane opens.

4   Click **Network** to view your network-related settings.

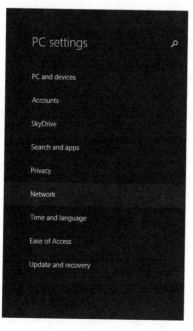

5   Click **Connections** to view the available network connections.

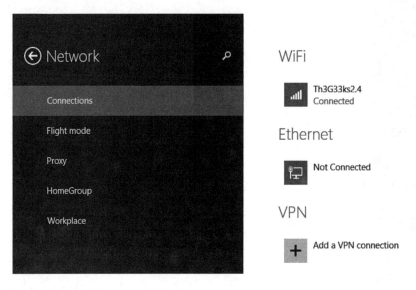

6   Click the network connection for which you want to view more details and settings.

⊗ CLEAN UP
When you are done setting the active network connection, close PC Settings.

Changing the network profile of a network

A network profile in Windows 8.1 is a collection of network and sharing settings that are applied to your active network. Setting this correctly is important to protect you when connecting to public networks and using network-sharing features when connected to trusted home or work networks.

When you connect for the first time to a network, you are asked whether you want to turn on sharing and connect to other devices.

Depending on your answer, one of the following two available network profiles is assigned to that network connection:

- **Private network**   This profile is assigned if you select Yes. You should set a network as private if it is your home or work network, used by people and devices you trust. By default, network discovery will be turned on, and you will be able to see other computers and devices that are part of the network. This allows other computers from the network to access your computer, and you will be able to create or join a HomeGroup.

- **Public network**   This profile is perfect when you are in public places such as air-ports, cafes, libraries, and so on. Network discovery and sharing are turned off. Other computers from the network will not be able to see your computer. This setting is also useful when your computer is directly connected to the Internet (direct cable/modem connection, mobile Internet, and so on). To assign this profile, select No when con-necting for the first time to the network.

TIP There is a third network location profile, called Domain Network, which cannot be set by a normal user. It is available for enterprise workplaces and can be set only by the network administrator. Under this profile, the network and sharing settings applied are the settings set by your workplace, and you cannot change them. The default settings can be changed for both profiles. To learn how to do this, check the instructions detailed in Chapter 13, "Sharing files and folders with my network."

11

These network profiles are useful to people who are very mobile and connect their computers to many networks. For example, you could use your work laptop to connect to your company network, take it home at the end of the day and connect to your home network, or connect to a few public networks at the airport and in a hotel while on a business trip. Each time you connect to a new network, Windows asks about assigning the correct profile. With one choice, you get the entire set of network settings correctly updated; you won't compromise your security, and you have enabled only the network features that you need for each network connection.

If you made a mistake when setting the network profile for the network to which you are connected, you can change it later. In this exercise, you'll learn how.

 SET UP
Open PC Settings and from there, go to the Networks section.

1   Click **Connections** and then click the network connection you want to edit.

2   Look for the **Find Devices And Content** category and its switch.

Find devices and content

Find PCs, devices and content on this network and automatically connect to devices like
printers and TVs. Turn this off for public networks to help keep your stuff safe.

On

3   Move the switch from **On** to **Off** or the other way around, depending on whether you want to set the network connection as **Public** or **Private**.

Find devices and content

Find PCs, devices and content on this network and automatically connect to devices like
printers and TVs. Turn this off for public networks to help keep your stuff safe.

Off

CLEAN UP
Close PC Settings.

The network profile is updated along with the relevant network and sharing settings based on the choice you made.

Key points

- Before working with network connections, it's best to understand the basic jargon so that you know what each term means when you encounter it.

- The Network And Sharing Center is the window from which you can access most network configuration settings.

- You can also manage your network connections from PC Settings.

- Most wireless networks require a password (also called a security key) to connect to them successfully.

- Before connecting to a hidden wireless network, ensure that you know all the important connection details.

- The network profile contains a collection of network and sharing settings that are applied to the network to which you are connected, depending on how you set it.

11

Chapter at a glance

Find

Find the settings related to your user account in the new Accounts pane, page 337

Add

Add a Microsoft account, page 342

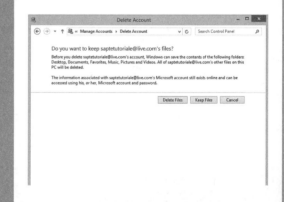

Create

Create a picture password to use instead of your normal password, page 356

Delete

Delete a user account, page 371

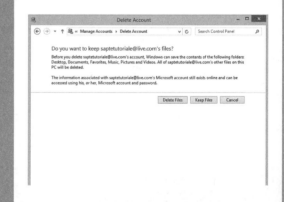

Allowing others to use the computer

12

IN THIS CHAPTER, YOU WILL LEARN HOW TO

- Create a new user account.
- Switch between user accounts.
- Create picture passwords and PINs.
- Change a user account password, picture, name, and type.
- Delete a user account.

In a typical family, there might be only one person who uses one or more computers. For these computers, you need only the user account you created when you first started using them. However, you might have a computer that more than one person uses; it can be a computer your children, your parents, or the whole family uses. If that's the case in your home, it is best to create a user account for each person, so that settings, files, and folders don't become mixed up, which can be frustrating for everyone.

In this chapter, you'll learn what user accounts are, understand how many you need to have on a computer, and learn how to manage and configure them.

PRACTICE FILES To complete the exercises in this chapter, you need the practice files contained in the Chapter12 practice file folder. For more information, see the section "Download the practice files" in the Introduction of this book.

What is a user account and how many do I need?

User accounts make it possible for multiple people to share a computer, with each person having his or her own private Documents folder, email inbox, Windows settings, and so on. When you have your own account, you can do all the customization you want to your Windows 8.1 environment without affecting other user accounts. Other users will have their own visual customization, their own app settings, and so forth.

You can use multiple types of accounts in Windows. You can use your Microsoft account (formerly known as a Windows Live ID) across multiple computers with Windows 8 or Windows 8.1, whereas you can use a local account only on your local computer. These accounts can then have *administrator* permissions (the word "Administrator" is specified near their name). A user account that is not an Administrator account is considered a *standard user account* and has limited permissions. A third type of user account is the *Guest account*.

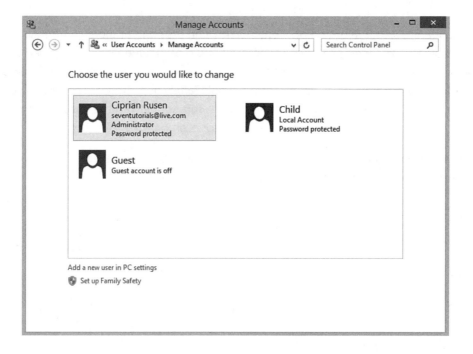

The administrator has full access to all user accounts. He can create and delete user accounts and change the name, password, and account types for other accounts. The administrator can also install software and hardware and configure every aspect of the operating system. As a rule, every computer must have at least one administrator.

A user with standard privileges has access to apps that have already been installed on the computer and cannot install other software without the administrator password. A standard user can change her password but cannot change the account name or type without the administrator password.

The Guest account is a special type of limited user account that has the following characteristics and restrictions:

- It does not require a password.
- The user can't install software or hardware.
- The user can't change the account type.
- The user can't create a password for the account.

When you install Windows 8.1 or when you use it for the first time (as is the case with devices that have Windows 8.1 installed already), you are prompted to create a default user account. That user account always has administrator permissions. You should create a new account when another person needs to work on the same computer.

For example, if you are a parent sharing the computer with your child, it is best to have two user accounts: one for you with administrator permissions and one for your child with standard user permissions. By doing this, you ensure that your child can use the computer but cannot change important configuration aspects.

TIP If children use a computer, consider using Family Safety. If you want to know more about Family Safety, read Chapter 16, "Supervising a child's computer use."

If you have temporary guests who need to use one of your computers to browse the Internet, check their email, and perform other light computing activities, it is best to set up a Guest account for them to use.

12

Introducing the Microsoft account

A major change that was first implemented in Windows 8, is the introduction of the Microsoft account and its mandatory use for working with features such as synchronizing your settings across the many computers you use or accessing the Windows Store to purchase apps. In addition, each time you create a user account, Windows 8.1 first asks for a Microsoft account.

The Microsoft account is an ID composed of an email address and password, which you can use to log on to most Microsoft websites, services, and properties such as Hotmail, Outlook.com, Xbox Live, and all Microsoft services (including SkyDrive and Skype). You also use it in Windows 8.1 for synchronizing your computer settings, using the Windows Store to purchase apps, and other activities.

How do you know whether you have a Microsoft account? If you are already using any of these services—Hotmail, Outlook.com, SkyDrive, or Xbox Live—you already have a Microsoft account. Use the same email address and password in Windows 8.1.

If you don't have a Microsoft account, you can easily create one in Windows 8.1 or on the Microsoft websites.

Using this account in Windows 8.1 is highly recommended, particularly if you want to access all the features it has to offer without problems or limitations. In addition, a Microsoft account gives you access to almost all Microsoft products, services, properties, and websites. The Microsoft account will also be useful in the following scenarios:

- You want to use any of the tools included in the Windows Essentials suite.
- You want to use devices such as Microsoft Xbox consoles, Surface tablets or Windows Phones.
- You need a free email account from Microsoft on Outlook.com.
- You want to purchase and use an Office 365 subscription.

Accessing the user accounts settings

Windows 8.1 offers two places from which you can manage user accounts on your computer. In PC Settings, in the Accounts section, you can manage settings related to your user account (the account picture, your password, picture password, and PIN), the password policy used when waking your computer from sleep, add new user accounts and edit them.

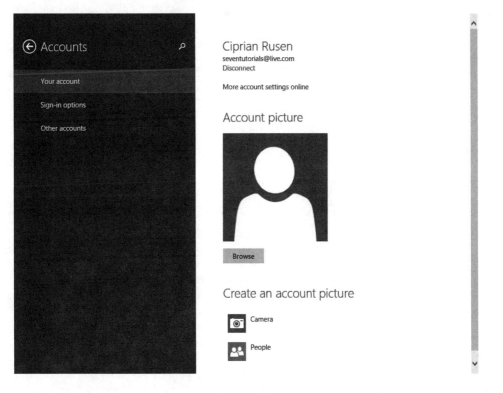

In Control Panel, you can manage other existing user accounts, change your account type, or configure the settings for User Account Control (UAC).

12

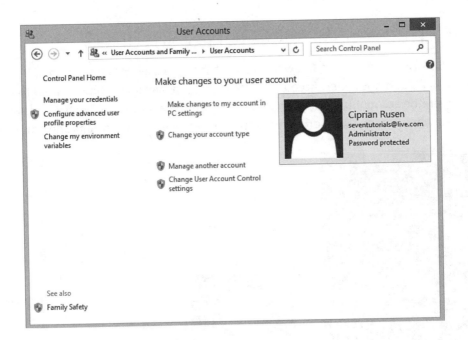

TIP If you want to know more about the UAC and how it works, read the dedicated section in Chapter 14, "Keeping Windows 8.1 safe and secure."

In this exercise, you'll learn how to access both methods for managing user accounts, starting with the one in Control Panel and ending with the one in PC Settings.

 SET UP
Open Control Panel.

1 Click **User Accounts and Family Safety**.

2 Click **User Accounts**.

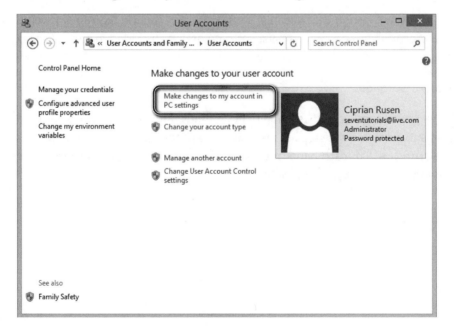

The User Accounts window, with settings related to your user account, opens.

3   Click **Make Changes To My Account In PC Settings**.

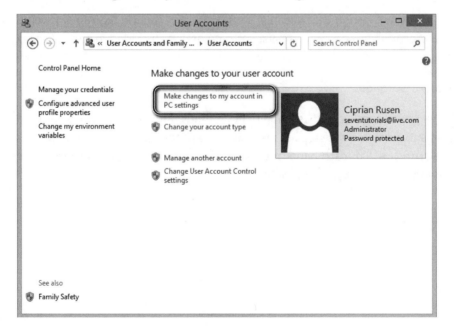

The Accounts pane in PC Settings opens.

4   Browse through the available sections (**Your Account**, **Sign-in Options**, **Other Accounts**) to become familiar with the options included in each of them.

⊗ CLEAN UP
Close PC Settings.

You can open the Accounts section in PC Settings directly, without going first to Control Panel and following the steps in the preceding procedure. This exercise was meant to familiarize you with each panel and its location before you learn how to manage the user accounts defined on your computer.

Adding a new user account

Anyone with administrator permissions can add a user account via PC Settings. When you add a user, Windows 8.1 first asks for a Microsoft account. If one is provided, the user is immediately given access to the computer and can log on by using the password associated with that Microsoft account. Keep in mind that when you add a user, you must have an active Internet connection. This also applies when the user logs on for the first time.

After the user account is created, a new folder with the new account name is created in the *C:\Users* folder, where all the personal files of the new user are kept. No users except administrator(s) and the newly added user have access to this folder.

In this exercise, you'll learn how to create a new user account on your Windows 8.1 computer or device, using a Microsoft account.

SET UP

Log on as a user who has administrator permissions. Ensure that your Internet connection is working correctly, so that the procedure works smoothly. Then, open PC Settings

1   In PC Settings, click **Accounts**.

2   In the **Accounts** pane, click **Other Accounts**.

3   Click **Add An Account**.

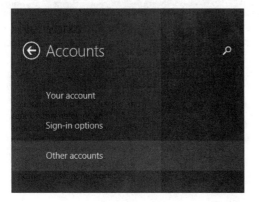

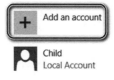

A wizard opens, asking how the new person will sign in.

12

4   Type the email address associated with her Microsoft account, and then click **Next**.

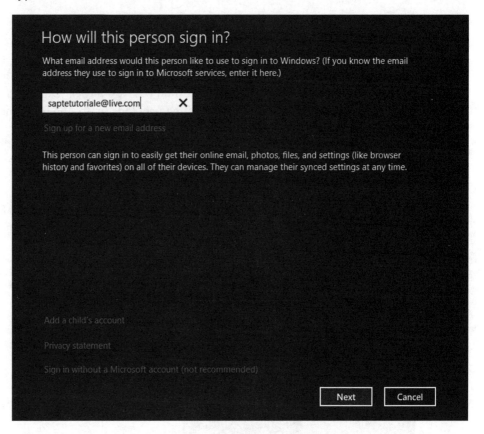

The Add A User page opens, informing you that the user has been added.

Add a user

Let this person know they'll need to be connected to the Internet to sign in for the first time.

saptetutoriale@live.com

☐ Is this a child's account? Turn on Family Safety to get reports of their PC use.

Finish   Cancel

5   Click **Finish**.

Windows returns you to the Accounts pane in PC Settings.

✖ CLEAN UP
Close PC Settings, sign out and ask the person you have added to sign in by using their Microsoft account password.

The user account has been created and the first time that person logs in, she will go through a brief configuration wizard, plus the Windows 8.1 introductory tutorial. This is prior to being able to use your computer or device.

12

Adding a local user account

If you are not interested in using a Microsoft account, you can create a local account, which is created on your local computer, and with which a user can log on and use Windows 8.1. However, the user of this account will not be able to use any synchronization features provided by Microsoft for Windows 8.1 and won't be able to make purchases in the Windows Store unless a Microsoft account is associated with it later. Another important difference is that a local account can have a blank (empty) password, whereas a Microsoft account does not allow blank passwords. Further, a local account does not need an active Internet connection to log on for the first time or for subsequent logons.

After the user account is created, a new folder with the new account name is created in the *C:\Users* folder, where all the personal files of the new user are kept. No users except administrator(s) and the newly added user have access to this folder.

In this exercise, you'll learn how to create a new local user account on your computer.

 SET UP
Log on as a user who has administrator permissions and then open PC Settings.

1   In **PC Settings**, click **Accounts**.

2   In the **Accounts** pane **Other Accounts**.

3   Click **Add An Account**.

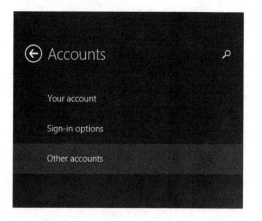

A wizard opens, asking how the new person will sign in.

4   Toward the bottom of the page, click the **Sign In Without A Microsoft Account (Not Recommended)** link.

You are shown more information about the options for adding a user.

5   Click **Local Account**.

You are asked to type the user name, password, and password hint.

12

Add a user

Choose a password that will be easy for you to remember but hard for others to guess. If you forget, we'll show the hint.

User name	Child
Password	••••
Reenter password	••••
Password hint	t ✕

Next   Cancel

6   Complete all the fields and then click **Next**.

You are informed that the user you created will be able to sign in to your computer.

7   Click **Finish**.

Windows returns you to the Accounts pane in PC Settings.

CLEAN UP
Close PC Settings.

The user account is created using the password you provided. When the new user signs in for the first time, he will be shown the Windows 8.1 introductory tutorial, prior to being able to use your computer or device.

Creating a Microsoft account

You can create a Microsoft account several ways. One way is to do it from Windows 8.1 during the procedure for adding a new user account.

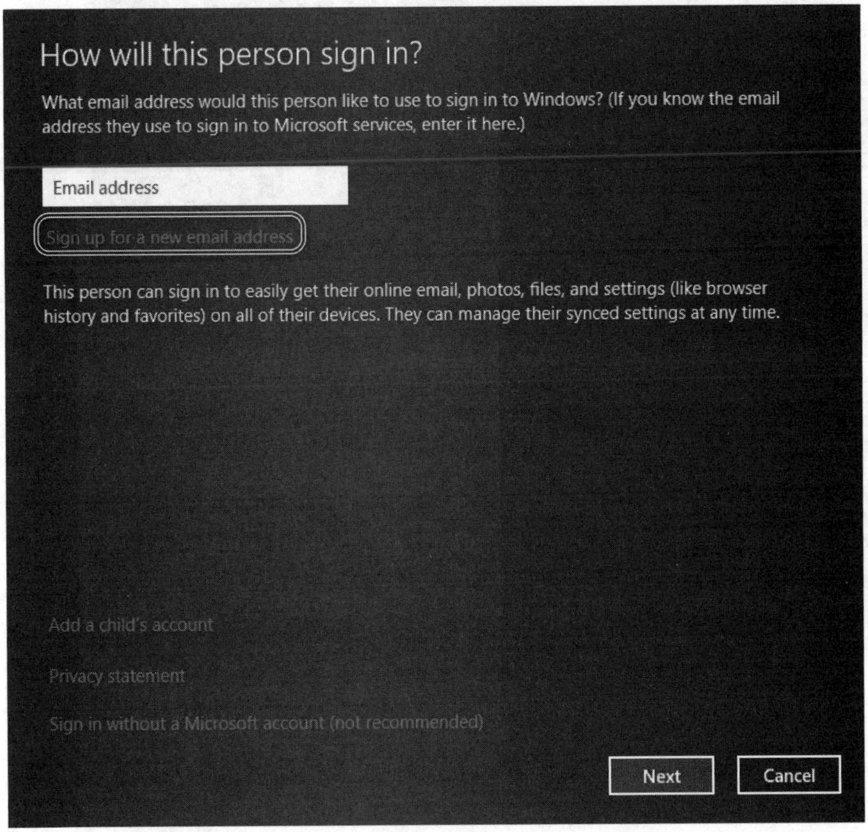

How will this person sign in?

What email address would this person like to use to sign in to Windows? (If you know the email address they use to sign in to Microsoft services, enter it here.)

Email address

Sign up for a new email address

This person can sign in to easily get their online email, photos, files, and settings (like browser history and favorites) on all of their devices. They can manage their synced settings at any time.

Add a child's account

Privacy statement

Sign in without a Microsoft account (not recommended)

Next   Cancel

If Windows has a connection to the Internet, it will ask for all the required details for creating the account, send them to Microsoft to confirm your details, and allow the newly created account to log on to your computer or device.

12

Create a Microsoft account

Create a new email address. You'll be able to use it with Outlook.com, Xbox, Skype, Windows Phone, and SkyDrive, to keep all of your info together on this PC.

Email address	ciprian	@	outlook.com

Or use an existing email address

New password	••••••••
Reenter password	••••••••
First name	Ciprian
Last name	Rusen
Country/region	United States

Next   Cancel

As an alternative, using any web browser, visit *https://signup.live.com*, and enter all the details requested.

Switching between user accounts

When you switch between user accounts, you leave the current user account logged on (with all running apps) and log on to a separate user account. You can switch back and forth between user accounts whenever you want. The user account from which you switched remains active with all apps running, and you can switch back to it at any time by entering its password, PIN, or picture password. This can be useful if you need to work on multiple accounts at the same time.

In this exercise, you'll learn how to switch between two user accounts. This is possible only if you have two or more user accounts on your computer.

 SET UP
Log on by using one of the user accounts existing on your computer and open the Start screen.

1 In the upper-right corner of the screen, click the icon that represents your user account.

A contextual menu with several options opens.

2 Click the user account to which you want to switch.

You are asked to complete logon details for the selected user.

3 Type the password for the selected user account and then click the **Submit** arrow.

You are now logged on to the selected user account.

12

TIP Depending on how the user account you selected is set up, you'll need to type one of the logon details, such as password, PIN, or picture password, at step 3. For example, if you have set up a PIN, you will be requested to type the PIN instead of the password.

⊗ CLEAN UP

When you finish working with this user account, sign out.

Changing the password for your user account

The owners of every user account except Guest can change the password for their account. Making the change doesn't require any administrator permissions as long as you do not want to change the password of a user account other than your own.

If you are using a user account associated with a Microsoft account, the password change is applied to both your Windows-based computer and all Microsoft services that account uses. If you are using a local user account, the password change applies only to the user account defined on your local computer.

TIP To keep your account safe, it is recommended that you use strong passwords. Strong passwords contain a combination of letters, numbers, and special characters (such as @, #, or &). Ideally, the password should be something that is easy for you to remember but difficult for anyone else to figure out.

In this exercise, you'll learn how to change the password of a user associated with a Microsoft account.

➡ SET UP

Log on to Windows 8.1 by using the user account whose password you want to change. Then, open PC Settings.

1 In **PC Settings**, click **Accounts**.

2 In the **Accounts** pane, click **Sign-In Options**.

Several password-related options are shown.

3 In the **Password** section, click the **Change** button.

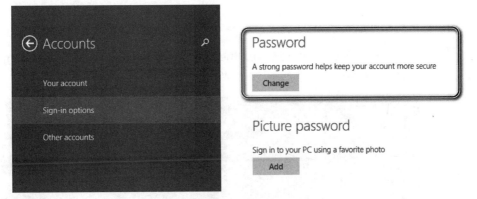

The wizard for changing your password opens.

4 Type your current password and then click **Finish**.

5   You are asked to enter your current password again as well as the new password for your Microsoft account.

6   In the **Old Password** box, type the existing password that you want to change.

7   In the **New Password** box, type the new password, and then, in the **Reenter Password** box, type the new password again.

Change your Microsoft account password

Ciprian Rusen
seventutorials@live.com

Old password

Forgot your password?

New password

Reenter password

Next   Cancel

8   Click **Next**.

You are informed that you have changed your password.

9   Click **Finish**.

CLEAN UP
Close PC Settings.

TIP If you are changing the password for a local user account, the procedure and the data being requested is the same, with a minor difference: you will be asked to also enter a password hint that is shown when logging on to Windows, in case you have entered your password incorrectly.

Removing the password for a user account

Unlike in earlier versions of Windows, in Windows 8.1 you cannot remove the password of a user account if a Microsoft account is associated with it. Having a password is critical to a Microsoft account and secures it from unauthorized access to your computer and all Microsoft services you are using. However, you can create local user accounts, which have no password, or change their existing password to a blank (empty) one.

Creating a picture password for your user account

One of the features first introduced by Windows 8 is the use of picture passwords. This concept entails using a specific picture on which you draw gestures. These gestures can be simple taps or clicks, circles, or lines. If your user account is using a Microsoft account with a complicated password, creating a picture password to be used as a complement can be a good way to make it easy to log on to your Windows 8.1–based devices.

Even though this feature is particularly recommended for use on touch-enabled devices such as tablets, you can also employ it on a desktop computer by using a mouse.

In this exercise, you'll learn how to create a picture password for your user account. To make things fast and easy, the exercise will use only taps or clicks.

12

SET UP

To complete this exercise, you need the PictureA.jpg file, which is in the Chapter12 folder in your practice files. When you have this file available, open PC Settings.

1   In **PC Settings**, click **Accounts**.

2   In the **Accounts** pane, click **Sign-In Options**.

Several password-related options are shown.

3   In the **Picture Password** section, click **Add**.

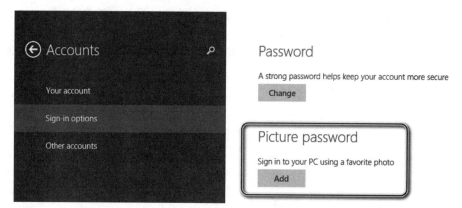

You are asked to first verify your account information.

4   Type your user account password and then click **OK**.

You are informed about picture passwords.

5   Click **Choose Picture**.

A browsing window opens.

6   Click **This PC** and navigate to where you stored the PictureA.jpg practice file.

7   Select **PictureA.jpg** and then click **Open**.

You are asked whether to use the picture as is or position it another way.

8   Click **Use This Picture**.

You are asked to set up the three gestures that will serve as your picture password.

9   Click or tap the picture as highlighted in the following screen shot, on the head of
     each figure, one by one.

You are immediately asked to confirm your gestures.

10   Click or tap the picture again as you just did, on the head of each figure, one by one. You are informed that the picture password has been created successfully.

11   Click **Finish**.

 CLEAN UP
Close PC Settings.

The picture password is now set, and you can use it instead of your normal user account password each time you log on to your computer.

Creating a PIN for your user account

To further simplify the way you log on to your computer, especially if you are using a Microsoft account with a long password, Windows 8.1 allows the creation of a four-digit PIN associated with your user account. After you create a PIN, you can use it to log on quickly to your user account.

In this exercise, you'll learn how to create a PIN for your user account.

 SET UP
Open PC Settings.

1　In **PC Settings**, click **Accounts**.

2　In the **Account** pane, click **Sign-In Options**.

　　Several password-related options are shown.

3　In the **PIN** section, click **Add.**

Accounts

- Your account
- Sign-in options
- Other accounts

Password

A strong password helps keep your account more secure

Change

Picture password

Sign in to your PC using a favorite photo

Change　　Remove

PIN

Sign in quickly with a four-digit number

Add

Password policy

Password is not required when waking this PC from sleep

Change

You are asked to first verify your account.

4   Type your user account password and then click **OK**.

You are asked to enter the 4-digit code you want to use as your PIN.

5   Type the same PIN in the **Enter PIN** and **Confirm PIN** boxes.

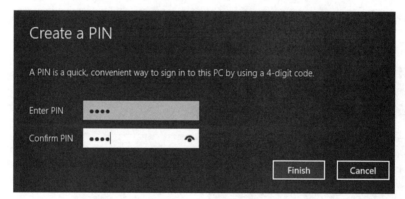

6   Click **Finish**.

 CLEAN UP
Close PC Settings.

You can now use the PIN you just set instead of your password to log on to your user account.

Changing the picture password or the PIN

You can change both your picture password and PIN if you decide to use these features. The change process is always started in the Accounts pane, in the Sign-In Options section.

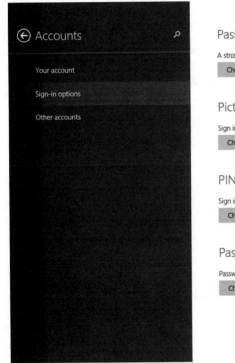

Windows 8.1 first asks you to type the current password associated with the user account and then allows you to change the picture password and the PIN. From here on, the procedures for changing them are the same as for creating them.

Changing a user account picture

As with any earlier version of Windows, you can change the picture for your user account at any time. The procedure involved is not complicated.

In this exercise, you'll learn how to change a user account picture.

SET UP
To complete this exercise, you need the PictureB.jpg file, which is in the Chapter12 folder in your practice files. When this file is available, open the Start screen.

1   In the upper-right corner of the screen, click the icon that represents your user account.

    A contextual menu with several options opens.

2   Click **Change Account Picture**.

    The Accounts pane in PC Settings opens.

3   Under **Your Account**, in the **Account Picture** section, click **Browse**.

A file browsing window opens.

4   Click **This PC** and navigate to where you stored the PictureB.jpg practice file.

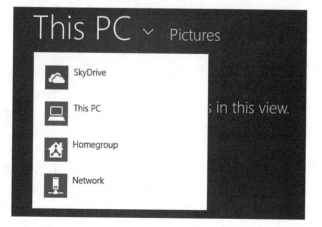

12

5   Select **PictureB.jpg** and then click **Choose Image**.

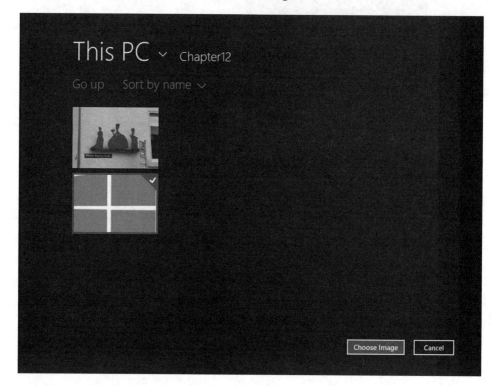

You return to the Accounts pane in PC Settings.

 CLEAN UP
Close PC Settings.

Your user account picture has been changed.

Changing a user account name

In Windows 8.1, changing the name of a user account is possible only for local accounts. You cannot change Microsoft account names from Windows. It is best to make this change from another user account with administrator permissions.

In this exercise, you'll learn how to change the name of a local user account.

→ SET UP

Log on by using a user account that has administrator permissions. In Control Panel, open the User Accounts window by clicking User Accounts And Family Safety, and then click User Accounts.

1   Click **Manage Another Account**.

A list of all the existing user accounts opens.

2   Click the user account whose name you want to change.

The Change An Account window opens.

3   Click **Change The Account Name.**

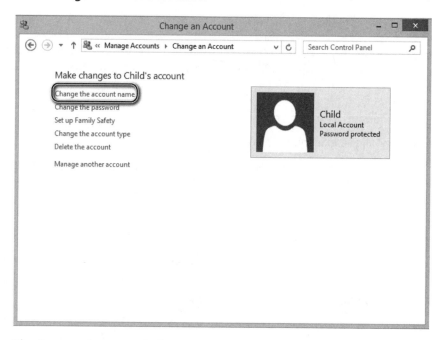

The Rename Account window opens.

4   Type the new name that you want to use for that user account.

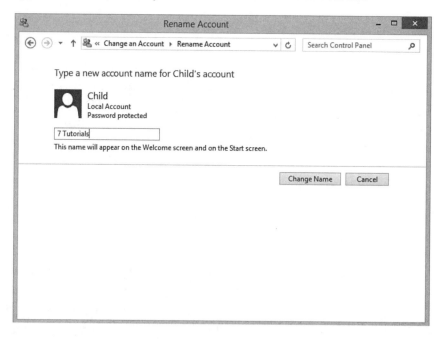

5   Click **Change Name**.

You return to the Change An Account window, where you can see that the selected user account has been renamed.

⊗ CLEAN UP
Close the Change An Account window.

The name of the selected user account is now changed.

Changing a user account type

All users except Guest can change their user account type. However, making the change requires administrator permissions. If you are trying to change the type for a user account with standard permissions, you need to know the password of the Administrator account or have someone log on by using the Administrator account and change the account type.

You must have at least one user account with administrator permissions on your Windows 8.1–based computer. If you have only one such user account, you can't change its type to standard user. However, you can change any number of standard user accounts to Administrator.

In this exercise, you'll learn how to change the type of a user account from standard to Administrator.

→ SET UP
Log on by using a user account that has administrator permissions. In Control Panel, open User Accounts window by clicking User Accounts And Family Safety, and then click User Accounts.

1   Click **Manage Another Account**.

A list of all the existing user accounts opens.

12

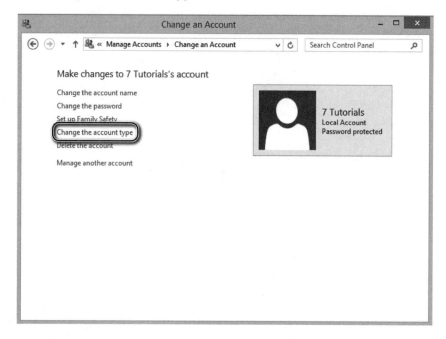

2   Click the user account whose type you want to change.

The Change An Account window opens.

3   Click **Change The Account Type**.

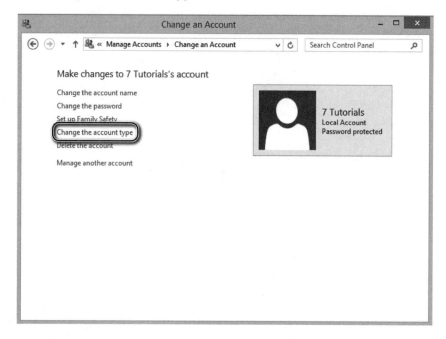

The Change Account Type window opens.

4   Select the new account type that you want to use, in this case, **Administrator**.

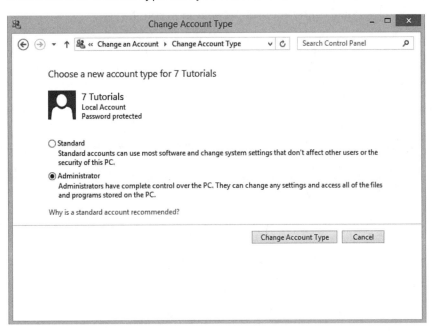

5   Click **Change Account Type**.

You return to the Change An Account window.

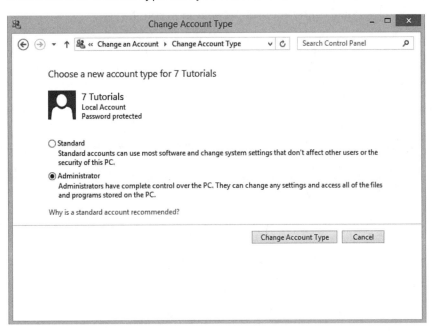 CLEAN UP
Close the Change An Account window.

The type of the selected user account is now changed.

Deleting a user account

Deleting user accounts is a task that only administrators can do. When an account is deleted, all the settings and files belonging to that user account are also deleted. This activity is best done by logging on to another user account and making the deletion from there. Ensure that the user account you are about to delete is not logged on when executing the deletion.

Before you delete a user account, back up all the important files created in its user files and folders so that they can be used later.

In this exercise, you'll learn how to delete a user account.

 SET UP
Log on by using a user account that has administrator permissions. In Control Panel, open the User Accounts window.

1 Click **Manage Another Account**.

A list of all the existing user accounts opens.

2 Click the user account that you want to delete.

The Change An Account window opens.

3 Click the **Delete The Account** link.

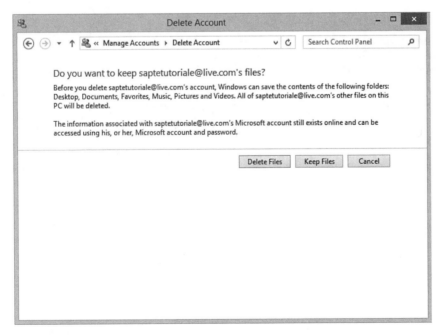

The Delete Account window opens.

4   Click **Delete Files**.

You are asked to confirm the deletion.

5   Click **Delete Account**.

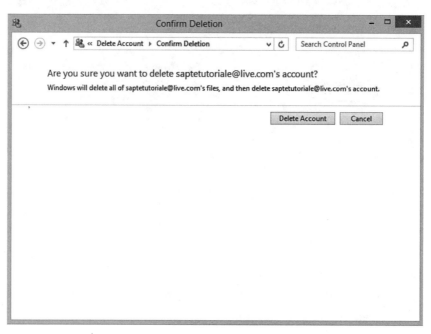

You return to the Manage Accounts window.

 CLEAN UP
Close the Manage Accounts window.

The selected user account is now deleted.

TIP If you decide to keep the user's files, they will be saved in a folder on the Desktop of the user account from which you are making the deletion. The folder name will be that of the deleted user account.

Key points

- If more than one person is using a computer, it is best to create a separate user account for each person.

- Windows 8.1 allows you to use Microsoft accounts as user accounts on your device.

- With a Microsoft account, you can use all the features included in Windows 8.1, including the Windows Store.

- Any user can create picture passwords or PINs for quicker logon procedures.

- To create a user account, change user account names or types, and delete user accounts, you need administrator permissions.

- The deletion of a user account is best done from another user account and only after you have backed up all the important files created by that user.

12

Chapter at a glance

Find

Find the Advanced Sharing Settings window that contains all your network-sharing settings, page 381

Create

Create a homegroup to easily share libraries, folders, and devices, page 384

Use

Use the Sharing Wizard for quick file sharing, page 397

Share

Share all printers and devices with one setting, page 405

Sharing files and folders with my network

13

IN THIS CHAPTER, YOU WILL LEARN HOW TO

- Turn on the Sharing Wizard.

- Find the network sharing settings.

- Set up a homegroup.

- Join other computers and devices to the homegroup.

- Share files and folders.

- Share printers.

- Stop sharing files, folders, or printers.

In Windows 8 and Windows 8.1, Microsoft continued its efforts to simplify the network sharing experience. Features such as HomeGroup have been further improved, and network sharing settings and wizards have been simplified so that they require fewer steps.

In this chapter, you'll learn about the default network sharing settings and how they affect your network sharing experience. You'll learn everything about the HomeGroup feature: how to create one, join other computers to it, find and change the current password, and leave an existing homegroup. Finally, you'll learn about sharing your libraries, folders, and devices such as printers, including how to stop sharing them when necessary.

PRACTICE FILES You do not need any practice files to complete the exercises in this chapter. For more information about practice file requirements, see the section "Using the practice files" in the Introduction of this book.

Turning on the Sharing Wizard

The Sharing Wizard in Windows is designed so that you can easily share anything you want with the other computers and devices on the network. By default, the wizard is turned on in Windows 8.1. However, if it is turned off on your computer, the exercises included as part of this chapter about sharing over the network won't work, and you will see a completely different set of sharing options and buttons. Therefore, before we go any further, this section shows how to turn on the Sharing Wizard so that you can complete the previous exercises without problems and have the easiest network-sharing experience possible with Windows 8.1.

In this exercise, you'll learn how to turn on the Sharing Wizard.

 SET UP
Open File Explorer. If the ribbon is collapsed, double-click it to expand it.

1   Click the **View** tab.

2   On the right side of the ribbon, click the **Options** button.

The Folder Options window box opens.

3   Click the **View** tab.

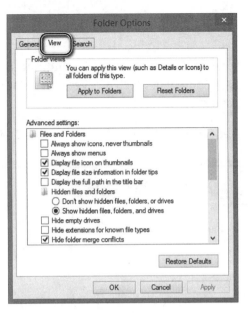

4   Scroll down the **Advanced Settings** list and select the **Use Sharing Wizard (Recommended)** check box.

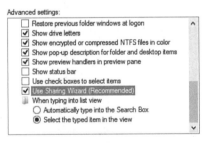

5   Click **OK**.

You return to the File Explorer window.

✖ CLEAN UP
Close File Explorer.

The Sharing Wizard is now turned on, and you can use it to complete the exercises detailed in this chapter.

Understanding the default network sharing settings

Windows 8.1 organizes most of your network sharing settings in the Advanced Sharing Settings window in the Network And Sharing Center, which is covered in detail in Chapter 11, "Connecting to a network and the Internet."

To access it, in the left column of the Network And Sharing Center, click the Change Advanced Sharing Settings link.

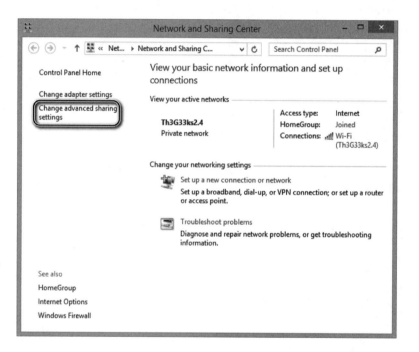

The network sharing settings are split by network profile. Each network profile has different settings, and a combination of settings is applied to all networks to which you connect.

The profile assigned to your current network connection is indicated by the Current Profile statement beside the name of one of the two profiles. If you want to access the settings for only one of the network locations, use the arrows to the right of each profile. Clicking the arrow once collapses the list of settings for that network location. Clicking it again expands the list.

13

The profile assigned
to the active network

Minimize/Maximize
list of settings

TIP To learn more about network profiles and assigning them to a network connection, see the section "Changing the network profile of a network" in Chapter 11.

The Private profile has the following default settings:

- **Network Discovery Is Turned On**   When this setting is applied, Windows can search for other devices on the network to which it is connected, and it allows other computers and devices on the same network to find your Windows–based computer or device.

- **File And Printer Sharing Is Turned On**   When this setting is applied, you can share content and printers with other computers and devices on your network.

- **Windows Is Allowed To Manage HomeGroup Connections**   After you join or create a homegroup, Windows automatically manages HomeGroup connections. If you choose the other available option, you must manually type a user name and password when you connect to other computers.

The default settings for the Private profile are very effective and do not need changing unless you don't want to or don't need to use the available network sharing features on the network to which you are connected. If this is the case, it is best to switch the network profile to Guest Or Public instead of changing the default settings of the Private profile.

The Guest Or Public profile has the following default settings:

- **Network Discovery Is Turned Off**   When this setting is applied, other computers and devices on the network can't discover your Windows–based computer or device unless they utilize its direct network address.

- **File And Printer Sharing Is Turned Off**   When this setting is applied, all network sharing features are disabled and can't be used on this network. If your computer is accessed by others, they cannot view any files, folders, or devices being shared.

These default settings are great when connecting to networks that you don't trust and with which you do not want to share any folders, libraries, or devices.

13

Last, a combination of settings is applied to all network connections. You can find and customize them in the All Networks section. The available settings are the following:

- **Public Folder Sharing**   When this setting is turned on, the C:\Users\Public\ folder is shared with all the computers and devices on the network. This folder contains the following subfolders: Public Documents, Public Downloads, Public Music, Public Pictures, and Public Videos. Other folders are also contained here, but they are hidden to users. Users on the same computer or from other computers and devices can read the contents of the Public folder and write files inside it and its subfolders. When this setting is turned off, this folder is not shared with your network. Turning off Public folder sharing is recommended unless using this folder for sharing is useful to you. Depending on your personal preference, you might choose to share files and folders directly with others instead of copying them to the Public folder.

- **Media Streaming**   With this setting, you can stream multimedia files (pictures, video, and music) by using Windows Media Player. When this setting is turned on, you can stream your media with the network and the Internet. When it's turned off, no media streaming is possible by using Windows Media Player. You should only turn on this feature if you plan to use it. By default, it is turned off, unless you have used Windows Media Player at least once.

- **File Sharing Connections**   This setting determines the type of encryption used for file sharing connections. By default, it's set to 128-bit encryption. You can also set it to the less secure 40-bit or 56-bit encryption. However, it is best to leave this set at 128-bit encryption unless you have issues with older devices or computers that cannot properly access your shared files and folders.

- **Password Protected Sharing**   With this setting, people can only access your shared files and folders if they have a user account and password set on your computer. If they don't have these details, they cannot connect to your shared folders and devices unless the shared folders and devices are shared with everyone. Turning off this feature is useful only when connecting to trusted home or work networks with diverse operating systems that have trouble connecting to your Windows 8.1 shared folders and devices. However, this setting should be used only as a last resort.

If you make any changes to the default network sharing settings, don't forget to click the Save Changes button so that they are applied. Also, keep in mind that making changes to these settings requires administrator permissions. User accounts with no administrator permissions cannot modify them in any way.

Setting up a homegroup

HomeGroup is a network feature first introduced in Windows 7 and further improved in Windows 8 and Windows 8.1. It aims to simplify the process of sharing content and devices on trusted small networks. In earlier versions of Windows, sharing content was a tedious and sometimes painful process.

By using the HomeGroup, you can access all shared files and devices in your network with very few clicks and without typing user names and passwords. The HomeGroup manages all security and authentication for you and ensures that computers and devices outside the homegroup cannot access what you are sharing. This feature is designed primarily for computers and devices connected to a small home or work network.

Each time you connect the computer to a new network, Windows 8.1 asks you to set network sharing. If you turn on sharing and connect to devices, you are in a trusted and private network of computers and devices. In this scenario, Windows 8.1 enables you to use the HomeGroup. If you do not turn on sharing, this feature will not be available.

13

Even though this feature is useful and easy to use, it has an important limitation: It is available only for computers and devices running Windows 7, Windows 8, and Windows 8.1. Only these operating systems can join a homegroup and take advantage of it without any special configuration.

After you have connected to your network and customized the network sharing settings, you can create the homegroup for your network computers to join and exchange libraries, files, folders, and devices. You can create the homegroup from either Control Panel or PC Settings; however, the creation process is slightly faster when you use PC Settings.

When you create a homegroup, Windows automatically generates a random and secure password that will be used by all computers and devices to join the homegroup and share items among them. You can't set this password when you create the homegroup initially, but you can change it later on.

After the homegroup is created, you can select from a standard list of items to share with others. A limited list of libraries is available for sharing: Documents, Music, Pictures, and Videos. You can also share installed printers and devices (scanners, multifunctional printers, and so on) and allow devices such as TVs and game consoles to play the content you have shared with the homegroup. Sharing other libraries, folders, or devices can be set up after you create the homegroup.

TIP To learn more about libraries in Windows 8.1, read Chapter 4, "Organizing files and folders."

In this exercise, you'll learn how to create a homegroup.

➡ SET UP
Open PC Settings.

1 In **PC Settings**, at the bottom of the window, click **Network**.

2 In the **Network** pane, click **HomeGroup**.

TROUBLESHOOTING If, when you click the HomeGroup link, you do not see a window similar to the one shown here, but something with the settings of an existing homegroup, the computer is already part of a homegroup. In this scenario, you either keep the computer as part of that homegroup or leave that homegroup and create a new one. To learn how to leave a homegroup, read the section "Leaving a homegroup" later in this chapter.

3 Click **Create**.

Windows takes a few seconds to create the homegroup.

13

4   Set the permissions to **On** by changing the positions of the switches for the items you want shared with the homegroup.

5   Scroll down to the **Password** section to learn the password generated for your homegroup.

can change it.

Documents
Off

⊖ Network   🔍

Music
Off

Connections

Pictures
Off

Airplane mode

Proxy

Videos
Off

HomeGroup

Workplace

Printers
Off

Let devices on this network (like TVs and game consoles) stream my music and videos
Off

If you leave the homegroup, you won't be able to get to shared libraries and devices

Leave

Password

If someone else wants to join your homegroup, give them this password

fU8ND8ZW1e

6   Write down the password.

 CLEAN UP
Close PC Settings.

The homegroup is now created, and other computers and devices running Windows 7, Windows 8, or Windows 8.1 can join it by using the same password.

Joining a homegroup

After the homegroup is created, other computers can join so that you can exchange files and folders and share devices. Any computer on the network can be part of a homegroup, but it can be in only one homegroup at a time.

In PC Settings, go to Network and then HomeGroup. There, Windows 8.1 informs you whether it detects a homegroup created by another computer. When joining a homegroup, you are asked to type the password that was generated during its creation. If you remember the password from the previous section, use that one. If not, ask the person who created the homegroup for the password.

In this exercise, you'll learn how to join a computer running Windows 8.1 to a previously created homegroup.

 SET UP
Open PC Settings.

1 In **PC Settings**, at the bottom of the window, click **Network**.

2 In the **Network** pane, click **HomeGroup**.

13

3   In the **Enter The HomeGroup Password** box, type the homegroup password, and then click **Join**.

Windows takes a few seconds to join you to the homegroup.

4   Set the permissions to **On** by changing the positions of the switches for the items you want shared with the homegroup.

 CLEAN UP
Close PC Settings. Repeat this procedure for all the computers and devices on your network that you want in the homegroup.

The computer is now part of the homegroup and has shared the items you selected.

Finding your homegroup password

If you want to add another computer or device to the homegroup and you forgot the password, you can find it easily on any of the computers that are part of the homegroup.

In this exercise, you'll learn how to find the password for your homegroup so that you can share it with the people who need to know it.

SET UP
Open PC Settings.

1   In **PC Settings**, at the bottom of the window, click **Network**.

2   In the **Network** pane, click **HomeGroup**.

3   Scroll down to the **Password** section where the homegroup password is displayed.

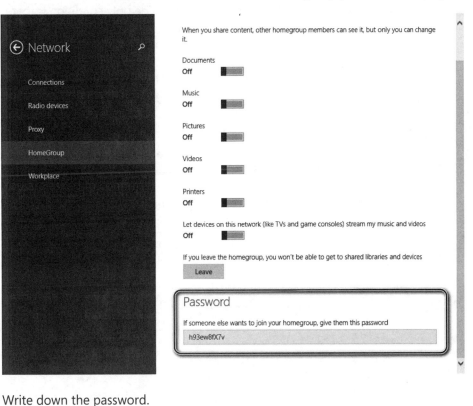

4   Write down the password.

❌ CLEAN UP
Close PC Settings.

Changing the password of a homegroup

You can change the password of a homegroup from any computer that joined it, but only from Control Panel, not from PC Settings. If you change the password after other computers and devices have joined the homegroup, the password change will disconnect the other computers and devices. After the password is changed, all the other computers and devices must rejoin the homegroup by using the new password.

13

When changing the password, Windows generates a new random and secure password for you, but you can type a password of your own. The only condition is that the password must be at least eight characters long; otherwise, Windows won't accept it as a valid password.

In this exercise, you'll learn how to change the password of an existing homegroup to one of your own choosing.

SET UP

Start a computer that is part of the homegroup and then open the Network And Sharing Center.

1. In the **Network And Sharing Center**, click the **HomeGroup** link.

   The HomeGroup window opens.

2. Click **Change The Password**.

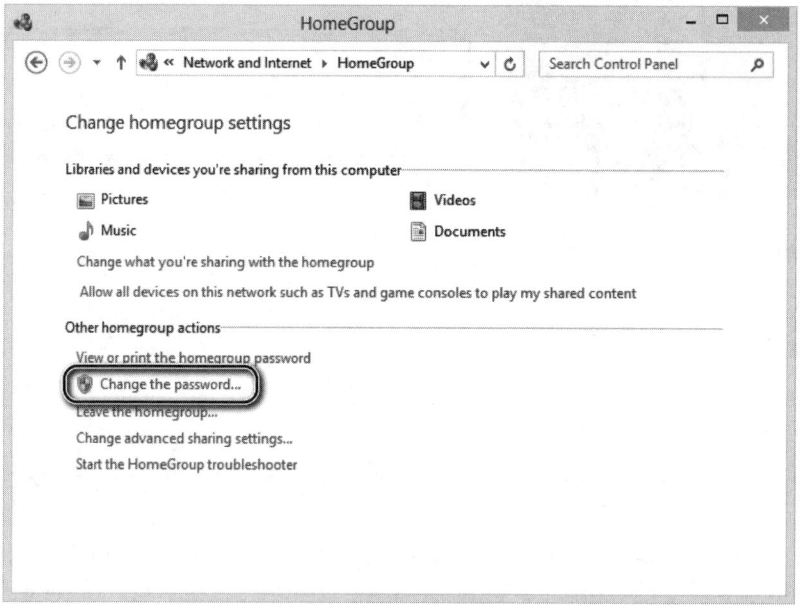
HomeGroup
Network and Internet ▸ HomeGroup
Search Control Panel
Change homegroup settings
Libraries and devices you're sharing from this computer
Pictures
Videos
Music
Documents
Change what you're sharing with the homegroup
Allow all devices on this network such as TVs and game consoles to play my shared content
Other homegroup actions
View or print the homegroup password
Change the password...
Leave the homegroup...
Change advanced sharing settings...
Start the HomeGroup troubleshooter

You are asked to confirm that you want to change the password.

3   Click **Change The Password**.

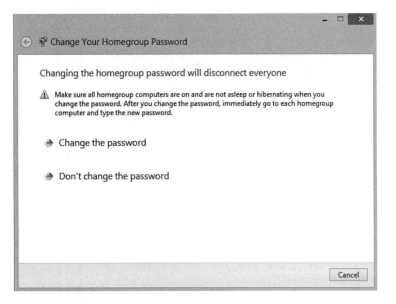

Windows generates a new random password.

4   In the **Type Your Own Password Or Use This One** box, type a new password that is at least eight characters long.

5   Click **Next**.

Windows makes the necessary changes.

6   Click **Finish**.

 CLEAN UP
Close the HomeGroup window. Rejoin all computers and devices that were disconnected due to the password change.

The password for the homegroup is now changed.

Accessing homegroup computers and devices

After the homegroup is created and all computers and devices are joined, accessing their shared content is simple. All it takes is a few clicks. You no longer need to type any user names and passwords to access what is being shared.

Open File Explorer and then, in the navigation pane on the left, click the HomeGroup section. You'll see a list of user accounts and computers that are part of the homegroup and running at that moment. Double-click any of the shared folders and libraries to access their content.

TIP By default, libraries and folders are shared with the other homegroup computers as Read Only. Therefore, you can access them or copy their content to your computer, but you can't delete them or change them unless the permissions are changed to Read/Write.

Leaving a homegroup

Leaving a homegroup is as easy as joining one. If you leave a homegroup, you stop sharing files, folders, and devices with other members of the group, and you won't be able to access what is shared as part of that homegroup. You can create another homegroup or join the existing one again at any time.

In this exercise, you'll learn how to leave a homegroup to which your computer is joined.

13

SET UP
Open PC Settings.

1   In **PC Settings**, at the bottom of the window, click **Network**.

2   In the **Network** pane, click **HomeGroup**.

3   Scroll down until you find the **Leave** button and then click it.

Windows 8.1 takes a few seconds to leave the homegroup.

 CLEAN UP
Close PC Settings.

Your computer is no longer a part of the homegroup.

Using the Sharing Wizard to share with the homegroup

If you have set up a homegroup and you want to share something with other computers that have joined it, the Sharing Wizard makes the procedure simple. The sharing options are on the Share tab of File Explorer.

For any library or folder you select for sharing, you have the following options:

- **HomeGroup (View)**   This option shares the selected item with the homegroup and gives Read-Only permissions to all computers and devices in the homegroup. The item will be shared only when you are connected to the homegroup, and others will be able to view and read the shared item but not modify it or delete it.

- **HomeGroup (View And Edit)**   This shares the item with others in your homegroup and gives full permissions to modify it or delete it. The item will not be shared when you disconnect from the homegroup or connect to another network.

- **User Accounts Names**   You will see other user accounts existing in Windows 8.1, in the list. If you select a user account name, you will share the item (with Read-Only permissions) with that user account.

- **Specific People**   With this option, you can share the selected item with whomever you want, including with computers that are not part of the homegroup or specific user accounts. This option is described in more detail in the next section of this chapter.

In this exercise, you'll learn how to use the Sharing Wizard to share a folder with the homegroup.

13

SET UP

Open File Explorer and browse to the folder that you want to share. If the ribbon is collapsed, double-click it to expand it.

1　Select the folder without opening it.

2　Click the **Share** tab.

The list of sharing options opens.

3　In the **Share with** section, click **HomeGroup (View)**.

IMPORTANT Depending on what you have shared, you might see a File Sharing window asking you to confirm that you want to share the selected folder. If that is the case for you, click **Yes, Share The Item**. However, for most folders this window doesn't appear.

⊗ CLEAN UP
Repeat the procedure for all the items you want to share. When you have finished, close File Explorer.

The selected folder is now shared with the homegroup.

TIP If you could not reproduce the steps in this exercise, because the options available for sharing were different, most probably the Sharing Wizard is turned off on your computer. Read the first section in this chapter to learn how to turn it on.

Using the Sharing Wizard to share with specific people

If you have computers that are not running Windows 8.1, Windows 8, or Windows 7, you can use the Sharing Wizard to share libraries and folders with them without using the HomeGroup. However, the procedure takes slightly longer.

During the sharing procedure, a drop-down menu appears that shows all the user accounts defined on your computer, the homegroup you have joined, and a user account called Everyone. The homegroup user account represents all the computers and devices from your homegroup, whereas Everyone is a generic user account; this can be any user on the list. If you want to share something with computers that have different operating systems installed, it is best to share items by using the Everyone user account. The other operating systems will have an easier time accessing what you have shared.

13

By default, all the user accounts with which you choose to share are granted Read permissions to the shared item. If you want to change that, click the Permission Level assigned. A list appears showing the available permission levels.

In this exercise, you'll learn how to use the Sharing Wizard to share a folder with everyone and assign Read/Write permissions.

 SET UP
Open File Explorer and browse to the folder that you want to share. If the ribbon is collapsed, double-click it to expand it.

1 Select the folder without opening it.

2 Click the **Share** tab.

3 Scroll down the **Share With** list of options.

4   Click **Specific People**.

The File Sharing Wizard opens.

5   Click the drop-down list to see the user accounts with which you can share.

6   Select the user account named **Everyone**.

7   Click **Add**.

The user account is added to the existing accounts that appear below the drop-down list.

8   Click **Permission Level** for **Everyone** and select **Read/Write**.

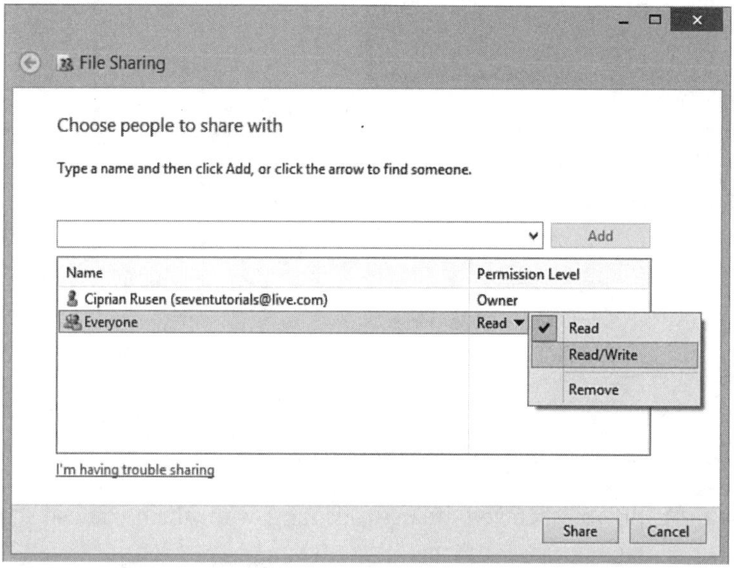

9   Click **Share**.

You are informed that the selected folder has been shared.

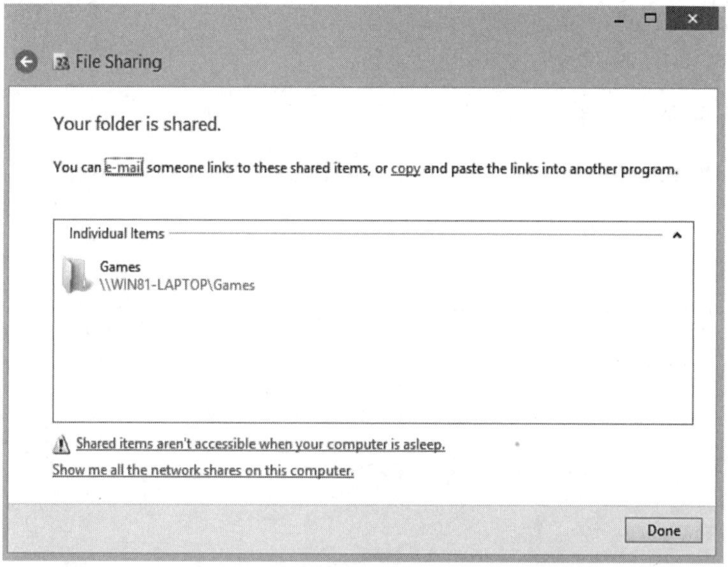

10   Click **Done**.

 CLEAN UP
Close File Explorer.

The selected folder is now shared with everyone on your network.

Stop sharing a library or folder

At some point in your networking experience, you might want to stop sharing a folder or library. The procedure for this is the same as for sharing it. The only difference is that you need to click the Stop Sharing button on the Share tab.

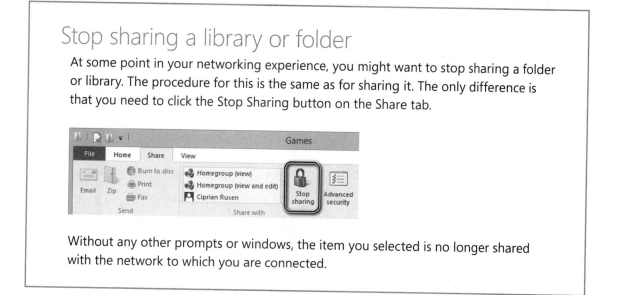

Without any other prompts or windows, the item you selected is no longer shared with the network to which you are connected.

Sharing a printer with computers on your network

Installed devices such as printers and scanners are accessible in the Devices And Printers window. From there, you can configure everything, including sharing devices with the other computers on your network.

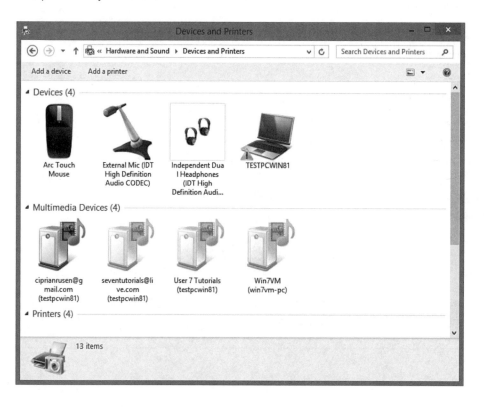

When sharing a printer, its default Share Name is its model name. If you want to change it, in the Properties dialog box for the printer, type a new name during the sharing procedure.

A shared printer on the network is shared with the entire network, including computers and devices that are outside the homegroup. If you want to share a printer with only the homegroup, check the instructions in the next section.

13

In this exercise, you'll learn how to share a printer with your network. The exercise and illustrations were created using a Canon Pixma MX410 printer; however, the same steps apply to almost any model of printer and should not vary much from what you see here. Please keep in mind that the number of printers and devices you see mentioned in the screenshots of this exercise will vary depending on your setup.

SET UP
Connect the printer to your computer, start it, and then install the latest drivers for it.

1   Open **Control Panel**.

2   In the **Hardware And Sound** section, click **View Devices And Printers**.

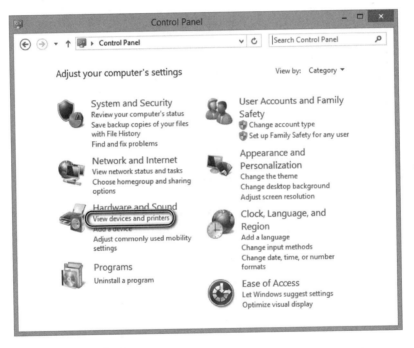

The Devices And Printers pane opens.

3   Scroll down to the **Printers** section to view the printers installed on your computer.

4   Right-click the printer that you want to share.

A shortcut menu opens.

5   Click **Printer Properties**.

The Printer Properties dialog box opens.

6   Click the **Sharing** tab.

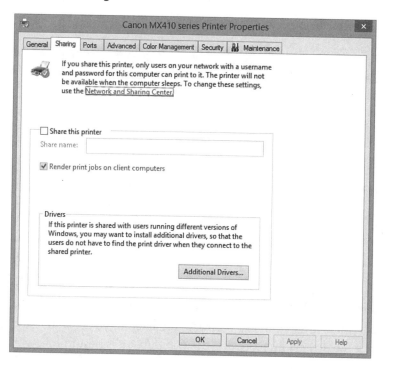

13

7   Select the **Share This Printer** check box.

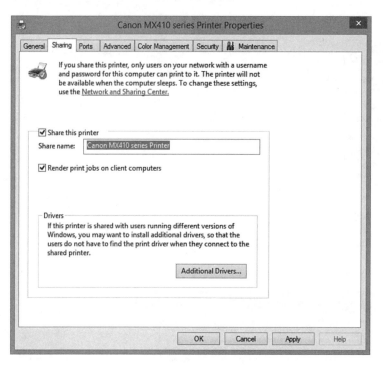

8   Click **OK**.

☒ CLEAN UP
Close Devices And Printers.

The printer is now shared with the other computers on your network.

Sharing a printer with your homegroup

Sharing a printer with your homegroup is very easy. However, the sharing procedure does not offer control over the specific devices being shared. With one setting, you can share with the homegroup all the printers and devices attached to your computer. If you want to share only one of the devices attached to your computer, it is best to follow the procedure detailed in the previous section.

In this exercise, you'll learn how to share all your connected printers and devices with others on the homegroup.

 SET UP
Open PC Settings.

1   In **PC Settings**, at the bottom of the window, click **Network**.

2   In the **Network** pane, click **HomeGroup**.

3   Look for the **Printers** switch.

4   Change the position of the switch from **Off** to **On**.

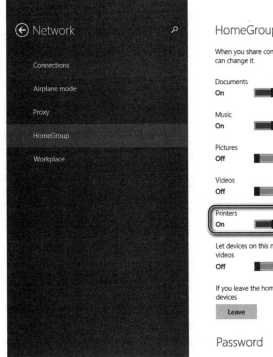

13

CLEAN UP

Close PC Settings.

All your printers and devices are now shared with the homegroup.

Stop sharing the printer

If you want to discontinue sharing a printer, use the same steps you took to share. For example, if you shared a printer with the network, to stop sharing it go through the steps detailed in the section "Sharing a printer with computers on your network" and clear the Share This Printer box at step 7. All the other steps are the same.

To stop sharing a printer with the homegroup, go through the same steps you took to share it and then, at step 4, turn the switch to Off instead of to On. All the other steps are identical.

Key points

- The appropriate network sharing settings are applied automatically to the network to which you are connected, depending on whether you turned on sharing when first connecting to it.

- The HomeGroup works only on computers running Windows 7, Windows 8, and Windows 8.1. It allows easy sharing of files, folders, libraries, and devices without having to type user names and passwords each time you want to access something that is shared over the network.

- To join a homegroup, you need to type the homegroup password defined on the computer on which it was created.

- A computer can join only one homegroup at a time. To join another homegroup, the computer must first leave the current one.

- You can share your printer with both your homegroup and the computers that are not in your homegroup but are part of the network to which you are connected.

- The Sharing Wizard makes it easy for you to share libraries and folders with your home network.

13

Chapter at a glance

Change

Change the UAC level, page 417

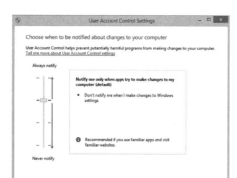

Work

Work with Windows Firewall, page 419

Restore

Restore Windows Firewall settings to their defaults, page 431

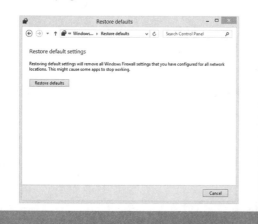

Use

Use Windows Defender to secure your system, page 433

Keeping Windows 8.1 safe and secure

14

IN THIS CHAPTER, YOU WILL LEARN HOW TO

- Work with the User Account Control.

- Use Windows Firewall.

- Use Windows Defender.

- Enhance the security of your passwords.

Security is very important in the modern era of computers and devices. Microsoft has spent quite a bit of effort to enhance the security provided by Windows 8.1. This operating system offers improved versions of all its main security tools: User Account Control (UAC), Windows Firewall, and Windows Defender.

In this chapter, you'll learn how the UAC works, how to tweak it, and why you should never turn it off. In addition, you'll learn the basics of working with Windows Firewall to secure your network and Internet traffic and about the new and improved Windows Defender and how to use it to keep your system safe from viruses and spyware. Finally, you'll learn how to improve your passwords to make it more difficult for unwanted people to use the Internet to access your Microsoft account, your email, and other important accounts.

PRACTICE FILES You don't need any practice files to complete the exercises in this chapter. For more information about practice file requirements, see the section "Using the practice files" In the Introduction of this book.

Understanding the UAC

The UAC is a security feature that was introduced in Windows Vista and improved in all subsequent versions of Windows. It is present in Windows 8.1, as well, and it helps prevent unauthorized changes to your computer. These changes can be initiated by users, apps, viruses, or other types of malware. UAC ensures that these changes are made only with approval from the administrator of the computer. If these changes are not approved by the administrator, they will never be executed, and the system will remain unchanged.

Unlike in Windows XP, desktop apps in Windows 8.1 do not run with administrator permissions and consequently cannot make any automatic changes to the operating system. When a desktop app wants to make system changes such as modifications that affect other user accounts, modifications of system files and folders, or installation of new software, UAC prompts the user to ask for permission.

If the user clicks No, the changes won't be performed. If the user clicks Yes, the app receives administrator permissions and makes the system changes it is programmed to make. These permissions will be granted until it stops running or is closed by the user. The next time it runs, it starts without receiving any administrator permissions.

To illustrate this process, the UAC algorithm is explained in the following diagram.

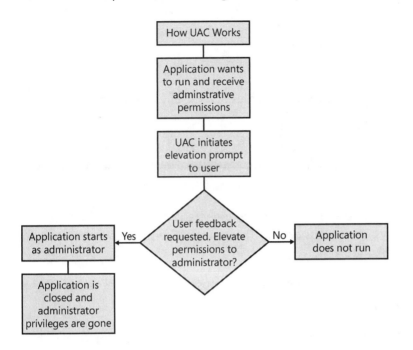

Many changes require administrator privileges and, depending on how UAC is configured on your computer, they can cause a UAC prompt to ask for permissions. Here are those changes:

- Running a desktop app as an administrator
- Changes to system-wide settings or to files in the Windows and Program Files folders
- Installing and uninstalling drivers and desktop apps
- Installing ActiveX controls
- Changing settings to Windows Firewall
- Changing UAC settings
- Configuring Windows Update
- Adding or removing user accounts

14

- Changing a user's account type

- Configuring parental controls

- Running the Task Scheduler

- Restoring backed-up system files

- Viewing or changing the folders and files of another user account

- Changing the system date and time

If UAC is turned off, any user and any desktop app can make any of these changes without a prompt for permissions. This would make it possible viruses and other forms of malware to infect and take control of your system more easily than when UAC is turned on.

When using Windows Store apps, UAC is never triggered because, by design, these apps cannot modify any system settings or files. Therefore, UAC prompts are displayed only when working with desktop apps.

Windows 8.1 has four UAC levels from which to choose. The differences between them are described in the following.

- **Always Notify**   At this level, you are notified before desktop apps make changes that require administrator permissions or before you or another user changes Windows settings. When a UAC prompt appears, your desktop is dimmed, and you must choose Yes or No before you can do anything else on your computer.

  Security Impact: This is the most secure setting but also the most annoying. If you do not like the UAC implementation from Windows Vista, you won't like this level either.

- **Notify Me Only When Apps Try To Make Changes To My Computer (Default)**   This is the default level; it only notifies you before desktop apps make changes to your computer that require administrator permissions. If you manually make changes to Windows, UAC doesn't notify you. This level is less annoying because it doesn't stop the user from making changes to the system; it only shows prompts if an app wants to make changes. When a UAC prompt appears, the desktop is dimmed, and you must choose Yes or No before you can do anything else on your computer.

  Security Impact: This is less secure because malicious desktop apps can be created that simulate the keystrokes or mouse moves of a user and change Windows settings. However, if you are using a good security solution, these scenarios should never occur.

- **Notify Me Only When Apps Try To Make Changes To My Computer (Do Not Dim My Desktop)** This level is identical to the preceding one except that when a UAC prompt appears, the desktop is not dimmed and other apps might be able to interfere with the UAC dialog box.

  Security Impact: This level is even less secure because it is easier for malicious desktop apps to simulate keystrokes or mouse moves that interfere with the UAC prompt. Again, a good security solution can compensate for the slight decrease in security.

- **Never Notify** At this level, UAC is turned off and offers no protection against unauthorized system changes. Any user or desktop app can make system changes without any prompts for permission.

  Security Impact: If you don't have a good security solution, you are very likely to have security problems. With UAC turned off, it is easier for malicious desktop apps to infect your computer and take control of it and its settings.

> **IMPORTANT** If you do not have administrator access, you can't set any exceptions, and the programs that do not comply with the standard set of rules are automatically blocked.

Changing the UAC level

Now that you know what this feature does and how it works, you'll learn how to configure it to offer the level of security you desire. In this exercise, you'll learn how to change the UAC level.

IMPORTANT Before changing the UAC level, review the previous section in this chapter. It is very important to understand the differences among the levels before making any changes.

➡ SET UP
Open Control Panel.

1   Click **System And Security**.

    The System And Security window opens.

2   In the **Action Center** section, click **Change User Account Control Settings**.

14

The User Account Control Settings window opens.

3   Move the slider to the UAC level you want to use.

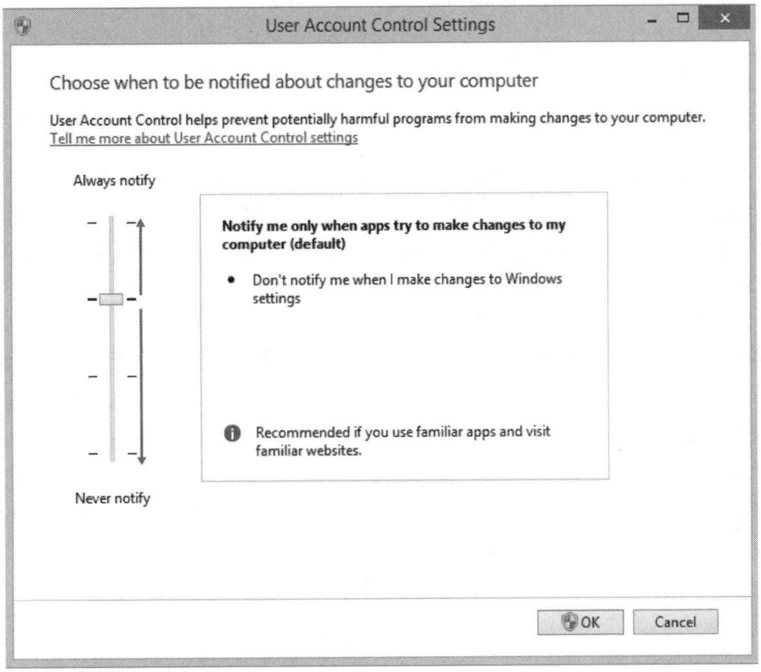

User Account Control Settings

Choose when to be notified about changes to your computer

User Account Control helps prevent potentially harmful programs from making changes to your computer.
Tell me more about User Account Control settings

Always notify

Notify me only when apps try to make changes to my computer (default)

- Don't notify me when I make changes to Windows settings

🛈 Recommended if you use familiar apps and visit familiar websites.

Never notify

OK   Cancel

4 Click **OK**.

5 Depending on the UAC level set before making the change, you might receive a UAC prompt. Click **Yes** if you do.

❌ CLEAN UP
Close the System And Security window.

The UAC is set to the level you selected and will provide you with the appropriate security level according to that choice.

14

Should I turn off UAC when I install my apps and turn it on afterward?

The biggest annoyance UAC causes is when you install all your daily desktop apps. At this time, you can receive many UAC prompts (one for each app you install). You might be tempted to turn off UAC temporarily while you install your desktop apps and turn it on again when you're finished. In some scenarios, this can be a bad idea. Certain desktop apps, which make many system changes, can fail to work if you turn on UAC after their installation even though they work if you install them with UAC turned on. These failures happen because when UAC is turned off, the virtualization techniques UAC uses for all apps are inactive. This causes certain user settings and files to be installed to a different place and no longer work when UAC is turned back on. To avoid these problems, it is better to leave UAC turned on at all times.

Using the Windows Firewall

Windows Firewall is a security desktop app built in to Windows that helps block unauthorized access to your computer while permitting authorized communications to and from your computer. It has been improved in each new version of Windows.

With Windows 8.1, this tool can filter both inbound and outbound traffic or set rules and exceptions, depending on the type of network to which you're connected. If you aren't using a third-party security suite that includes a firewall, it is highly recommended that you use Windows Firewall because it provides a good level of security.

Windows Firewall has a predefined set of rules that are applied as soon as it is turned on. By default, it allows you to do many things: browse the Internet; use instant messaging apps; connect to a homegroup; share files, folders, and devices with other computers; and so on. The rules are applied differently depending on the network profile set for your active network connection.

SEE ALSO For more information about network profiles, see Chapter 11, "Connecting to a network and the Internet."

Most apps you install on your computer automatically add an exception to Windows Firewall so that they receive network and Internet access as soon as you start them. However, if they don't add such an exception, Windows Firewall asks if you want to allow them access to the network. At this point, you receive a security alert similar to the following one, in which you are asked to select the network profiles to which you allow access for the app: private networks (such as home and work networks) or public networks (such as those in airports, coffee shops, and so on).

By default, Windows Firewall selects the check box relevant to the network you are currently using. However, you can select either of the options or both, depending on what you want to do. When you've decided, click Allow Access, and the desktop app is allowed to communicate on the selected type(s) of network. To block access, just click Cancel.

IMPORTANT If you do not have administrator access, you can't set any exceptions, and the apps that do not comply with the standard set of rules are automatically blocked.

Windows Firewall is turned on by default in Windows 8.1, and it runs silently in the background as a service. It prompts you whenever you need to make a decision, and you don't need to open it unless you want to see its status or configure it to better meet your needs.

To open Windows Firewall, on the Start screen type firewall, and then click the Windows Firewall search result. As an alternative, you can open Control Panel and click System And Security to open the System And Security window, which has all tools and configuration options available for this category.

Click Windows Firewall to open the Windows Firewall desktop app. In the center of its window, you can see information about the status of your network connections and how Windows Firewall is set for each type of connection.

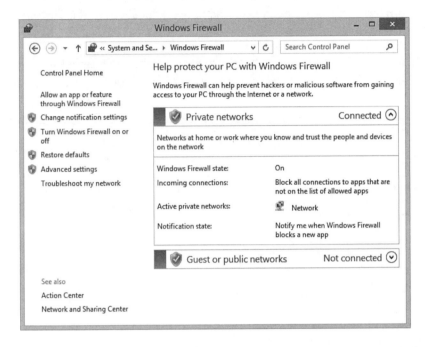

In the left column are links to different configuration options for Windows Firewall and other tools such as the Action Center.

14

Turning Windows Firewall off or on

By default, Windows Firewall is turned on for both types of network profiles, Private and Public. You can turn it on or off for one or both the network locations in the Customize Settings window.

If you choose to install a third-party security app, such as a complete Internet security suite or another firewall, it is best to disable Windows Firewall so that it doesn't create conflicts and problems.

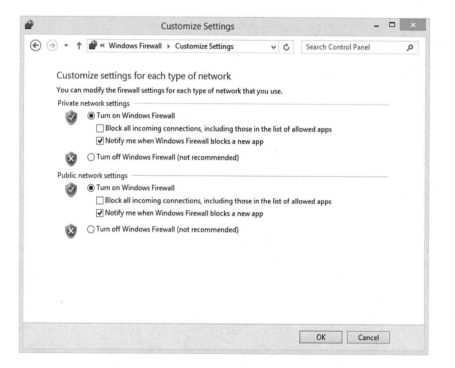

Beneath the Turn On Windows Firewall option, there are two other settings you can choose. The first is to block all incoming connections to your computer. Don't choose this unless you want your computer to be unavailable to anyone or any app. The second is to receive notifications when Windows Firewall blocks a new app. You should select this option; otherwise, you won't know why an app doesn't access the network or the Internet correctly.

You can only turn Windows Firewall on or off if you are logged on as an administrator. This setting will apply to all user accounts defined on your computer. Also, if you turn off Windows Firewall, make sure your user account and others have proper security alternatives installed.

In this exercise, you'll learn how to turn off Windows Firewall.

 SET UP
Log on by using a user account that has administrator rights and then open Windows Firewall.

1   In the left column, click **Turn Windows Firewall On Or Off**.

The Customize Settings window, which shows whether the Windows Firewall is turned on, opens.

2   Select **Turn Off Windows Firewall (Not Recommended)** for both **Private Network Settings** and **Public Network Settings**.

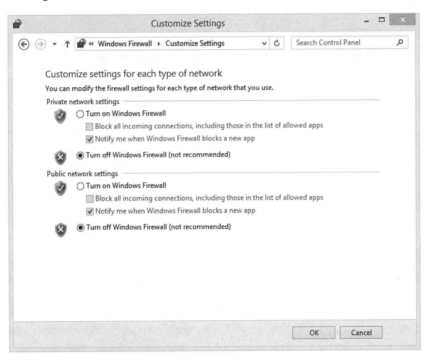

3   To apply your settings, click **OK**.

 CLEAN UP
Close the Windows Firewall window.

To turn Windows Firewall on, perform the same steps. However, in step 2, you select Turn On Windows Firewall for both Private Network Settings and Public Network Settings.

14

Customizing the list of allowed apps

The Allowed Apps window contains all the apps that are allowed to go through Windows Firewall. By default, you cannot edit the list. Click the Change Settings button to edit the list of allowed apps. The button will then be dimmed, and you will be able to edit the list of allowed apps, programs, and features.

The check boxes for some apps are selected, indicating that the rules defined for those apps are active and used by Windows Firewall. The apps with with clear check boxes don't have any active rules used by Windows Firewall. For those apps for which Windows Firewall is active, certain Private and Public check boxes are also selected. If a check box is selected in any of these columns, it means that the rule defined for that app is applied to the network profile that is selected. Some apps have rules for one network profile, whereas others have rules for both. The rules are active only for the network profiles that are selected.

With Windows Firewall, you can edit its communication rules so that you can permit or deny network access for certain apps or services. In this exercise, you'll learn how to customize the list of allowed apps.

➡ SET UP
Log on by using a user account that has administrator rights and then open Windows Firewall.

1   In the left column, click **Allow An App Or Feature Through Windows Firewall**.

       The Allowed Apps window opens.

2   Click **Change Settings**.

3   Select the app whose permissions you want to change.

14

4   Click **Details**.

A window displaying the apps properties opens.

5   Read the information to confirm that this is the app whose permissions you want changed and then click **OK**.

6   Clear the **Private** and **Public** check boxes for the app to block its access to both network profiles, and then click **OK**.

⊗ CLEAN UP
Close the Windows Firewall window.

The changes you made for the selected app are now applied.

TIP For the Windows apps that are bundled with the operating system (for example, Bing Food & Drink, Music, Mail, Maps, and so on), the Details button is not available and you cannot view more infomation about these apps. But, you can edit the rules applied for them.

Adding new apps to the allowed list

You can easily add new apps to the list of apps allowed through Windows Firewall. In this exercise, you'll learn how to add new apps to the allowed list.

➡ SET UP
Log on by using a user account that has administrator rights and then open Windows Firewall.

1   In the left column, click the **Allow An App Or Feature Through Windows Firewall**.

The Allowed Apps window opens.

2   Click **Change Settings** if required.

3   Click **Allow Another App**.

The Add An App window opens.

4   Select the app that you want to add and then then click **Network Types**.

The Choose Network Types window opens.

NOTE If you don't find the app you want to add in the Add An App list, click Browse to locate it. Select it and then continue with the instructions in this exercise.

5   Select the network locations through which you want to allow the app to communicate, and then click **OK**.

14

6   In the Add An App window, click **Add**.

You return to the Allowed Apps window, in which you can see the newly added app on the list.

7   Click **OK**.

CLEAN UP
Repeat this procedure for all the apps you want to add and then close the Windows Firewall window.

The change is now applied to the list of active rules Windows Firewall uses.

Removing apps from the allowed list

Removing apps from the list of allowed apps through Windows Firewall or disabling access to certain types of networks is easy. Both tasks are done from the Allowed Apps window. If you want to disable a rule allowing access to a certain app or feature, simply clear the check box to the left side of its name. Windows Firewall will no longer use it.

If you only want to disable network and Internet access for an app when connected to a certain type of network profile, clear the check box in the column of that network profile. For example, if you want to prevent an app from receiving network and Internet access when you are connected to a public network, clear the check box in the Public column. If the Private column is selected for that app, it will only have access to private networks.

When removing entries from the allowed list, keep in mind that you can remove only apps and entries that were not included with Windows 8.1. For example, you cannot remove an entry about Windows Media Player because it is part of Windows 8.1, although you can re-move an entry about a third-party app you installed, such as Steam or uTorrent. The entries that are included in the default configuration of Windows Firewall can only be disabled, not removed.

In this exercise, you'll learn how to remove an app from the allowed list.

→ SET UP

Log on by using a user account that has administrator rights and then open Windows Firewall.

1   In the left column, click the **Allow An App Or Feature Through Windows Firewall**.

The Allowed Apps window opens.

2   Click **Change Settings**, if required.

3   Select the app or feature that you want to remove, and then click **Remove**.

14

4   Click **Remove**.

You are asked to confirm the removal.

5   Click **Yes**.

You return to the Allowed Apps window.

6   Click **OK**.

⊗ CLEAN UP
Close the Windows Firewall window.

The change is now applied to the list of active rules Windows Firewall uses.

Restoring the Windows Firewall default settings

If you have used this tool for a long time and you have made many changes to its settings, the chances are good that some things might stop working. In such cases, it is best to reset all rules to the default settings and values created by Microsoft. Then, you can start from the beginning, defining the rules that you want to apply to your apps so that everything works as it should.

In this exercise, you'll learn how to restore the default settings of Windows Firewall.

➡ SET UP
Log on by using a user account that has administrator rights and then open Windows Firewall.

1   In the left column, click **Restore Defaults**.

The Restore Defaults window opens.

2   Read the information shown and then click **Restore Defaults**.

You are asked to confirm your choice.

> **Restore Defaults Confirmation**
>
> ⚠ Restoring the default settings will delete all settings of Windows Firewall that you have made since Windows was installed. This may cause some apps to stop working
>
> Do you want to continue?
>
> [Yes]   [No]

3   Click **Yes**.

You are returned to the Windows Firewall window.

 CLEAN UP
Close the Windows Firewall window.

All the Windows Firewall settings you created are deleted. Everything is now reset to the initial settings and values as they were when Windows 8.1 was installed on your computer.

Using Windows Defender

Windows Defender was originally a tool that provided protection only against spyware threats. Then Microsoft introduced Microsoft Security Essentials, a product that added antivirus protection. It quickly became one of the most popular free anti-malware products among Windows users. With Windows 8, Microsoft has decided to include the features initially released in Microsoft Security Essentials in the earlier Windows Defender product. In Windows 8.1, further improvements have been made to this product.

Windows Defender now provides basic anti-malware protection that will keep you safe from viruses, spyware, and other types of malware. It doesn't compare in number of features and efficiency with most commercial security solutions, but it is one of the best free security solutions you can find for Windows. Windows Defender is turned on by default in Windows 8.1, and it can be launched by searching for the word "defender" on the Start screen and clicking the appropriate search result.

The Windows Defender interface is simple and easy to use. At the top of the window, four tabs are available:

- **Home** This tab shows an overview of Windows Defender: whether any threats and problems were detected, whether the real-time protection is turned on, and whether the virus and spyware definitions are up to date. On the right side, you can start a manual scan for malware; on the bottom, you can view when the last scan was made.

Green means no problems were detected.
Red means problems were found, while
orange means there are warnings to consider.

Options for starting
a manual scan.

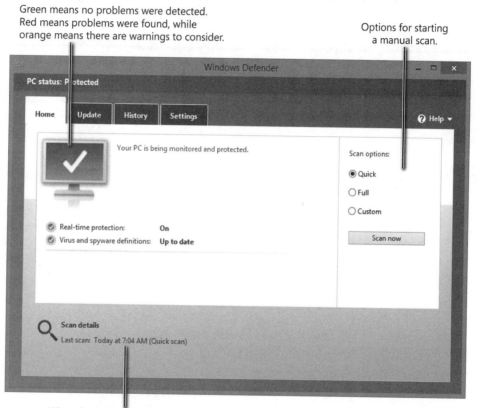

When the last scan was made and
what type of scan it was.

14

- **Update** This tab displays details about the latest update of definitions Windows Defender made. You can also manually start an update if the definitions are more than a day or two old.

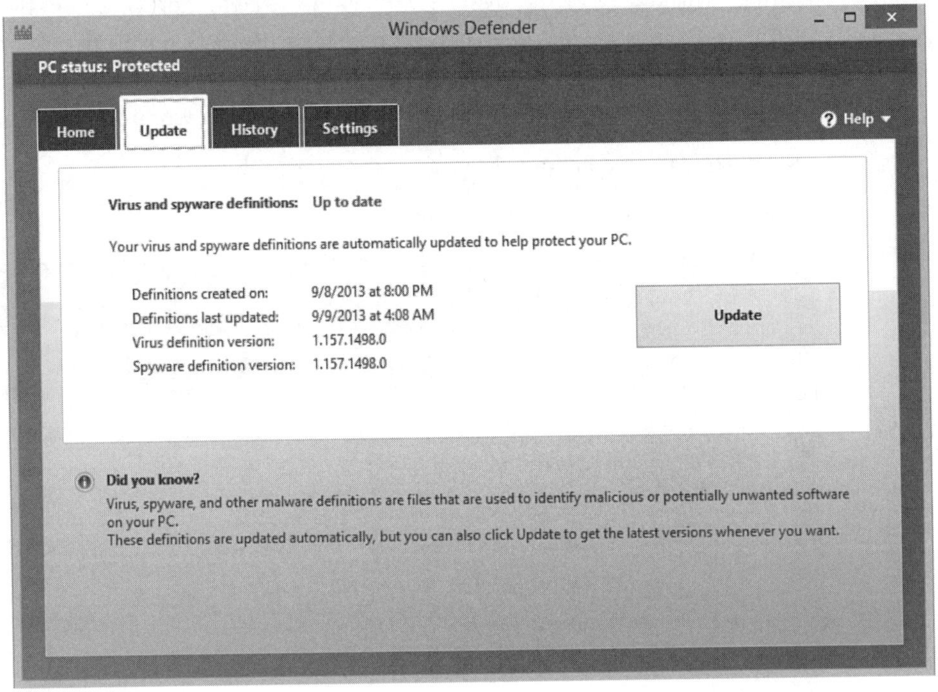

Windows Defender

PC status: Protected

| Home | Update | History | Settings | | ❓ Help ▾ |

Virus and spyware definitions: Up to date

Your virus and spyware definitions are automatically updated to help protect your PC.

Definitions created on:	9/8/2013 at 8:00 PM
Definitions last updated:	9/9/2013 at 4:08 AM
Virus definition version:	1.157.1498.0
Spyware definition version:	1.157.1498.0

Update

ⓘ **Did you know?**

Virus, spyware, and other malware definitions are files that are used to identify malicious or potentially unwanted software on your PC.
These definitions are updated automatically, but you can also click Update to get the latest versions whenever you want.

- **History** This tab is for viewing details about the threats Windows Defender has detected. You can view the items that were quarantined, the items that you allowed to run despite the recommendations received from Windows Defender, and all the items that were detected as malicious.

14

- **Settings** On this tab, you can customize how Windows Defender runs. You can turn on or off its real-time protection engine; exclude files, locations, or processes from being scanned; tweak more advanced settings; choose whether you want to join the Microsoft Active Protection Service; or completely disable Windows Defender.

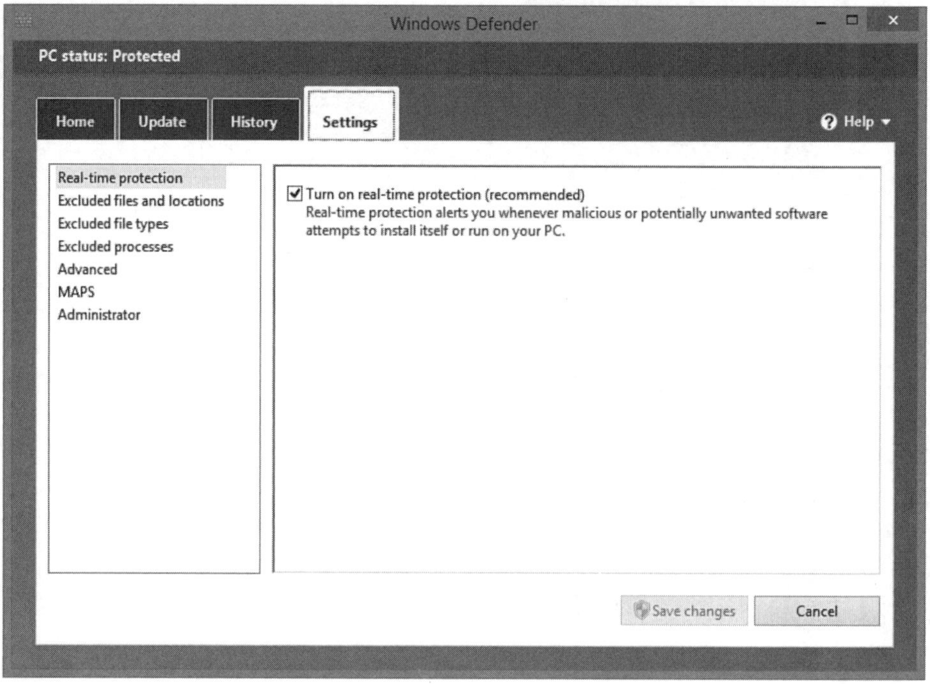

Removing quarantined files

Windows Defender automatically scans all the files and folders through which you browse. If a threat is identified, it is immediately quarantined, and you are informed of this action.

Each time you see a warning similar to the following one, Windows Defender cleaned some threats it detected.

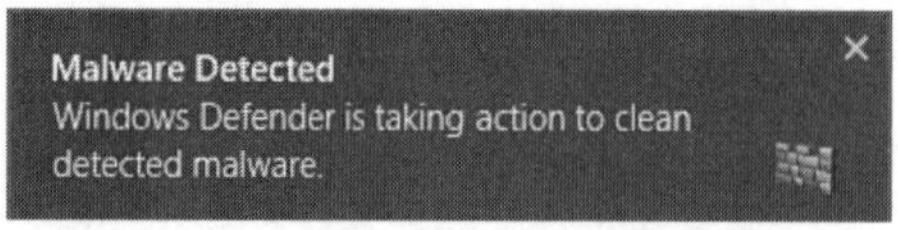

Detected threats are automatically isolated and placed into quarantine. You can only access the items that were quarantined from Windows Defender and decide whether you want to remove them completely from your system or keep them and set Windows Defender to allow them. However, to remove them or keep them you need to have administrator permissions.

In this exercise, you'll learn how to access the items that were detected as malicious by Windows Defender and remove them from your computer.

 SET UP
Log on by using a user account that has administrator rights and then open Windows Defender.

1   Click the **History** tab.

2   Choose **All Detected Items**.

3   Click **View Details** to see all the items that were detected as malware.

Windows Defender

PC status: Protected

| Home | Update | **History** | Settings | | ? Help ▾ |

View the items that were detected as potentially harmful and the actions that you took on them:

○ Quarantined items
   Items that were prevented from running but not removed from your PC.
○ Allowed items
   Items that you've allowed to run on your PC.
◉ All detected items
   Items that were detected on your PC.

To help protect user privacy, these items are hidden.
Click View details to see the items.

View details

4   Scroll through the infected items that were detected and read the information being displayed, to learn more about them.

	Windows Defender	_ □ ✕

PC status: Protected

Home	Update	**History**	Settings		❓ Help ▼

View the items that were detected as potentially harmful and the actions that you took on them:

○ Quarantined items
    Items that were prevented from running but not removed from your PC.
○ Allowed items
    Items that you've allowed to run on your PC.
◉ **All detected items**
    Items that were detected on your PC.

Detected item	Alert level	Date	Action taken	
☑ ⊗ Rogue:Win32/FakeDef	Severe	9/9/2013 5:19 AM	Removed	
☑ ⊗ Trojan:Win32/Meredrop	Severe	9/9/2013 5:19 AM	Removed	
☑ ⊗ Trojan:Win32/Provis!rts	High	9/9/2013 5:19 AM	Quarantined	
☑ ⊗ VirTool:Win32/Obfuscator.C	Severe	9/9/2013 5:19 AM	Quarantined	

Category: Backdoor

Description: This program provides remote access to the computer it is installed on.

Recommended action: Remove this software immediately.

⊗ Remove all   🛡 Allow item

5   Click **Remove All**.

 CLEAN UP
Close Windows Defender.

All the items that were detected as threats have now been completely removed from your computer.

Don't ignore the warnings and recommendations from SmartScreen filter

In Chapter 5, the section "Understanding the SmartScreen filter in Internet Explorer" covers in detail how the SmartScreen feature included in Internet Explorer and Windows 8.1 can help prevent security problems with your computer or device.

This chapter reinforces that recommendation to consider the warning messages from SmartScreen filter.

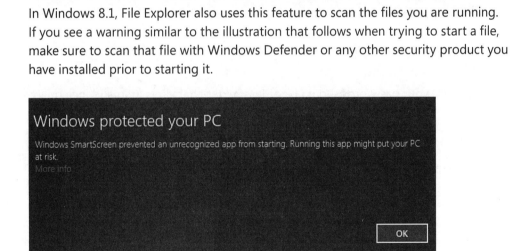

In Windows 8.1, File Explorer also uses this feature to scan the files you are running. If you see a warning similar to the illustration that follows when trying to start a file, make sure to scan that file with Windows Defender or any other security product you have installed prior to starting it.

Following this recommendation will help keep your Windows system safe and secure.

14

Improving your password habits

No matter how good the security products you are using are, you are still vulnerable to many security problems if your habits related to password use are poor. Many people tend to use the same one-two-three passwords everywhere. This is a sure recipe for security problems, including security problems with your Microsoft account, your Facebook and Google accounts, and any other accounts. If you use the same password everywhere, a malicious user might break into a forum or social website you are using and steal your password from there. That user can then use the same password and the email address with which you registered to access more of your personal data and information from your Inbox, accounts on social networks, and so on.

To make sure it is much more difficult for unwanted parties to access your Windows-based computer, your Microsoft account, your email inbox, and any online services you are using, consider the following recommendations regarding password use.

- Do not use passwords with fewer than six characters. They are especially easy to break.

- Ideally, your passwords should be at least eight characters long and include letters, numbers, and special characters such as +, #, $, and so on.

- Do not use the same password twice or more.

- Having different passwords for different accounts can be difficult to manage, so using password management solutions such as LastPass, KeePass, or Roboform is also recommended. You can find them easily with a search on Bing. These solutions help you identify your duplicate passwords, change them to new random passwords, generate secure passwords automatically, and store them safely so that you can use them whenever needed and not lose them again.

Reasons to consider commercial security solutions

Windows Defender together with Windows Firewall and Internet Explorer can provide a good level of security. If you are not willing or able to invest in security software, they are the best free security tools available for Windows 8.1, and you won't need to install other free products.

However, if you want the maximum level of security possible and premium features such as anti-spam, ad blockers for your Internet browser, remote location of your computers and devices if they are stolen, the possibility to command a remote wipe of your data (if your computers and devices are stolen), and more advanced malware detection algorithms and other features, it is best to consider purchasing and installing security products provided by specialized vendors. The best way to be fully protected is to use a complete security package, generally called an Internet Security Suite. These packages include antivirus, anti-spyware, and firewall protection plus other security modules such as the ones previously mentioned.

Before making a choice, it is best to understand which options are available. To make an informed decision, it is recommend that you check the following Internet sources.

- **Antimalware apps for Windows *(http://bit.ly/15Q3xQU)*** The Compatibility Center also lists the security software providers that offer solutions compatible with Windows. Search for the security product you are interested in, and you can easily view whether it is compatible with Windows 8.1.

- **Security for Everyone at 7 Tutorials *(http://bit.ly/12jjvrs)*** The 7 Tutorials website provides a series of reviews for Internet security suites. The team from the website regularly tests the latest offerings from both a security and a usability perspective. The aim of the team is to highlight solutions that provide the best mix of effective security and user friendliness.

14

- **AV Comparatives** *(http://av-comparatives.org)*   This is the website of an independent security organization that regularly tests the quality of security provided by antivirus products. Its tests are very professional and evaluate all the important security aspects for an antivirus solution. If you want to know which security company has the best detection engine for viruses, this website is the place to visit.

- **AV Test** *(http://www.av-test.org)*   This website is run by the AV-Test GmbH company, which offers security testing and consulting services. It runs regular reviews of the latest security products on the market and publishes the results of its evaluations. Just like AV Comparatives, this website is a great destination for learning how effective the latest security offerings are.

Key points

- Never turn off UAC; it's a key feature that contributes to a good level of security on your system.

- Windows Firewall filters both inbound and outbound traffic depending on the type of network to which you are connected. It is an important tool in securing your network and Internet traffic.

- Windows Defender now includes both antivirus and anti-spyware protection.

- Improving your password habits is a key component of a secure computing experience.

14

Chapter at a glance

Check

Check for Windows updates, page 446

Learn

Learn File History and how to use it, page 451

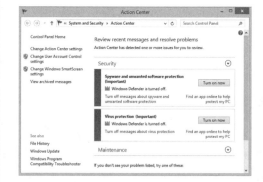

Restore

Restore your system to a previous state with System Restore, page 465

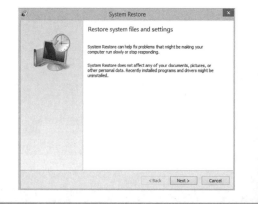

Use

Use the Action Center to prevent problems, page 470

Preventing problems

15

IN THIS CHAPTER, YOU WILL LEARN HOW TO

- Keep your system up to date.

- Check for Windows updates and install them.

- Turn on File History.

- Restore files by using File History.

- Use System Restore to revert Windows 8.1 to a previous state.

- Use the Action Center to prevent problems.

Prevention is an important part of having a safe and pleasant computing experience. Windows 8.1 offers a few tools to help you stay away from trouble for as long as possible and, if you do have trouble, restore your lost user files.

The first and most important tool for preventing problems is Windows Update. In this chapter, you'll learn about its role in keeping your computer running smoothly, how it works, and how to use it to keep your system up to date. You'll learn how to use the File History feature in Windows 8.1 to make automated backups of your user folders, libraries, and files and to restore files from those backups. In addition, you'll learn about System Restore and how to use it to revert to an earlier and more stable state if you encounter problems. Finally, you'll see how to use the Action Center to stay informed about the maintenance and security of your system so that you can spot problems before they have a major impact on your system.

PRACTICE FILES You don't need any practice files to complete the exercises in this chapter. For more information about practice file requirements, see the section "Using the practice files" in the Introduction of this book.

Keeping your system up to date by using Windows Update

Keeping your system up to date is important for maintaining it as secure and trouble-free as possible. Viruses and other forms of malware that exploit security vulnerabilities in Windows and other operating systems appear on a daily basis. Being up to date means having fewer security issues and fewer chances for your computer to become infected and exploited by unauthorized parties.

Windows Update also includes stability and compatibility fixes that solve problems you might encounter with your system; other updates can add functionality. Another important type of update is drivers for your computer's components. Windows Update automatically installs the newest versions of signed drivers for your system's components, which keep your system's performance at optimum levels.

All these are good reasons for you to have Windows Update turned on at all times and configured to install the most important updates automatically. It is enabled by default in Windows 8.1, and it should be active and working on your system. The only exceptions are business computers and devices on which the updates and the update policy are handled by the IT support staff.

You can find Windows Update in both PC Settings and Control Panel. In PC Settings, you can view information about available updates, check for new updates manually, install those that are available, view your update history, and choose how updates get installed in Windows 8.1.

In Control Panel, open System And Security and then Windows Update.

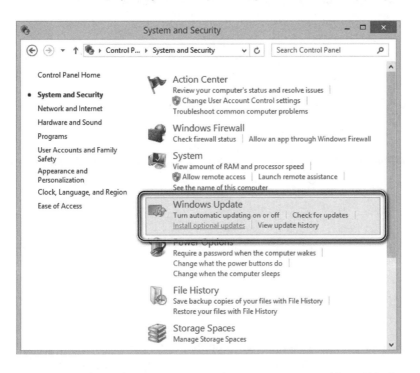

From Control Panel, you can customize many aspects of how Windows Update works by using the options presented in the column on the left, which are described here:

- **Check For Updates**   With this option, you can check for new updates manually.

- **Change Settings**   This option opens a list of all the Windows Update settings that you can customize.

- **View Update History**   This option shows a list of all the updates that have been installed on your system, with complete information about what they do, when they were installed, and so on.

- **Restore Hidden Updates**   With this option, you can restore updates that have been hidden and marked as unavailable for your system.

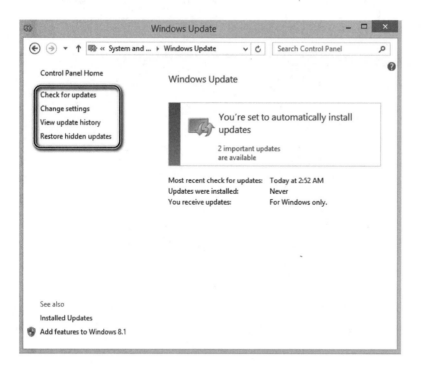

If you are using Windows 8.1 on a traditional computer, don't hesitate to experiment with using and configuring Windows Update from Control Panel. You will be able to learn a lot about the way it works and tweak its behavior in detail.

Checking for and installing available updates

Windows handles the installation of updates automatically. However, you can check for updates manually and install them at any time.

In this exercise, you'll learn how to check for updates manually and install the available updates from PC Settings.

 SET UP
Ensure that you have a working Internet connection and then open PC Settings.

1   In **PC Settings**, click **Update And Recovery** and then click **Windows Update**.

Windows Update

You're set to automatically install updates.

We found new updates today, and we'll install them for you soon. We'll continue to check daily for newer updates.

View details

Check now

View your update history

Choose how updates get installed

2   Click **Check Now** and wait a few seconds for the process to finish.

3   Click **View Details** to see a list of the updates found.

⊖ View details

Total Selected: 6.4 MB

Install

☑ Select all important updates

Important

Windows Defender

☑ Definition Update for Windows Defender - KB2267602 (Definition 1.157.1798.0)   Details

Windows 8.1

☑ Security Update for Internet Explorer Flash Player for Windows 8.1 (KB2880289)   Details

4   Select the updates that you want to install and then click **Install.**

❌ CLEAN UP

Close PC Settings at any time, even if the updates are still being downloaded and installed.

The download and installation process for all the available updates is handled in the background by Windows Update. Its window does not need to remain open. You can continue your normal computing activities while the updates are installed.

Using File History in Windows 8.1

File History was introduced in Windows 8. With it, users can back up the files in their Libraries, Contacts, Favorites, and Desktop. The backup is handled automatically by Windows after this feature is turned on and the backup location is available.

File History backs up only your users' libraries and the aforementioned folders. If you want to have file copies made for other folders, you must include them in one of your user libraries.

SEE ALSO To learn more about libraries and how to create a library and add folders to it, see Chapter 4, "Organizing files and folders."

File History also stores the versions you create for any file, depending on how you set it, so you can revert to a previous version of a file if you need to.

File History works best with external storage devices such as hard disks or large USB memory sticks that have sufficient space for the file copies. You can also make copies on network locations such as folders from another computer or a home server if you have one available.

File copies can be restored at any time on the same computer or on other Windows devices and computers. This can be useful if your system crashes or encounters problems with data corruption. By using File History, you can ensure that your important data is always backed up and available.

The file copies are made on the target drive (or network location) by using the following folder structure: File History\<Your User Account Name>\Your Computer Name. There, you will find the following two folders:

- **Configuration**   Files with File History settings
- **Data**   The file copies

You can access File History both from PC Settings and Control Panel. PC settings offers a simplified version with which you can only turn this feature on or off, select the drive where the backup is made and perform a manual backup.

The File History window in Control Panel is organized as follows:

- On the left is a column of links that gives you access to different configuration options.

- In the center you can view the File History status: on or off.

- In the center you can also see where file copies are stored.

- Below that you can view when the last file copies were made.

- On the right is a button for turning File History on and off.

Access to different
configuration options

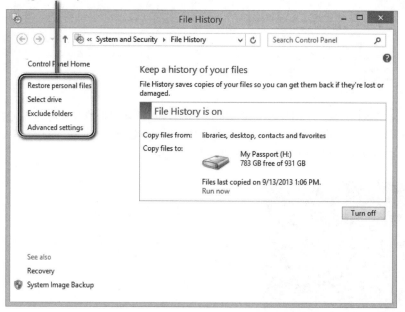

The column on the left side of the File History window has the following links:

- **Restore Personal Files**   Starts the wizard for restoring files using the existing copies. This will be covered in a step-by-step exercise later in this chapter.

- **Select Drive**   Use this to change the drive on which file copies are made. You can also add a network location if that suits your needs better.

Exclude Folders Use this to exclude specific folders and libraries from backup by File History.

- **Advanced Settings**   Click this link to access and change the following settings.

  - **Save Copies Of Files**   Sets how often file copies are made. The default is to save copies of files every hour. The interval can be changed to almost anything, from every 10 minutes to daily.

  - **Size Of Offline Cache**   Sets the percentage of space that file copies can occupy on the target storage device. The default is 5 percent. It can be changed to values ranging from 2 percent to 20 percent.

  - **Keep Saved Versions**   Sets how long you want to keep the different versions of files. The default is to keep file versions forever. It can be set to keep versions until space is needed on the target storgae device or for a set time ranging from one month to two years.

  - **Recommend This Drive**   Enabling this setting can be done only if your computer is part of a homegroup. When enabled, your storage drive is recommended to other homegroup members so that they can store their data by using File History.

Turning File History on or off

After File History is turned on, it automatically starts creating copies of your files based on its default schedule settings. If copies were created, you are shown the date and time when they were last copied.

One important aspect to keep in mind is that File History is turned on only for your own user account. If you want the files in other user accounts on the same Windows 8.1–based computer or device to be backed up, turn on File History for each account.

In this exercise, you'll learn how to turn on File History in Windows 8.1, from PC Settings.

SET UP
Plug in an external hard disk or a USB memory stick, wait for Windows 8.1 to detect it, and then open PC Settings.

1   In **PC Settings**, click **Update And Recovery.**

2   Click **File History.**

Save copies of your files automatically

Automatically back up copies of your personal files on this PC in Documents, Music, Pictures, Videos, and Desktop to a drive so you can get them back if they're lost or damaged.

File History
On   .

Back up your personal files on this PC to
My Passport (H:), 783 GB free of 931 GB

Select a different drive

Your files were last backed up on 9/13/2013 1:06 PM.

Back up now

3   Slide the File History switch to **On.**

CLEAN UP
Close PC Settings and leave the external drive plugged into your computer or device.

File History is now turned on and will automatically save copies of your files according to its default settings and when the external drive is available for making the copies. You can turn off File History by using the steps in the preceding exercise but, instead, slide the File History switch to Off.

Restoring files by using File History

It's easy to use File History to restore files, and you can do it at any time. You can restore complete folders and libraries as well as individual files. If you want to restore a library, you select it; If you want to restore only one file, browse to its location and select it.

To select more than one item, press and hold the Ctrl key on your keyboard while selecting each item with the mouse.

You can restore files to the location on your computer from which files were initially copied or to a different location. If you want to restore a file to a different location, select it, click the Options button, and then, on the menu that appears, click Restore To.

In this exercise, you'll learn how to restore folders and libraries previously backed up by using File History. You'll restore individual files by using the same steps but selecting files instead of folders or libraries.

➡ SET UP

Plug in the drive on which your File History is stored, wait for Windows 8.1 to detect it, and then open Control Panel.

1   Click **System And Security** and then **File History.**

The File History window opens.

2   Click **Restore Personal Files** to open the File History wizard.

3   Select the libraries and folders that you want to restore.

4   Click the **Restore** button to start the restoration procedure.

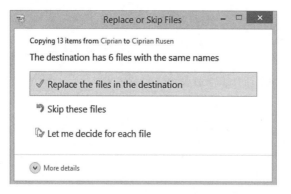

Restore
button

You are asked to confirm that you want to replace the existing files with the ones from your backup.

5   Click **Replace The Files In The Destination** and wait for the files to be copied.

After the copying process completes, a File Explorer window opens, showing the files, folders, and libraries you copied.

CLEAN UP

Close File Explorer and the File History window.

The selected folders and libraries are now restored to their original location.

Using System Restore

System Restore is a time-tested and useful desktop app that can restore your system and settings to a previous state. It can be used when you encounter problems and you need to revert quickly to a previously working state without removing all of your installed desktop apps, as is the case when using the Refresh Your PC feature.

This feature is turned on by default in Windows 8.1 for the partition in which the operating system is installed. It automatically creates a new restore point each time you install a new app or make important changes to your system such as installing a long list of updates and drivers. These restore points can then be used to restore your system to an earlier but stable state if you encounter some stability or performance issues later.

System Properties

Computer Name | Hardware | Advanced | System Protection | Remote

Use system protection to undo unwanted system changes.

System Restore

You can undo system changes by reverting your computer to a previous restore point.

[System Restore...] ⟶ Restore your system by using a previous restore point

Protection Settings

Available Drives	Protection
Local Disk (C:) (System)	On

Configure restore settings, manage disk space, and delete restore points.

[Configure...] ⟶ Configure System Restore

Create a restore point right now for the drives that have system protection turned on.

[Create...] ⟶ Create a manual restore point

[OK] [Cancel] [Apply]

To access System Restore settings, in the System Properties window, click the System Protection tab. The tool is straightforward and easy to use. Following are descriptions of the items you need to set up restore points:

- Use the System Restore button to start the wizard for restoring your system by using a previous restore point.

- The Protection Settings section contains a list of all the partitions available on your computer or device. You can see whether the System Restore protection is turned on or off in each partition.

- When you select a partition, you can change its protection settings by using the Configure button.

- Use the Create button when you want to create a manual system restore point.

Having System Restore turned on is a good prevention practice. If you encounter issues, the first and easiest step is to use this tool to restore your system to a previous and more stable state.

Starting System Restore

In Windows 8.1, the System Restore tool is hidden behind menus and options, so it is not easy to find. In this exercise, you'll learn how to start System Restore.

 SET UP
Open Control Panel.

1   Click **System And Security**.

2   In the **System And Security** window, click **System**.

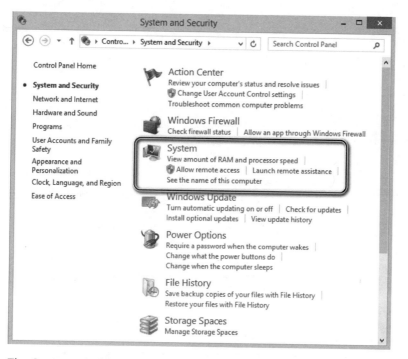

The System window opens, presenting information about your system's hardware and software configuration.

3   In the left column, click **System Protection**.

The System Properties window opens, in which you can start and configure System Restore.

⊗ CLEAN UP
When done working with System Restore, close the System Properties window.

The System Properties window is opened directly at the System Protection tab, where you can find System Restore.

Restoring to a previous state by using System Restore

If you have installed some new drivers that make your system unstable or you have insti-gated some performance issues, you can use System Restore to revert to an earlier and hopefully more stable state.

Before starting the restoration process, start System Restore, and then click Scan For Affected Programs.

This opens a new window in which you are shown a summary of the changes that will be made to your system when the restoration process is complete. If you don't like the number of changes that will be executed, you can select a more recent restore point (if available) that makes fewer changes. Unfortunately, System Restore does not display the Windows Store apps that will be deleted during the process. It only displays traditional desktop apps.

System Restore		×

Description: Scheduled Checkpoint

Date: 9/9/2013 11:57:47 AM

Any programs that were added since the last restore point will be deleted and any that were removed will be restored.

Programs and drivers that will be deleted:

Description	Type
Mozilla Firefox 23.0.1 (x86 en-US) 23.0.1	Program
Update for Package_for_KB2880289 (KB2880289)	Windows Update

Programs and drivers that might be restored. These programs might not work correctly after restore and might need to be reinstalled:

Description	Type
None detected.	

Close

After the restore process is started, it cannot be interrupted. It also involves a restart, so before you go ahead with the process, it is best to close any apps and current work.

In this exercise, you'll learn how to use System Restore to return Windows 8.1 to a previous state.

SET UP
Open System Restore.

1   Click **System Restore**.

The System Restore Wizard opens.

2   Click **Next**.

You are asked to select the restore point to which you want to restore.

3   Select the restore point you want to use and then click **Next**.

You are informed of the changes that will be made.

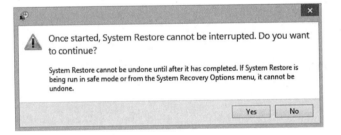

4   Click **Finish**.

You are asked to confirm that you want to continue the process.

5   Click **Yes** and wait for Windows to restart and revert to the selected restore point.

 CLEAN UP

Log on to Windows and resume your computing activities. When System Restore informs you that the restoration process has been completed, click Close.

Windows 8.1 is now restored to the selected restore point. Any changes made to your system as well as any apps that were installed after the restore point was created are no longer available.

Using the Action Center

Windows 8.1 comes with a convenient way to help you review the state of your system and find solutions to security and maintenance issues. This feature is called Action Center, and it is built upon the foundation set by the Windows Security Center, which was first introduced in Windows XP Service Pack 2 and then revised in all Windows versions that have been released since.

Action Center continuously monitors the state of your system. If it notices any kind of problem related to the security or good maintenance of your system, it immediately notifies you so that you can take corrective action. Action Center monitors the following aspects of Windows 8.1:

- Whether Windows Update is turned on and working well.

- Whether all Internet Security settings are set to their recommended levels.

- Whether the network firewall is actively protecting your computer or device.

- Whether your Microsoft account is working properly.

- Whether there are any issues with the activation of your Windows installation.

- Whether you have an active tool providing spyware and related protection.

- Whether User Account Control (UAC) is turned on.

- Whether virus protection exists and is working well.

- Whether the SmartScreen technology used in Internet Explorer and File Explorer is turned on.

- Whether Windows Backup is working well when Windows users use this feature.

- Whether automatic maintenance scheduled and performed automatically by Windows is active and working well. This maintenance includes checking for the latest software updates, making a security scan of your system, and running some quick system diagnostics to search for new problems.

- Whether all your drives are working well.

- Whether you need additional drivers and software installed for some of your computer's hardware devices.

- Whether apps running on the Windows startup have a big performance impact on the system's boot timings.

- Whether there are any ongoing problems that can be fixed by using Windows troubleshooting tools.

- Whether a homegroup is available.

- Whether File History is turned on and working well.

- Whether Storage Space is working well when Windows users use this more advanced feature.

- Whether Work Folders are working well when business users use this more advanced feature.

When a problem is detected, you are notified and provided with guidance regarding what you can do to fix it. As you can see, Action Center is an important tool for preventing problems with your system.

On the Desktop, in the notification area of the Windows taskbar, you'll see a small white flag. This is the Action Center icon. When there are messages for the user, one of two additional graphics appears just below the flag: an x in a red circle or a black clock. The x in the red circle means there is at least one important message, so you need to pay attention. The black clock overlay means a scheduled task is running in the background (for example, a scheduled Windows Defender scan).

Hover over the flag icon to see a tooltip, giving you some brief information about what is happening with your system.

To see the list of messages you should read, click the Action Center icon.

To open Action Center and view more details, click Open Action Center.

As an alternative, on the Start screen, you can type the words action center and then click the appropriate search result.

Reviewing the list of messages displayed by Action Center is simple. No complicated jargon is involved, and all you need to do is follow what the tool recommends to keep your computer in top shape. Each message has a button that takes you directly to where you need to fix things. For example, in the following screen shot, Action Center strongly recommends to Turn On Windows Defender. Click Turn On Now to activate this Windows security feature.

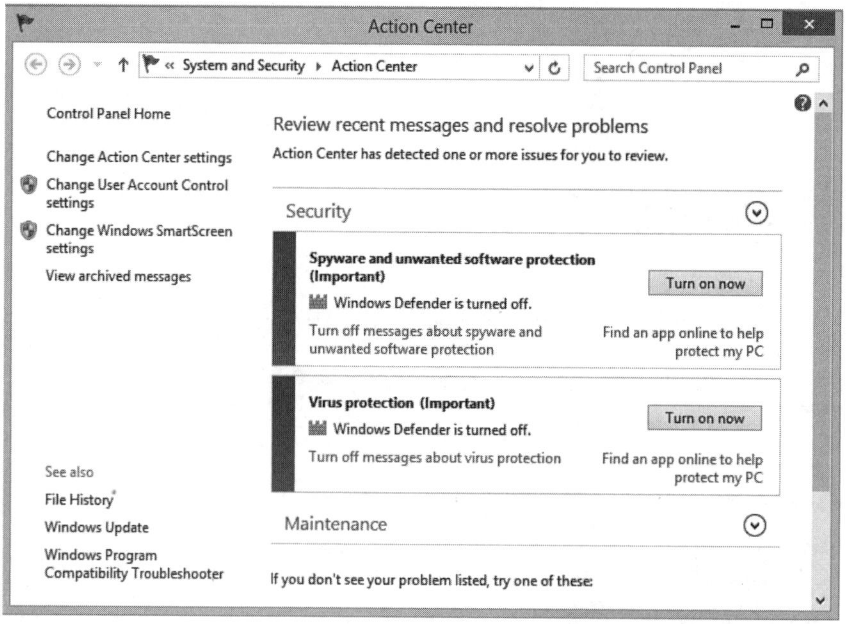

The same thing happens with the recommendation to install software for your devices. Clicking Install Automatically starts the download and installation process for that missing software.

TIP All messages that Action Center displays have the following color coding: Red means a very important message that you should not ignore; yellow means a recommendation that can be ignored if you do not consider it important.

Configuring the messages Action Center shows

Another great thing about Action Center is that you can configure it to fit your needs. You can easily customize which types of alerts and messages you want to receive, depending on how you have configured your Windows 8.1 installation and the additional software you have installed.

In this exercise, you'll learn how to configure the list of messages Action Center shows you.

 SET UP
Open Action Center.

1 In the upper-left corner of the Action Center window, click **Change Action Center Settings**.

2 Select the check boxes adjacent to the messages you want to receive.

3   Clear the check boxes for the messages you do not want to receive.

Change Action Center settings

« Action Cen... ▸ Change Action Center settings   Search Control Panel

Turn messages on or off

For each selected item, Windows will check for problems and send you a message if problems are found.
How does Action Center check for problems?

Security messages

☑ Windows Update   ☑ Spyware and unwanted software protection
☑ Internet security settings   ☑ User Account Control
☑ Network firewall   ☑ Virus protection
☑ Microsoft account   ☑ SmartScreen
☑ Windows activation

Maintenance messages

☑ Windows Backup   ☑ Windows Troubleshooting
☑ Automatic Maintenance   ☑ HomeGroup

OK   Cancel

4   Click **OK**.

❌ CLEAN UP
Close Action Center.

Action Center will now show only messages for the items that you want it to monitor on a
continuous basis.

> **IMPORTANT** It's strongly recommended not to disable the messages from the Security
> category. If there are security issues with your computer, you would miss important alerts that
> could help you fix them.

Key points

- Windows Update is a key feature for preventing problems and for securing your system.

- You can set File History to back up your important user folders, libraries, and files automatically.

- With File History, you can restore files to the location where they were originally stored or to a new, custom location.

- You can use System Restore when you have stability or performance problems to revert to an earlier and more stable system state.

- Action Center keeps you informed of the status of your system's security and regular maintenance tasks.

15

Chapter at a glance

Enable

Enable Family Safety for your child's account, page 477

Set

Set time limits and app restrictions, page 478

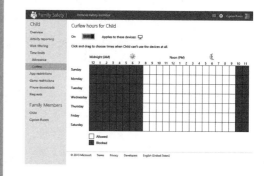

Define

Define restrictions for games and apps, page 488

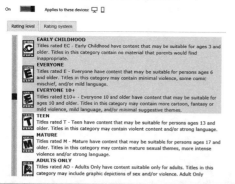

Create

Create restrictions for websites and downloads, page 490

Supervising a child's computer use

16

IN THIS CHAPTER, YOU WILL LEARN HOW TO

- Turn on Family Safety.

- Set time limits and app restrictions.

- Define restrictions for games.

- Create restrictions for websites and downloads.

Children use computers and gadgets at a very young age and for many purposes: to have fun, to learn, to communicate, socialize, and so on. In today's world, such devices are an integral part of their life. That's why, as a parent, it is important to educate children not only about how to use these devices and how to stay safe, but also about the implications of using them for long periods of time.

Windows 8.1 has a great feature named, Family Safety that can help parents educate children and control their computing habits. This feature makes it possible for parents to define when children can use the computer, what games they are allowed to play, which apps they are allowed to use, and what kinds of websites they can browse on the Internet.

In this chapter, you'll learn how to turn on Family Safety for your child's user account; how to define time limits; and how to apply restrictions for games, apps, websites, and downloads.

PRACTICE FILES You don't need any practice files to complete the exercises in this chapter. For more information about practice file requirements, see the section "Using the practice files" in the Introduction of this book.

Turning on Family Safety for your child

Before setting up Family Safety, you need to create a standard user account with no administrator permissions for your child. If your child's user account has administrator permissions, he or she will have all the required rights to override any controls you apply. Also, your child must have used his account at least once, so that Windows 8.1 can generate all the appropriate settings and install the default apps.

TIP To learn more about user accounts and how to set them up, see Chapter 12, "Allowing others to use the computer."

After you have created a user account for your child, you can turn on Family Safety and configure all the limitations that can be defined (allowed websites, time limits, game, and apps ratings). At the beginning, the setting for these limitations is Off. Even if Family Safety is turned on, no limitations are defined for your child's user account. He is free to do anything on the computer, so configure the limitations you want applied one by one. You'll learn how to do this throughout the sections of this chapter.

In this exercise, you'll learn how to turn on Family Safety for your child's user account.

 SET UP
Open PC Settings.

1   In **PC Settings**, click **Accounts** and then click **Other Accounts** to access the list of user accounts existing on your computer or device.

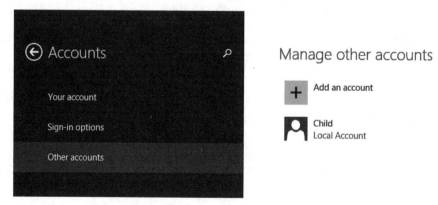

2   Click the user account that you set up for your child (which, for the purposes of illustration in this exercise, is named **Child**).

Two buttons are displayed.

3   Click **Edit**.

The Edit Account pane opens.

4   Click the **Account Type** list and then select **Child**.

5   Click **OK**.

You are returned to the Accounts section in PC Settings.

CLEAN UP
Close PC Settings.

Family Safety is now turned on, using the default settings, which do not impose any restrictions.

Setting time limits and app restrictions

Now that Family Safety is on, you can apply the restrictions you want. All types of restrictions are created using the new Family Safety website. You can access it from the Family Safety section in Control Panel or you can browse to *https://familysafety.microsoft. com* in any Internet browser of your choosing. The easiest restrictions you can define are related to the times when your child can use the computer and which apps she is allowed to use.

Time restrictions can be defined for each day of the week and for the hours in a day. A simple table displays the hours you want to block. When selected, all the blocked hours appear blue. The hours that appear white represent hours when computer usage is allowed. You can change a time slot from Allowed to Blocked, and vice versa, by clicking it.

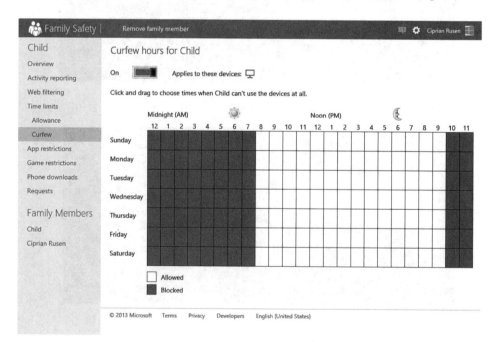

You can also set restrictions on how many hours and minutes your child is allowed to use the computer each day. You can set the restrictions independently for each day of the week or for weekdays and the weekend.

When you turn on Family Safety, no app restrictions are enforced; you need to create such restrictions and manually select which desktop apps your child is allowed to use. The list of apps is organized into folders. Expanding each folder displays the app executables that are part of it. You can allow or block each app executable individually or the whole folder with just one setting.

![Family Safety App restrictions screen for Child]

NOTE When defining restrictions for apps, keep in mind that all the new Windows 8.1 apps that you can download from the Windows Store have a separate set of rules, different than those applied to traditional desktop apps. You will learn how to set restrictions for modern apps in the next section of this chapter.

In this exercise, you'll learn how to set restrictions for time limits and set allowed apps. The exercise will start by setting time limits to block computer usage for your child's user account between 10 P.M. and 7 A.M. each day. Then, you'll allow usage of specific subset of desktop apps.

SET UP
Family Safety must be turned on for your child's user account. If it is not, follow the instructions provided in the previous section. If Family Safety is turned on, open Control Panel.

1   Click **User Accounts And Family Safety**.

2   Click **Family Safety**.

3   Click **Manage Settings** on the **Family Safety** website.

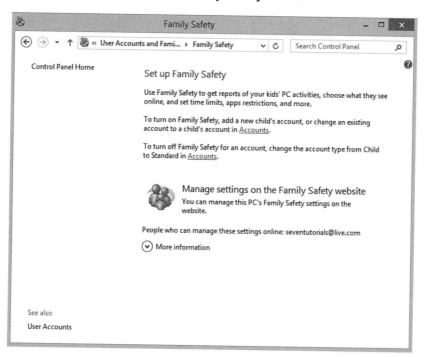

The Family Safety website is loaded in your default browser and you are asked to log on with your Microsoft account.

4   Type your Microsoft account password and click **Sign In**.

The Family Safety control panel is displayed.

5   Click the user account used by your child (for this exercise the user account is called **Child**). The complete list of settings that can be customized, are displayed.

6   Click **Time Limits**, then click **Curfew**.

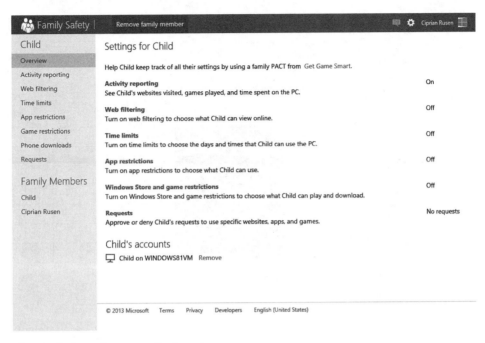

The Curfew settings are displayed.

7   Set the **Curfew** switch to **On**.

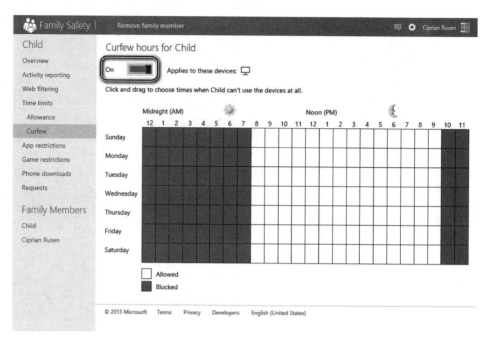

8   Highlight the squares in the table such that your child is not allowed to use the computer each day between 10 P.M. and 7 A.M. The table should look similar to the preceding screen shot.

9   To set restrictions for apps, click **App Restrictions**.

10 Change the position of the **App Restrictions** switch to **On**.

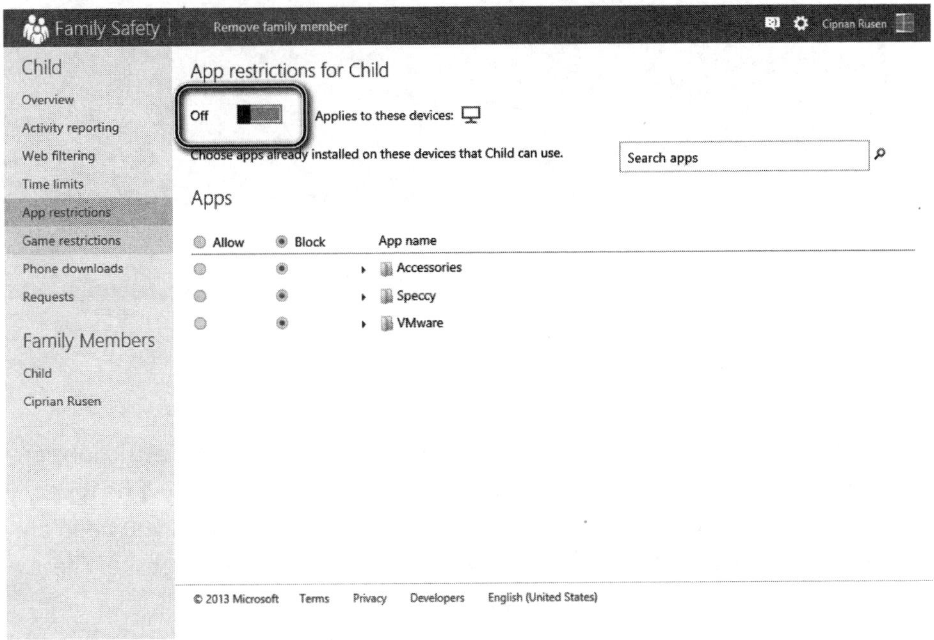

The list of all apps installed on your computer is shown below the On switch.

11 Check **Allow** for all the apps you want your child to use and **Block** for those you don't.

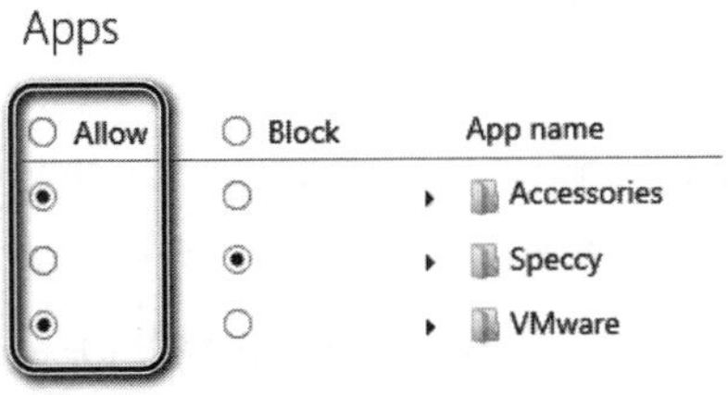

CLEAN UP

Sign out from the Family Safety website.

IMPORTANT The tricky part about blocked apps is that Family Safety will allow some of the Windows-specific apps to run even if they are not marked as allowed (such as Calculator and Internet Explorer). However, any third-party desktop apps that are installed on the computer won't be allowed to run on your child's user account unless marked as allowed. In addition, when you want to allow a desktop app that uses more than one executable file while you run it, it is best to allow all its executable files, not just the main one. This helps to ensure that an app won't fail because only some of its executable files are allowed to run.

Setting restrictions for games and Windows Store apps

Another control feature that you might want to use configures restrictions on the kinds of games your child can play. This can be very important, especially if he is very young. Family Safety makes it very easy to set such restrictions. All the options you need are in the Game And Windows Store Restrictions section, on the Family Safety website. These options make it possible for you to do the following:

- You can approve and block games based on their rating on the Entertainment Software Rating Board (ESRB), as well as other well known rating systems. You are shown a detailed description of what each rating means so that you can make an informed choice.

- You can allow or block individual games and apps. The individual overrides you choose overrule other general restrictions you have set.

The restrictions you set for ratings are also applied to the apps that your child can install from the Windows Store. Apps that don't conform to the rating you set won't be allowed.

In this exercise, you'll learn how to set restrictions for the games and Windows Store apps your child is allowed to play or use. You'll allow games and apps that have a rating of up to Everyone 10+. You'll also block your child from playing any of the individual games or Windows Store apps installed on the computer.

SET UP

Go to the Family Safety website, log on with your Microsoft account, and select your child's user account.

1   In the column on the left, click **Game Restrictions**.

2   Slide the ratings switch on the top from **Off** to **On**.

The list of ratings is now editable.

3   Select **EVERYONE 10+** to allow titles with this maximum rating.

Set ratings for Windows Store apps and other games Child can install

On ▬▬   Applies to these devices: 🖥 ▯

| Rating level | Rating system |

EARLY CHILDHOOD
Titles rated EC - Early Childhood have content that may be suitable for ages 3 and older. Titles in this category contain no material that parents would find inappropriate.

EVERYONE
Titles rated E - Everyone have content that may be suitable for persons ages 6 and older. Titles in this category may contain minimal violence, some comic mischief, and/or mild language.

EVERYONE 10+
Titles rated E10+ - Everyone 10 and older have content that may be suitable for ages 10 and older. Titles in this category may contain more cartoon, fantasy or mild violence, mild language, and/or minimal suggestive themes.

TEEN
Titles rated T - Teen have content that may be suitable for persons ages 13 and older. Titles in this category may contain violent content and/or strong language.

MATURE
Titles rated M - Mature have content that may be suitable for persons ages 17 and older. Titles in this category may contain mature sexual themes, more intense violence and/or strong language.

ADULTS ONLY
Titles rated AO - Adults Only have content suitable only for adults. Titles in this category may include graphic depictions of sex and/or violence. Adult Only

4   In the column on the left, in the Game Restrictions section, click **Game List**.

A list with the installed games and Windows 8.1 apps is shown.

5   Check the **Allow** box for the games and apps that you want to allow your child to use.

Choose which installed games Child can play on this PC

On ▬▬   Applies to these devices: 🖥

Games   Search games   🔎

Allow	Use game rating	Block	Name
●	○	○	⤵ 7 Tutorials
●	○	○	▦ Bing Food & Drink
●	○	○	▦ Bing Health & Fitness
●	○	○	▦ Cut The Rope
●	○	○	Finance

6   Check the **Block** box for the games and apps that you don't want to your child to run.

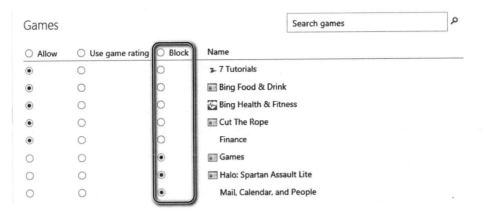

 CLEAN UP
When you are done editing your restrictions, sign out from the Family Safety website.

The game and apps restrictions you have defined are now applied to your child's user account. Before setting these restrictions, take the time to look through all the types of content that can be blocked and select all those that you consider appropriate. The preceding exercise showed only the steps involved to accomplish this and was not making recommendations for the types of content that should be blocked for a child depending on her age.

Setting restrictions for websites and downloads

Another important feature in Family Safety is the ability to filter the websites to which your child has access. Microsoft has a large database that categorizes websites and the type of content found on them. By using just one setting, you can ensure that your child is blocked from accessing websites that are not appropriate for his age. Turning on web restrictions also turns on the SafeSearch settings found in all popular search engines such as Bing and Google. The web searches your child initiates will be filtered to prevent access to adult content of any kind.

You have five restriction levels from which to choose:

- **Allow List Only** Your child can view only the websites you have added to the Allow List. All other sites, including adult sites, are blocked.

- **Designed For Children** Your child can view only websites you specifically marked as allowed as well as those with child-friendly content. Adult sites are blocked.

- **General Interest** Your child can view only websites you specifically marked as allowed, those with child-friendly content, and those with content of general interest. Adult sites are blocked.

- **Online Communication** This setting applies the same restrictions as the General Interest level, but it also allows social networking sites, web chat, and webmail. Adult sites are blocked.

- **Warn On Adult** Your child is allowed to view all websites but receives a warning when a site has adult content.

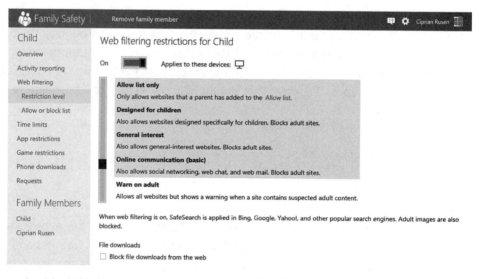

You can also block file downloads by selecting **Block File Downloads From The Web** to ensure that your child can't download files that you do not approve.

You can also add specific websites to be allowed or blocked. As with games, these individual overrides overrule other general restrictions you have set for websites.

The restrictions you define are applied to all major browsers, not just Internet Explorer. For example, if your child is using Mozilla Firefox or Google Chrome instead of Internet Explorer, the restrictions will still be in force.

In this exercise, you'll learn how to block web content automatically and how to block file downloads.

SET UP
Open the Family Safety website, log on with your Microsoft account, and select your child's user account.

1   In the column on the left, click **Web Filtering**.

    Here you set the websites your child can view.

2   Slide the Web Filtering switch on the top, from **Off** to **On**.

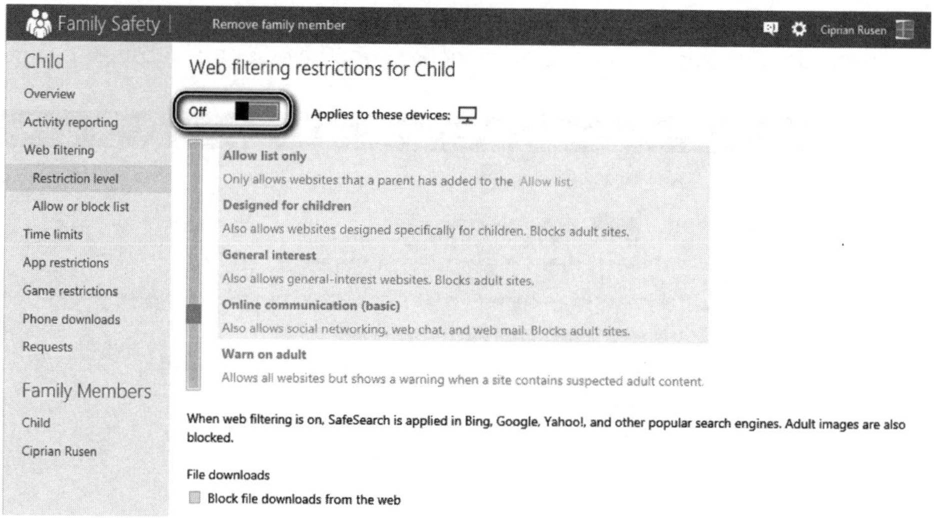
Family Safety
Remove family member
Ciprian Rusen
Child
Overview
Activity reporting
Web filtering
Restriction level
Allow or block list
Time limits
App restrictions
Game restrictions
Phone downloads
Requests
Family Members
Child
Ciprian Rusen
Web filtering restrictions for Child
Off
Applies to these devices:
Allow list only
Only allows websites that a parent has added to the Allow list.
Designed for children
Also allows websites designed specifically for children. Blocks adult sites.
General interest
Also allows general-interest websites. Blocks adult sites.
Online communication (basic)
Also allows social networking, web chat, and web mail. Blocks adult sites.
Warn on adult
Allows all websites but shows a warning when a site contains suspected adult content.
When web filtering is on, SafeSearch is applied in Bing, Google, Yahoo!, and other popular search engines. Adult images are also blocked.
File downloads
Block file downloads from the web

3 Choose **General Interest**.

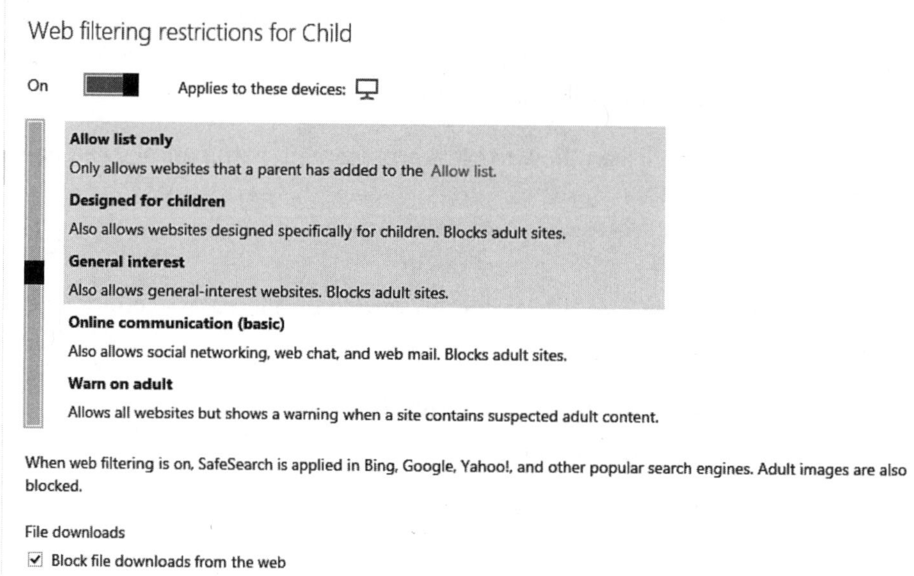
Web filtering restrictions for Child
On
Applies to these devices:
Allow list only
Only allows websites that a parent has added to the Allow list.
Designed for children
Also allows websites designed specifically for children. Blocks adult sites.
General interest
Also allows general-interest websites. Blocks adult sites.
Online communication (basic)
Also allows social networking, web chat, and web mail. Blocks adult sites.
Warn on adult
Allows all websites but shows a warning when a site contains suspected adult content.
When web filtering is on, SafeSearch is applied in Bing, Google, Yahoo!, and other popular search engines. Adult images are also blocked.
File downloads
Block file downloads from the web

4 At the bottom of the window, select **Block File Downloads From The Web**.

CLEAN UP

Close the Web Restrictions window.

The web restrictions you have set are now applied to your child's user account.

Understanding the messages shown by Family Safety

When your child wants to log on to the computer during a time slot that is blocked, he receives the message "Time's up! It's past the curfew time your parent set."

Your child cannot log on unless you set that specific time slot as allowed.

If your child tries to run a blocked app or game, a pop-up appears with the message "Blocked by Family Safety."

Blocked by Family Safety
Request permission to use ThinPrint
AutoConnect component.

If your child tries to access a blocked website, that website will not be loaded and she is notified that "This page is blocked."

When he tries to download a file and downloads have been blocked, the message "Family Safety has blocked this download" appears. The download does not proceed. Unfortunately, this feature of Family Safety does not work well with all Internet browsers. Currently, it is guaranteed to block downloads only if you use Internet Explorer (if you have this setting turned on, of course); however, with other browsers it might not succeed at blocking all undesirable downloads.

Each time something is blocked, your child is given the chance to ask for permission and receive access. Parents can review her permission requests and approve them when appropriate. If you are at the computer, you can also type your user account password and her request is immediately approved, without you having to log on separately. However, you might want to pay attention because your child can see what keys you press on the keyboard and figure out the password.

Managing Family Safety settings and viewing activity reports

You can view your child's activity from the Family Safety website.

In the left column, click Activity reporting to find all the reports made available by Family Safety.

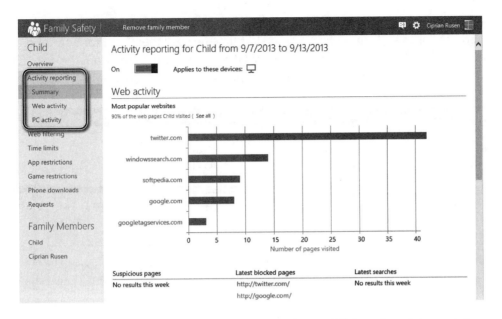

The Summary report, first displays a summary of your child's web activity and then a summary of his PC activity.

In the column on the left, access the Web Activity report to get a more detailed look into what he is doing.

The detailed PC Activity report shares information about when your child used the computer, what apps and games he used, the last time he used them, and for how long. Then, the report shares information about the files that were downloaded from the web as well as the apps and games that he downloaded from the Windows Store.

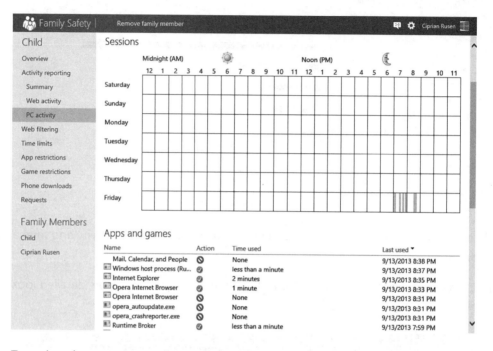

To review the requests you have received from your child and make a decision as to whether you want to approve them or not, in the left column, click Requests. The complete list of requests is displayed and you can click Allow or Ignore for each, depending on what you think is best for your child.

If your child has a Windows Phone device and a Microsoft account, you can also set restrictions for his smartphone. Almost every type of restriction in Family Safety can be applied to your child's computer(s) and his smartphone. Also, there is a Phone Downloads section with rules that apply only to his Windows Phone device.

Key points

- You can only turn on Family Safety if your child has a standard user account.

- You can easily set time limits and restrictions on apps and games.

- You can set restrictions for games and Windows Store apps by using their ESRB rating.

- Setting restrictions on the types of websites that can be visited helps to ensure that your child doesn't visit websites with content that is inappropriate for his age.

- Your child is notified each time he tries to log on at a restricted time or run a blocked game or app.

- Family Safety restrictions, activity reports, and requests are managed from the Family Safety website, which can be accessed from any browser or device.

Chapter at a glance

Configure
Configure visual notifications, page 502

Recommended settings

These settings can help you set up your computer to meet ⁝
below and select the options that you want to use.

☐ Turn on visual notifications for sounds (Sound Sent

Choose visual warning

○ None
○ Flash active caption bar
◉ Flash active window
○ Flash desktop

User
User Magnifier, page 506

Use
Use the On-Screen Keyboard, 512

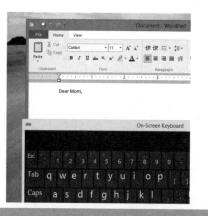

Give
Give verbal commands, 515

Making my computer accessible

17

IN THIS CHAPTER, YOU WILL LEARN HOW TO

- Locate the Ease of Access options.

- Let Windows suggest Ease of Access settings.

- Use the Magnifier.

- Use Narrator.

- Use the On-Screen Keyboard.

- Set up and use Windows Speech Recognition.

- Log on to Windows 8.1 without a password.

Windows 8.1 offers several options to help you use your computer if you have any kind of impairment or disability. These are referred to cumulatively as Ease of Access features; there are many ease of access features and options from which to choose.

If you need to wear reading glasses to see what's on the screen, you can take the glasses off and simply make the text larger; if you are visually impaired, you can turn on Narrator to have what's on the screen read to you. If you have difficulty hearing, you can turn up the volume on your speakers or turn on text captions for spoken dialog; if you are unable to hear at all, you can turn on visual notifications with Sound Sentry. If you have difficulty using the mouse or keyboard, options exist to help you, including Toggle Keys, Sticky Keys, Filter Keys, and so on. You can also turn on and configure Windows Speech Recognition so that you can talk to your computer to give commands and perform tasks. Finally, if you have trouble entering a password to unlock Windows 8.1, you can log on without one (although this isn't recommended due to security issues).

PRACTICE FILES You do not need any practice files to complete this chapter. For more information about practice file requirements, see the section "Using the practice files" in the Introduction of this book.

Locating the Ease of Access options

There are several ways to get to the Ease of Access options. You can search for a specific option on the Start screen; for instance, you can type High Contrast and then, from the results, click to open the options with which you can turn high contrast on or off. You can locate the Ease of Access options from PC Settings; you've explored many of the options there already, including personalizing the lock screen with your favorite picture and adding users. You can also get to the features from the Ease of Access Center, which offers all of the access options in one place and on the desktop (PC Settings doesn't offer all of the options). Here are the options from PC Settings:

TIP Many more accessibility settings are available than those in PC Settings. To see everything that's available, open Control Panel and then click Ease Of Access. You can then select Ease Of Access Center or Speech Recognition. You'll learn more about this later in the chapter.

In this exercise, you'll search for the High Contrast option from the Start screen and then open the PC Settings app and turn on High Contrast.

SET UP

Start your computer and unlock the lock screen. You need access to the Start screen.

1   On the **Start** screen, type High Contrast.

2   Click **High Contrast Settings.**

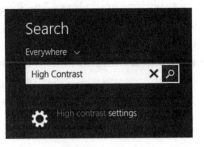

3   In the **Choose A Theme** section, click the arrow next to **None** to display the list of available themes.

4   In the list, click **High Contrast Black**.

5   Click **Apply.**

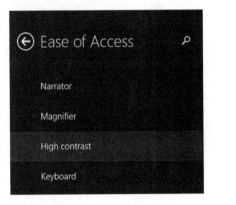

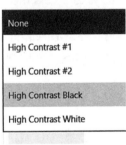

CLEAN UP

Change the setting back to normal by repeating the steps, but this time selecting None and clicking Apply.

Letting Windows suggest Ease of Access settings

Because you can't access all the Ease of Access options from PC Settings, and because you might not even be sure what options to use, it's often best to let Windows suggest the settings it deems best for you based on a series of questions you answer. The five questions are easy to understand, and after you answer them, options to turn on the suggested accessibility features are presented. For example, if you work through the wizard and state only that you are hard of hearing, Windows will suggest that you turn on Sound Sentry and choose a type of visual warning for when audio warnings are presented. (If you state that "it is often difficult for me to concentrate," more options are presented.)

Recommended settings

These settings can help you set up your computer to meet :
below and select the options that you want to use.

☐ Turn on visual notifications for sounds (Sound Sent

Choose visual warning

◯ None
◯ Flash active caption bar
◉ Flash active window
◯ Flash desktop

There are several ways to access the wizard that helps you decide which options are best for you, but the best way is to open Control Panel and then open Ease Of Access. You can access Control Panel by right-clicking the Start button that appears in the lower-left corner of the screen when you position your pointer there. After Control Panel is open, click Ease Of Access (not shown).

Network Connections
Disk Management
Computer Management
Command Prompt
Command Prompt (Admin)

Task Manager
Control Panel
File Explorer
Search
Run

Shut down or sign out   ▶
Desktop

From Control Panel, click Ease Of Access, and in the Ease Of Access Center, you can select Let Windows Suggest Settings. The rest is simple; you just answer the questions as they pertain to you and let Windows figure out what needs to be turned on.

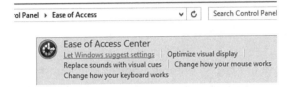

Here are a few of the items (and a few related items) that you might be prompted to turn on based on the answers you give in the wizard.

- **Narrator**   Narrator reads aloud any text on the screen. You'll need speakers. (You might also want to turn on audio descriptions to hear what's happening on the screen when that feature is available for the items being viewed.)

- **Magnifier**   Magnifier zooms in anywhere on the screen and makes everything in that area larger. You can move the magnifier around on the screen just as you would if you had a magnifying glass in your hand. (You might also want to turn on High Contrast, change the thickness of the cursor, adjust the color and transparency of the window borders, and so on if prompted to do so.)

- **On-Screen Keyboard**   Use the On-Screen Keyboard to type by using the mouse, your finger (on a touch screen), or another pointing device, such as a joystick, by selecting keys that appear on the screen.

- **Speech Recognition**   Use speech recognition to speak into a microphone to control the computer, open apps, and dictate text.

- **Mouse Keys, Sticky Keys, and Filter Keys**   With Mouse Keys, you use the numeric keypad to move the mouse around the screen; with Sticky Keys, you press keyboard shortcuts such as Ctrl+Alt+Del one key at a time instead of all at once; enabling Filter Keys causes Windows to ignore or slow down brief or repeated keystrokes and adjust keyboard repeat rates. (You might also try Toggle Keys, which sound a tone when you press specific keys such as Caps Lock, Num Lock, or others.)

- **Visual Notifications and Time Limits**   Sound Sentry provides visual notification for sounds, and you can enable visual warnings that flash on the screen when a notification is active. You can also turn off time limits and flashing visuals if you find it difficult to concentrate, or set how long Windows notification boxes should stay open.

(You might also want to turn off unnecessary animations, prevent windows from being automatically arranged when you move them to the edges of the screen, or turn on caret browsing.)

Using the Magnifier

You can turn on Magnifier from the Ease of Access Center in Control Panel, from the landing page. You can also type Magnifier on the Start screen to access the options to turn it on. Another way is to enable Magnifer in PC Settings.

Whatever you choose, when you turn on Magnifier a window appears for a second or two that contains options to change the magnification level and how Magnifier shows its magnified data.

If you don't immediately click any option from this window, it changes to a magnifying glass. (You click the magnifying glass to cause the window to reappear when you need it.) With the settings configured, you just move your cursor around the screen to use Magnifier. As you can see here, the image degrades and pixelates at higher settings.

Invert colors

Off

Start Magnifi

Off

Many keyboard shortcuts are available for Magnifier, including those you can use to start and exit it.

- **Start Magnifier**   Windows key+Plus Sign

- **Zoom out or in while Magnifier is running**   Windows key+Minus Sign or Windows key+Plus Sign

- **Exit Magnifier**   Windows key+Esc

You'll want to explore each available view in the Views list, and the settings available by clicking the Settings icon in the Magnifier window if you decide to use Magnifier regularly. One view is Full Screen. When you use it, the entire screen is magnified at the percentage you select, and you move around the screen with your mouse.

Docked view is another option. In this view and while on the desktop, you'll see an area at the top of the screen that shows what's being magnified (where you've placed your pointer). Docked is not an option on the Start screen or while using an app. Docked is available only on the desktop.

If you aren't on the desktop but instead on the Start screen or in an app, you can choose between Lens and Full Screen. You've seen Full Screen; Lens offers a rectangle on the screen that holds the magnified data.

In this exercise, you'll start Magnifier and use it at 200% and 300% in Full Screen view. You'll then exit the Magnifier app.

 SET UP
Start your computer and unlock the lock screen. You need access to the Start screen.

1   On the **Start** screen, press **Window key+Plus Sign**.

2   Move the cursor over the Magnifier window or the magnifying glass (whichever is available).

3   If the Magnifier is available, click the right-facing double arrows.

4   Click the **Views** list arrow. Verify that **Full Screen** is selected.

5   If it disappears, click the magnifying glass icon, and then click the + button to zoom in.

6   Using the keyboard, press **Windows key+Minus Sign** two times.

7   Press **Windows key+Esc** to close Magnifier.

⊗ CLEAN UP
No cleanup is required.

Using Narrator

You can start Narrator from Ease of Access Center in Control Panel. As with Magnifier, you can start Narrator from PC Settings, too. You can also start Narrator on the Start screen. Just start typing Narrator and then, in the results, click Narrator when it appears.

TIP If you have a touch-enabled screen, you can use Narrator Touch, a new feature that supports four-finger input. Otherwise, you can control and use Narrator with a keyboard and mouse.

NOTE It's best to open Narrator from PC Settings the first time you use it. This makes it possible for you see what options are available and when you're finished using it, you can turn it off.

Hear text and controls on the screen

Narrator is a screen reader that reads all the elements on screen, like text and buttons.

Narrator
On

To turn Narrator off with a touchscreen, tap the Narrator slider, and then double-tap anywhere on the screen.

Start Narrator automatically
Off

Voice

Choose a voice
Microsoft David

Speed

Pitch

Sounds you hear

As you explore, you'll discover that you can press any key on the keyboard to hear the name of the key. You can press Caps Lock+F1 to review and have read to you a full set of Narrator commands. You can also change the various settings, including the speed, pitch, and volume of the narrator, as well as how and when the app starts. Each time you click an option, you are prompted to save or discard the changes before you can return to the previous screen. To use Narrator, use the computer as you normally would, via the keyboard and mouse or the touch screen.

Understand that Narrator won't read all of the *content* you encounter; however, it will always let you know what's happening on the screen itself. It might read what's on a webpage, and it will read URLs, dialog boxes, text entry boxes, and so on. When you start a app, Narrator will announce that you've opened a window, state the name of the app, and describe the available tooltips. It can't tell you what's on a Microsoft PowerPoint slide, though, or what a picture on the screen looks like. It will state which key you press on the keyboard, such as Print Screen (PrtSc), but it won't describe what you've copied. Instead, it tells you when you start and exit desktop apps and apps, the commands available under your pointer, the commands you've selected, and other pertinent information.

Narrator does work with some apps. This is an ever-expanding technology, so you can expect more features and functionality in the future. As an example of what is available now, however, you can start the Weather app and click the current temperature; Narrator will read the temperature aloud to you if you place your pointer appropriately. If you open Calendar and create an event, it will read some of the information, such as the month you select, the number of hours you configure for the event, and so on.

If you decide to use Narrator regularly, you'll need to spend some time exploring the features, configuring the settings, and learning about keyboard, mouse, and touch-screen shortcuts.

TIP If you've started Narrator and want to stop it, open PC Settings, and then, in the Ease Of Access area, turn Narrator from On to Off.

Using the On-Screen Keyboard

The On-Screen Keyboard is another accessibility option in the Ease Of Access Center. It is available on all computers, even those that do not support touch, and you can use the keyboard with a mouse or input device designed for people with disabilities. Start On-Screen Keyboard is an option in Control Panel and in the Ease Of Access Center. An easier way to open it is to type **Keyboard** on the Start screen and click On-Screen Keyboard in the results. The keyboard appears immediately when you do this. It offers a Minimize button so that you can easily hide it when you aren't using it.

TIP You can drag from the corners of the keyboard to make it larger and easier to use. You can configure it to be quite large.

The keyboard is similar to most; you click or tap keys to use them, and there are even specialty keys such as Tab, Caps, and Shift; Alt, Ctrl, and Del; the Windows key; arrow keys; and PgUp, PgDn, PrtScn, and so on. In addition, the keyboard has a few extra entries such as Nav, Mv Up, Mv Dn, Dock, Fade, Help, ScrLk, and Options, among others. To get the most from the On-Screen Keyboard, you need to know how to use most of these extra entries.

TIP If you plan to use the On-Screen Keyboard regularly, on the keyboard click the Options key and configure the settings as desired.

The On-Screen Keyboard special keys include but are not limited to the following:

- **Nav**   Use this to hide the full keyboard and show only the navigation options. Click General to return to the full On-Screen Keyboard.

- **Mv Up**   Press this to reposition the On-Screen Keyboard near the top of the screen.

- **Mv Dn**   Press this to reposition the On-Screen Keyboard near the bottom of the screen.

- **Dock**   Use this to dock the On-Screen Keyboard to hide it, show it, or otherwise manage it. This option is not available (and dimmed) on computers but might be available on tablets.

- **Fade**   Press this to make the keyboard transparent. Click Fade again to show it.

- **Help**   Press this to get help using the On-Screen Keyboard.

- **ScrLk**   This is the same as the Scroll Lock key you find on many keyboards. When the ScrLk key is enabled, it is white.

- **Options**   Use this to configure options for the On-Screen Keyboard. These include but are not limited to setting a click sound when keys are pressed, turning on a numeric keypad, using text prediction, and turning on the option to hover over a key for a specific amount of time to use it (versus actually clicking the key with a mouse or other device).

TIP To open the On-Screen Keyboard by using keyboard shortcuts, press Windows key+R and then, in the Run dialog box, type **osk** and press Enter.

In this exercise, you'll open the On-Screen Keyboard on the Start screen and use it to type a short note by using Microsoft WordPad.

 SET UP
Open WordPad by using any method desired. Return to the Start screen.

1   On the **Start** screen, type Keyboard. From the results, click **On-Screen Keyboard**.

2 If desired, drag from any corner of the keyboard to enlarge it.

3 Position WordPad and the On-Screen Keyboard where you can access both easily.

4 Click inside **WordPad** to place your cursor there.

5 Use your mouse or another pointing device (such as your finger) to select keys on the keyboard. Note that they appear on the screen in WordPad.

6 Use the **Shift** and **Enter** keys as required.

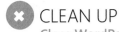 CLEAN UP
Close WordPad and save the document if desired.

Set up and use Windows Speech Recognition

Like Narrator, Windows Speech Recognition takes a little time to master. You have to set it up, train it to understand your voice, and then learn the commands for using it. You can then use Windows Speech Recognition to start and exit apps, open and select items from menus, click buttons and objects, and even dictate text. Just about everything you can do with a keyboard and mouse, you can do with only your voice.

The set up wizard can take a while to get through, so it's best to start when you have at least 30 minutes for the process. You open Speech Recognition the same way you open any Ease of Access feature, by typing related keywords on the Start screen or by using Control Panel.

Configure your Speech Recognition experience

Start Speech Recognition
Start using your voice to control your computer.

☒

⬅ 🎤 Set up Speech Recognition

Welcome to Speech Recognition

Speech Recognition allows you to control your computer by voice.

Using only your voice, you can start programs, open menus, click buttons and other objects on the screen, dictate text into documents, and write and send e-mails. Just about everything you do with your keyboard and mouse can be done with only your voice.

First, you will set up this computer to recognize your voice.

Note: You will be able to control your computer by voice once you have completed this setup wizard.

17

During the setup process, you are required to do the following:

- **Configure a microphone**   You choose and test a microphone. This can be one built in to a headset, one that sits on the desk, or one built in to your computer (or device).

- **Enable document review**   Speech Recognition will work better if you let it review the documents and email that have already been indexed for search by Windows. The computer can learn words and phrases you use often and can understand better when you speak.

- **Choose how to activate and deactivate the app**   Start Listening and Stop Listening are the two commands you'll learn to use first. You can choose what happens when you say these commands. You can configure it so that when you say "Stop listening," Windows Speech Recognition closes (Manual), or you can configure it so that when you say "Stop listening," it stays active and waits for you to use the Start Listening command to reactivate it.

- **Print the speech reference card**   You can print the speech reference card if you have a printer so that you will always have a quick reference of the available commands. You can also view the reference sheet. If the sheet does not automatically appear, search for Controlling Your PC With Speech Recognition.

- **Run Speech Recognition at startup**   If you know you'll use Windows Speech Recognition every time you use your computer, turn on this feature; otherwise, turn it off.

- **Work through the tutorial**   After Windows Speech Recognition is set up, work through the tutorial. It teaches you how to use Windows Speech Recognition and is well worth the time it takes to go through it.

After you've worked through the tutorial, you're ready to use Windows Speech Recognition. You'll see the Speech Recognition window on the desktop and Start screen when it's running, and it will appear on top of any open windows (until you minimize it to the taskbar).

In this exercise, you'll start Windows Speech Recognition, use it to access the desktop, and use it to open and close the Recycle Bin on the desktop.

SET UP
Start your computer and unlock the lock screen. You need access to the Start screen.

TIP If you did not print out the list of commands offered in the Windows Speech Recognition tutorial, you can access commands from www.microsoft.com. Search for Speech Recognition commands. You can also say, "What can I say?" while Windows Speech Recognition is listening.

1   On the **Start** screen, type Speech.

2   In the search results, click **Windows Speech Recognition** to open it.
     Speech Recognition shows it is "listening".

3   Say "**Click desktop.**"

4   Say "**Double-click Recycle Bin.**"

5   Say "**Close Recycle Bin.**"

6   Say "**Stop listening.**"

✖ CLEAN UP
No cleanup is required.

Finally, understand that there are multiple ways to configure Windows Speech Recognition. You can access the options by right-clicking the Speech Recognition dialog box on the screen, from which you can access many configuration options, including but not limited to the following:

- Choosing how Windows Speech Recognition should start, stop, and listen.
- Starting or restarting the Speech tutorial.
- Getting help.
- Performing steps to improve voice recognition.
- Opening the Speech Dictionary and adding a word.
- Exiting Windows Speech Recognition.

TIP If you plan to use Windows Speech Recognition regularly, explore each option available, work through the tutorial, and let the app review the documents on your computer.

Log on to Windows 8.1 without a password

If you have trouble entering your password when you log on to windows, consider creating a PIN or a Picture Password. These might be easier for you than typing a longer, more complicated password. If you simply can't log on with any of these due to a disability, it is possible to configure Windows 8.1 to let you in without one. Take note that this isn't recommended, and you'll have to go to great lengths to keep your computer safe if you do this. Without a password, anyone can access your device.

You'll need to access the hidden options to disable the password you use on your computer. Do this by opening the User Accounts dialog box. On the Start screen type netplwiz. Click **netplwiz** in the results. Choose your user account in the list of users.

By default, the Users Must Enter A User Name And Password To Use This Computer check box is selected. Clear this check box and then Apply and enter your existing credentials. Click OK and then click OK in the remaining dialog box.

Automatically sign in

You can set up your computer so that users do not have to type a user name and password to sign in. To do this, specify a user that will be automatically signed in below:

User name: JenniferV

Password:

Confirm Password:

[OK] [Cancel]

Key points

- You can configure basic accessibility options in PC Settings.

- If you're unsure of which accessibility options are right for you, you can work through the available wizard to let Windows make suggestions.

- To access all accessibility options, open the Ease of Access Center from Control Panel; this is the desktop version.

- You can use Magnifier in various modes and views; you can choose the one that's right for you.

- Narrator can read what's happening on the screen and inform you when you start or exit an app, name the URL of the website you're visiting, and read what's under your pointer. It can sometimes read content in apps, although that feature is expected to become more robust in the future.

- The On-Screen Keyboard can be used with alternative input devices, with a mouse, and with touch (on compatible monitors).

- By using Windows Speech Recognition, you can issue commands verbally such as, "Click desktop," "Double-click Recycle Bin," "Scroll up," "Scroll down," and so on.

- It is possible to log on to Windows 8.1 without a password, but it isn't recommended.

Chapter at a glance

Use

Use the Windows Mobility Center, page 520

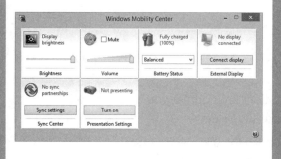

Start

Start Presentation mode, page 524

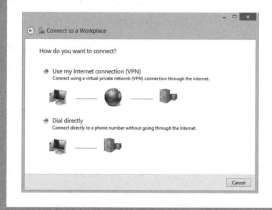

Encrypt

Encrypt the operating system drive by using BitLocker, page 530

Set

Set up a VPN connection, page 541

Using Windows 8.1 at work

18

IN THIS CHAPTER, YOU WILL LEARN HOW TO

- Learn to use the Windows Mobility Center.

- Turn on Presentation mode.

- Use BitLocker to encrypt the operating system drive.

- Use BitLocker to secure removable data drives.

- Set up a VPN connection to your workplace.

The chances are pretty good that you will also be using Windows 8.1 at your workplace. Although the tools covered in this book can be used both at home and at work, there are a few that you are likely to use mostly at work, not at home.

The first is Windows Mobility Center, which is targeted at laptop or netbook users who are mobile and need to connect to multiple devices and external displays. The second is BitLocker, a feature by which you can encrypt your computer and ensure that your data is safe and accessed only by you and other authorized people. The third tool is one with which you can connect to your workplace when working from home or other remote places by setting up a Virtual Private Network (VPN) connection.

In this chapter, you'll learn how to use the Windows Mobility Center, connect to external displays, and use Presentation mode to deliver presentations without any unwanted interruptions. Then, you'll learn how to encrypt and decrypt hard disks by using BitLocker. Last but not least, you will learn how to set up a VPN connection to your company's network.

PRACTICE FILES You don't need any practice files to complete the exercises in this chapter. For more information about practice file requirements, see the section "Using the practice files" in the Introduction of this book.

Using the Windows Mobility Center

The Windows Mobility Center is a tool that works only on mobile computers and devices such as laptops and netbooks. It is not available on desktop computers. Its role is to help users be mobile and quickly take the following actions:

- Change the display brightness of the screen

- Change the sound volume of the Windows 8.1 computer or device

- Change the power plan

- Connect or disconnect external displays

- Set synchronized partnerships with portable music players, USB memory sticks, or smartphones that provide support for this feature

- Turn Presentation mode on or off

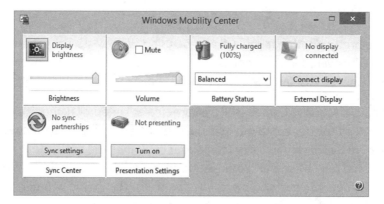

Although all the settings that you can manage through the Windows Mobility Center are important, two will be especially appreciated during office hours: the ability to connect external displays, and the ability to turn on Presentation mode.

These settings are very useful when switching among different office rooms and connecting the laptop to different kinds of external displays, from monitors to TVs and projectors.

The Connect Display button is the equivalent of pressing the Windows key+P on your keyboard. It opens a window that asks how you want to set the second screen The following are your options:

- **PC Screen Only**   The second screen is ignored and no image is displayed on it.
- **Duplicate**   The image on your laptop's screen is duplicated on the external display.
- **Extend**   The second screen extends your laptop's screen, which you can use as an additional desktop.
- **Second Screen Only**   The second screen becomes your main screen, and the laptop's screen is turned off.

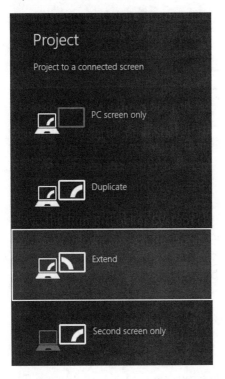

18

To start the Windows Mobility Center, open Control Panel, choose Hardware And Sound, and then select Windows Mobility Center.

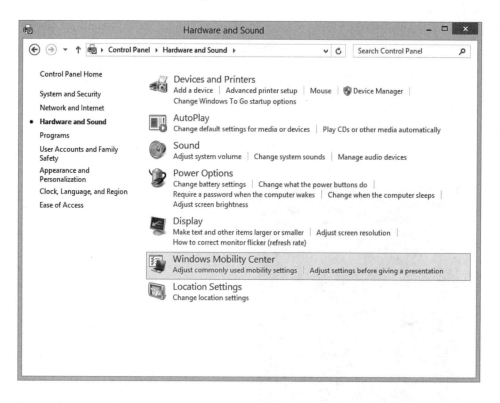

As an alternative, you can type Mobility on the Start screen and then, in the search results area, click the appropriate item. Last but not least, you can find its shortcut in the Windows+X or WinX menu as it is named by some.

Turning on Presentation mode

Presentation mode is very useful when delivering any kind of presentation. Take some time to configure Presentation mode exactly the way you want so that your presentation runs smoothly without unwanted hiccups and interruptions (such as the screen saver showing up when you don't need it).

In this exercise, you'll learn how to turn on Presentation mode and configure it.

 SET UP

Open Windows Mobility Center and connect the external display that you want to use with your computer.

1   In Windows Mobility Center, click **Connect Display** to set how you want to connect the second screen.

2   Click **Extend**.

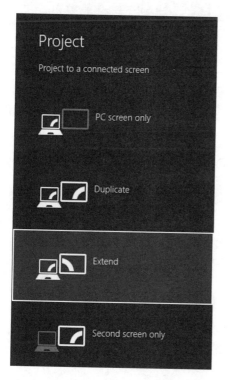

The second external display now acts as a second Desktop.

3   Back in the Windows Mobility Center, in the **Presentation Settings** section, click the
     projector icon.

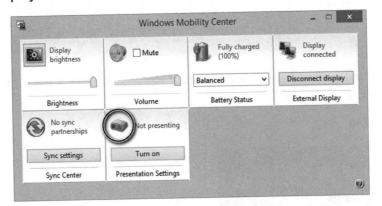

The Presentation Settings window opens.

4   Select the check boxes for **I Am Currently Giving A Presentation** and **Turn Off The
     Screen Saver**.

5   Set the volume and the background as you want them to be and then click **OK**.

You return to the Windows Mobility Center window.

After you have delivered your presentation, click the Turn Off button under Presentation Settings and close Windows Mobility Center.

Now, you can move the documents and presentations you want to show to the second display and start your presentation. You don't have to worry about unwanted screen savers turning on, distracting wallpapers appearing, and so on.

Using BitLocker to encrypt drives

Many companies use different encryption solutions to ensure the security of the data stored on the companies' systems. If a business laptop is stolen or a USB memory stick with company data is lost, it's important for the stored data to be inaccessible to unwanted people. In such scenarios, encryption is the only solution which ensures that the data is accessed only by people who have the appropriate access keys and passwords. Some businesses also have policies that forbid the distribution of company data on removable media such as USB memory sticks. Be sure you comply with such policies. However, if you need to have important business data on a mobile device when you're away from the office and you won't break any company policies by doing so, use encryption. It is the only sensible solution to the challenge of protecting your data.

BitLocker is available only for the business editions of Windows 8.1 (Windows 8.1 Pro and Windows 8.1 Enterprise). That's why it is very likely that you will use it only on your work computers. In addition, it works only on computers with Trusted Platform Module (TPM) chips. These chips can store the cryptographic keys BitLocker and other encryption solutions use. TPM chips are included in most business computers but not in computers sold to consumers and home users.

One important change in Windows 8.1 is that it features what Microsoft calls Pervasive Device Encryption. Device encryption previously found on Windows RT and Windows Phone 8 is now available in all editions of Windows. It is active right out of the box if your hardware supports this feature. Your Windows 8.1 devices are automatically encrypted and protected when using a Microsoft account. Data on any Windows connected standby device is automatically protected (encrypted) with device encryption. BitLocker is now an additional layer that provides more protection options and manageability.

You can find BitLocker by opening Control Panel, choosing System And Security, and then selecting BitLocker Drive Encryption.

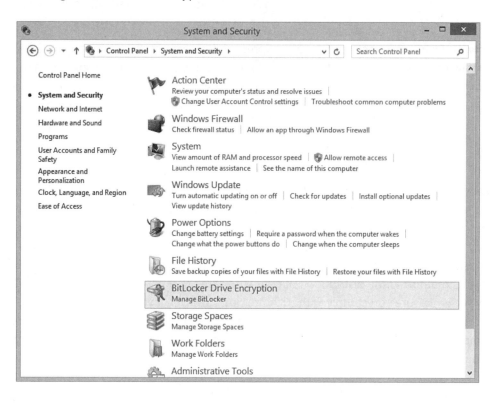

BitLocker's main window is well organized and easy to understand and use. You can see the drive on which Windows is as well as other fixed data drives that might exist on your computer. You can also see the removable storage devices that are plugged into your computer.

You can use BitLocker to encrypt all of these devices. After a drive is encrypted, its status changes from BitLocker Off to BitLocker On. In addition, you can perform tasks such as the following:

- Suspending the BitLocker protection for a time
- Backing up the recovery key again in case you lose it
- Changing the password used to access the encrypted drive
- Removing the existing password
- Copying the Bitlocker startup key to a removable USB flash drive
- Turning off BitLocker and decrypting the device

Operating system drive

C: BitLocker on   ⊙

🛡 Suspend protection
🛡 Back up your recovery key
   Change password
🛡 Remove password
🛡 Copy startup key
🛡 Turn off BitLocker

Encrypting the operating system drive by using BitLocker

The encryption process is rather lengthy and first involves setting a password that will be used prior to starting Windows and using any encrypted drive. It is important to remember this password. Without it, you won't be able to access the encrypted drive.

To prevent you from losing access to the encrypted drive, the encryption process includes a step to save a backup recovery key. You can use it if you forget the password and need to recover the encrypted data. You can save the recovery key automatically to your Microsoft account (if you log on to Windows 8.1 with a Microsoft account), to a file on a USB memory stick, on a different drive, or it can be printed on a piece of paper.

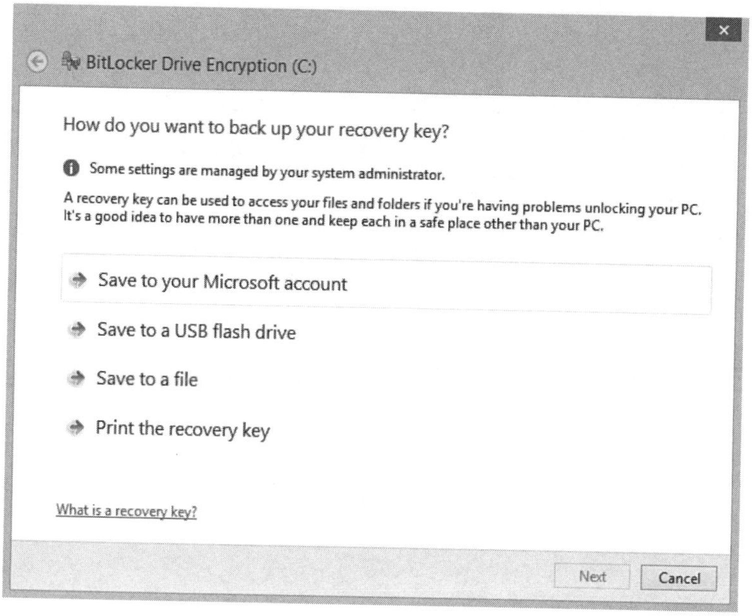

The dialog box shown:

BitLocker Drive Encryption (C:)

How do you want to back up your recovery key?

ⓘ Some settings are managed by your system administrator.

A recovery key can be used to access your files and folders if you're having problems unlocking your PC. It's a good idea to have more than one and keep each in a safe place other than your PC.

→ Save to your Microsoft account

→ Save to a USB flash drive

→ Save to a file

→ Print the recovery key

What is a recovery key?

Next   Cancel

18

TIP When encrypting a drive other than the operating system drive, the text displayed will be slightly different. However, the options you can choose remain the same.

Before the encryption process begins, you are asked whether you want to encrypt only the used disk space or the entire drive. Both methods work well. If you have a newer computer with a fresh installation of Windows 8.1, it is best to choose the first option. If your computer has been used for quite some time, it is best to encrypt the entire drive. However, the second option takes longer than the first.

As soon as the encryption process begins, each time you start your computer you are asked to enter the password you set earlier. Without it, you can't start Windows or access the encrypted drive.

Prior to encrypting the drive, you are asked to restart the computer. When you log on again, you see the Encryption In Progress notification on the Desktop.

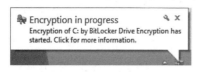

You can click the notification to see a progress indicator for the encryption process.

During the encryption process, you can use your computer normally. You can run apps, work on documents, and so on. You can restart your computer even if the encryption is not yet finished; it will resume automatically the next time you start Windows.

In this exercise, you'll learn how to encrypt your operating system drive by using BitLocker.

 SET UP
Close any apps or work you have open and then open the BitLocker Drive Encryption window.

1   Adjacent to the operating system drive, click **Turn On BitLocker** to start the BitLocker Drive Encryption Wizard.

You are asked to choose how to unlock your drive at startup.

2   Choose **Enter A Password** and you are asked to enter the password twice.

3   In the **Enter Your Password** and **Reenter Your Password** boxes, type the password that you want to use, and then click **Next**.

18

BitLocker Drive Encryption (C:)

Create a password to unlock this drive

You should create a strong password that uses uppercase and lowercase letters, numbers, symbols, and spaces.

Enter your password

[••••••••••]

Reenter your password

[••••••••••]

Tips for creating a strong password.

[Next]   [Cancel]

4   Save the recovery key by using the method you prefer and then click **Next**.

How do you want to back up your recovery key?

ℹ Some settings are managed by your system administrator.

A recovery key can be used to access your files and folders if you're having problems unlocking your PC. It's a good idea to have more than one and keep each in a safe place other than your PC.

➔ Save to your Microsoft account

➔ Save to a USB flash drive

➔ Save to a file

➔ Print the recovery key

What is a recovery key?

You are asked to choose how much of your drive you want to encrypt.

5   Select the option that best fits your needs and then click **Next**.

Choose how much of your drive to encrypt

If you're setting up BitLocker on a new drive or a new PC, you only need to encrypt the part of the drive that's currently being used. BitLocker encrypts new data automatically as you add it.

If you're enabling BitLocker on a PC or drive that's already in use, consider encrypting the entire drive. Encrypting the entire drive ensures that all data is protected–even data that you deleted but that might still contain retrievable info.

◉ Encrypt used disk space only (faster and best for new PCs and drives)

○ Encrypt entire drive (slower but best for PCs and drives already in use)

6   Leave the **Run BitLocker System** check box selected and click **Continue**.

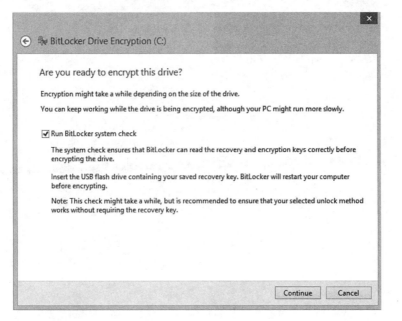

You are informed that the encryption will be completed after the computer is restarted.

7   Restart the computer and enter the BitLocker password you set in step 3.

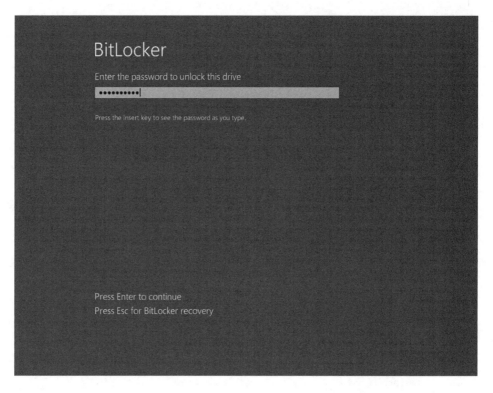

8   Log on to Windows 8.1.

You are notified that the encryption is in progress.

⊗ CLEAN UP
Continue using your computer while the encryption process runs in the background.

The time it takes for the operating system drive to be encrypted depends on its size and how much data is stored on it. The speed of your computer's processor will also affect the amount of time it takes. The faster the processor, the faster the encryption process will be. It can take from 30 minutes to a few hours, so be patient.

Encrypting removable storage devices by using BitLocker

Encrypting a removable data storage device such as a USB memory stick doesn't take long, and it involves fewer steps than encrypting the operating system drive. After the encryption process ends, each time you plug that device into a Windows computer, it will be displayed in File Explorer using a lock icon, signaling that it is encrypted. To access its content, you must enter the password that was set during the encryption process.

In this exercise, you'll learn how to use BitLocker to encrypt a USB memory stick. The process is the same for other types of removable storage devices, such as external hard disks.

 SET UP
Plug in the USB flash drive that you want to encrypt and then open the BitLocker Drive Encryption window.

1   Click **Turn On BitLocker** next to the storage device to start the BitLocker Drive Encryption Wizard.

2   On the first page of the wizard, select the **Use A Password To Unlock The Drive** check box.

> **⊗** **BitLocker Drive Encryption (H:)**
>
> Choose how you want to unlock this drive
>
> ☑ Use a password to unlock the drive
>   Passwords should contain uppercase and lowercase letters, numbers, spaces, and symbols.
>
>   Enter your password   ••••••••••
>
>   Reenter your password   ••••••••••
>
> ☐ Use my smart card to unlock the drive
>   You'll need to insert your smart card. The smart card PIN will be required when you unlock the drive.
>
>   Next   Cancel

3   In the **Enter Your Password** and **Reenter Your Password** boxes, type the password that you want to use, and then click **Next**.

TIP Depending on the USB memory stick you are encrypting, you might see an additional option on the screen: Automatically Unlock This Drive On This Computer. If you are storing very sensitive data, it is best not to select this option.

4   Save the recovery key by using the method you prefer and then click **Next**.

You are asked to choose how much of your drive you want to encrypt.

5   Select the option that best fits your needs and then click **Next**.

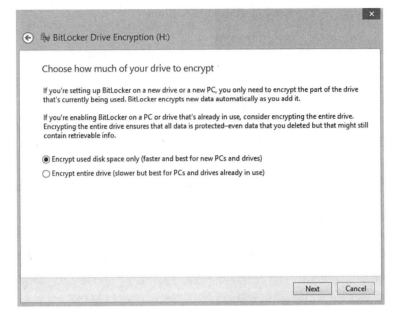

You are asked to confirm that you are ready to encrypt the drive.

6   Click **Start Encrypting**.

A progress window appears.

7   Wait for the process to finish and then click **Close**.

You can now use the USB memory stick as you normally would. All the data stored on it is now encrypted and can be accessed only by using the password you have set. You can encrypt other removable devices, including external hard disks, by using the same procedure. The steps will be the same, but some of the options will appear slightly different depending on the device.

Accessing an encrypted removable storage device

Each time you plug the encrypted removable storage device into any computer running Windows 8.1, including your own, a notification appears saying that the drive is BitLocker-protected.

Click the notification, and you are asked to type the password you set during the encryption process. Type the password and click Unlock. If you click More Options, you can also set Windows to unlock this drive automatically each time you insert it.

BitLocker (H:)

Enter password to unlock this drive.

●●●●●●●●●●   👁

More options

Unlock

If notifications are turned off in Windows 8.1, you can access the encrypted device from File Explorer. When you double-click the device, a prompt for entering the password is shown, just like the one in the preceding screen shot.

Only after typing the correct password are you able to view and use the data stored on the device.

Decrypting a BitLocker-protected drive

The process for decrypting a BitLocker-protected drive is easy. First, unlock the drive it by providing the appropriate encryption password. Then, open the BitLocker Drive Encryption window and click Turn Off BitLocker for the drive you want to decrypt.

Removable data drives - BitLocker To Go

H: BitLocker on   (⌃)

Back up your recovery key
Change password
Remove password
Add smart card
Turn on auto-unlock
Turn off BitLocker

Confirm that you want to decrypt the drive and wait for the process to finish. When the decryption is complete, BitLocker no longer protects the device.

Setting up a VPN connection

A VPN is a link between your computer or device and your company's network. Such connections extend access to your company's private network across public networks such as your home network. VPN connections are useful because they enable you to send and receive data across public networks as if you were connected to your workplace's network. This makes it possible for you to access apps and services available on your company's network even though you are working remotely.

VPN connections benefit also from increased security because all transferred data is encrypted. These connections cannot be easily sniffed by unauthorized parties which might be trying to monitor your public network connection and the data you send and receive through it. VPNs are also cost effective because they can connect geographically disparate offices of an organization creating one cohesive virtual network, without spending too much money and resources to set them up.

If your company uses VPN connections for its remote employees, you will receive a specific user account and password to establish VPN connections to your company's network. Before you go ahead and try to connect via VPN, ensure that you are aware of all the technical details required to set it up. The list of details varies depending on your company's setup, but it will include at least the following details: the IP address (Internet address) of the VPN server, the connection name, and a username and password.

You can establish VPN connections by using third-party tools or you can do it directly from Windows 8.1. It depends on the VPN solution adopted by your company. If your company is using Microsoft solutions, including for VPN, Windows 8.1 makes it easy for you to connect to your workplace's network.

In this exercise, you'll learn how to connect to your workplace through a VPN.

 SET UP

Ensure that you know the technical details required for setting up a VPN connection: Internet address of the VPN server, its name, credentials, and other parameters. They will be given to you by the company's IT department, when it sets up your VPN account. Then, on your work laptop or device, connect to the Internet and open the Network And Sharing Center.

1   In the **Network And Sharing Center**, click **Set Up A New Connection Or Network**, to open a wizard of the same name.

2   Select **Connect To A Workplace** and then click **Next**.

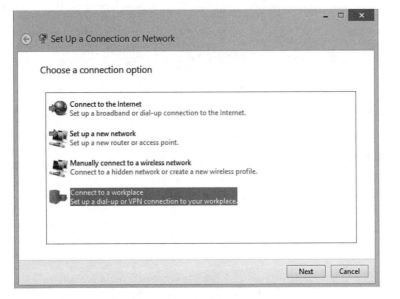

You are asked to select how you want to connect.

3   Select **Use My Internet Connection (VPN)**.

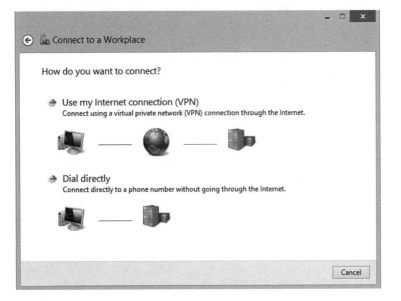

You are asked to enter the details of the VPN connection.

4 Type the Internet address of the VPN server, the destination name, and select or clear the appropriate options, as instructed by your company's IT staff.

5 When ready, click **Create**.

You are taken to the Desktop.

6   Click the network icon in the notification area of the taskbar to open the Networks pane.

7   In the **Connections** section, click the VPN connection you just created and then click **Connect**.

You are asked to enter your username and password.

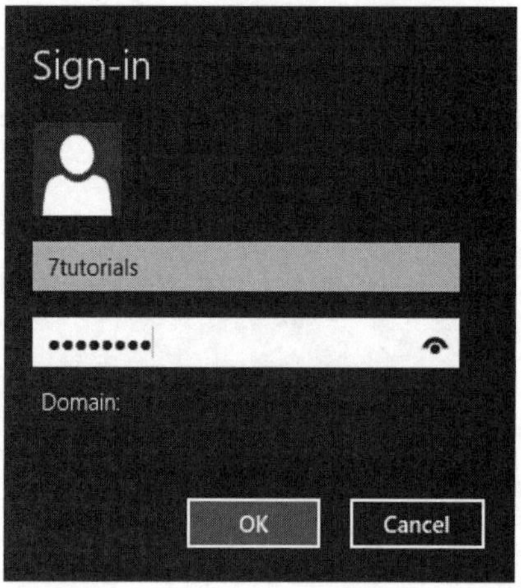

```
Sign-in

[user icon]

7tutorials

•••••••••                                    ⌒

Domain:


            OK              Cancel
```

8   Enter the requested details and click **OK**.

9   You are now connected to your workplace through VPN.

⊗ CLEAN UP
Use the VPN connection to your workplace and then, when done, disconnect from the Networks pane.

Other enterprise-friendly features

Windows 8.1 also offers other enterprise-friendly features. Because the space available for this book is limited, we could not cover all of them in detail. However, there are a few features we would like to mention:

- **Storage Spaces**   This is a feature designed for IT enthusiasts and professionals who need a lot of flexibility when working with drives and storage space. This feature makes it possible for you to group together physical storage drives in a storage pool. Then, you can use the pool's capacity to create storage spaces. These spaces are virtual drives that appear in File Explorer. You can use them like any other drive and do whatever you need to do with them. If you happen to run low on capacity, you can add more drives at any time and increase the capacity available for your storage spaces.

Storage Spaces also offer resiliency features, such as two-way mirroring, 3-way mirroring and parity, to secure your data and prevent its loss when disk failures take place. By enabling resiliency, you will have at least two copies of your data on separate physical disks. Since the data saved in the storage space is always mirrored, you will be able to access it even though one physical drive fails.

- **Work Folders** You can use these to store and access work files on any kind of computer or device. You will have a location where you can store work files and access them from anywhere, even when connected to remote networks. Businesses can use this feature to store files on centrally managed file servers and set in place policies such as encryption and lock-screen passwords when users try to access their data from remote computers. Using Work Folders, users can access their work files while offline and synchronize them with the central file server when their computer or device has an Internet connection available.

- **Windows to Go** This is a feature for enterprise users with which they can boot a full version of Windows 8.1 from external USB drives on any computer, including their personal computer. When booting from the USB drive, a full Windows 8.1 instance is started and the user can work with it as with any other Windows edition. In a business environment, only the IT administrator(s) will provision Windows to Go drives to the company's employees. The users cannot create these themselves from Windows 8.1.

Key points

- Windows Mobility Center is a helpful tool when you are mobile and you need to connect your laptop to multiple devices and displays.

- Turning on Presentation mode is helpful when you need to deliver presentations at work or anywhere else.

- Encryption is a great solution for ensuring that your data cannot be accessed by unwanted people.

- With BitLocker, you can encrypt both your computer's drives and removable data storage devices such as USB flash memory sticks.

- VPNs offers a fast and secure way to connect remotely to your company's network and access its apps and services.

18

Chapter at a glance

Use

Use touch to view all running apps, page 554

Configure

Configure how fast a double-tap should be, page 556

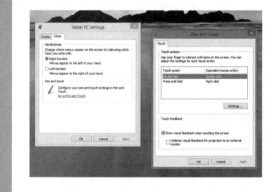

Configure

Configure Pen and Touch settings in Control Panel, page 557

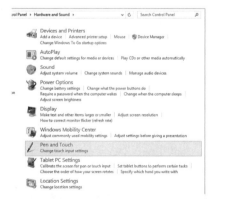

Show

Show or hide touch feedback, page 559

Using touch-compatible devices

19

IN THIS CHAPTER, YOU WILL LEARN HOW TO

- Set up your screen and calibrate it.

- Use general touch gestures.

- Explore and use multitouch gestures.

- Change touch input settings.

- Access touch settings from PC settings.

If you have a Windows 8.1 computer, laptop, tablet, or other compatible device that accepts touch gestures, you can use the single-touch and multitouch features available with Windows 8.1 in lieu of using a mouse or other pointing device. There are several features to explore beyond touch gestures, however; you can use a pen (stylus) to draw on the screen and use the On-Screen Keyboard to type (see Chapter 17, "Making my computer accessible"). You can use the Touch Keyboard on the desktop. You can configure touch settings, too, including how you want to use a double-tap or long press. You should also configure and calibrate your display (even if it seems to work fine now). The touch and pen settings are configurable, so you can personalize them to suit your needs exactly.

PRACTICE FILES You do not need any practice files to complete this chapter. For more information about practice file requirements, the section "Using the practice files" in the Introduction of this book.

Setting up touch hardware

If you've used touch before, you know you can touch tiles to open their respective apps, double-tap desktop apps and desktop items such as Recycle Bin to open them, and use your finger to swipe and scroll while within various apps and desktop apps, including Microsoft Internet Explorer. You know you can tap and hold some items and swipe up from the bottom or down from the top to access an app's charms features. You might think that because touch works, your hardware does not need to be set up, but it does. At the very least, it should be calibrated.

During the calibration process, you'll be prompted to do the following:

- **Choose the screen to use**   If more than one screen is available (or if Windows thinks there are multiple screens available), you choose which screen to use.

- **Calibrate the screen**   This involves touching the screen in various places upon prompting to calibrate Windows 8.1 properly.

- **Choose a rotation option**   If your screen rotates, you can configure how the screen's orientation changes when you rotate it.

In this exercise, you'll access the touch options and work through the wizard to complete the setup process.

 SET UP
Start your computer and unlock the lock screen. You need access to the Start screen.

TIP In this book, if an instruction requires you to click something with a mouse, you can generally touch or tap the item to achieve the same result. If a right-click is required, you might need to touch and hold, swipe up from the bottom, or perform some other gesture.

1   On the **Start** screen, type Calibrate.

2   In the search results area, click or touch **Calibrate The Screen For Pen Or Touch Input**.

3   In the **Tablet PC Settings** dialog box, tap **Setup**.

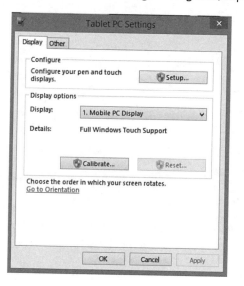

4   Tap the screen to choose a monitor if prompted.

5   Tap **Calibrate**.

6   Work through the wizard as instructed. Tap **Yes** to save the calibration data.

7   If your screen rotates, tap **Go To Orientation**.

8   Configure the orientation options as desired and then tap **OK**. Tap **OK** again to close all dialog boxes.

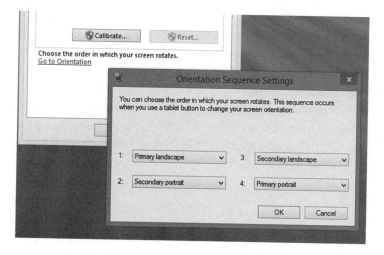

9   Flick or swipe in from the right side of the screen to access the charms.

10   Tap **Start** to return to the Start screen.

> **TIP** It might take some practice to learn how to swipe from the right side of the screen to the left to access the charms. Keep trying; it will work!

⊗ CLEAN UP
No cleanup is required.

Learning general touch gestures

You might already be familiar with a few touch gestures; you can certainly tap a tile on the Start screen to open an app. You can apply many more touch techniques, too.

Here are the general single-touch gestures you'll want to learn right away:

- **One tap**   Tap once to open an app, to select a desktop icon, to apply a rating in the Windows Store, to open a link in Internet Explorer, to use a Back or Forward button, to install an app, to select an email, or to perform any other task that can be applied with a single mouse click.

- **A double-tap**   Tap twice in rapid succession to open an item on the desktop, to zoom in on a webpage (and tap twice to zoom back out), or to perform any other task that can be applied with a traditional double-click with the mouse.

> **TIP** Use a pinching motion with your thumb and forefinger to zoom in and out of the screen. This works on the Start screen, too. Technically, this is a multitouch gesture and is outlined in the next section.

- **A long touch (touch and hold)**   In some cases, to obtain results consistent with a traditional right-click with the mouse. Long-touch a folder on the desktop to access the shortcut menu; long-touch a link in Internet Explorer to access options to copy and open the link. Use a long touch on the Start screen to drag an app to a new position or to simply select it

- **A fast swipe from the left edge inward**   When multiple apps and desktop apps are open, this one-finger motion switches among them.

  TROUBLESHOOTING If you have trouble getting the desired result when you swipe from the edges of the screen with a finger, try swiping with your thumb, instead.

- **A fast swipe from right to left or from left to right (while not at the edge of the screen)**   Use this motion to scroll quickly through a map with the Maps app; to view additional information about the current weather from the Weather app; to change months quickly in the Calendar; to scroll through pages in the Store, Music, Video, and similar apps; to move among webpages you've visited in the Internet Explorer app; or to perform tasks such as scrolling from right to left with a traditional scroll bar and mouse.

- **A fast swipe from the right edge inward**   Do this to show the charms (Search, Share, Start, Devices, Settings).

  TIP To access settings for any app quickly, while in the app, swipe from the middle right edge inward to show the charms and then tap Settings.

- **A slow swipe from left to right (in the middle of the left edge)**   If you perform this gesture while using an app when multiple apps are open, you can snap one app so that it takes a part of the screen and another app takes up the rest of it. When you do this, you can run two apps side by side (such as Calendar and Weather) and interact with both. If you hardware supports it, you can have up to four apps open at once.

  TIP When you have multiple apps open at one time on the screen, use the bar that appears between them to make the smaller one larger and the larger one smaller. In this mode, you can still pinch to zoom and use other touch techniques.

> **IMPORTANT** You won't be able to snap apps (and perform some other touch gestures) if your resolution is set too low or your monitor doesn't support the required resolution (as of this writing, that resolution is 1366 × 768).

19

- **A fast swipe out and back from the middle of the left side of the screen** Use this motion to show all running apps in a bar on the left side of the screen. (You can then tap any app to open it.)

- **Pull (flick) down from top** Depending on your display and resolution and the app you have open, you might be able to pull down from the top of an app and drag it off the screen to close it. If you flick down from the top quickly you might be able to view additional features.

  TIP Open the Internet Explorer app and pull down from the top somewhat slowly to see additional options.

- **Pull (flick) up from the bottom**   While in an app, this gesture might display the available charms for that app.

- **Tap, hold, and pull**   Do this to select and move an item such as a tile on the Start screen.

TIP   Try all these gestures before moving on.

Using multitouch gestures

In the previous section, you learned how to use the most common one-finger gestures. You learned about tapping, double-tapping, long-touching, swiping, and others. There are also a few multitouch gestures you can use, and these require more than one finger to perform.

One of the most-used multitouch gestures is the pinch. With two fingers, you can pinch inward and outward to zoom out and in, respectively. You can do this even on the Start screen. When you pinch inward, all the icons on the Start screen become smaller; pinch outward, and they return to their original size (or zoom out) You can also perform this task with four or five fingers if desired and if your monitor supports it.

If you have compatible hardware, a screen set to the proper resolution, and if you are using an app that supports it, you can use two fingers to rotate what's on the screen 90 degrees. In addition, as newer releases, updates, and hardware improvements become available, more multitouch gestures will become available, as well.

Changing touch-input settings

Touch settings exist. You saw some earlier if you worked through the calibration options. You can access some touch settings from PC Settings, but not many. If you use a tablet, you might have more settings than described in this section if they are provided by the manufacturer. Here, you'll be concerned only with what's available with Windows 8.1 and what is common to all Windows 8.1 touch-compatible computers, tablets, and devices.

TIP   The manufacturer of your device might include additional features for it, such as a Windows button on the device itself (which returns you to the Start screen).

To see a few of the touch features and configuration options that are available, on the Start screen, type Tablet PC Settings. In the search results area, click Tablet PC Settings. This opens the dialog box you used earlier to calibrate your device. The settings you'll want to explore here are available on the Other tab and include but might not be limited to the following:

- **Change multi-touch gesture settings** To change handedness settings, access the Tablet PC Settings dialog box and then tap Other.

- **Pen and touch** To configure options that require you to use your finger to interact with items on the screen. You can configure settings for Double-Tap and Press And Hold and settings to show visual feedback when touching the screen and when using a projector or external monitor.

You can access these settings and more from the traditional Control Panel, too. On the Hardware And Sound page, you have easy access to Mouse settings, Display settings, Pen And Touch input settings, and Tablet PC Settings.

In this exercise, you'll access Pen And Touch settings and configure how quickly you tap the screen when you double-tap and the tolerance for the distance you can move between taps.

→ SET UP

Start your computer and unlock the lock screen. You need access to the Start screen.

1   On the **Start** screen, type Pen and Touch.

2   In the search results area, tap **Pen And Touch**.

3   On the **Touch** tab, select **Double-Tap**, and then tap **Settings**.

4   In the **Double-Tap Settings** window, move the slider for **Speed** to the right or left to make the speed required for a double-tap faster or slower, respectively.

5   Double-tap in **Test Settings**. If the door opens and you are happy with the set speed, continue. Otherwise, repeat step 4 to change it.

6   Repeat the process with **Spatial Tolerance**.

7   Tap **OK** to close the **Double-Tap Settings** window. Tap **OK** in the **Pen and Touch** window to close it.

> **TIP** If you have a disability and find it difficult to use your hands effectively, increase the Spatial Tolerance to Large. This will give you the most leeway possible if your hands shake or you have other issues that prevent you from tapping the screen in the same place twice in a row.

CLEAN UP
Return to the Start screen.

Access touch settings from PC Settings

A few of the touch options are available in PC Settings. To see these, from the Settings charm click Change PC Settings. Then, take a look at what is available in the following sections:

- **PC And Devices, the Display tab**   Click this tab to change the resolution and orientation quickly.

- **PC And Devices, the Mouse and Touchpad tab**   Click this tab to change the settings for a mouse or touchpad.

- **Ease of Access tab, and Other Options tab**   Click this to change touch feedback options.

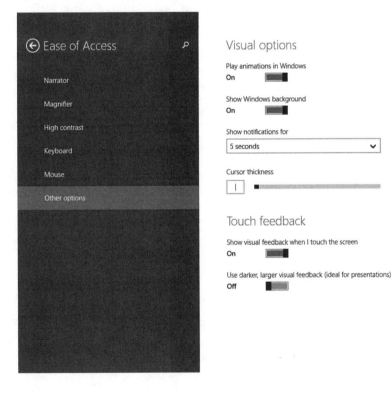

Key points

- You should calibrate your monitor, even if it worked correctly right out of the box.

- You can use many single-touch and single-finger gestures to navigate Windows 8.1.

- A handful of multitouch gestures, such as pinching, require more than one finger to perform.

- You can change many aspects of touch features, including how fast a double-tap should be and how close or far apart from each other those taps must occur.

- A few touch (and touchpad) settings are available from PC Settings.

Chapter at a glance

Add

Add the Shut Down, Restart, Sign Out, and other shortcuts to the Start screen, page 564

Lock - Switch User

Restart

Shut Down

Sign out

Sleep

Stop Shut Down

Name

Name groups of shortcuts on the Start screen, page 567

Set

Set Windows 8.1 to boot to the desktop, page 570

Optimize

Optimize startup items by using Task Manager, page 590

Tips for improving your computing experience

20

IN THIS CHAPTER, YOU WILL LEARN HOW TO

- Add useful shortcuts for use on the Windows 8.1 Start screen and desktop.

- Customize the Windows taskbar.

- Use the WinX system menu.

- Use Task Manager to optimize the Windows 8.1 startup.

The learning doesn't stop with the tips mentioned in the preceding list. This chapter aims to teach you twenty useful tricks to optimize your Windows 8.1 experience.

Because the Start screen represents a major change from earlier versions of Windows, you'll find quite a few tricks to help you be more organized and productive when using it. You'll see some tips for the desktop and the Windows taskbar you've grown to love from earlier versions of Windows.

Next, you'll learn how to log on to Windows 8.1 automatically, without typing your password each time; run older apps as an administrator; add or remove features in Windows 8.1; turn off notifications; and optimize your drives. You'll learn a few tricks about using Microsofts SkyDrive and the new Task Manager, too.

This chapter ends with tips on how to change the defaults for apps, file extensions, and AutoPlay dialog boxes.

PRACTICE FILES Before you can complete the exercises in this chapter, you need to copy the book's practice files to your computer. The practice files you'll use to complete the exercises in this chapter are in the Chapter20 folder. A complete list of practice files is provided in the section "Using the practice files" in the Introduction of this book.

Adding Shut Down, Restart, Sign Out, and other shortcuts to the Start screen

In the folder with practice files for this chapter are quite a few shortcuts for handy commands such as Shut Down, Restart, Sign Out, Sleep, Lock - Switch User, and Stop Shut Down.

Each shortcut does what its name says, and all shortcuts work on all editions of Windows 8.1. There are a few things to keep in mind, though:

- The Shut Down shortcut won't shut down your system immediately. It initiates the shutdown procedure, which takes a few seconds to finish.

- The Stop Shut Down shortcut works only if you have used the Shut Down shortcut to shut down your system. If you have started the shutdown procedure by other means, running this shortcut probably won't have any effect on your system.

In this exercise, you'll learn how to add each of these shortcuts to the Start screen.

➡ SET UP
To complete this exercise, you need the shortcut files in the Chapter20 practice files folder. After these files are downloaded to your computer, open File Explorer and browse to their location.

1   Right-click one of the shortcuts that you want to pin to the Start screen.

2   On the right-click menu that opens, click **Pin To Start**.

3   Repeat steps 1 and 2 for all the shortcuts that you want pinned to the Start screen and then open the Start screen.

4   Drag and drop the shortcuts on the Start screen so that they are in the same group and placed in the order you want.

 CLEAN UP
Close File Explorer.

Ensure that you don't delete the shortcuts from the location to which you downloaded them. If you do, they will stop working because the Start screen will point to files that no longer exist.

Adding a Control Panel shortcut to the Start screen

Another useful shortcut you might want to have on your Start screen is a shortcut for Control Panel. In this exercise, you'll learn how to add this shortcut to the Start screen.

 SET UP
Open the Start screen.

1 Type control and then, in the search results, look for **Control Panel**.

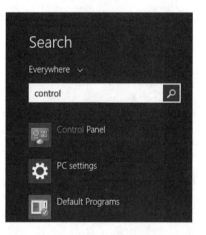

2 Right-click the **Control Panel** search result.

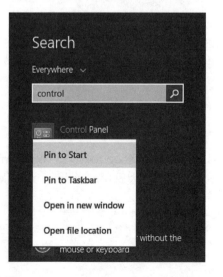

3   On the right-click menu, click **Pin To Start**.

 CLEAN UP
Switch from the list of search results back to the Start screen.

A Control Panel shortcut is now pinned and visible on the Start screen. Using the same procedure you can add lots of apps and Windows features to the Start screen, including File Explorer or any desktop app you install on your Windows 8.1 computer.

Naming groups of shortcuts on the Start screen

On the Start screen, you can drag shortcuts and tiles into groups and apply custom names to those groups.

If you like your Start screen well organized, you'll want to name each group of shortcuts and tiles. In this exercise, you'll learn how to to do just that.

 SET UP
Open the Start screen.

1   Right-click somewhere in the empty space of the **Start** screen.

2   On the toolbar that appears at the bottom of the screen, click **Customize**.

3   Each group of shortcuts and tiles on the **Start** screen has a text box above it labeled **Name Group** or with a label you have created previously.

4   Click the text box above the group that you want to name.

5   Type the new name that you want to apply to the group.

 CLEAN UP
Click the empty space of the Start screen to return it to normal.

The selected group of shortcuts and tiles now displays the name you have set. You can rename it by following the same steps and typing a new name in place of the old one.

Booting to the desktop in Windows 8.1

An important new feature in Windows 8.1 is the ability to change how it starts and what is loaded first, the Start screen or the desktop. If you are a traditional computer user who doesn't use modern Windows 8.1 apps, you can also disable the charms and hot upper-right and upper-left corners. All these things and more are set from the Taskbar And Navigation Properties window.

In this exercise, you'll learn how to set Windows 8.1 to boot to the desktop instead of the Start screen.

→ SET UP
Open the desktop.

1   Right-click the empty space on the taskbar.

2   On the right-click menu that appears, click **Properties**.

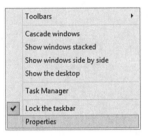

The Taskbar And Navigation Properties window opens.

3   Click the **Navigation** tab.

4   In the **Start Screen** section, select the check boxes for **When I Sign In Or Close All Apps On A Screen, Go To The Desktop Instead Of Start** and **Show Start On The Display I'm Using When I Press The Windows Logo Key**.

Taskbar and Navigation properties

| Taskbar | Navigation | Jump Lists | Toolbars |

Corner navigation

☑ When I point to the upper-right corner, show the charms

☑ When I click the upper-left corner, switch between my recent apps

☐ Replace Command Prompt with Windows PowerShell in the menu when I right-click the lower-left corner or press Windows key+X

Start screen

☑ When I sign in or close all apps on a screen, go to the desktop instead of Start

☐ Show my desktop background on Start

☑ Show Start on the display I'm using when I press the Windows logo key

☐ Show the Apps view automatically when I go to Start

☐ Search everywhere instead of just my apps when I search from the Apps view

☐ List desktop apps first in the Apps view when it's sorted by category

| OK | Cancel | Apply |

5   Click **OK**.

 CLEAN UP

No cleanup is required.

Windows 8.1 will now boot to the desktop, instead of the Start screen. To access the Start screen you can press the Start button on the desktop or the Windows key on your keyboard.

Transforming the Start screen into a full screen Start menu

Another important change that that you can do from the Taskbar And Navigation Properties window is to set Windows 8.1 to display the Apps view when you press the Start button or the Windows key on your keyboard. This view is a full screen Start Menu, which looks familiar to die-hard Windows users. You see shortcuts for all apps and desktop apps, organized by folders, just like they were in the Windows 7 Start menu.

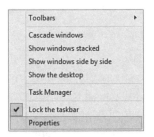

Apps by category ∨

Desktop		Windows Ease of Access		File Explorer
Desktop	Remote Desktop Connection			
	Snipping Tool	Magnifier	Help and Support	
Windows Media Player	Sound Recorder	Narrator	Run	
Windows Accessories	Steps Recorder	On-Screen Keyboard	Task Manager	
Calculator	Sticky Notes	Windows Speech Recognition	This PC	
Character Map	Windows Fax and Scan	Windows System	Windows Defender	
Math Input Panel	Windows Journal	Command Prompt	Windows Easy Transfer	
Notepad	WordPad	Control Panel	Windows PowerShell	
Paint	XPS Viewer	Default Programs		

If you are one of those die-hard users and you would prefer this view, in this exercise you'll learn how to set Windows 8.1 to display the Apps view instead of the Start screen. Also, you'll learn how to prioritize desktop apps when using with this view.

 SET UP
Open the desktop.

1   Right-click the empty space on the taskbar.

2   On the right-click menu that appears, click **Properties**.

Toolbars ▸
Cascade windows
Show windows stacked
Show windows side by side
Show the desktop
Task Manager
✓ Lock the taskbar
Properties

The Taskbar And Navigation Properties window opens.

3   Go to the **Navigation** tab.

4   In the **Start screen** section, select the check boxes for **Show The Apps View Automatically When I Go To Start** and **List Desktop Apps First In The Apps View When It's Sorted By Category**.

5   Click **OK**.

 CLEAN UP
No cleanup is required.

The Apps view is now displayed each time you press the Start button or the Windows key on your keyboard. You can still access the Start screen by pressing the Up arrow in the lower-left corner of the Apps view.

Using the WinX system menu

In Windows 8 and Windows 8.1, Microsoft removed the classic Start menu. In its place is a system menu that provides quick and easy access to many useful tools such as Computer Management, the Command Prompt, Task Manager, Control Panel, the Run window, and many others. In a further improvement, there are now options for shutting down or restarting your computer or device.

Programs and Features
Mobility Center
Power Options
Event Viewer
System
Device Manager
Network Connections
Disk Management
Computer Management
Command Prompt
Command Prompt (Admin)

Task Manager
Control Panel
File Explorer
Search
Run

Shut down or sign out ▸
Desktop

The fastest way to open this menu is to press Windows key+X on your keyboard, but in this exercise, you'll learn how to access the hidden system menu by using the mouse.

 SET UP
Open the desktop.

1   Using the mouse, point to the Start button.

2   Right-click the Start button.

3   On the menu that appears, click the tool that you want to start.

❌ CLEAN UP
No cleanup is required.

Don't hesitate to experiment with this procedure until you are comfortable accessing and using this menu.

Running a desktop app as Administrator

In Windows 8.1, apps run by default without administrator permissions. This is a security feature which ensures that apps do not have the permission to make unwanted system changes. However, earlier apps that don't run so well on newer versions of Windows might need to be run with administrator permissions so that they function without problems.

If the app has a shortcut on the Start screen, right-click to select it. On the menu that appears at the bottom of the screen, click Run As Administrator.

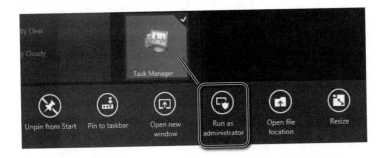

If you want to run the app from the desktop or File Explorer, right-click its shortcut or main executable and then, on the menu that appears, click Run As Administrator.

In this exercise, you'll learn how to edit the properties of the app shortcut or main executable and have it always run as administrator.

SET UP
Open File Explorer.

1   Browse to where the main executable file of the app or its shortcut is stored.

2   Right-click the shortcut or executable, and then, on the menu that appears, click **Properties** to open the **Properties** dialog box.

3   Click the **Compatibility** tab.

4   In the **Settings** section, select the **Run This Program As An Administrator**.

5   Click **OK**.

⊗ CLEAN UP
Close File Explorer.

From this point forward, each time you run the selected app, a User Account Control (UAC) prompt appears asking for your permission to run the app as administrator. After you approve it, the app will be allowed to run with administrator permissions.

> **IMPORTANT** Remember that the new Windows Store apps don't run with administrator permissions and cannot be set to run with administrator permissions.

Printing documents from Windows Store apps

If you're working with desktop apps, printing in the new Windows is the same as in earlier versions. However, when using Windows Store apps, printing is done by using the Devices charm. With this charm, you can interact with other devices in your network, including your printers.

Before you print, you are shown a preview and given access to several printing options. You can set how many copies you can print, which pages, the size of the document, its orientation and other parameters.

In this exercise you'll learn how to print from Windows Store apps via the Devices charm.

 SET UP
To complete this exercise, you need the ForPrinting.pdf file in the Chapter20 practice files folder. Also, a printer must be installed and turned on, and be accessible on your Windows 8.1 computer or device. Then, open File Explorer.

1   Open the folder where you stored the ForPrinting.pdf practice file.

2   Select the file and then, on the ribbon, click the **Home** tab.

Name	Date modified	Type
ForPrinting.pdf	8/5/2013 5:27 AM	PDF File
Lock - Switch User	10/4/2009 3:28 AM	Shortcut
Restart	10/4/2009 3:26 AM	Shortcut
Shut Down	10/4/2009 3:22 AM	Shortcut
Sign out	10/4/2009 3:28 AM	Shortcut
Sleep	10/4/2009 4:28 AM	Shortcut
Stop Shut Down	3/8/2012 10:07 AM	Shortcut

3   In the **Open** section, click the down-pointing arrow, near the **Open** button.

4   From the list of options, click **Reader**.

The ForPrinting.pdf file is opened in the Reader app.

5   Access the charms and then select **Devices** (**Windows key+K**).

This document will be used as a practice file, so that you learn how to print from Windows 8.1 apps.

6   In the **Devices** charm, select **Print**.

A list with all installed printers is shown.

7   Click the printer with which you want to print the document.

You can now set how you want to print the document.

8 Set the available printing options as you want them and then click **Print**.

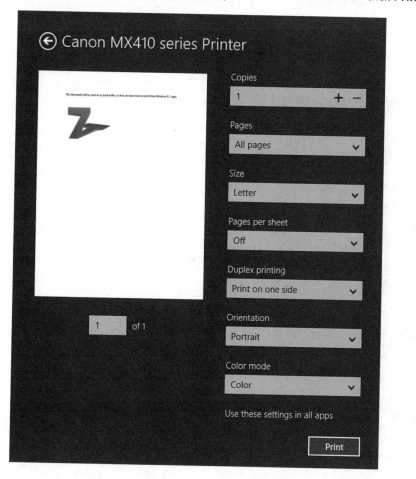

9   The document is now sent to the printer, for printing.

❌ CLEAN UP
Close the Reader app.

The process for printing from all modern Windows 8.1 apps is the same. When you work with a modern app, bring up the Devices charm and follow the steps presented in this exercise.

Turning off notifications for Windows Store apps

Windows has a new system for showing notifications that is more verbose than earlier versions, which you will notice after you download and install a number of apps.

You can customize in detail, at an app level, which notifications you receive. To configure this, access PC Settings, click Search and Apps, and then click Notifications.

At the top are the following four settings with switches that affect all app notifications:

- **Show App Notifications**   When this set to Off, you do not receive notifications from all apps.

- **Show App Notifications On The Lock Screen**   When set to Off, no notifications appear on the lock screen.

- **Play Notification Sounds**   When set to Off, notifications are not accompanied by sounds.

- **Turn On My Screen When I Get A Call**   When set to Off, your screen won't be turned on when you get a call via messaging apps like Skype.

Below Notifications is the Quiet Hours section, which includes several settings and switches. Quiet Hours are the times in a day during which you don't want to be bothered by app notifications of any kind. By default, they are set from 12:00 AM to 6:00 AM, when most people are likely to sleep.

Slide the Quiet Hours switch to On to activate this feature.

Quiet hours

Stop app notifications during certain hours of the day. Notifications turn back on if you start using your PC or when quiet hours end.

Quiet hours
On   ▮▮▮▮▮▯

From
| 12 ⌄ | 00 ⌄ | AM ⌄ |

To
| 6 ⌄ | 00 ⌄ | AM ⌄ |

Receive calls during quiet hours
On   ▮▮▮▮▮▯

Then, you can set the time interval when you don't want to be bothered. Last but not least, you can control whether you receive calls during quiet hours. By default, this is set to On, but if you would rather not be bothered by calls, switch this setting to Off.

Scroll down a bit and you'll see the section named Show Notifications From These Apps. Here you have individual switches for all Windows Store apps. Setting the switch for an app to Off stops notifications from that app. Keep in mind that the list of apps displayed depends on the apps you install on your computer or device. On your Windows installation, probably won't see the same number of apps listed as in the screen shots included in this section.

In this exercise, you'll learn how to disable notifications for a group of apps.

SET UP
Open PC Settings.

1   Click **Search And Apps** and then click **Notifications**.

2   Scroll down until you find the list of notifications that can be turned on or off and then identify those that you want to turn off.

← Search and apps	🔍	Show notifications from these apps		
Search		🕐 Alarms	On	▭
Share		📅 Calendar	On	▭
Notifications		🖨 Canon Inkjet Print Utility	On	▭
App sizes		🍴 Food & Drink	On	▭
Defaults		🎮 Games	On	▭
		ℯ Internet Explorer	On	▭
		✉ Mail	On	▭
		🎧 Music	On	▭
		📰 News	On	▭
		🖼 Photos	On	▭
		📖 Reader	On	▭
		📐 Scan	On	▭

3   For the apps for which you no longer want to receive notifications, turn the switch from On to Off.

Show notifications from these apps

Alarms	On	
Calendar	On	
Canon Inkjet Print Utility	Off	
Food & Drink	Off	

 CLEAN UP
Close PC Settings.

Your notification settings are now applied.

Adding or removing Windows features

Windows 8.1 comes with many features. Some of them are installed and enabled by default, whereas others are not and need to be added manually. You add or remove Windows features in the Windows Features window.

The features for which the check box is selected are turned on; those with clear check boxes are turned off. Similar features are grouped into folders that you can expand. Click the plus sign to the left of a folder name to view the individual features that are included. You can turn on or off the entire set of features in that folder or just individual features.

In this exercise, you'll learn how to remove a Windows feature. To demonstrate the procedure, you'll remove XPS Viewer, which you can add back after the exercise. However, for this exercise you can remove any Windows feature you don't plan to use.

 SET UP
Open Control Panel.

1   Click **Programs** and then choose **Programs And Features**.

2   In the **Program And Features** window, in the column on the left, click **Turn Windows Features On Or Off** to open the **Windows Features** window.

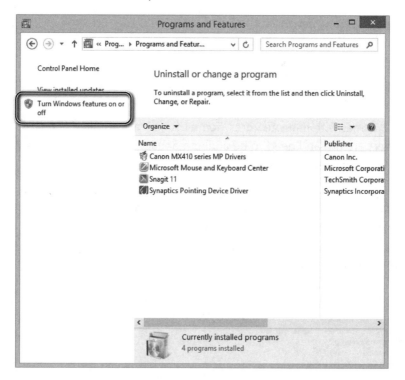

3   Scroll down until you find the **XPS Viewer** entry.

4   Clear the check box for **XPS Viewer**.

You are warned that this might affect other Windows features and programs.

5   Click **Yes** and then **OK.** Wait for Windows to complete the requested changes.

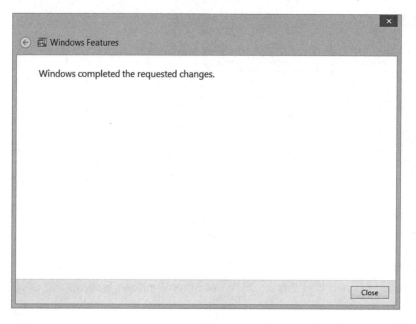

6   Click **Close**.

 CLEAN UP
Close Programs And Features.

To add a Windows feature, go through the same steps. At step 4, you just choose the feature you want to add.

IMPORTANT Depending on the feature you are removing or adding, you might be asked to restart your system or to provide the Windows installation disc so that files can be copied from it. For most features, a disc won't be required.

Six ways to start the Task Manager

Chapter 21, "Troubleshooting problems," covers the basics of using the Task Manager to manage running apps and services. However, it does not cover in detail the many ways by which you can access this tool.

The first and best-known method to access Task Manager is not necessarily the fastest: press Ctrl+Alt+Del and then click Task Manager.

If you prefer to use your keyboard, the fastest way to start Task Manager is to press Ctrl+Shift+Esc. That will open the tool without an additional click.

Another rapid method is to use the WinX system menu for power users, detailed in a previous tip in this chapter. To access that, press Windows key+X and then click Task Manager.

20

Programs and Features
Mobility Center
Power Options
Event Viewer
System
Device Manager
Network Connections
Disk Management
Computer Management
Command Prompt
Command Prompt (Admin)
Task Manager
Control Panel
File Explorer
Search
Run
Shut down or sign out ▶
Desktop

You can also perform a search on the Start screen; just type the word task and then click the appropriate search result.

You can use the Apps view, which you can open from the Start screen. The Task Manager shortcut is in the Windows System section of shortcuts.

Finally, you can go to the desktop and right-click the notification area on the taskbar (on the right end, where the date and time are displayed). In the right click menu, select Task Manager.

Optimizing startup items by using the Task Manager

When you open the new Task Manager for the first time, you might have the impression that you can only use it to manage the apps that are currently running. This is a consequence of its rather simple interface and the apparent lack of options.

However, you can click the More Details button to enlarge the window and display several tabs and options. On the Startup tab, you can view the apps that run at the Windows startup. For each app, Task Manager shows its name, its publisher, its status (whether it is enabled or disabled to run at startup), and its impact on the startup procedure.

Name	Publisher	Status	Startup impact
CCleaner	Piriform Ltd	Enabled	High
▷ Synaptics TouchPad Enhanc...	Synaptics Incorporated	Enabled	High

(Task Manager — File, Options, View menu; tabs: Processes, Performance, App history, Startup, Users, Details, Services. Fewer details / Disable.)

Based on this information, you can choose to prevent some apps from running at startup so that Windows 8.1 starts up more quickly.

In this exercise, you'll learn how to disable apps from running at startup by using Task Manager.

 SET UP
Open Task Manager.

1   Click **More Details**.

2   Click the **Startup** tab to view a list of all the apps running at startup.

3   Select the app that you want to prevent from running at startup, and then click
     Disable.

20

CLEAN UP
Close Task Manager.

By using this method, you can disable all the items running at startup. However, it's recommended that you disable only those apps that you don't need to run at startup. You should not disable apps that are installed by the drivers of your hardware components (video card drivers, keyboard and mouse drivers, sound card drivers, and so on). If you disable them, you might encounter issues with the functioning of your hardware components.

Adding clocks and time zones to the Windows taskbar

If you interact with people all over the world, it is useful to quickly access the time for more than just your time zone. You can set Windows to display up to two additional clocks when you click or use the mouse to point to the clock shown on the taskbar.

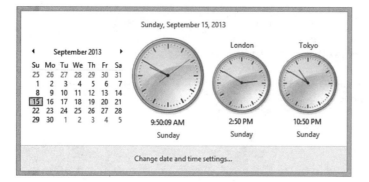

In this exercise, you'll learn how to add two clocks to the Windows taskbar.

 **SET UP**
Open the desktop.

1   Click the area of the taskbar where the clock is displayed to open a window with details about the current date and time.

2   Click **Change Date And Time Settings** to open the **Date And Time** window.

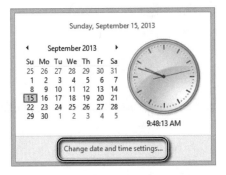

3   Click the **Additional Clocks** tab.

4   Select the **Show This Clock** check box and then select the time zone you want displayed for the first additional clock.

5   In the **Enter Display Name** box, type the name that you want to display for the first additional clock.

Date and Time

| Date and Time | Additional Clocks | Internet Time |

Additional clocks can display the time in other time zones. You can view them by clicking on or hovering over the taskbar clock.

☑ Show this clock

Select time zone:

(UTC) Dublin, Edinburgh, Lisbon, London

Enter display name:

London

☑ Show this clock

Select time zone:

(UTC+09:00) Osaka, Sapporo, Tokyo

Enter display name:

Tokyo

| OK | Cancel | Apply |

6   Repeat steps 4 and 5 for the second clock.

7   Click **OK**.

 CLEAN UP
No cleanup is required.

The additional clocks now appear each time you use the mouse to point to the clock on the taskbar or when you click the taskbar.

Changing the location of the Downloads folder and other user folders

Windows stores all your user files and folders in C:\Users, followed by your user name. There, you will find folders such as Desktop, Downloads, Documents, Music, Pictures, and so on. In Windows 8.1 they are also displayed in File Explorer, under This PC.

You might want to change the location of one or more of your user folders. For example, you might want to move the Downloads folder to another partition, so that you have enough room left on your system drive. This will help to ensure that your user folders and their contents are safe if Windows fails and you need to reinstall it. If you have a solid-state storage device (SSD) with little space available, moving your user folders to another drive makes even more sense. This way, you can use the precious space available on the SSD for apps and games that will benefit from its performance.

IMPORTANT When carrying out this operation, it is important to avoid this mistake: do not move the location of one user folder inside another user folder. This will break the internal references used by Windows and its apps and might cause malfunctions. For example, if you move the Downloads folder somewhere inside the desktop, Windows will display two desktop folders instead of a Downloads and a desktop folder. Also, some apps won't know how to deal with two desktop folders and no Downloads folder.

In Windows 8.1, you can easily change the location of your user folders. In this exercise, you'll learn how to change the location of your Downloads folder.

SET UP

Open File Explorer and browse to This PC.

1 Right-click the **Downloads** folder to open the shortcut menu.

2 Click **Properties** to open the properties window for the **Downloads** folder.

Open
Open in new window
Share with ▸
Include in library ▸
Pin to Start
Send to ▸
Copy
Create shortcut
Properties

3 Click the **Location** tab.

Downloads Properties

General | Sharing | Security | Location | Customize

Files in the Downloads folder are stored in the target location below.

You can change where files in this folder are stored to another place on this hard drive, another drive, or another computer on your network.

C:\Users\Ciprian\Downloads

[Restore Default] [Move...] [Find Target...]

[OK] [Cancel] [Apply]

4   Click **Move**, select the new location for the Downloads folder and then click **Select Folder**.

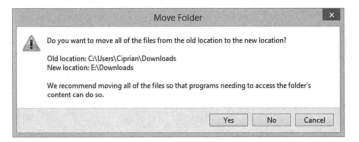

5   Click **OK**.

You are asked to confirm whether you want to move all the files from the old location to the new location.

6   Click **Yes** and wait for the process to finish.

CLEAN UP

Close File Explorer.

The Downloads folder and all its content has been moved to the new location. You can repeat the same procedure for other user folders that you would like to move to a different location.

Burning a disc with File Explorer

You can burn a disc directly from File Explorer without the need for a third-party solution. Even though third-party solutions are more complex and offer more features, File Explorer can do the job when you need to write a simple disc with files on it. When starting the burn process, you are prompted to choose between the following two types of discs:

- **Like A USB Flash Drive (Live File System)**   Discs formatted with this method work like a USB flash drive or floppy disk, meaning you can copy files to disc immediately. They are a good choice if you want to keep a disc in the burning drive and copy files whenever you need to. These discs are compatible only with Windows XP and later versions of Windows.

- **With A CD/DVD Player (Mastered)**   Discs formatted with this method don't copy files immediately, meaning you need to select the entire collection of files that you want to copy to the disc and then burn them all at once. This is convenient when you want to burn a large collection of files at one time. These discs are compatible with older computers and devices such as CD players and DVD players.

In this exercise, you'll learn how to burn a disc like a USB flash drive by using the Live File System.

 SET UP
Open File Explorer and insert an empty disc (CD or DVD) into the burning drive. Wait for the disc to be detected.

1 In File Explorer, click **This PC**.

2 Double-click the **DVD-RW Drive**.

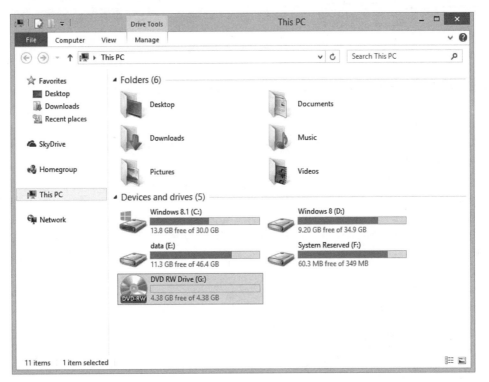

You are asked how you want to use the disc you are about to burn.

3 Select **Like A USB Flash Drive**.

4   In the **Disc title** box, type a name for the disc, and then click **Next**.

> **Burn a Disc**   ✕
>
> How do you want to use this disc?
>
> Disc title: My Disc
>
> ● **Like a USB flash drive**
>   Save, edit, and delete files on the disc anytime. The disc will
>   work on computers running Windows XP or later. (Live File
>   System)
>
> ○ **With a CD/DVD player**
>   Burn files in groups and individual files can't be edited or
>   removed after burning. The disc will also work on most
>   computers. (Mastered)
>
> Which one should I choose?
>
>   Next   Cancel

5   Wait for the disc to be formatted and become ready for writing.

       When the disc is ready, use the newly opened File Explorer window to access the disc.

6   Drag or copy and paste the files and folders that you want to burn to the disc in to the newly opened File Explorer window.

7   Wait for the burn process to end.

36% complete	– □ ×
Copying 14 items from Downloads to DVD RW Drive (G:) My Disc	
36% complete	II ×

⌄ More details

8   Eject the disc and wait for the burning session to be closed so that the disc can be used later.

 CLEAN UP
Close File Explorer.

You can continue to add content to the disc until it becomes full, either on the same computer or on any other computer running Windows.

20

Freeing up disk space by using Disk Cleanup

When you are running out of space, a good solution to free up some capacity is to use the Disk Cleanup tool. This tool scans a selected drive and looks for temporary files and log files that are no longer needed, cache files used by different apps such as Internet Explorer, file history data, and so on.

It's recommended to use this tool once every few months to ensure that your hard disk doesn't get overloaded with files that are not useful and to make more space available.

In this exercise, you'll learn how to use the Disk Cleanup tool to save space on one of your drives.

SET UP
Open Control Panel.

1   Click **System And Security** and then **Administrative Tools**.

2   Click the **Disk Cleanup** shortcut.

	Name	Date modified	Type
	Component Services	8/22/2013 9:57 AM	Shortcut
	Computer Management	8/22/2013 9:54 AM	Shortcut
	Defragment and Optimize Drives	8/22/2013 9:47 AM	Shortcut
	Disk Cleanup	8/22/2013 9:57 AM	Shortcut
	Event Viewer	8/22/2013 9:55 AM	Shortcut
	iSCSI Initiator	8/22/2013 9:57 AM	Shortcut
	ODBC Data Sources (32-bit)	8/22/2013 2:56 AM	Shortcut
	ODBC Data Sources (64-bit)	8/22/2013 9:59 AM	Shortcut
	Performance Monitor	8/22/2013 9:52 AM	Shortcut
	Resource Monitor	8/22/2013 9:52 AM	Shortcut
	Services	8/22/2013 9:54 AM	Shortcut
	System Configuration	8/22/2013 9:53 AM	Shortcut
	System Information	8/22/2013 9:53 AM	Shortcut
	Task Scheduler	8/22/2013 9:55 AM	Shortcut
	Windows Firewall with Advanced Security	8/22/2013 9:45 AM	Shortcut
	Windows Memory Diagnostic	8/22/2013 9:52 AM	Shortcut
	Windows PowerShell (x86)	8/22/2013 6:34 PM	Shortcut
	Windows PowerShell ISE (x86)	8/22/2013 9:55 AM	Shortcut

3   If you have more than one drive in your computer, select the drive on which Windows is installed (by default, it's the C drive), and then click **OK**. Otherwise, skip to the next step.

4   Wait for the tool to scan the selected drive and present its suggestions for files to delete.

5   Select all the types of files that can be deleted.

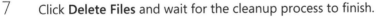

6   Click **OK**.

You are asked to confirm your choice.

7   Click **Delete Files** and wait for the cleanup process to finish.

⊗ CLEAN UP
No cleanup is required.

The selected files are deleted, and now more space is available on the selected drive. You can repeat the procedure on other drives in your Windows computer or device. If you want to clean up even more unneeded files, at step 5 you can press the Clean Up System Files button and have Disk Cleanup scan the selected partition also for system files that can be safely removed. Using this option, you can remove old Windows Update files that are no longer needed, old Windows installation files, and so on.

Changing the defaults for apps, file extensions, and AutoPlay dialog boxes

Windows 8.1 users can change the defaults for apps, file types, and AutoPlay settings. You can change these values from Control Panel by clicking Programs and then choosing Default Programs.

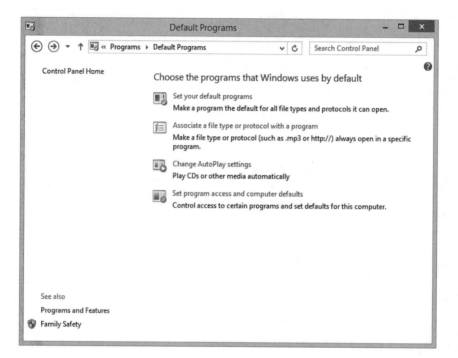

The following list describes the options that are available to you in the Default Programs window:

- **Set Your Default Programs** This setting lists all the apps you have installed so that you can choose the default file types and protocols that each will open.

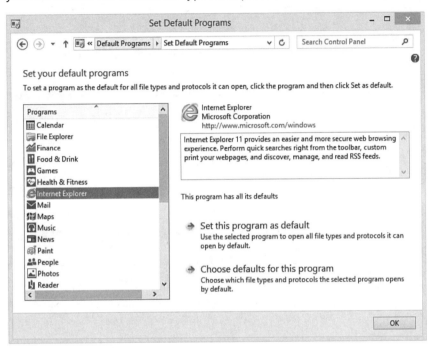

- **Associate A File Type Or Protocol With A Specific Program**   This setting lists all the file extensions registered on your Windows computer or device so that you can change the default app used to open each file extension.

■ **Change AutoPlay Settings** These settings determine the behavior of the AutoPlay dialog boxes displayed for the following types of media and devices: removable storage devices, video and photo storage, DVDs, Blu-ray discs, CDs, software, and games.

- **Set Program Access And Computer Defaults**   This setting changes the default apps you use for the most common computing activities: web browsing, email, playing multimedia, instant messaging, and the virtual machine used for Java. You can change the default apps so that they are the Microsoft Windows defaults, third-party apps you installed, or you can choose a different app for each type of activity.

These tools come in handy after you have installed many apps on your Windows computer or device, which can cause your defaults to change in ways you don't want. You can use these tools to customize default apps and have the computing experience you want.

Logging on to Windows automatically, without entering your password each time

If you are using only one user account on your Windows computer or device, and you are using it where it is safe from strangers gaining unwanted access, you might want to set Windows to log you on automatically, without entering your password each time. Even though this isn't a best practice recommended by Microsoft because it can lead to some complications detailed at the end of this section, it can make your life easier in certain scenarios.

In this exercise, you'll learn how to set Windows 8.1 to log on to your user account automatically.

➡ SET UP
Open the Start screen.

1   Type netplwiz.

2   In the search results, click **netplwiz** to open the **User Accounts** window.

3   Select your user account.

4   Clear the **Users Must Enter A User Name And Password To Use This Computer** check box.

5   Click **OK**.

You are asked to enter and confirm your password.

6   In both the **Password** and **Confirm Password** boxes, type your user account password, and then click **OK**.

CLEAN UP

No cleanup is required.

The next time you start Windows, you will be logged on automatically to the user account you just selected. This user account will become the default logon user to Windows 8.1.

If you have multiple user accounts on your computer or device, setting this up might be an inconvenience. Windows will always log on automatically to the user account you selected during this procedure. To log on by using another user account, you need to wait for Windows 8.1 to start up and log on automatically. Then, you must sign out and select the other user account to which you want to log on. If you want to reverse this setting, follow the same procedure and then, in step 4, select Users Must Enter A User Name And Password To Use This Computer.

If your Windows computer or device is part of a network domain, such as a corporate network, this procedure will not work. In network domains, the policies regarding the logon procedure are set by the network administrator and you cannot overwrite them.

Using shortened URLs when you want to share files from SkyDrive

You can share files and folders from SkyDrive by using both the SkyDrive app and File Explorer in Windows 8.1 and from the browser. When sharing a file from the browser, you have access to more options for sharing, including using a shortened URL instead of a complete one.

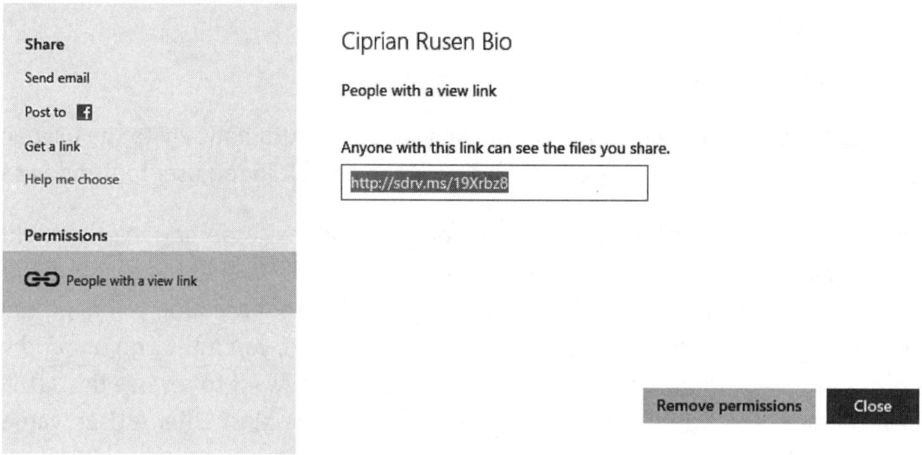

Share

Send email

Post to **f**

Get a link

Help me choose

Permissions

🔗 People with a view link

Ciprian Rusen Bio

People with a view link

Anyone with this link can see the files you share.

http://sdrv.ms/19Xrbz8

[Remove permissions] [Close]

When generating the link for the file, you can also set permissions for accessing the file. The default is View Only permissions, but you can set them to View And Edit or to Public. Setting these kinds of sharing permissions is not available in the SkyDrive app. Therefore, if you want to share files and folders and set very specific permissions, it is best to use the browser and visit the SkyDrive website.

In this exercise, you'll learn how to share a file from SkyDrive by using a shortened URL.

➡ SET UP
Open Internet Explorer, browse to *https://skydrive.live.com*, and then log on by using your Microsoft account.

1 In SkyDrive, browse and select the file that you want to share.

2 On the toolbar at the top of the page, click the **Sharing** button.

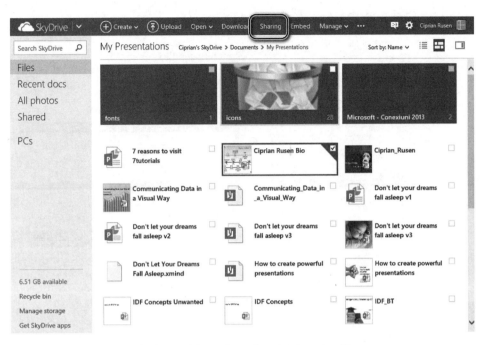

This opens a pop-up window with options for sharing the file.

3   Click **Get A Link**.

4   In the **View Only** section, click **Create**.

5   Click **Shorten**.

Share	Ciprian Rusen Bio
Send email	People with a view link
Post to [f]	Anyone with this link can see the files you share.
Get a link	https://skydrive.live.com/redir?resid=4DC0B8D6E0D68FC6!677&a **Shorten**
Help me choose	
Permissions	
⚭ People with a view link	
	Remove permissions Close

6   Copy the short URL and use it to share the file with others.

✖ CLEAN UP
When you are done using SkyDrive in the browser, sign out.

Changing the default SkyDrive folder

One of the subtle but important changes in Windows 8.1 is that SkyDrive is now embedded into the operating system. Therefore, SkyDrive now has a Windows app, a synchronization service running in the background, a special section in File Explorer, and its own user folder. Microsoft accounts in Windows 8.1 now include in their user folder (found at C:\Users, followed by their user name) the SkyDrive folder, alongside traditional user folders such as Desktop, Downloads, Documents, Music, Pictures, and so on.

What does this mean? Well, it means that your entire SkyDrive data is stored at the following location: C:\Users\Your User Name\SkyDrive.

Name	Date modified	Type	Size
Contacts	9/5/2013 4:57 PM	File folder	
Desktop	9/15/2013 5:24 PM	File folder	
Documents	9/5/2013 5:06 PM	File folder	
Favorites	9/5/2013 4:57 PM	File folder	
Links	9/5/2013 4:57 PM	File folder	
Music	9/5/2013 4:57 PM	File folder	
Pictures	9/5/2013 5:07 PM	File folder	
Saved Games	9/5/2013 4:57 PM	File folder	
Searches	9/5/2013 4:57 PM	File folder	
SkyDrive	9/16/2013 11:31 AM	File folder	
Videos	9/5/2013 5:13 PM	File folder	

If you have multiple hard disks and very little space available on the hard disk where Windows is installed, this might constitute a problem because you will run out of space relatively quickly. What is the best solution when this problem occurs? Move the location of the SkyDrive user folder to another storage device where more space is available. When undertaking this operation, it is important that you do not move the SkyDrive user folder within another user folder. This will break the internal references used by Windows and its apps and might cause malfunctions.

In Windows 8.1, you can easily change the location of the SkyDrive user folder. In this exercise, you'll learn how.

➜ SET UP
Open File Explorer.

1   In File Explorer, on the left side of the window, right-click the **SkyDrive** folder.

2   Click **Properties** to open the **Properties** window for this folder.

3   Click the **Location** tab.

4 Click **Move**, select the new location for the **SkyDrive** folder, and then click **Select Folder**.

5 Click **OK**.

You are asked to confirm whether you want to move all the files from the old location to the new location.

6 Click **Yes** and wait for the process to finish.

⊗ CLEAN UP
Close File Explorer.

The SkyDrive folder and all its content is moved to the new location.

Key points

- You can use the shortcuts that are available in the practice files folders of this chapter to shut down, restart, or lock Windows.

- One of the many improvements in Windows 8.1 is the ability to boot directly to the desktop instead of the Start screen.

- Notifications for Windows 8.1 apps can be set on a per-app level and you can also set quiet hours when you don't want to be disturbed by any notifications.

- You can use Task Manager not only to end apps that don't respond to your commands but also to optimize the list of apps running at startup.

20

Chapter at a glance

Check

Check for solutions using Action Center, page 621

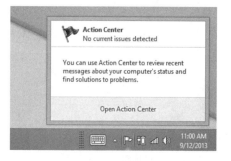

Fix

Fix screen rotation problems, page 627

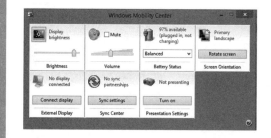

Get

Get Remote Assistance from a friend, page 636

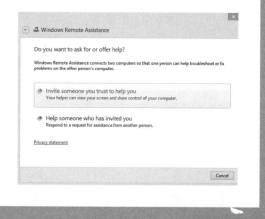

Use

Use Task Manager to view resource allocation and usage, page 644

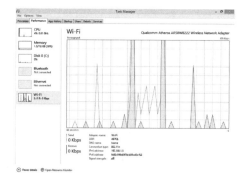

Troubleshooting problems

IN THIS CHAPTER, YOU WILL LEARN HOW TO

- Apply common solutions.
- Resolve display problems.
- Let Windows fix problems for you.
- Use the Microsoft Fix It Solution Center.
- Get help and support.
- Ask for Remote Assistance.
- Explore advanced troubleshooting tools.
- Refresh your computer or device.
- Reset your computer or device.

Your Windows 8.1 computer or device will likely run smoothly for quite some time. However, as your computer or device ages and you install new apps, acquire Windows and software updates, and save data and media to your computer's hard drive, problems might begin to appear. Most problems can be fixed by applying common solutions such as restarting the computer or uninstalling problematic apps, but others can take a little more effort.

In this chapter, you'll learn how to troubleshoot problems. In general, you should apply the techniques in this chapter in the order in which they are presented. Try to apply the most common solutions first and then see whether Windows can fix the problem for you. You can also look at Windows and Microsoft Help files, webpages, and forums, and use the Microsoft Fix It Solution Center if applicable. If none of that works, you might be able to resolve the problem by using the Advanced Startup boot menu, and boot to a repair disk or recovery drive. If you can't find a solution on your own, you can ask for Remote Assistance from someone you know and trust. You can also experiment with advanced troubleshooting tools, and, finally, refresh or reset your computer or device.

Apply common solutions

Most problems can be resolved (at least in the short term) with one of a few common solutions. Restarting your computer is the first thing you should try. Restarting often resolves a problem temporarily and might allow you to get back to work quickly. You'll need to resolve the problem later and locate the root cause when you have more time.

Although there are several ways to restart your computer, the best way is to right-click the Start button. Then, point to Shut down or Sign out and click Restart.

After you restart your computer, one of a few things will happen. Most likely, your computer will restart without incident, and the problem will be resolved. However, Windows 8.1 should run without incident, so whatever problem exists will still need to be resolved. If you've restarted the computer and you can access the Start screen, and you find that the problem persists, try these common fixes as they apply to your particular problem. (You'll try other options if these don't work.)

NOTE If your computer won't start at all, your only option is to boot to a Windows 8.1 DVD or an available restore disk or partition. When you do you can opt to perform an upgrade, a repair, a system restore, or choose a recovery option. If your computer is not configured to boot to a DVD or recovery disk or partition, you'll need to change the boot order in the BIOS. Search the manufacturer's website to see what you have to do to enter BIOS and perform this task.

Listed next are things you can try when your computer or network isn't working correctly, and these are common and often successful solutions. Resetting devices, the first in the list, may help you resolve problems with peripherals such as printers and scanners. Restarting your network, the last in this list, may resolve connectivity problems among devices or to the internet.

- **Reset hardware devices** Turn off, disconnect, and then reconnect problematic sound devices, monitors, printers, scanners, and USB or FireWire devices. Turn the devices back on afterwards to see if the problem is resolved. Turn off Bluetooth devices and resync or relink them if the problem has to do with Bluetooth device connectivity.

- **Check for solutions from the Action Center** Make sure Windows is up to date from the Action Center and let the Action Center check for solutions to problems it knows about already. See Chapter 15, "Preventing Problems," for more information. To open the Action Center, on the desktop, click the flag that appears on the Taskbar in the Notification Center and then click Open Action Center. Anything in red means the Action Center needs your attention. (If you don't see the flag in the Notification area on the taskbar, click the up arrow that appears on it. You'll find the icon there.)

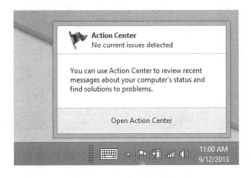

- **Update a driver with Device Manager** An internal piece of hardware may be causing a problem for your computer. You can use Device Manager to see if there are any problems with internal devices. Open Device Manager (type Device at the Start screen) and see whether specific hardware is the issue. If possible, install, reinstall, or roll back the device driver. If prompted, let Windows search for the appropriate driver.

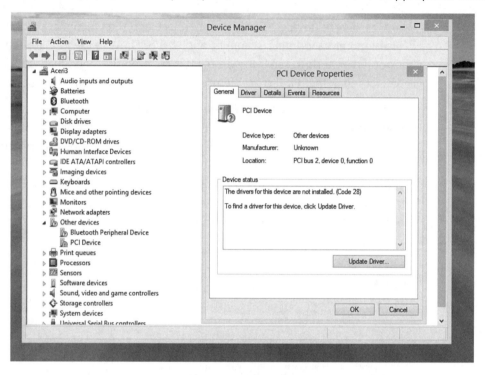

- **Uninstall and reinstall a problematic desktop app** If you are sure an installed desktop app is causing the issue, uninstall it. If the problem resolves, you can try reinstalling the app. If the problem reappears, uninstall the app permanently. You can uninstall desktop apps from Control Panel.

Programs
Uninstall a program

- **Uninstall a Windows Update** Windows Updates can cause problems, although they rarely do. If you are sure an update is to blame (perhaps because you were informed so by a technician or by your computer manufacturer) you can uninstall it. At the Start screen type update, and click Windows Update Settings. From there you can view your update history and uninstall the problematic one.

- **Restart your network** Restart a problematic network by turning everything off and then turning hardware back on in the following order, letting each piece of hardware finish initializing before moving to the next one: turn on modems first, then routers, and then computers.

TIP If you receive an error that says you are low on disk space, you'll need to delete some files. Video files are the largest so start there. If the error says that you are low on memory, you'll need to close open desktop apps, especially those that perform calculations and are resource-intensive. You may need to reboot your computer to resolve memory issues.

If your problem is not resolved by performing the tasks outlined in the previous bulleted list, you should reboot the computer and let Windows 8.1 run its own troubleshooting checks. You'll need to access the Advanced Settings employ these checks. To start with advanced startup settings, type Advanced at the Start screen and choose Change Advanced Startup Options from the results available from Settings. PC Settings opens; under Advanced Startup click Restart Now.

TIP If you need to restart your computer and access options that enable you to say, boot to a DVD or USB drive, you no longer press F8 during startup to do so. New computers may start too quickly to press F8 in time! Instead, use the Advanced Startup options in PC Settings, under Update and Recovery, from the Recovery tab.

Advanced startup

Start up from a device or disc (such as a USB drive or DVD), change Windows startup settings, or restore Windows from a system image. This will restart your PC.

Restart now

After the computer restarts, you'll have access to the following options.

- **Continue** Select this option to continue the start process. The only thing that happens is that the computer restarts.

- **Use A Device** Select this option to start the computer with an alternate hard drive or device such as a Windows recovery DVD or startable USB drive.

- **Troubleshoot** Select this option to reset or refresh your PC or to use Advanced Options. Advanced Options include options to use System Restore and Startup Repair, among others. Startup Repair will diagnose your PC and automatically fix problems it finds.

- **Turn Off Your PC** Turn off the PC and do nothing.

> **IMPORTANT** You will encounter problems if your computer's BIOS settings don't allow you to (or aren't configured to) start to a DVD or startable USB drive and you choose Use A Device in the advanced startup options. You might have to restart the computer again, enter BIOS settings (often by pressing F2 or some other key during startup), and change the start options so that you can start with the desired device.

In this exercise, you'll restart the computer, access the advanced options, and choose Automatic Repair. This will not harm your computer.

 SET UP
Start your computer and unlock the Lock screen. You need access to the Start screen.

1 From the **Start** screen, type Advanced.

2 Click **Settings** in the right pane and then click **Change Advanced Startup Options**.

3 Under **Advanced Startup**, click **Restart Now**.

4 From the boot options menu, click **Troubleshoot** and then **Advanced Options**.

5 Click Startup Repair. Wait while the computer restarts.

CLEAN UP
No cleanup is required.

TIP Read Chapter 14, "Keeping Windows 8.1 Safe and Secure," to learn how to use features such as System Restore, the Action Center, and Windows Defender.

Resolve display problems

Display problems come in several forms. If the screen resolution isn't set properly you can't snap apps (so that two or more appear on the screen at the same time). Peek won't work on the desktop if it isn't enabled. The taskbar may disappear or appear on the side or top of the screen. The computer may boot directly to Apps view instead of the Start screen. Finally, a laptop may get stuck in portrait mode when you really need landscape. You can resolve these problems and more from a few distinct areas of Windows 8.1.

Here are the more common display problems and their solutions.

- **Snap Apps** To snap two apps to the screen so you can view both side by side at the same time, your screen resolution must be set to 1366 x 768. You can access screen resolution settings by right-clicking the desktop. To snap 3 or 4 apps, the screen resolution must be even higher. To see how many apps you can snap, configure the screen resolution to its highest setting and test it.

- **Enable Peek** Peek lets you position your cursor in the bottom right corner of the screen while on the desktop to see behind open windows. It must be enabled to work. To enable this, right-click the taskbar, click Properties, and from the Taskbar tab select Use Peek To Preview The Desktop When You Move Your Mouse To The Show Desktop Button At The End Of The Taskbar.

- **Move or show the Taskbar** The taskbar can be accidentally moved if it is unlocked. If this happens, simply drag the taskbar from wherever it is (left, right, or top) and move it to the desired position (probably the bottom of the screen). The taskbar will be hidden if the taskbar properties are configured to auto-hide it when not in use. You can prevent both of these by right-clicking the taskbar, clicking Properties, and from the Taskbar tab, select Lock The Taskbar and deselect Auto-hide The Taskbar.

- **Configure Start view** If you don't see the Start screen when you power on your computer, and you want to, you'll need to reconfigure the settings. To do this, right-click the taskbar and click Properties. Use the Navigation tab to configure the desired settings. To return to the defaults, deselect When I Sign In Or Close All Apps On A Screen, Go To The Desktop Instead Of Start, and deselect Show The Apps View Automatically When I Go To Start.

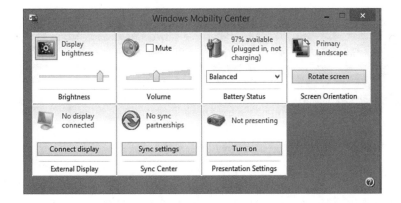

- **Fix a rotation problem** Occasionally a mobile computer will get stuck in the wrong mode. If this happens, open Windows Mobility Center and reset the Primary Landscape option.

TIP If the hot corners bother you, disable them. Right-click the taskbar, click Properties, and from the Navigation tab, configure options for Corner Navigation.

21

Letting Windows fix problems for you

If you are experiencing problems that can't be fixed by restarting the computer, device, or network, and reconfiguring related settings didn't help, and if the problem doesn't seem to have anything to do with the startup process, the troubleshooting options presented so far in this chapter probably didn't help any. Sometimes a problem is very specific, like an inability to access a single computer in a Homegroup, an inability to print to a new printer you just installed, or using a program that appears to be incompatible with Windows 8.1. When this happens, your next step is to explore the available troubleshooting wizards. To access the wizards, type Find and fix problems at the Start screen, and from the Settings results, choose **Find And Fix Problems**.

The resulting screen in Control Panel shows four categories; when you click one of these categories, new options appear.

- **Programs** Choose this option to run programs (now called desktop apps) that were made for previous versions of Windows on your Windows 8.1 computer or device. This opens Program Compatibility Troubleshooter. Work through the wizard to select the problematic program and choose the operating system for which it was designed. This resolves almost all problems with earlier programs because it lets those programs run in their native operating system space.

Troubleshoot computer problems

Click on a task to automatically troubleshoot and fix common computer problems. To view more troubleshooters, click on a category or use the Search box.

Programs
Run programs made for previous versions of Windows

Hardware and Sound
Configure a device | Use a printer | Troubleshoot audio recording | Troubleshoot audio playback

Network and Internet
Connect to the Internet | Access shared files and folders on other computers

System and Security
Fix problems with Windows Update | Run maintenance tasks | Improve power usage

- **Hardware And Sound** Click this option to access troubleshooting wizards that relate to hardware and sound. You can choose from Sound, Device, Network, Printing, and Media Player options. Continue to work your way through these wizards by selecting the associated entry in this window.

- **Network And Internet** Choose this option if you've restarted your network as detailed earlier but are still having problems. You can let Windows troubleshoot and fix advanced network problems, including those that deal with Internet connections, shared folders, homegroups, network adapters, incoming connections, and more. You can also troubleshoot network printer problems.

- **System And Security** Choose this option if you have problems with Internet Explorer, system maintenance, power, search and indexing, or Windows Update. As with the other options, when you open the desired wizard, it asks for input from you. Often, Windows will suggest a fix for your problem, and the fix will resolve it.

In this exercise, you'll use a wizard to run a maintenance check.

SET UP
Start your computer and unlock the Lock screen. You need access to the Start screen.

1   From the **Start** screen, type Find and Fix Problems. Click **Find And Fix Problems**. Maximize the window if desired.

2   Under System And Security, click **Run Maintenance Tasks**.

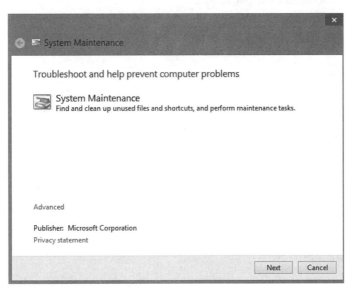

3   Click **Next**.

4   If problems are found, let Windows 8.1 resolve them. Click Close.

CLEAN UP
Close Control Panel.

Using the Microsoft Fix It Solution Center

The Microsoft Fix It Solution Center can automatically fix some problems for you. To access this website, on the Start screen type Microsoft fix it solution center, and click it in the results. You can also navigate to it directly at *http://www.support.microsoft.com/fixit.*

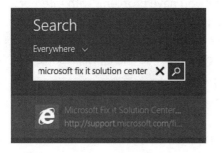

From the Microsoft Support website, choose the category for the type of problem you're having or choose from a list of problems. In this example, Print, Fax, Scan, Share, Or Save is selected and four solutions are ready to run. All you have to do is click Run Now and click through the resulting screens as applicable.

1 Select a problem area (Optional)

Top Solutions

Windows

Internet Explorer

Windows Media Player

Entertainme

2 What are you trying to do?

All problem areas
Use Desktop features, or open programs & files
Play games, music or sounds, pictures or video
Connect to the Internet or networks
Install or upgrade software or hardware
Print, fax, scan, share or save
Fix performance, errors or crashes
Fix security, privacy or user accounts

3 View or run solutions for Print, fax, scan, share or save   Filter Solutions

Run Now
Learn More
> **Diagnose and fix printer and printing problems automatically**
> Automatically fix printing issues like printer does not work, unable to install printer, other printing errors.

Run Now
Learn More
> **Diagnose and fix Windows Firewall service problems automatically**
> Automatically repair Windows Firewall problems, such as Windows fails to start Win missing, or Windows remote assistance is not working.

Run Now
Learn More
> **Fix Windows Desktop Search when it crashes or not showing results**
> Automatically repair Windows Desktop Search problems, when search is not started desktop search shows no results.

Run Now
Learn More
> **Diagnose and repair Windows File and Folder Problems automatically**
> Automatically diagnose and repair problems with files and folders in Windows, like bin, or trying to copy, move, rename or delete a file.

TIP Occasionally you'll receive an error that displays an error code. Write down the code and then type it in the Microsoft Support Center. Chances are good you'll find a solution to your problem quickly.

Getting help and support

Your Windows 8.1 operating system comes with built-in Help files for common problems and issues. You can access these files by typing Help and Support on the Start screen.

After clicking Help and Support in the results, the Windows Help and Support window opens on the desktop. By default, the Help And Support Center accesses online Help files so that the results you get are the latest available. To get the most from Help And Support, you should be connected to the Internet.

You search for information and solutions in the Help And Support Center the same way you'd search for them on the Internet: type your keywords in the Search window and click the Search icon. You can use the Back and Forward buttons and access web links to find more information. The Windows Help And Support Center offers access to both the Windows website and the Microsoft Community website.

You can use Help And Support to troubleshoot hardware, network, and security issues, just as you can with the wizards, although most people find the wizards easier to use. However, the Help And Support pages also offer information related to more general problems. Suppose your child keeps accessing your user account and you can't figure out how to re-strict such access. You can search Help And Support for information on how to create user accounts and create stronger passwords that your kids can't easily guess. That's a form of troubleshooting; it's resolving a problem!

Windows also offers a Help + Tips tile on the Start screen. You click that tile to open a more graphical and user-friendly way to search for help and support. There are six categories: Start and apps, Get around, Basic actions, Your account and files, Settings, and What's new. You'll explore these in the exercise that follows.

In this exercise, you'll browse the Help and Support files to learn how to secure your com-puter with a user account for every user as well as create strong passwords.

SET UP

Start your computer and unlock the Lock screen. You need access to the Start screen.

1 From the **Start** screen, type Help and Support.

2 Click **Help And Support** in the results.

3 Click **Security, Privacy, & Accounts**.

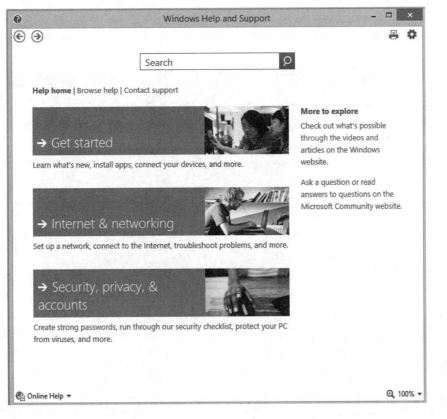

4 Click **Create A User Account**. Read the data and click the **Back** button.

5 In the **Search** window, type Strong passwords. Click the **Search** icon.

6 Review the results as desired.

CLEAN UP

Close the Help and Support window. There is also a Help + Tips app available from the Start screen.

The Help + Tips app offers information that can help you learn your way around Windows 8.1, create accounts and configure settings, learn what's new, and more. You click any item in the Help + Tips app to go to that section, and you'll have access to a back arrow to help you navigate your way back to the landing page. You can also right-click anywhere in the app to access the available toolbar, which offers access to the six categories you see here.

Asking for Remote Assistance

Remote Assistance is a feature available in Windows 8.1 (and previous operating systems) by which you can ask a friend, relative, colleague, or support professional for assistance in resolving a problem. You have to know someone who is willing to help, has a connection to the Internet, and also runs a compatible version of Windows. After you ask for assistance and the other person agrees to give it, the helper can view your computer screen to see the problem in action. (This happens over the Internet.) By viewing your computer screen and the problem, they can often help you figure out how to fix it. After you're connected with a helper by Remote Assistance, you can also give them permission to take control of the computer screen and resolve the problem directly. It's a technology that enables someone who is not physically close to you to access your computer as if he or she were sitting in front of it.

Before you can use Remote Assistance, you must verify that Remote Assistance invitations can be sent from your computer. By default, this feature is enabled, but it doesn't hurt to check. To access this setting, type Remote Assistance at the Start screen and in the results click Allow Remote Assistance Invitations To Be Sent From This Computer. Verify that the option is enabled, and if it isn't, select it and click OK.

TIP Remote Desktop is different from Remote Assistance. Remote Desktop lets you access your computer remotely so that you can work from it, as if you were sitting at it, even when you are not. Remote Assistance lets others access your computer with your permission to resolve problems (while you are sitting at it).

When you're ready to send a Remote Assistance invitation, you must access the option to send an invitation. You can do this by typing Invite at the Start screen. Click Settings, and the option to Invite Someone To Connect To Your PC And Help You, Or Offer To Help Someone Else appears.

When the Windows Remote Assistance window opens, select Invite Someone You Trust To Help You and then follow the rest of the prompts as required.

There are three ways to send the required invitation to ask for help by using Remote Assistance.

- **Save This Invitation As A File** Choose this option to send your invitation as an attachment when you use a web-based email account such as Gmail or Yahoo!.

- **Use Email To Send An Invitation** Choose this option if you use a compatible email program on your computer, such as Microsoft Outlook or the Mail app, to send the invitation as an attachment.

- **Use Easy Connect** Choose this option if your helper also has access to Easy Connect. When you choose this option, you'll receive an Easy Connect password, which you'll relay to your helper by phone, email, fax, or text. (Try this option first and then work through the exercise offered later if this option doesn't work.)

After your helper receives an invitation by email or as a message from you by another means, he or she will open Remote Assistance on that computer and type the password you've given him or her. You'll be prompted to accept his or her help through Remote Assistance, a connection will be established, and the other user will be able to see your screen.

During the session, the helper can see and take control of your screen by using his or her own monitor and mouse. You can hold chats to relay the problem, stop sharing your screen (if you are), pause the session, and so on. You're always in control and can stop the session at any time by clicking the red X in the Remote Assistance window.

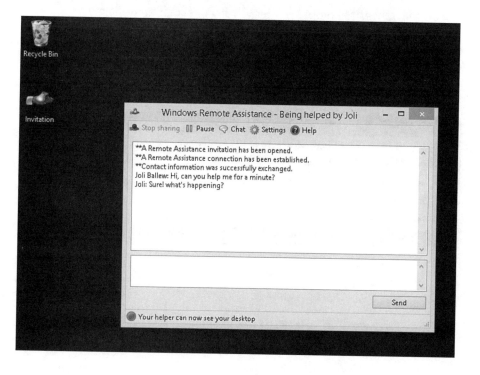

In this exercise, you'll create a Remote Assistance invitation code and relay that code to your helper by using your preferred method of communication.

 SET UP
Start your computer and unlock the Lock screen. You need access to the Start screen. You also need someone available to help you, who has access to the Internet, and who runs a compatible version of Windows.

1   At the **Start** screen, type Invite.

2   Click **Invite Someone To Connect To Your PC And Help You, Or Offer To Help Someone Else**.

3   Click **Invite Someone You Trust To Help You**.

     TIP If you've received help from someone before by using Remote Assistance, that person will appear as an option after you invite someone to help you.

4   Click **Save This Invitation As A File**. In the **Save As** dialog box, click **Desktop** and then choose **Save**.

     The invitation file and password opens.

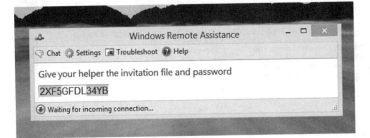

5   Relay the information to your helper as desired.

      The helper inputs the 12-character password he or she receives, and a session begins.

6   Follow the helper's instructions to resolve your problem.

✖ CLEAN UP
If the helper responds with an offer to help, accept the offer. When desired, close the Remote Assistance window to end the session.

Exploring advanced troubleshooting tools

Windows 8.1 comes with many more troubleshooting tools than can be detailed here. You can access the tools from the Start screen by typing **Troubleshooting**, **Diagnose**, **Performance**, **Repair**, or similar keywords. These options can be more complex than you are ready for, such as using Task Manager to close processes or services or viewing and drawing conclusions from what you see in event logs, Performance Monitor, Resource Monitor, and similar programs. However, it's important to know at least some of the advanced tools that are available in case your troubleshooting efforts continue to go unresolved or if a technician asks you to supply information you can get only by using these tools.

TIP Although advanced tools are detailed here, it might be best to try to refresh or reset your PC before you spend too much time working with these tools if you don't have professional help.

Here are a few of the tools you can use to troubleshoot difficult-to-diagnose problems.

- **Performance Options** To adjust visual effects for best appearance or performance; to choose allocate processor resources to either programs or background services; and to turn on Data Execution Prevention which helps protect against damage from viruses and other security threats. Access the Performance Options dialog box from System Properties (Advanced tab, Performance Settings button) Both are shown here. You'll use this mostly when you need to enhance performance.

21

- **Administrative Tools** A window that offers access to the available administrative tools including but not limited to Disk Cleanup, Event Viewer, Performance Monitor, Resources Monitor, Task Scheduler and so on. Search for Administrative Tools from the Start screen to access this. You'll use this to access advanced tools.

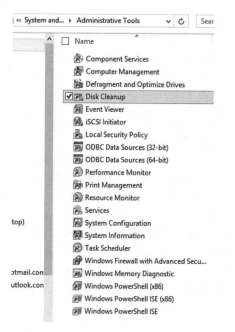

■ **Disk Cleanup** To free disk space by deleting unnecessary files stored in the Recycle Bin, and those saved when you download programs, surf the internet, report errors to Microsoft, and more. Search Disk Cleanup from the Start screen to access this. You'll use this when you need to free up disk space and you've already cleaned your personal file folders.

- **Event Viewer** To view information about errors that have occurred on your computer, warnings that have been generated, and critical events. Although the information here is rather cryptic, a technical support professional (or a good web search) might help you understand the information. You'll use this when asked to by a support professional or to view a list of errors to try to self-diagnose the problem. Access this from Administrative Tools or by searching for it from the Start screen.

- **Performance Monitor** To view performance information in logs by configuring specific criteria detailing what you'd like to monitor. You can monitor memory, CPU, and other components. Access Performance Monitor when you think a specific component is causing problems, from Administrative Tools.

- **Resource Monitor** To view live information about how resources are currently being used along with other data regarding those resources. Access Resource Monitor when you think a specific component is causing problems, from Administrative Tools, to view the component live.

One specific tool with which you'll want to become familiar is Task Manager. If you've used a computer running Windows before, you're probably already familiar with it. After you open Task Manager, click More Details. Task Manager offers seven tabs, and each performs specific functions. You should access Task Manager when you want to review running processes, see how resources like RAM and CPU are being used, view the demands placed on your computer from running apps, limit what starts when you boot your computer, see information about logged in users' allocated resources, view details about what's running and the CPU and Memory usage of those items, and the services that are running.

TIP You can open Task Manager by using the Ctrl+Alt+Del key combination. Click Task Manager. When it opens, click More Details.

- **Processes** To see which apps, background processes, and Windows processes are currently running. If an app is frozen, you can right-click it from this tab and end the task (close the app). You can also view how much of your computer's resources the app is using. Likewise, if you know that a particular process is unresponsive, you can exit that process.

- **Performance** To see how your computer's resources are currently being allocated. You have options for CPU, Memory, Disk, and likely Wi-Fi and Ethernet, although you might see others. You can use this information to find out which resource is being overworked or overwhelmed.

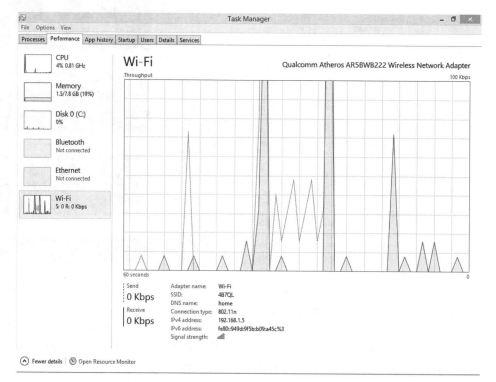

TIP There are some general rules for deciding whether a resource is overwhelmed. For instance, average CPU usage when the computer is idle or only running a word processing program should be around 10 percent, and when average usage hits 90 percent or higher, the CPU is working hard to keep up with the demands placed on it. You can expect spikes for components at any time, however; spikes are normal.

- **App History** To view the total resources that your installed apps have used for the past month. You can use this tab to discover resource-intensive apps and uninstall them if you feel one app might be causing performance problems.

- **Startup** To see which applications start when your computer starts (and thus run in the background all the time). The more enabled apps you see here, the longer it will take the computer to start. You can right-click to disable any app so that it does not start when your computer starts to improve start time and computer performance.

- **Users** To view the users who are currently logged on and how many resources they are using.

- **Details** To view details about running apps and programs, including how much CPU and memory they use, their status, and their descriptions. You probably won't make too many changes here; you'll use other tabs to troubleshoot.

- **Services** To view the services that are currently running. Services run so that Windows features can work, including Plug and Play, Themes, Task Scheduler, and more. Programs and apps need services to run, so stopping a service could cause problems for the computer. Sometimes you can use this option to troubleshoot a nonworking service and start (or restart) the service if it's inadvertently been stopped or is not working properly.

In this exercise, you'll explore Task Manager and view CPU usage as you perform calculations.

21

SET UP
Start your computer and unlock the Lock screen. You need access to the Start screen.

1   From the **Start** screen, type Calculator. Click **Calculator** in the results to open it.

2   Press **Ctrl+Alt+Del** and then click **Task Manager**; click the **Performance** tab.

3   Under Performance, click CPU.

4   Position Calculator off to the side of the Task Manager window.

5   Perform several complex computations and note the change (if any) in the CPU's performance graph.

CLEAN UP
Close Calculator and Task Manager.

To view additional resources, type keywords on the Start screen. *Troubleshooting* is a great keyword to try. Try *Performance* and *Identify*, too, as time allows.

Refreshing your PC

If your PC just isn't running well, or if you have problems that you think are related to missing operating system files, third-party programs, malware, or some hard-to-fix Windows-related issue, you can refresh your PC. This is a good option if you've tried everything else and nothing seems to work. It isn't a new install; it's just a refresh of the operating system and a removal of potentially problematic third-party applications and add-ons.

A refresh will revert Windows 8.1 to its system defaults, while at the same time preserves quite a few things too, including user settings, user data, and apps purchased through the Windows Store. It keeps all your photos, music, documents, and videos. It keeps your personal settings, too. However, everything else is removed, including desktop programs you've installed. Toolbars for Internet Explorer will be uninstalled. Third-party software, such as software you might acquire with a new printer or scanner, will also be removed.

In this exercise, you'll refresh your PC. Do not perform this exercise unless you have tried other troubleshooting techniques and you are sure this is the only option remaining.

SET UP
Start your computer and unlock the Lock screen. You need access to the Start screen.

1   From the **Start** screen, type **Refresh**.

2   Click Refresh Your PC Without Affecting Your Files.

3   Under Refresh Your PC Without Affect Your Files, click Get Started.

4   Read the information and click **Next**.

5   Wait while the computer is prepared for the refresh and then follow any additional prompts.

6   When the process completes, enter your password on the **Lock** screen.

❌ CLEAN UP
Reinstall third-party programs as applicable.

Create a Recovery Drive

One way to recover quickly from a computer disaster is to use a recovery drive that you've already created. You have to have already created a recovery drive to use it. A Recovery Drive is like the older Recovery disks and Restore disks you may be familiar with.

To create a recovery drive, type Recovery Drive at the Start screen and click "Create a Recovery Drive" in the results. Click Next to get started, point to drive to use (it may be a USB drive, DVD, external drive, or network drive), and work through the wizard.

Keep the drive in a safe place. If you ever need to use it for recovery, connect the drive to your PC, restart the PC using the Advanced Startup options, and then choose the drive from the startup options as prompted. You can access Advanced Startup from PC Settings, Update and Recovery, Advanced Startup.

Resetting your PC

You reset your PC by using the same method you used to refresh it. Resetting is a good option if you've already tried all the other troubleshooting tips in this chapter and others, if you've refreshed your PC, and if you've been told by a professional that resetting is the only option (or if you plan to sell or give away your PC).

When you reset your PC, all your personal files, apps, and third-party programs are removed. All your personalization settings will be reset. Your network settings, Internet settings, installed hardware, and any other personalization you've made are erased, and all your PC settings are changed to their defaults. This option restores your computer to a like-new state. You'll find the option to remove everything and reinstall Windows from PC Settings, in Update and Recovery, from the Recovery tab.

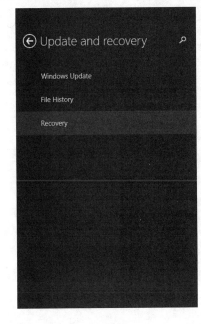

Refresh your PC without affecting your files

If your PC isn't running well, you can refresh it without losing your photos, music, videos, and other personal files.

Get started

Remove everything and reinstall Windows

If you want to recycle your PC or start over completely, you can reset it to its factory settings.

Get started

Advanced startup

Start up from a device or disc (such as a USB drive or DVD), change your PC's firmware settings, change Windows startup settings, or restore Windows from a system image. This will restart your PC.

Restart now

Key points

- Restarting your computer will resolve many problems in the short term without further troubleshooting. However, you'll need to get to the root of the problem to resolve it permanently.

- Resetting devices or your network can easily resolve many related problems.

- Advanced startup options are no longer available by pressing F8 during startup; instead, you restart the PC with Advanced Startup from PC Settings, Update and Recovery.

- Troubleshooting wizards are available that can help you fix all kinds of problems, including those that are related to program, hardware, network, Internet, security, and so on.

- The Windows Help + Tips app offers resources you can use to learn more about Windows 8.1. The Help and Support Center offers troubleshooting tools.

- With Remote Assistance, you can easily ask a friend, colleague, relative, or other person for help.

- When all else fails, there are myriad advanced troubleshooting tools to try.

- Refresh and Reset are options to return your PC to a previous state.

Using keyboard shortcuts and touch gestures

A

IN THIS APPENDIX, YOU WILL LEARN HOW TO

- Use the keyboard shortcuts for Windows 8.1.

- Explore touch keyboard shortcuts.

- Use touch gestures in Windows 8.1.

As long as there have been Windows operating systems, there have been keyboard short-cuts. You might know some already. You might even know that you can press the Windows key to return to the Start screen from anywhere in Windows 8.1, for instance, or that Windows key+C displays the default charms. There are many more shortcuts; you will likely be surprised at just how many there are and the extent to which you can use them.

In this appendix, you'll first learn the keyboard shortcuts that work in Windows 8.1 and how to experiment with touch keyboard shortcuts. Then, you'll see the touch gestures you can use in Windows 8.1 when running it on a computer or device with touch capabilities.

PRACTICE FILES You do not need any practice files for this Appendix. A complete list of practice files is provided in the section "Using the practice files" in the Introduction of this book.

Learning keyboard shortcuts for Windows 8.1

Some keyboard shortcuts are unique to Windows 8.1, such as pressing the Windows key to return to the Start screen, mentioned earlier. Some keyboard shortcuts are traditional, such as using Ctrl+x to delete selected text, Ctrl+z to undo what you've just done (perhaps restoring text you've just deleted), and so on. These have been around for decades and al-most always produce the same results.

TIP See Chapter 17, "Making my computer accessible," for more information about personalizing the keyboard to use Sticky Keys, Toggle Keys, Filter Keys, Mouse Keys, and so on.

The following list contains a few keyboard shortcuts that are extremely useful in Windows 8.1, and you can use most of them no matter where you are (in an app, on the desktop, using Internet Explorer, and so on) on the computer.

TIP If you prefer the On-Screen Keyboard to a traditional keyboard, you can use these shortcuts there. However, because you can't hold down two keys at the same time, click the first required key (such as the Windows key) and then the second (such as D or C).

- **Access the Start screen**   Press the Windows key
- **Access the desktop**   Windows key+D
- **Show the Charms**   Windows key+C. Shortcuts for the charms are:
  - **Search**   Windows key+Q or just start typing when you are on the Start menu
  - **Share**   Windows key+H
  - **Start screen**   Press the Windows key
  - **Devices**   Windows key+K
  - **Settings**   Windows key+I

  TIP When you're ready to shut down your computer, use Windows key+I and then click the Power button, located in the lower-right. You can also right-click the Start button to access the Shut Down options.

- **Show the app bar while in any app**   Windows key+Z
- **Cycle through open apps**   Windows key+Tab or Alt+Tab
- **Zoom in and out**   Ctrl+– to zoom out and Ctrl++ to zoom in

TIP You'll find that many of the traditional shortcuts you've always used still exist, such as Windows key+L to lock and Windows key+P to project to another display.

The following is a list of common keyboard shortcuts that you can use in Windows 8.1:

- **Windows key**   Opens the Start screen.
- **Right Shift key**   If you press it for eight seconds, it turns on Filter Keys. If you press it five times in a row, it turns on Sticky Keys.

- **Ctrl+mouse wheel**   This changes the size of things. When used on the desktop in an app like WordPad, it changes the view. When used on the Start screen, it zooms in and out. When used in some apps, it zooms or scrolls.

- **Ctrl+A**   Select all.

- **Windows key+C**   Open the charms.

- **Ctrl+C**   Copy selected text or items.

- **Windows key+D**   Show the desktop.

- **Alt+D**   Select the address bar in Internet Explorer.

- **Windows key+E**   Open File Explorer.

- **Ctrl+E**   Select the search box in File Explorer.

- **Windows key+F**   Show Files in the Search charm.

- **Windows key+Ctrl+F**   Open the Find Computers window, which can find computers on a network (used mostly in business networks).

- **Windows key+H**   Open the Share charm.

- **Windows key+I**   Open the Settings charm.

- **Windows key+J**   Switch the focus between snapped apps and larger apps.

- **Windows key+K**   Open the Devices charm.

- **Windows key+L**   Lock the computer and display the lock screen.

- **Windows key+M**   Minimize all the windows on the desktop.

- **Ctrl+N**   Open a new File Explorer window.

- **Ctrl+Shift+N**   Create a new folder in File Explorer.

- **Windows key+P**   Open the project options for a second screen.

- **Windows key+Q**   Open the Search charm.

- **Windows key+R**   Open the Run window.

- **Ctrl+R**   Refresh the screen.

- **Windows key+T**   Set the focus on the taskbar and cycle through the running desktop apps.

- **Windows key+U**   Start the Ease of Access Center.

- **Ctrl+V**   Paste.

- **Windows key+W**   Open Settings in the search charm.

- **Windows key+X**   Open the WinX menu.

- **Ctrl+X**   Cut.

- **Ctrl+Y**   Redo (only works after using Ctrl+Z to undo something)

- **Windows key+Z**   Opens the app bar. It works only in Windows 8-based apps.

- **Ctrl+Z**   Undo.

- **Windows key+keys from 1 to 9**   Display the app at the given position on the taskbar.

- **Windows key++ (plus sign)**   Zoom in while using the Magnifier tool, Internet Explorer and in some other instances.

- **Windows key+– (minus sign)**   Zoom out while using the Magnifier tool, Internet Explorer, and some other instances.

- **Windows key+, (comma)**   Peek at the desktop.

- **Windows key+Enter**   Start Narrator.

- **Windows key+Alt+Enter**   Start Windows Media Center if installed.

- **Alt+Enter**   Open the Properties window for the item selected in File Explorer.

- **Space**   Select or clear an active check box (but not a check mark that appears on a selected item on a touch screen, like a folder).

- **Tab**   Move forward through options.

- **Windows key+Tab**   Cycle through Windows 8.1 app history.

- **Alt+Tab**   Switch between opened apps (including desktop apps).

- **Shift+Tab**   Move backward through options.

- **Esc**   Cancel.

- **Ctrl+Esc**   Show the Start screen.

- **Ctrl+Shift+Esc**   Start Task Manager.

- **PrtScn**   Copy an image of your screen to the Clipboard.

- **Left Alt+Left Shift+PrtScn**   Turn on High Contrast.

- **NumLock**   Press for five seconds to turn on Toggle Keys.
- **Windows key+PageUp**   Move the Start screen to the left monitor.
- **Windows key+PageDown**   Move the Start screen to the right monitor.
- **Left arrow**   Open the previous menu or close the current submenu.
- **Windows key+Left arrow**   Snap the active desktop window to the left.
- **Windows key+Shift+Left arrow**   Snap the active desktop window to the left monitor.
- **Ctrl+Left arrow**   Show the previous word or element.
- **Alt+Left arrow**   Show the previous folder in File Explorer.
- **Right arrow**   Open the next menu or submenu.
- **Windows key+Right arrow**   Snap the active desktop window to the right.
- **Windows key+Shift+Right arrow**   Snap the active desktop window to the right monitor.
- **Ctrl+Right arrow**   Show the next word or element.
- **Ctrl+Shift+Right arrow**   Select a block of text from the current cursor position to the right.
- **Windows key+Up arrow**   Maximize the active desktop window.
- **Windows key+Shift+Up arrow**   Maximize the active desktop window and keep the current width.
- **Alt+Up arrow**   Advance up one level in File Explorer.
- **Windows key+Down arrow**   Minimize the active desktop window.
- **F1**   Display Help if available.
- **Windows key+F1**   Start Windows Help and Support.
- **F2**   Rename the selected item.
- **F3**   Search for a file or folder.
- **F4**   Display items in the active list (works only for desktop apps).
- **Ctrl+F4**   Close the active document.
- **Alt+F4**   Close the active item or app.
- **F5**   Refresh.

Exploring touch keyboard shortcuts

If you have a touch-based device, you can use the touch keyboard. It's available on the desktop taskbar by clicking the keyboard icon. You can then use it to type in any compatible app.

On the right side of the touch keyboard, there are several icons that you can tap to configure the keyboard to display in different ways. In the illustration that follows, a traditional keyboard is selected, but it's easy to see the others. If you don't like the traditional keyboard, you can select the split keyboard. You can also write with a pen in the designated writing area and hide the keyboard when you no longer need it.

You can also configure how you want the touch keyboard to work. On the Start screen, type keyboard. In the search results area, select Ease Of Access Keyboard Settings, and then choose the option to change.

You can make changes to how you type from the Typing tab in PC Settings. From the Settings charm, click Change PC Settings, click PC And Devices, and then click Typing.

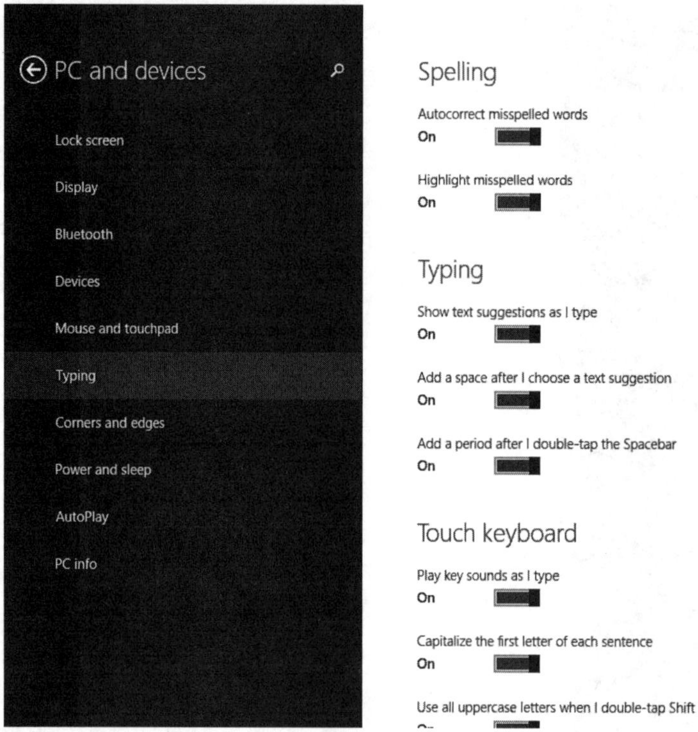

Spelling

Autocorrect misspelled words
On

Highlight misspelled words
On

Typing

Show text suggestions as I type
On

Add a space after I choose a text suggestion
On

Add a period after I double-tap the Spacebar
On

Touch keyboard

Play key sounds as I type
On

Capitalize the first letter of each sentence
On

Use all uppercase letters when I double-tap Shift
On

You might want to make note of the following options in particular:

- Add A Period After I Double-Tap The Spacebar
- Capitalize The First Letter Of Each Sentence
- Play Key Sounds As I Type

Using touch gestures in Windows 8.1

You can use Windows 8.1 on a multitude of touch-based input devices such as tablets, compatible monitors, laptops with trackpad gesture support, and so on. Before using Windows 8.1 on such devices on a daily basis, becoming thoroughly familiar with the touch gestures and their mouse equivalents will quickly make you more productive.

The touch gestures you can use in Windows 8.1 are the following (the mouse equivalents are presented after each one).

- **Access the Search, Share, Start, Devices, and Settings charms**

    - **Touch gesture** Swipe from the right to access the Search, Share, Start, Devices, and Settings charms.

    - **Mouse equivalent** Position your mouse in the lower-right or upper-right corner to access the charms.

- **Snap apps**

  - **Touch gesture**   Swipe from the left edge to swipe in the last used app. If you swipe quickly, the app will fill the entire screen. If you swipe slowly, you can snap the app to take up only part of the screen.

  - **Mouse equivalent**   Place the mouse in the upper-left corner and slide down the left side of the screen to see the most recently used apps. Click to select one for fullscreen viewing or drag it inward slowly to snap it.

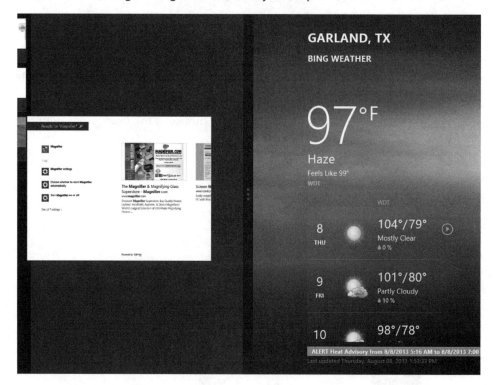

- **Open an app**

  - **Touch gesture**   Swipe quickly from the left edge inward and then outward again to see a list of open apps. You can then tap an app to open it.

  - **Mouse equivalent**   Place the mouse in the upper-left corner and slide down the left side of the screen to see the most recently used apps.

- **View app commands**

  - **Touch gesture**   Swipe from the bottom or top edge. App commands are re-
    vealed by swiping from the bottom or top edge.

  - **Mouse equivalent**   Right-click the app to see the app commands.

- **Close an app**

  - **Touch gesture**   Drag an app down from the top to close it. You don't have to close apps. They won't slow down your computer or device, and they'll close on their own if you don't use them for a while. If you want to close an app, drag the app to the bottom of the screen.

  - **Mouse equivalent**   Click the top of the app and drag it to the bottom of the screen.

- **See details about an item**

  - **Touch gesture**   Press and hold to learn more about an item, or to copy, paste, and to perform other tasks that are dependent on the item being held. You can almost always see details when you press and hold an item, as shown here. In some cases, pressing and holding opens a menu with more options.

  - **Mouse equivalent**   Point to an item to see more options; if nothing happens, right-click the item. You will likely have to click Properties after you right-click.

- **Perform an action**

  - **Touch gesture** Tap to perform an action. Tapping an item causes an action such as starting an app or following a link.

  - **Mouse equivalent** Click an item to perform an action.

- **Pan and scroll**

  - **Touch gesture** Slide to drag. This is used mostly to pan or scroll through lists and pages, but you can use it for other interactions, such as moving an object or drawing and writing.

  - **Mouse equivalent** Click, hold, and drag to pan or scroll. In addition, when you use a mouse and keyboard, a scroll bar appears at the bottom of the screen so you can scroll horizontally. You might be able to use your mouse wheel to scroll.

- **Zoom in and out**

  - **Touch gesture** Pinch or stretch to zoom. Zooming provides a way to jump to the beginning, the end, or a specific location within a list. You can start zooming by pinching or stretching two fingers on the screen. You can pinch on the Start screen to zoom in and out on app tiles.

  - **Mouse and keyboard equivalent** Hold down the Control key on the keyboard while using the mouse wheel to expand or shrink an item or tile on the screen.

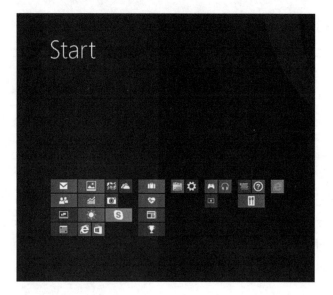

- **Rotate an item**

    - **Touch gesture** Rotate to turn. Rotating two or more fingers turns an object. You can turn the whole screen 90 degrees when you rotate your device, too.

    - **Mouse equivalent** Support for rotating an object depends on whether the specific app supports it.

Key points

- You can use keyboard shortcuts to navigate in Windows 8.1 just as you could in previous versions of Windows.

- If you have a touch screen, you can use the touch keyboard to type text, including keyboard shortcuts you would use on a physical keyboard.

- Learn the touch gestures Windows 8.1 supports if you plan to use it and be productive on a device with touch input.

Enhancements for using multiple displays

B

IN THIS APPENDIX, YOU WILL LEARN HOW TO

- Use Windows 8.1 with multiple monitors.

- Customize the way the image is displayed on multiple monitors.

Windows 8.1 provides better support for dual or multiple-monitor setups than any previous version. For example, on a dual-monitor setup, you can display the Start screen on the main monitor and the desktop on the second. You can also display the desktop on both monitors, and unlike Windows 7, you can have the taskbar visible on both, provided your displays and video drivers support this.

In this appendix, you'll learn in detail how to use Windows 8.1 with a dual-monitor setup and how to customize how each display is used.

PRACTICE FILES You do not need any practice files for this Appendix. A complete list of practice files is provided in the section "Using the practice files" in the Introduction of this book.

Using Windows 8.1 with a dual-monitor setup

When using Windows 8.1 with a dual-monitor setup, you can opt to leave the second monitor blank and not use it at all (PC Screen Only), show what is on the original monitor on the second one, too (Duplicate), show the Start screen on the original monitor and the desktop on the second one (Extend), or make the original monitor blank and show only the screen on the second monitor (Second Screen Only). You use the Windows key+P keyboard shortcut to choose.

To customize in detail how the image is displayed on each monitor, right-click the desktop, and then, on the shortcut menu that appears, click Screen Resolution.

The Screen Resolution window opens, in which both monitors and their relative positions are displayed as identified by Windows 8.1. You can drag each monitor to a different position or switch between them.

When selecting each monitor, you can also customize the following parameters:

- **Display** This is the display that you want to customize
- **Resolution** Use this to set the resolution of the selected display
- **Orientation** Select the orientation of the selected display
- **Multiple Displays** Choose how to use the available displays

After you make your changes, click OK to apply them. Don't hesitate to experiment until you find the setup that works best for you.

Key points

- Windows 8.1 provides support for multiple monitor configurations.
- Windows 8.1 can also work with touch screens with different sizes and aspect ratios.
- You can customize the available display options when using a dual-monitor setup so that everything is displayed the way you want it to be.

Installing and upgrading to Windows 8.1

C

IN THIS APPENDIX, YOU WILL LEARN HOW TO

- Make a clean installation of Windows 8.1.
- Dual-boot Windows 8.1 with earlier versions of Windows.
- Upgrade to Windows 8.1 from Windows 8 by using the Windows Store.

When you have a new computer or device, you'll want to learn how to install Windows 8.1. In this appendix, you'll learn how to perform a clean installation. If you want to use Windows 8.1 alongside other versions, that's entirely possible, and this appendix presents the basics you need to know about how to create a dual-boot setup.

In addition, you'll learn how to perform an upgrade to Windows 8.1 from an earlier version of Windows.

PRACTICE FILES You do not need any practice files for this Appendix. A complete list of practice files is provided in the section "Using the practice files" in the Introduction of this book.

Installing Windows 8.1

Installing Windows 8.1 is not a complicated procedure. As long as your system meets at least the minimum hardware requirements to run, you can install it yourself.

TIP If you want to learn more about the hardware requirements of Windows 8.1, read Chapter 1, "Introducing Windows 8.1."

Before you start the installation procedure, look for the activation code (also called the product key) that is required for the entire process to begin. Without it, you cannot install Windows 8.1. The code is distributed with your retail copy of Windows.

Insert the installation disc into your computer or device and boot your computer or device from it. Depending on how it is configured, you might need to edit the basic input-output system (BIOS) and change the boot order so that your system starts first from your DVD or Blu-ray drive.

Early in the installation process, you are asked to select the partition on which you want to install Windows. If you are installing it on a new computer or device, you'll see your hard disk as one chunk of unallocated space. You must create a new partition for it. When creating the partition, keep in mind that it is best to allocate at least 25 GB for Windows to ensure that you have space for it and the apps that you will install while using it. If you plan to install many apps and games, allocate even more space.

When creating this partition, Windows Setup automatically creates another partition named System Reserved, about 350 MB in size. Leave this partition untouched and don't delete it. It stores recovery tools that will be necessary if you should encounter failures and problems.

If you have partitions, all you need to do is select the one on which you want to install Windows. It is best to format that partition so that there is no data on it, making all the space available for Windows 8.1.

After the installation process is complete, start customizing your Windows installation. You are asked to select whether you want to use the Express Settings (the default settings) or customize your environment in detail.

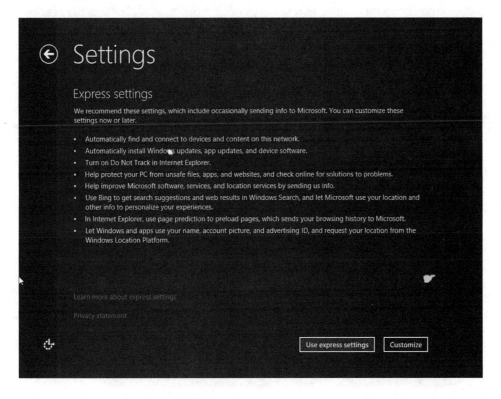

To be certain that Windows will work the way you want it to, select Customize and go through a few additional steps.

Prior to the first logon, you will be asked to enter the details of your Microsoft account (email address and password). If you do not have a Microsoft account, it is best to create one on a computer or device with an Internet connection prior to the installation process.

TIP If you want to learn more about Microsoft account, see the section "Introducing the Microsoft account in Chapter 12, "Allowing others to use the computer."

In this exercise, you'll learn how to install Windows 8.1 from the beginning on a new computer or device.

SET UP

Insert the Windows 8.1 installation disc into your DVD or Blu-ray reader. Start the computer or device from the disc. Depending on how your system is set up, you might need to enter your computer's BIOS and set it to boot from the DVD or Blu-ray reader.

1   When instructed, press a key on your keyboard to start the Windows setup process.

2   Select the language you want to install, the time and currency format you want to use, and the keyboard or input method, and then click **Next**.

3   Click **Install Now.**

You are asked to enter the product key.

4   Type the product key for your Windows installation and then click **Next.**

You are asked to accept the license terms.

5   Read the license terms, select the **I Accept The License Terms** check box, and then click **Next**.

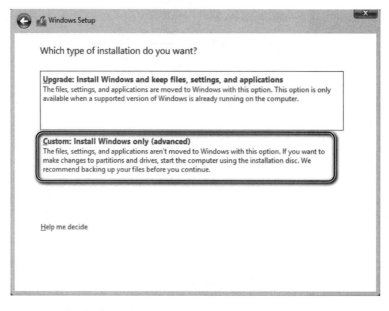

You are asked to select the type of installation you want to perform.

6   Click **Custom: Install Windows Only (Advanced)**.

You are asked where you want to install Windows.

7   Click **New** and specify the size of the partition that will be created for Windows 8.1.

> **IMPORTANT** If your computer or device has formatted partitions, select the partition on which you want to install Windows and then skip to Step 12.

8   Click **Apply**.

You are informed that Windows might create additional partitions for system files.

9   Click **OK**.

10   Select the partition you just created and click **Format**.

You are informed that all the data on this partition will be lost.

11   Click **OK** to confirm that you want the partition to be formatted.

12   Click **Next** to start the installation process.

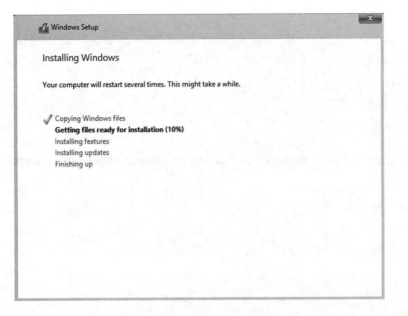

13   Wait for the installation process to finish and for your system to restart.

The customization process for your Windows installation begins.

14 Select the color that you want to use for your Windows installation and type the
    name for your computer or device.

NOTE If you are installing Windows 8.1 on a laptop or device with a wireless network
card, you are asked to select a wireless network to which to connect and introduce the
appropriate connection details.

15 Click **Next** to start configuring other important settings.

16   Click **Customize** to customize the settings for Windows in detail.

17 Select whether you want to find other computers, devices, and content on your net-
    work, and automatically connect to devices such as printers and TVs.

18   Select how you want Windows 8.1 to protect and update your computer or device by turning the relevant switches On or Off, and then click **Next**.

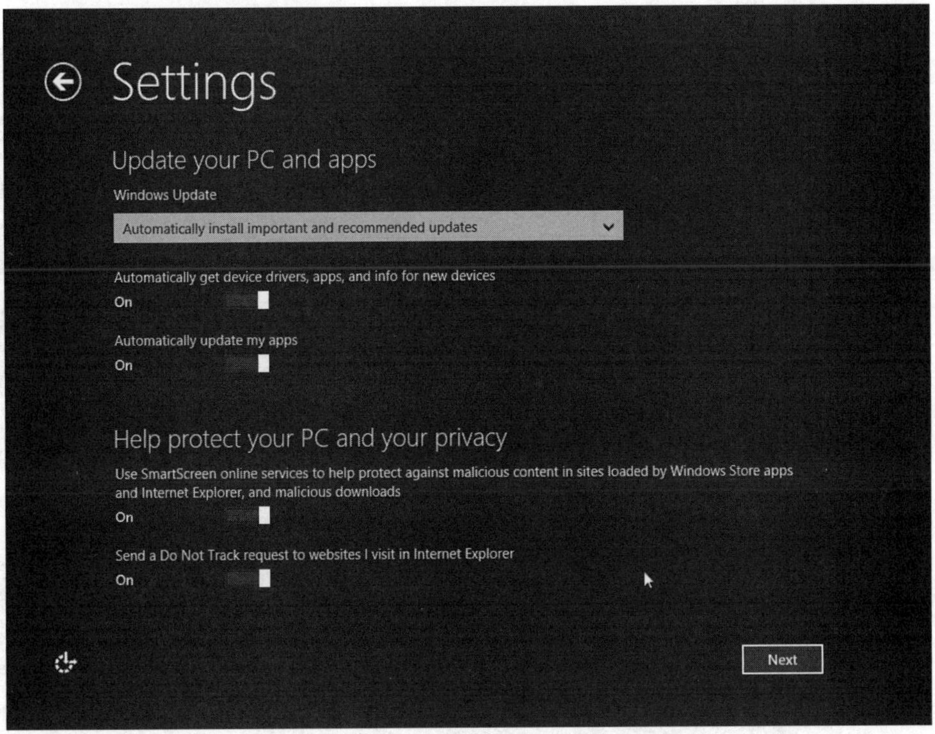

← Settings

Update your PC and apps

Windows Update

Automatically install important and recommended updates

Automatically get device drivers, apps, and info for new devices
On

Automatically update my apps
On

Help protect your PC and your privacy

Use SmartScreen online services to help protect against malicious content in sites loaded by Windows Store apps and Internet Explorer, and malicious downloads
On

Send a Do Not Track request to websites I visit in Internet Explorer
On

Next

19 Select whether you would like to let Windows check online for solutions to problems and whether you want to send different types of information to Microsoft, and then click **Next**.

20   Select whether you want to share information with Microsoft and the different services existing in Windows 8.1, and then click **Next**.

You are asked for a Microsoft account to sign in.

> **IMPORTANT** If the Windows 8.1 setup doesn't detect a working Internet connection, you won't be asked to log on by using a Microsoft account. You are given the option to create a local user account. The personalization process ends here and Windows 8.1 will display a brief tutorial while it prepares for your first logon.

21 Type the email address and password for your Microsoft account and click **Next**.

You are informed that you will need to enter a security code that is used to verify your account.

22   Select how you would like to receive that code: via a text message on your phone, via a phone call, or via email. Then, click **Next**.

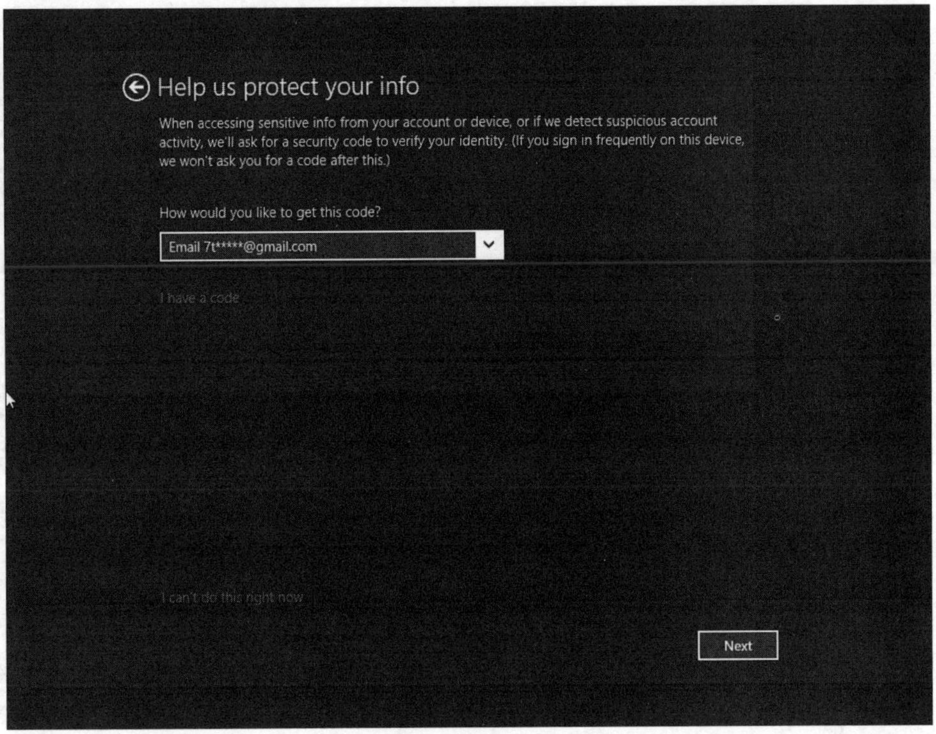

⊖ Help us protect your info

When accessing sensitive info from your account or device, or if we detect suspicious account activity, we'll ask for a security code to verify your identity. (If you sign in frequently on this device, we won't ask you for a code after this.)

How would you like to get this code?

Email 7t*****@gmail.com

I have a code

I can't do this right now

Next

23 Enter the security code you just received via the method you selected and then click **Next**.

You are informed about Microsoft SkyDrive and how it is going to be used to back up your data, documents, and settings to the cloud.

24   Click **Next** and wait for Windows 8.1 to finalize the preparations for the first logon.

NOTE If you previously installed Windows 8.1 on another computer or device, you won't be shown information about SkyDrive and what it is going to back up to the cloud. Instead you are asked whether you want to set up this computer using the settings synchronized from other Windows installations you have made. Make a choice and then click Next.

25   While you wait for the preparations to complete, watch the tutorial about how to navigate Windows.

     You are logged on to Windows 8.1 for the first time.

✖ CLEAN UP
When you are logged on, don't forget to eject the installation disc and store it in a safe location.

You can now use Windows 8.1 and all the available features. If you have used Windows 8 or Windows 8.1 on another computer or device with the same Microsoft account you used to log on, your settings from the other device are automatically migrated to this installation.

TIP After you have installed Windows 8.1, don't forget to activate it. You won't be able to customize it fully until the activation is performed from PC Settings.

Dual-booting Windows 8.1 and other Windows versions

You can create a multiboot setup on your computer or device. For example, you can run Windows 8.1 alongside Windows 7 and switch between operating systems effortlessly.

Installing Windows 8.1 in a dual-boot configuration is not much different from the procedure for making a clean installation. You must have a separate partition just for Windows 8.1. After you create that, follow the steps detailed in the installation guide from the previous section. At step 7, you select the partition created just for Windows 8.1 and continue with the installation.

Windows 8.1 automatically detects the other Windows operating systems you have installed and creates the appropriate boot entries for them. When you start your computer or device, you can select the operating system into which you want to boot.

When creating a multiboot setup with multiple versions of Windows, it is best to install Windows 8.1 last. Earlier Windows versions cannot set the boot entry for Windows 8.1 correctly, because it is a newer operating system using different technologies. However, Windows 8.1 can manage the boot entries for earlier versions of Windows correctly.

If you install earlier versions of Windows after Windows 8.1, they will overwrite the Windows 8.1 boot entry and you won't be able to access Windows 8.1. To fix this issue, you would need to use third-party solutions with which you can edit the boot loader on your computer and add back the Windows 8.1 entry. You will find many solutions online, including the popular EasyBCD utility.

Upgrading to Windows 8.1 from earlier versions of Windows

You can upgrade to Windows 8.1 from Windows 7 and Windows 8. Users of earlier versions of Windows may try to perform an upgrade and it might work, but there's no official support from Microsoft on this. The process is similar for each of these operating systems, but there are differences when it comes to the settings, files, and apps that can be migrated to Windows 8.1. You can upgrade from Windows 7 retail editions to Windows 8.1 Pro. Although you can upgrade all retail editions of Windows 8 to Windows 8.1 Pro, you can only update the basic edition of Windows 8 to the basic edition of Windows 8.1. During the upgrade process, the Windows 8.1 setup will evaluate your system and ask you to choose what you would like to keep. The following are the possible choices:

- **Keep Windows Settings, Personal Files, And Apps**   This is available only when you're upgrading from Windows 8 to Windows 8.1.

- **Keep Personal Files Only**   This is available when you're upgrading from Windows 7 and Windows 8 to Windows 8.1.

- **Nothing**   This is available when you're upgrading from Windows 7 and Windows 8 to Windows 8.1.

You can also perform an upgrade from Windows 8 to Windows 8.1 via the Windows Store. If you have purchased a computer or device that had Windows 8 preinstalled, the upgrade will be available free of charge through the Windows Store. The procedure to carry it out is covered in the next section of this appendix.

If you purchased a Windows 8 installation disc, you can upgrade through the Windows Store or by using a Windows 8.1 installation disc.

You cannot upgrade volume license versions of Windows 8, Windows 8 Enterprise, and Windows 8 Enterprise Eval versions from the Windows Store. You must use media to upgrade these editions.

Finally, you must upgrade to Windows RT 8.1 from Windows RT by using the Windows Store. Media is not available for Windows RT 8.1 upgrades.

To upgrade from an earlier version of Windows to Windows 8.1, insert the Windows 8.1 installation disc into your DVD or Blu-ray drive and run the Setup.exe file. The Windows 8.1 Setup Wizard starts and guides you through all the steps. The upgrade process involves fewer steps than when installing from scratch, but more requirements must be met. For example, on the partition on which your current operating system is installed, you must have at least 5.9 GB of free space available for Windows to install itself and preserve the old operating system until the installation is done. The 5.9 GB are in addition to what the current operating system is using.

A great feature of the Upgrade Wizard is that it automatically checks to see whether all the prerequisites are met for the upgrade to continue. If they are not, the wizard presents a summary of the problems that were found and you are asked to take action prior to the upgrade procedure.

The old operating system is preserved so that if there are any problems with the upgrade you can revert to the previous Windows installation. The earlier version of Windows is removed only after the upgrade has finished successfully.

IMPORTANT One very important requirement is that you cannot upgrade from a 32-bit version of Windows to a 64-bit version of Windows 8.1 (or vice versa). If you have purchased a different version, you must perform a clean installation and move your files, settings, and apps manually.

In this exercise, you'll learn how to upgrade from Windows 7 to Windows 8.1. The process for upgrading from Windows 8 to Windows 8.1 is similar, and you can follow almost the same steps, although some options might be different.

SET UP

Insert the Windows 8.1 installation disc into your DVD or Blu-ray drive. Open Windows Explorer and run the Setup.exe file found on the disc. If an UAC prompt is shown, allow the setup to run. Make sure you close all active apps before performing the upgrade. Also, you need to have the Windows 8.1 product key available.

1   Wait for the setup files to be prepared.

     You are asked whether you want to get the latest updates during the upgrade process.

2   Leave **Download And Install Updates** selected, and click **Next**.

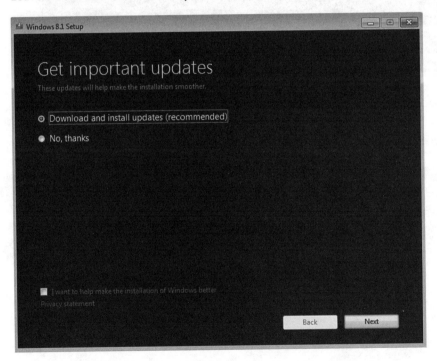

3   Type the Windows product key and click **Next**.

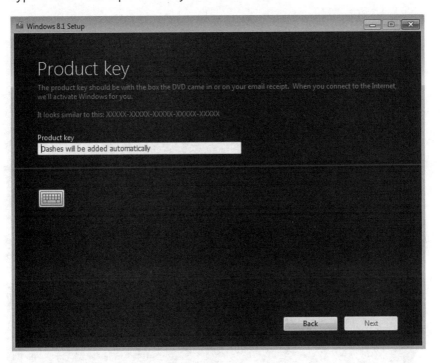

You are asked to accept the license terms.

4   Read the license terms, select the **I Accept The License Terms** check box, and then click **Accept**.

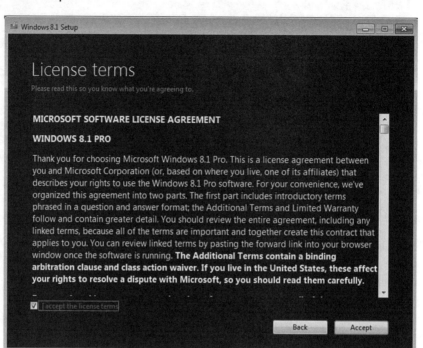

5   Choose what you want to keep during the upgrade process and then click **Next**.

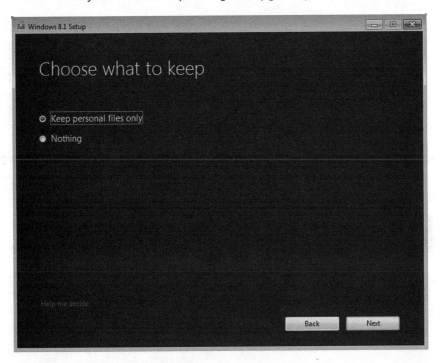

A summary of what the upgrade process will do opens.

IMPORTANT If any of the prerequisites for the upgrade process are not met, you will be shown a summary of the things that need to be changed at this point. You won't be able to continue the upgrade process until you resolve those issues.

6   If you are ready to go ahead with the upgrade, click **Install**.

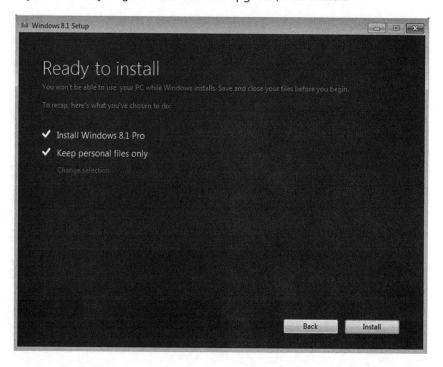

7   Wait for the installation process to finish.

If any problems are encountered, the previous Windows installation will be restored automatically. After several restarts, the personalization process begins.

8   Select the color you want to use for your Windows 8.1 installation.

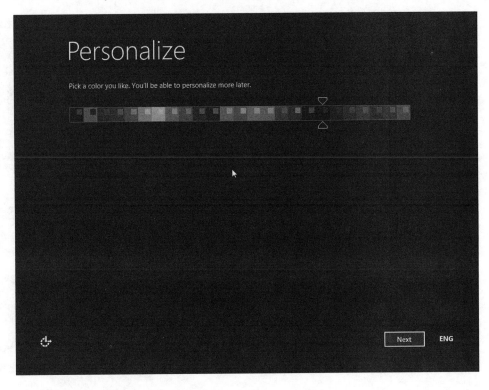

9   Click **Next** to start configuring other important settings.

10 Click **Customize** to customize Windows settings in detail.

11 Select whether you want to find other computers, devices, and content on your network, and automatically connect to devices such as printers and TVs.

12   Select how you want Windows 8.1 to protect and update your computer or device by turning the relevant switches On or Off, and then click **Next**.

13 Select whether you would like to let Windows check online for solutions to problems and whether you want to send different types of information to Microsoft, and then click **Next**.

14 Select whether you want to share information with Microsoft and the different services existing in Windows 8.1, and then click **Next**.

To sign in, you are asked to enter the password of the user account you used in the previous version of Windows.

15 Type the password and then click **Next**.

You are asked to type your Microsoft account address and then password.

16 Type the email address and password for your Microsoft account and then click **Next**.

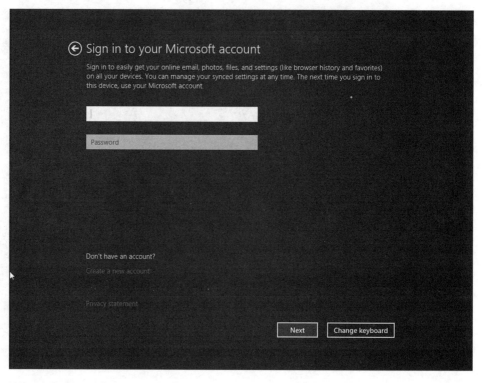

You are informed that you will need to enter a security code that is used to verify your account.

17   Select how you would like to receive that code: via a text message on your phone, via a phone call, or via email. Then, click **Next**.

18   Enter the security code you just received via the method you selected and then click **Next**.

You are informed about SkyDrive and that it will be used to automatically back up your data, documents, and settings to the cloud.

19   Click **Next** and wait for Windows to finalize the preparations for the first log in.

20   While you wait for the preparations to complete, watch the tutorial about how to navigate Windows.

You are logged on to Windows 8.1 for the first time.

CLEAN UP
When you are logged on, don't forget to eject the installation disc and store it in a safe location.

The upgrade has been performed, and your files, settings, and apps have been migrated according to your settings.

Upgrading to Windows 8.1 from Windows 8 by using the Windows Store

Windows 8 users who have purchased their systems with Windows 8 preinstalled or have used a retail copy of Windows 8 to install on their systems, can update for free to Windows 8.1, using the Windows Store.

However, this upgrade procedure doesn't work, for the following editions of Windows 8:

- Windows 8 Enterprise

- Editions of Windows 8 Pro that are installed by enterprises using KMS activation

- Editions of Windows 8 that are installed using an MSDN ISO, and activated using multiple activation keys

If you're running one of these editions, you can't install the free update to Windows 8.1 or Windows RT 8.1 from the Windows Store. If you installed Windows 8 using an MSDN ISO, you will be able to install Windows 8.1 using a similar ISO from MSDN.

To learn if you can update to Windows 8.1, simply open the Windows Store. There you should find a big entry named Update Windows with the recommendation to update to Windows 8.1 for free.

But, even if you meet the requirements shared above, this option might still not appear. That is because there are several other conditions that must be met before you can start the update process:

- You should log on with a Microsoft account. Local accounts can't be used for the upgrade process.

- You must have your Windows 8 installation up-to-date with the latest updates. If you just installed Windows 8 and you want to upgrade to Windows 8.1 without going through the many updates available for it, you can't.

- You should have 20 GB of empty space for the 64-bit edition of Windows 8.1 and 16GB of empty space for the 32-bit edition of Windows 8.1, on the partition where Windows 8 is installed. This space will be used to download and install the Windows 8.1 update. The download alone will use 3.6-4 GB of space.

- Your Windows 8 installation must be activated. If it isn't, the update won't be available in the Windows Store.

- You should back up your important files, to make sure you won't lose them. Problems should not occur but you never know how things may start to malfunction. If you don't know what tool to use, don't hesitate to try the built-in File History tool we covered in Chapter 15.

If you see Update Windows entry in the Windows Store, then go ahead and follow our step by step guide.

During the upgrade to Windows 8.1, if you have multiple display languages installed on your system, you will be informed that installing Windows 8.1 might change your display language. To change it back, you'll need to reinstall the language pack. This is because Windows 8.1 has many new features that need additional translation. Therefore, the language packs from Windows 8 are incomplete and Microsoft has provided new language packs for Windows 8.1.

After the first restart, you need to arm yourself with patience. You won't be able to use your computer for quite a while, because the upgrade process will reboot it several times and perform tasks like installing your devices, applying PC Settings, etc.

In this exercise, you'll learn how to upgrade from Windows 8 to Windows 8.1, through the Windows Store.

 SET UP Log on with a Microsoft account with administrative permissions. Then, open the Windows Store.

1 Click the **Update Windows** entry in the Windows Store.

2 You are shown information about Windows 8.1, its most important new features and the requirements that must be met before starting the upgrade process.

3 Click **Download**, so that the download and installation process begins.

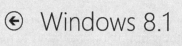

4   You are shown a progress indicator in the Windows Store.

5   You may continue to use your computer for other things while the download and installation process is performed in the background.

6   You will be prompted when it is time to restart your computer.

7   Close any work you have in progress and click **Restart Now**.

8   Wait for Windows to restart your computer or device and continue the installation
     process.

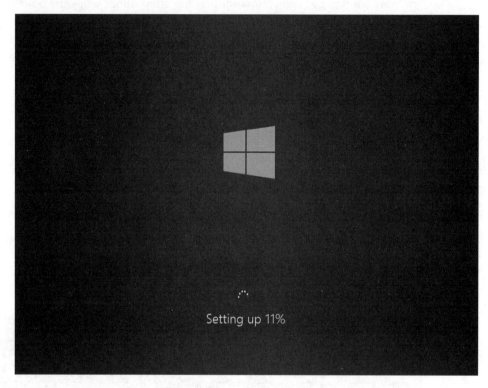

9   Read the license terms and click **I Accept**.

Licence terms

Please read this so you know what you're agreeing to.

MICROSOFT SOFTWARE LICENSE AGREEMENT WITH COMPUTER MANUFACTURER OR SOFTWARE INSTALLER, OR MICROSOFT

WINDOWS 8.1

Thank you for choosing a computer preinstalled with, or updating to, Microsoft Windows 8.1. This is a license agreement between you and the computer manufacturer or software installer that distributes Windows 8.1 with your computer; if you first obtain this software as an update to Windows 8 via the Windows Store, this is an agreement between you and Microsoft Corporation (or, based on where you live, one of its affiliates) instead. This agreement describes your rights to use the Windows 8.1 software. For your convenience, we've organized this agreement into two parts. The first part includes introductory terms phrased in a question and answer format; the Additional Terms and Limited Warranty follow and contain greater detail. You should review the entire agreement, including any linked terms, because all of the terms are important and together create this contract that applies to you. You can review linked terms by pasting the forward link into your browser window once the software is running. **The Additional Terms contain a binding arbitration clause and class action waiver. If you live in the United States, these affect your rights to resolve a dispute with the computer manufacturer or software installer, or with Microsoft, so you should read them carefully.**

By accepting this agreement or using the software, you agree to all of these terms and consent to the transmission of certain information during activation and for Internet-based features of the software. If you do not accept and comply with these terms, you may not use the software or its features. You

I don't accept

I accept   ENG

10   You are now asked to customize your Windows 8.1 installation.

11   Click **Customize** to customize Windows settings in detail.

12 Select whether you want to find other computers, devices, and content on your network, and automatically connect to devices such as printers and TVs.

13   Select how you want Windows 8.1 to protect and update your computer or device by turning the relevant switches On or Off, and then click **Next**.

14 Select whether you would like to let Windows check online for solutions to problems and whether you want to send different types of information to Microsoft, and then click **Next**.

15 Select whether you want to share information with Microsoft and the different services existing in Windows 8.1, and then click **Next**.

16   Type the password for your Microsoft account and then click **Next**.

17   You are informed that you will need to enter a security code that is used to verify your account.

18 Select how you would like to receive that code: via a text message on your phone, via a phone call, or via email. Then, click **Next**.

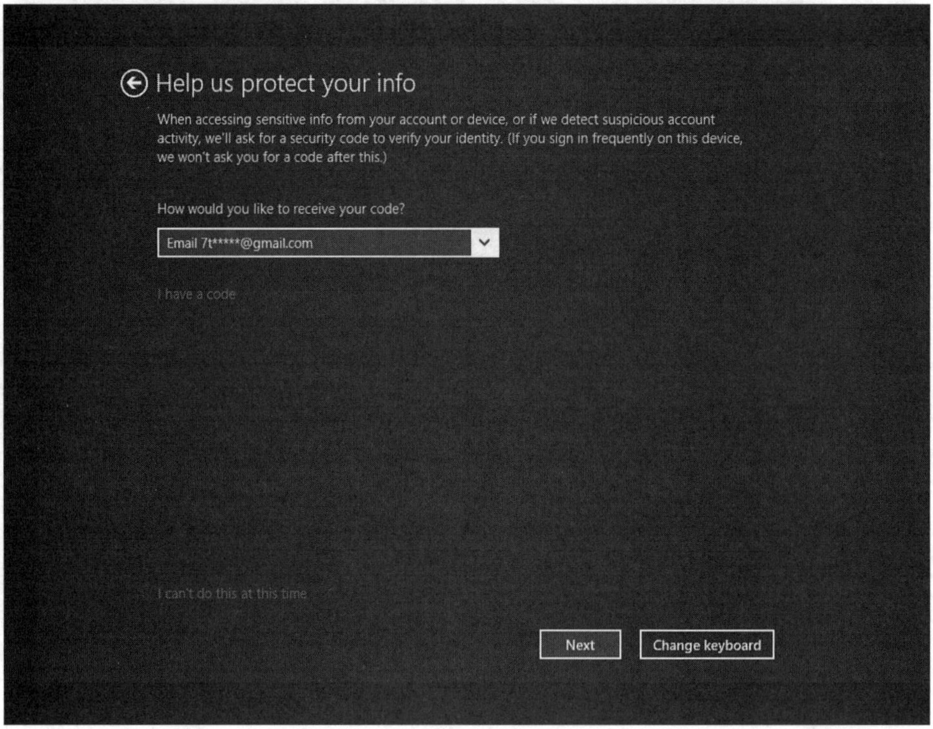

← **Help us protect your info**

When accessing sensitive info from your account or device, or if we detect suspicious account activity, we'll ask for a security code to verify your identity. (If you sign in frequently on this device, we won't ask you for a code after this.)

How would you like to receive your code?

Email 7t*****@gmail.com

I have a code

I can't do this at this time

Next   Change keyboard

19 Enter the security code you just received via the method you selected and then click **Next**.

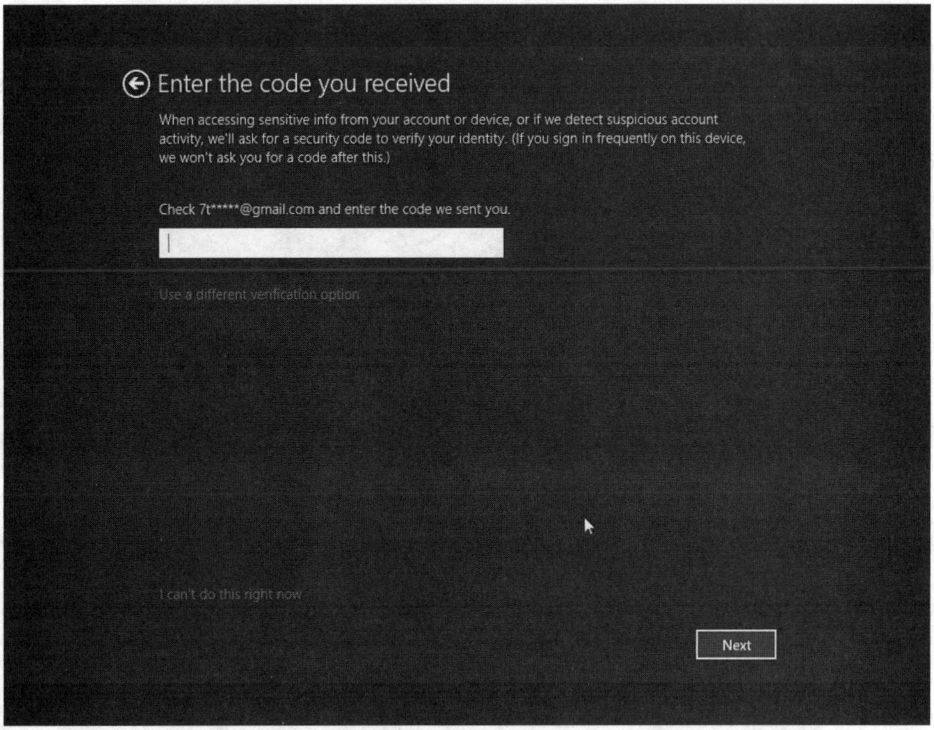
Enter the code you received
When accessing sensitive info from your account or device, or if we detect suspicious account activity, we'll ask for a security code to verify your identity. (If you sign in frequently on this device, we won't ask you for a code after this.)
Check 7t*****@gmail.com and enter the code we sent you.
Use a different verification option
I can't do this right now
Next

20 You are informed about SkyDrive and that it will be used to automatically back up your data, documents, and settings to the cloud.

21 Click **Next** and wait for Windows to finalize the preparations for the first login.

22 While you wait for the preparations to complete, watch the tutorial about how to navigate Windows.

23 You are logged on to Windows 8.1 for the first time.

✖ CLEAN UP
The old Windows 8 installation is stored in the Windows.old folder, on the C drive. To remove it and free up space, it is best to use the Disk Cleanup tool. Press the Clean Up System Files button and select the old Windows installation files.

TIP If you want to learn more about using Disk Cleanup, see the section "Freeing up disk space by using Disk Cleanup" in Chapter 20, "Tips for improving your computing experience."

The upgrade has been performed, and your files, settings, and apps have been migrated to Windows 8.1.

Key points

- Prior to installing Windows 8.1, ensure that you are aware of its system requirements and that you have a valid product key.

- When creating a dual-boot setup with another version of Windows, install Windows 8.1 last.

- You can upgrade to Windows 8.1 from Windows 7, and Windows 8 to Windows 8.1.

- Windows 8 upgrades to Windows 8.1 can also be performed not only through installation media, but also through the Windows Store.

Moving your data and settings to Windows 8.1

D

IN THIS APPENDIX, YOU WILL LEARN HOW TO

- Transfer your data and current settings from an older computer to a new computer running Windows 8.1.

- Use Easy Transfer.

If you bought a new computer or device that's running Windows 8.1, you might be interested in moving your data and settings from your older computer. If you you were running an earlier version of Windows on that computer, you can use one of many tools to do this job.

One of the best available tools is the free Windows Easy Transfer. In a nutshell, you make a backup of your data and settings on your older computer and then restore that backup on your new Windows 8.1 computer or device.

In this appendix, you'll learn how to use Windows Easy Transfer to restore your backed-up data and settings on your new Windows 8.1–based computer or device.

PRACTICE FILES You do not need any practice files for this Appendix. A complete list of practice files is provided in the section "Using the practice files" in the Introduction of this book.

Transferring your data to Windows 8.1 by using Windows Easy Transfer

Windows Easy Transfer is a tool that was first introduced with Windows XP. You can use it to switch files and settings between Windows-based computers or devices. You can use this tool to migrate your files and settings to Windows 8.1 from Windows 7, Windows 8 and Windows RT, or from other Windows 8.1 installations. Unfortunately, backups created on older versions of Windows like Windows XP or Windows Vista are not supported by the version of Windows Easy Transfer existing in Windows 8.1.

If you have upgraded to Windows 8.1 from an earlier version of Windows on the same computer or device, you don't need to use this tool because your data and settings have been migrated.

If you purchased a new computer or device with Windows 8.1 and you want to transfer files and settings from your old computer to the new one, Windows Easy Transfer is the tool for the job. Before you go ahead, there's another important restriction you should keep in mind: if your old computer is using a 64-bit operating system, you will be able to migrate your data and settings only to a 64-bit edition of Windows 8.1. You cannot migrate it to a 32-bit edition.

The tool can transfer items by using an external hard disk or USB flash drive. To use Windows Easy Transfer, you need to log on with a user account that is set as Administrator. Without an administrative account, you cannot start this tool successfully.

First, on the older computer or device, back up your data by using Windows Easy Transfer. This data is stored in a file with the .mig extension (for migration). The file is password protected to prevent unauthorized access.

On the computer or device to which you want to transfer your data, select the same file and type the password you have set.

Before transferring your data to the new computer or device, you can customize the items that will be migrated. By default, Windows Easy Transfer will transfer all the data included in the migration file. If you click Customize, you can select the type of items that you want to transfer.

Clicking Advanced Options gives you even more precise control over the items to be transferred. For example, you can set the storage device to which the data will be migrated.

In this exercise, you'll learn how to migrate your files and settings to Windows 8.1 by using Windows Easy Transfer.

➡ SET UP

On the older computer, back up your data by using Windows Easy Transfer. Then, on your new Windows 8.1 computer or device, log on with a user that has Administrator permissions. Go to the Start screen and type **windows transfer**. Click the Windows Easy Transfer search result to open Windows Easy Transfer. Plug in the external hard disk on which the Windows Easy Transfer backup file is stored.

1   Click **Next.**

You are asked if you have already used Windows Easy Transfer to save your files from your other computer.

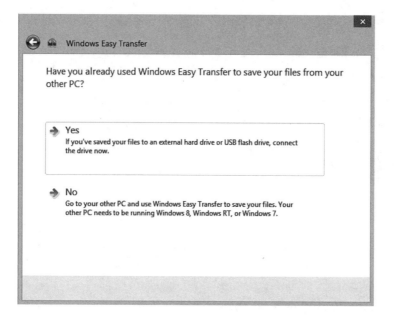

2   Click **Yes**.

The Open An Easy Transfer File window opens, in which you need to select the file where you saved your data from the other computer.

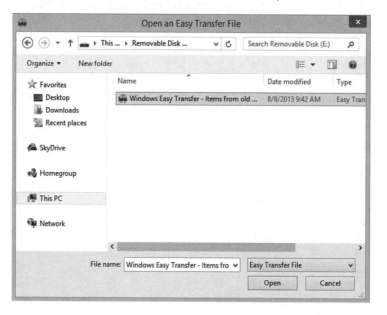

3   Select the appropriate transfer file (with the .mig file extension) and then click **Open**.

You are asked to enter the password you used to protect the transfer file.

4   Type the password and then click **Next**.

You are asked to choose what to transfer to the new computer.

5   Click **Customize** and then clear the items you do not want transferred, if any.

6   Click **Save** and then click **Transfer**. Wait for the transfer to finish.

Windows Easy Transfer informs you that your transfer is complete.

7   Click **Close**.

❌ CLEAN UP

Eject and then unplug the external hard disk drive in which the Windows Easy Transfer data is stored.

The selected data and settings have been transferred to your new Windows 8.1 computer or device.

Key points

- You can use Windows Easy Transfer to transfer data from an older Windows-based computer to your new computer that's running Windows 8.1.

- Before making the transfer, back up your data and settings on the older computer.

- For large transfers, it is best to use an external hard disk.

Glossary

Action Center A feature in Windows 8.1 by which you can view and fix problems and run automated troubleshooters, among other things.

Activation The process you must complete to verify that you have a valid copy of Windows 8.1, which includes a Product ID. You usually activate Windows 8.1 online the first time you turn on your computer or device, but there are other activation options. Activation is mandatory.

Active window The window that is in the foreground and currently in use.

ActiveX control A reusable software component that performs a specific function or set of functions in the Windows operating system, in an app that runs on Windows, or in the Internet Explorer environment.

Address bar In Internet Explorer or any web browser, the area in which you type Internet addresses, also known as URLs (uniform resource locators). Often, an Internet address takes the form of *http://www.companyname.com*.

Administrator account A type of Windows user account with access to all system files and settings and with permission to perform all operations. Every computer must have at least one administrator account. This account type is not recommended for daily use. See also **standard user account**.

App A software program available either on the Start screen or in Apps view, which can be opened by clicking its related tile. More apps can be obtained from the Windows Store. Apps from the Windows Store are created to use the entire screen (or snapped to a portion of it) and are tailored to work well on desktop computers, laptops, tablets, and Windows Phones. Desktop apps, which are also software programs, are typically more complex and perform many functions. Desktop apps open on the desktop. Windows Store apps have fewer features than their desktop counterparts but are more streamlined and often easier to use.

App bar A toolbar (available in almost all apps) that is typically hidden until needed. The app bar holds commands that might enable the user to configure the app, input a location, add an event, delete an item, view properties, and more.

Attachment Data you add to an email, such as a photograph, a short video, a sound recording, a document, or other data. Attachments can be dangerous to open because they can contain viruses.

Autorun file A file that automatically starts an installation app when you insert a disc in a drive or browse to the autorun file in a folder.

Bandwidth The transmission capacity of an electronic communications device or its rate of data transfer, usually expressed in bits per second.

BCC *Blind carbon copy.* If If you want to send an email to someone and you don't want other recipients to know you included that person in the email, add them to the Bcc line. BCC is like a secret copy.

BitLocker Drive Encryption BitLocker combines drive encryption and integrity checking to keep the hard disk from becoming accessed by unauthorized persons. Even if a thief steals the hard disk out of a computer and installs it in another computer, its data cannot be accessed.

Bitmap (.bmp) A patent-free digital image file format. A bitmap image consists of pixels in a grid. Each pixel is a specific color; the colors within the color palette are governed by the specific bitmap format. Common formats include monochrome bitmap, 16-color bitmap, 256-color bitmap, and 24-bit bitmap. The bitmap file format does not support transparency.

Blog Short for *weblog*. An online journal or news/opinion column. Contributors post entries consisting of text, graphics, or video clips. When permitted by the blog owner, readers can post comments responding to the entries or to other people's comments. Blogs are often used to publish personal or company information in an informal way.

Browse Browsing for a file, folder, picture, video, song, or app (among other things) is the process of navigating the operating system's folder structure to locate the desired item. *Browse* also describes the act of surfing the Internet.

Burn A term that describes the process of copying music, video, or data from a computer to a CD or DVD. The term originated because data is actually burned onto this media by using a laser. In many cases, music is burned to CDs because CDs can be played in cars and generic DVD players, and videos are burned to DVDs because videos require much more space and DVDs can be played on DVD players.

Byte A unit of measurement for data; a byte typically represents a single character, such as a letter, digit, or punctuation mark. Some single characters can take up more than one byte.

Central processing unit (CPU) The main circuit chip in a computer. It performs most of the calculations necessary to run the computer. Also called a *processor*.

CC Carbon copy. If you want to send an email to someone and you don't need that person to respond, you can put that person in the CC line. (BCC is a blind carbon copy; other recipients cannot see the BCC field address.)

Charm The default charms are a set of five icons that appear when you swipe inward from the right side of the screen or press Windows key+C. The charms icons are Search, Share, Start, Devices, and Settings. Apps have their own charms, generally available from the app bar found there.

Click The act of pointing to an interface element and then pressing the primary mouse button one time, usually for the purpose of selecting an item or positioning a cursor.

Cloud The cloud is a broad term that represents the Internet, specifically internet servers and data centers where data can be stored and apps can be hosted. A cloud is called a *Public cloud* when the services are rendered over a network that is open for public use. A *personal cloud* is an app of cloud computing for individuals.

Cloud Computing A technology wherein groups of computers are connected through a network for the purpose of accessing and sharing resources that are available off premises. Cloud computing can minimize the cost that companies pay for app management and on-site hosting.

Cloud Storage The ability to save data at an off-site location and to have it managed by a third party. In doing so, companies can save money by outsourcing data storage. Tablet, laptop, and even desktop users can store data in the cloud (rather than on their devices) and on Internet servers to make it accessible from anywhere. Microsoft SkyDrive is an example of cloud storage. You must be able to connect to the Internet to access data stored in the cloud.

Command An instruction you give to a computer app.

Command bar In Internet Explorer, a toolbar located above the Content pane that provides buttons for common tasks associated with the home page, printing, web content display, and safety, as well as tools for managing Internet Explorer.

Compatibility view An Internet Explorer feature that displays a website as though you were using an earlier version of the web browser. Compatibility view was first introduced with Internet Explorer 8.

Compress To reduce the size of a set of data, such as a file or group of files, within a compressed folder that can be stored in less space or transmitted using less bandwidth.

Compressed folder A folder containing a file or files whose contents have been compressed.

Connected Standby A new power management mode for ARM-based versions of Windows 8.1 (often installed on high-end tablet devices) that makes it possible for the device to sleep or hibernate efficiently for long periods of time. Thus, tablets and similar devices can remain turned on when not in use without draining the battery quickly.

Content pane In File Explorer, the pane that displays files and folders stored in the currently selected folder or storage device.

Control Panel The window in which you can change computer settings related to system and maintenance, networks, and the Internet; user accounts; appearance; security; hardware; and sounds, among others. Control Panel opens on the desktop and is not an app.

Cookies Small text files that include data that identify your preferences when you visit particular websites. Cookies are generally harmless and using them makes it possible for websites such as Amazon.com to greet you by name when you navigate there.

Copy A command that you can use to copy data to a virtual clipboard, which is a temporary holding area for data. You generally copy data so that you can paste it somewhere else.

Credentials Information that provides proof of identification that is used to gain access to local and network resources. Examples of credentials are user names and passwords, smart cards, and certificates.

Cursor The point at which text or graphics will be inserted. The cursor usually appears on screen as a blinking vertical line, or "I-beam".

Cut A command you use to remove the selected text, picture, or object and place it on the Clipboard. After it's pasted, the item is deleted from its original location.

Desktop Where desktop apps run; where windows open; where you browse File Explorer; and where you work with desktop apps to write letters, create spreadsheets, manage files and folders, install and uninstall desktop apps, and do everything else you're used to doing on Windows 7, Windows Vista, and other earlier operating systems.

Desktop folder A folder that contains icons that represent what's on your desktop. You can access this folder in File Explorer.

Desktop computer A computer designed for use at one location. A typical desktop computer system includes the computer case containing the actual computer components, a monitor, a keyboard, a mouse, and speakers.

Details pane In File Explorer, the pane that displays details about the selected item.

Dialog box An interface element (similar to a window) that appears on the screen, in which you can make changes to default settings in an app, make decisions when installing apps, set print options for a selected printer, configure sharing options for a file or folder, and perform similar tasks. Unlike a window, a dialog box does not include minimize and maximize buttons and you cannot resize it, but it does offer a Help button.

Digital signature An electronic signature that is composed of a secret code and a private key. Digital signatures are used to help verify file authenticity. Also called a *digital ID*.

Disk Cleanup A desktop app included with Windows 8.1 that offers a safe and effective way to remove unwanted and unnecessary data. You can remove temporary files, downloaded app files, and offline webpages; empty the Recycle Bin; and more, all in a single process.

Disk Defragmenter A desktop app included with Windows 8.1 that improves performance by analyzing the data stored on your hard disk and consolidating files that are not stored contiguously but are instead fragmented in chunks throughout the hard disk. Disk Defragmenter runs automatically on a schedule, so you should (theoretically) never have to invoke it manually.

Domain In Windows: A logical (rather than physical) group of resources—computers, servers, and other hardware devices—on a network, which is centrally administered through a Windows server. On the Internet: A name used as the base of website addresses and email addresses that identifies the entity owning the address.

Domain Name System (DNS) A technology that translates Internet address names into numerical addresses (IP addresses) so that the address can be found over the Internet. For example, if you type **www.microsoft.com** into a web browser, the name is translated into a numerical address and that address is used to connect you to the server hosting the Microsoft website.

Double-click To point to an interface element and press the primary mouse button two times in rapid succession, usually for the purpose of starting an app or opening a window, folder, or file.

Drag To move an item to another location on the screen by pointing to it, holding down the primary mouse button, and then moving the mouse.

Drafts A folder that holds email messages you've started and saved but not yet completed and sent.

Driver A software device driver enables Windows to communicate with a software program or hardware device (such as a printer, mouse, or keyboard) that is attached to your computer. Every device needs a driver for it to work. Many drivers, such as the keyboard driver, are built in to Windows.

Dynamic Host Configuration Protocol (DHCP) server A server that manages a pool of IP addresses and client confirmation parameters and assigns IP addresses to computers and devices on a network.

dynamic-link library (DLL) An operating system feature that allows executable routines (each generally serving a specific function or set of functions) to be stored separately as files with .dll extensions. These routines are loaded only when needed by the app that calls them.

Ethernet A technology that uses Ethernet cables to connect computers to routers and similar hardware for the purposes of transmitting data and connecting multiple computers to form a network.

Executable file A computer file that starts an app, such as a word processor, game, or Windows tool. You can identify executable files by their extension, .exe.

Expansion card A printed circuit board that when inserted into an expansion slot of a computer, provides additional functionality. There are many types of expansion cards, including audio cards, modems, network cards, security device cards, TV tuner cards, video cards, and video processing expansion cards.

Extensible Markup Language (XML) A text markup language, similar to HTML, used to define the structure of data independently of its formatting so that the data can be used for multiple purposes and by multiple apps.

External peripheral A peripheral device installed by connecting it to a port from outside the computer. Examples are a monitor, keyboard, mouse, and speakers.

Favorite A webpage for which you've created a shortcut in Internet Explorer. You can click a favorite instead of typing the web address to visit a website quickly.

Favorites bar In Internet Explorer, a toolbar located below the Address bar that provides buttons for storing web locations for easy future access, obtaining add-ons, and accessing sites that match your browsing history.

Favorites Center In Internet Explorer, a pane with three tabs: Favorites, on which you can save and organize links to websites and webpages; Feeds, on which you can save and organize RSS feeds; and History, on which you can view your browsing history.

Feed An information stream that contains frequently updated content published by a website. Feeds are often associated with news sites and blogs but are also used for distributing other types of digital content, including photos, music, and video. See also ***Really Simple Syndication***.

File A distinct piece of data. A file can be a single Microsoft Word document, a spreadsheet, a song, a movie, a picture, or even a very large single backup.

File Explorer A window in which you can browse all the data stored on your computer and your network. You use File Explorer to access your data libraries, personal and public folders, and networked computers.

File history The backup feature included with Windows 8.1 with which you can perform backups and, in the case of a computer failure, restore the backed-up data.

File name extension Characters appended to the name of a file by the app that created it and separated from the file name by a period. Some file name extensions identify the app that can open the file, such as .xlsx for Microsoft Office Excel 2010 or newer files, and some represent formats that more than one app can work with, such as .jpg graphics files.

Filter To display only items that match specified criteria.

FireWire port FireWire is the brand name given to the IEEE 1394 port by Apple, Inc., one of the patent holders of IEEE 1394 technology.

Flash drive See **USB flash drive**.

Flick To swipe a single finger quickly left, right, up, or down on a touch-enabled computer screen.

Flip A way to move through open windows, open apps, and run apps graphically instead of clicking the item on the desktop or flicking to it. You invoke this by pressing Alt+Tab.

Folder A data unit (similar to a folder in a filing cabinet) that holds files and subfolders. You use folders to organize data. Some folders come with Windows 8.1, including but not limited to Documents, Public Pictures, Videos, Downloads, Contacts, and Favorites.

Form data In Internet Explorer, this is personal data, such as your name and address, that's been saved using the Internet Explorer autocomplete form data functionality. If you don't want forms to be filled out automatically, turn this feature off.

Gesture A movement you make with your finger to perform a task. Flick, swipe, tap, double-tap, and others are considered gestures. See also **multitouch gesture**.

Gigabyte (GB) 1,024 megabytes of data storage; often interpreted as approximately 1 billion bytes.

Glyph An icon that appears on the new Windows 8.1 lock screen. You might see information about the network status, power, unread emails, and so on. You can decide which glyphs appear on the lock screen by using PC Settings.

Graphical user interface (GUI) A user interface that incorporates visual elements such as a desktop, icons, and menus with which you can perform operations by interacting with the visual interface rather than by typing commands.

Graphics Interchange Format (.gif) A digital image file format developed by CompuServe that is used for transmitting raster images on the Internet. An image in this format can contain up to 256 colors, including a transparent color. The size of the file depends on the number of colors used.

Guest account A built-in Windows user account that allows limited use of the computer. When logged on to a computer with the Guest account, a user can't install software or hardware, change settings, or create a password. The Guest account is turned off (unavailable) by default; you can turn it on in the User Accounts window of Control Panel.

Hardware Physical computing devices that are both inside a computer and attached to it externally. Common hardware includes printers, external USB drives, network interface cards, CPUs, RAM, and more.

Hibernate A power option by which the computer is still powered on but is using very little power.

History In Internet Explorer, this is the list of websites you've visited or typed in the address bar. Anyone who has access to your computer or device and to your user account can look at your History list to see where you've been, and often it's advisable to clear your History list if you share a computer and do not have separate user accounts.

HomeGroup A group of computers running Windows 7, Windows 8, and Windows 8.1 that have been configured to form a network. Homegroups make sharing easier because the most common sharing settings are already configured. After a homegroup is set up, you only need the proper operating system, access to the local network, and the homegroup password to join.

Home page The webpage that opens when you open Internet Explorer 11. You can set the home page and configure additional pages to open, as well.

Hosted datacenter A facility that houses and maintains computer systems, apps, resources, and associated components, such as telecommunications and storage systems. Datacenters manage the data stored there with backups, redundant power supplies, environmental controls, and so on. Hosted datacenters are in the cloud, on the Internet.

Hotspot A wireless public network where you can connect to the Internet without being tethered to a network cable. Sometimes access to a wireless hotspot service is free, provided you have the required wireless hardware and are at a location with an open connection. You'll find wireless hotspots in libraries, coffee shops, hotels, bars, and so on.

Hub A device used to connect multiple devices of one type. See also **network hub** and **USB hub**.

Hyperlink A link from a text, graphic, audio, or video element to a target location in the same document, another document, or a webpage.

Hypertext See **hyperlink**.

Hypertext Markup Language (HTML) A text markup language used to create documents for the web. HTML defines the structure and layout of a web document by using a variety of tags and attributes.

Icon A visual representation of a file, folder, app, or other interface elements such as buttons that you can click or double-click as applicable, and which then opens, activates, or executes the item that the icon represents. *Icon* is a term generally associated with the desktop and items you find in folders, whereas **tile** is a term generally used to represent the items available on the Start screen.

Information technology (IT) The development, installation, and implementation of computer systems and apps.

InPrivate Browsing A browsing mode that opens a separate Internet Explorer window in which the places you visit are not tracked. The pages and sites do not appear on the History tab, and temporary files and cookies are not saved on your computer.

Input device A piece of hardware with which you type, select, open, or otherwise interact with the computer. Common input devices include the mouse and keyboard. However, your finger can be an input device, and there are several specialty input devices for people with disabilities.

Interface What you see on the screen when working on a computer. In the WordPad interface, you see the ribbon, tabs, and the page itself, for instance.

Internal peripheral A device installed inside the computer's case, such as an expansion card, a hard disk, or a DVD drive. See also **external peripheral** and **peripheral device**.

Internet Explorer 11 The newest version of the Microsoft web browser. It's available as both a Windows Store–style app and a desktop app.

Internet Message Access Protocol (IMAP) A method computers use to send and receive email messages. Using this protocol, you can access email without downloading it to your computer.

Internet Protocol (IP) address An address that identifies a computer that is connected to the Internet or to a network. There are two types of IP addresses: IP version 4 (IPv4) and IP version 6 (IPv6). An IPv4 address usually consists of four groups of numbers separated by periods, such as 192.200.44.69. An IPv6 address has eight groups of hexadecimal characters (the numbers 0 through 9 and the letters a through f) separated by colons—for example, 3ffe:ffff:0000:2f3b: 02aa:00ff:fe28.1:9c5a.

Internet server A computer that stores data offsite, such as one that might store your email before you download it or hold backups you store in the cloud. Through Internet servers, you can access information from any computer that can access the Internet.

Internet service provider (ISP) A company that provides Internet access to individuals or companies. An ISP provides the connection information necessary for users to access the Internet through the ISP's computers. An ISP typically charges a monthly or hourly connection fee.

JPEG (.jpg) file format A digital image file format designed for compressing either full-color or gray-scale still images. It works well on photographs, naturalistic artwork, and similar material. Images saved in this format have .jpg or .jpeg file extensions.

Jump list An efficient method of accessing the features and files you are most likely to use with a desktop app. Right-clicking an app icon on the taskbar might offer quick access to recently opened files.

Kbps Kilobits per second; a unit of data transfer equal to 1,000 bits per second or 125 bytes per second.

Keyword A word or phrase assigned to a file or webpage so that it can be located in searches for that word or phrase.

Kilobyte (KB) 1,024 bytes of data storage. In reference to data transfer rates, 1,000 bytes.

Laptop An outdated term for a portable computer, referring to the fact that portable computers are small enough to set on your lap. See also **netbook**, **notebook**, and **portable computer**.

Library A virtual data unit that previously offered access to both the related private and public folders. As an example, the Documents library offered access to the Documents and Public Documents folders, and the data was grouped to appear as a unit. In Windows 8.1, libraries only represent what is available in the related personal folder and no longer offer access to what is in the related Public folder. You can create your own libraries.

Link A shortcut to a webpage. It might be contained in an email, document, or webpage and offers access to a site without actually typing the site's name.

Local area network (LAN) A computer network covering a small physical area such as a home or office, with a central connection point such as a network router and a shared Internet connection.

Local printer A printer that is directly connected to one of the ports on a computer. See also **remote printer**.

Lock To make your Windows computing session unavailable to other people. Locking is most effective when your user account is protected by a password.

Lock screen The Windows 8.1 welcome screen, which appears when the computer first starts. It features the time, date, and a series of notification glyphs; the screen can be personalized with your own background picture and the glyphs shown.

Log off To stop your computing session without affecting other users' sessions.

Log on To start a computing session.

Magnifier A tool in the Ease of Access suite of apps. You use Magnifier to increase the size of the information shown on the screen; three options are available for doing so. By default, you use your mouse to enlarge what's under it, and you can choose to what degree the material is magnified.

Mail server A computer that your ISP configures to transmit email. It often includes a POP3 incoming mail server and an SMTP outgoing mail server. You'll need to know the names of these servers if you use an ISP to configure Microsoft Mail. Often, the server names look similar to *pop.yourisp-namehere.com* and *smtp.yourispnamehere.com*.

Malware Malicious software. Malware includes viruses, worms, spyware, and so on.

Mbps Megabits per second; a unit of data transfer equal to 1,000 Kbps (kilobits per second).

Media Materials on which data is recorded or stored, such as CDs, DVDs, floppy disks, or USB flash drives.

Megabyte (MB) 1,024 kilobytes or 1,048.1,576 bytes of data storage; often interpreted as approximately 1 million bytes. In reference to data transfer rates, 1,000 kilobytes.

Menu A title on a menu bar (such as File, Edit, View). Clicking a menu name opens a drop-down list with additional choices (Open, Save, Print). Menus are being phased out by the ribbon in many apps, including those included with Windows 8.1, such as WordPad and Paint, among others.

Menu bar A toolbar on which you can access menus of commands.

Metadata Descriptive information, including keywords and properties, about a file or webpage. Title, subject, author, and size are examples of a file's metadata.

Microsoft account A sign in option by which you can synchronize settings and other data across computers, laptops, and other devices, which are applied when you log on by using the account. You need to be connected to the Internet when logging in for this to work effectively.

MiFi A term for wireless routers that act as mobile Wi-Fi hotspots. A MiFi device can be connected to a mobile phone carrier and provide Internet access for up to ten devices.

Modem A device through which computer information can be transmitted and received over a telephone line or through a broadband service.

Multimonitor A term used when more than one monitor is configured on a Windows computer. There are multimonitor capabilities that are new to Windows 8.1, for both the Start screen and the classic Windows desktop.

Multitouch gestures Gestures that require two (or more) fingers to perform, such as pinching the computer screen to zoom in and out.

Narrator A basic screen reader included with Windows 8.1 and part of the Ease of Access suite of apps. This app reads aloud text that appears on the screen while you navigate using the keyboard and mouse.

Navigate A term used to describe surfing the Internet by browsing webpages. It is the process of moving from one webpage to another or viewing items on a single webpage. You can also navigate the data on your computer by using File Explorer.

Navigation pane In Windows Explorer, the left pane of a folder window. It displays favorite links, access to SkyDrive, access to your HomeGroup, My PC, and an expandable list of storage devices and folders.

NET Passport See **Windows Live ID** or **Microsoft account**.

Netbook A small, lightweight portable computer designed primarily for web browsing and simple computing. Most netbooks have limited internal resources and a screen size of less than 11 inches.

Network A group of computers, printers, and other devices that communicate wirelessly or through wired connections, often for the purpose of sharing both data and physical resources (such as printers). Networks often contain routers, cable modems, hubs, switches, or similar hardware to connect the computers and offer them all access to the Internet.

Network adapter A piece of hardware that connects your computer to a network such as the Internet or a local network. Network adapters can offer wired capabilities, wireless capabilities, or both.

Network And Sharing Center A place in Windows 8.1 where you can view your basic network information and set up connections. You can also diagnose problems here, change adapter settings, and change advanced sharing settings.

Network discovery A feature that you must turn on so that computers can find other computers on the network. When connected to public networks, this feature is turned off by default.

Network domain A network whose security and settings are centrally administered through a Windows server computer and user accounts.

Network drive A shared folder or storage device on your network to which you assign a drive letter so that it appears in the My PC window as a named drive.

Network hub A device that connects computers on a network. The computers are connected to the hub with cables. The hub sends information received from one computer to all other computers on the network.

Network printer A printer that is connected directly to a network through a wired or wireless network connection or through a print server or printer hub.

Network profile Information about a specific network connection, such as the network name, type, and settings.

Network router A hardware device connecting computers on a network or connecting multiple networks (for example, connecting a LAN to an ISP).

Network share A shared folder on a computer on your network (not your local computer).

Newsgroup An online forum in which people participate (anonymously or not) to share ideas and opinions, get help, and meet other people with interests similar to theirs.

Notebook A standard portable computer designed for all types of computing. Notebooks have technical specifications that are comparable to those of desktop computers. Most notebooks have a screen size ranging from 11 to 17 inches.

Notification area The area at the right end of the Windows taskbar. It contains shortcuts to running apps and important status information.

Office 365 A product and services bundle from Microsoft that includes Microsoft Online Services as well as domain administration tools, additional account storage space, and increased vendor support.

Online Connected to a network or to the Internet. Also used to describe time that you will be working on your computer.

On-Screen Keyboard A feature that is available as part of Windows 8.1 with which you can input text and interact with the computer by using a virtual keyboard.

Operating system The underlying software instructions that direct your computer what to do and how to do it. The operating system coordinates interactions among the computer system components, acts as the interface between you and your computer, makes communication possible between your computer and other computers and peripheral devices, and interacts with apps installed on your computer.

Option One of a group of mutually exclusive values for a setting, usually in a dialog box.

Option button A standard Windows control that you use to select one from a set of options.

Original equipment manufacturer (OEM) A company that assembles a computer from components, brands the computer, and then sells the computer to the public. The OEM might also preinstall an operating system and other software on the computer.

Partition A hard disk has a certain amount of space to store data. That can be 120 GB, 500 GB, 1 TB or more. Sometimes, people or computer manufacturers separate this space into two or three distinct spaces called partitions (or drives or volumes). The purpose is to separate system files, data files, and app files, among other reasons. Windows 8.1 creates a small partition at the beginning of the hard disk to hold files needed to repair the computer if something goes wrong.

Password A security feature by which the user is required to input a personal password to access the computer, specific files, websites, and other data.

Password hint An entry you record when you create or change your password to remind you what the password is. Windows displays the password hint if you enter an incorrect password.

Password reset disk A file you create on a flash drive or other compatible media so that you can reset your password if you forget it.

Path A sequence of names of drives, directories, or folders, separated by backslashes (\), that leads to a specific file or folder.

Paste A command that enables you to place previously copied or cut data in a new location. You can cut, copy, and paste a single word, sentence, paragraph, or page; a file; a folder; a web link; and more.

PC Settings A user-friendly, graphical version of Control Panel that offers access to the most-configured settings, including changing the picture on the lock screen, adding users, viewing installed devices, and configuring Windows Update.

Peek To see what's on the desktop behind currently active windows and apps. To use Peek, you position your mouse in the lower-right corner. Peek must be turned on to work.

Peer-to-peer A network, such as a workgroup, in which computers and resources are connected directly and are not centrally managed by a server.

Peripheral device A device, such as a hard disk, printer, modem, or joystick, that is connected to a computer and is controlled by the computer's microprocessor but is not necessary to the computer's operation. See also **external peripheral** and **internal peripheral**.

Permissions Rules associated with a shared resource such as a folder, file, or printer that define who can use it and what users can do after they have access to it. You can set permissions to allow a user to print to a printer only during certain hours, for instance.

Personal folder In Windows, a storage folder created by Windows for each user account and containing subfolders and information that is specific to the user profile, such as Documents and Pictures. The personal folder is labeled with the name used to log on to the computer.

Phishing A hacking technique to entice you to divulge personal information such as bank account numbers. Internet Explorer 11 has a phishing filter to warn you of potential phishing websites.

Picture password A method of logging on to Windows 8.1. Instead of typing a password or PIN, you can use a series of touch gestures on a particular part of an image that you select.

PIN password A method of logging on to Windows 8.1. The PIN is similar to what you type in an ATM machine and is a four-digit numeric password.

Pinned taskbar button A button representing an app, which appears permanently at the left end of the taskbar. A button that is not pinned appears on the taskbar only when its app is running.

Pinning Attaching an app, folder, or file shortcut to a user interface element such as the taskbar or Start screen.

Playlist A collection of songs that you can save and then listen to as a group. You can also burn a playlist to a CD, copy a playlist to a portable music player, and more.

Plug and play A technology by which the computer can automatically discover and configure settings for a device connected to the computer through a USB or IEEE 1394 connection.

Podcast An online audio or video broadcast. Podcasts are generally free and can be synchronized to many types of portable music devices.

Pointer The onscreen image that moves around the screen in conjunction with movements of the mouse. Depending on the current action, the pointer might resemble an arrow, a hand, an I-beam, or another shape.

Pointing device A device such as a mouse that controls a pointer with which you can interact with items displayed on the screen.

POP3 A standard method that computers use to send and receive email messages. POP3 messages are typically held on an email server until you download them to your computer, and then they are deleted from the server. With other email protocols, such as IMAP, email messages are held on the server until you delete them.

Pop-up window (pop-up) A small web browser window that opens on top of (or sometimes below) the web browser window when you display a website or click an advertising link.

Port An interface through which data is transferred between a computer and other devices, a network, or a direct connection to another computer.

Portable computer A computer, such as a notebook, laptop, or netbook, with a built-in monitor, keyboard, and pointing device, designed to be used in multiple locations.

Portable Network Graphic (.png) A digital image file format that uses lossless compression (compression that doesn't lose data) and was created as a patent-free alternative to the .gif file format.

Power plan A group of settings that specify when and whether to turn off the computer monitor or display and when or whether to put the computer to sleep. You can create your own power plan if desired.

Preview pane In File Explorer, a pane used to show a preview of a file selected in the Content pane. See also **Content pane**, **Details pane**, and **Navigation pane**.

Primary display In a multimonitor system, the monitor is specifically configured to be the main display. Most app windows appear on the primary display when they first open. See also **secondary display**.

Product key A unique registration code issued by the manufacturer of a desktop app. The key must be supplied during the setup process to verify that you have a valid license to install and use the app.

Progress ring The Windows 8.1 progress indicator that informs the user that a task is in progress.

Public folder Folders from which you can easily share data with other users. Anyone with an account on the computer can access the data here.

Quick Access toolbar The small, thin toolbar that appears across the top of the ribbon in many apps on which you can quickly access common commands (such as Save). You can personalize this toolbar by adding your most-used commands and by repositioning it below the ribbon if desired.

RAM *Random access memory.* This is the hardware inside your computer that temporarily stores data the operating system or apps are using. Theoretically, the more RAM you have, the faster your computer will run. Temporary data can include a document you have written but not saved and have subsequently sent to the printer, or calculations required when resizing or otherwise editing a photo.

ReadyBoost A technology with which you can improve the performance of your computer by adding additional paging file space. ReadyBoost increases performance in a way that is similar to adding internal RAM, but ReadyBoost is not RAM. Often, you use an external USB flash drive for this.

Really Simple Syndication (RSS) A method of distributing information from a website or blog to subscribers for display in an RSS reader or aggregator.

Recycle Bin The Recycle Bin holds deleted files until you manually empty it. The Recycle Bin is a safeguard that makes it possible for you to recover items you've accidentally deleted or items you thought you no longer wanted but later decide you need. Note that after you empty the Recycle Bin, the items that were in it are gone forever.

Refresh Your PC This is a service in Windows 8.1 that, when invoked, automatically backs up all your photos, music, videos, and other personal files, reinstalls new operating system files on your computer, and then puts your data back on it for you. It also backs up and restores your customizations, changes you've made to apps, and more. By using Refresh Your PC, you can completely reinstall Windows and then easily put your data back on your computer.

Registry A repository for information about the computer's configuration. The registry stores settings related to the hardware and software installed on the computer. Registry settings are typically updated through the proper install and uninstall procedures and apps.

Relative path A path that defines the position of a file or folder in relation to the current location. For example, ..\Images\Picture.png defines a path up one level to the parent folder of the current location, down one level into the Images folder, to the Picture image. Relative paths are frequently used in website navigational code.

Remote Desktop Connection An app included in Windows 8.1 by which you can access your computer from somewhere else, such as an office or hotel room.

Remote printer A printer that is not connected directly to your computer.

Reset Your PC A service in Windows 8.1 that reverts your computer to its factory settings. It does this by wiping all the data from it and reinstalling Windows, after which the computer will appear as it did the first time you turned it on, right out of the box.

Resolution The measure of how many pixels are shown on a computer screen. A pixel is a very small square unit of display. Choosing 1024 × 768 pixels means that the desktop displays by using 1024 pixels across and 768 pixels down. When you increase the resolution, you increase the number of pixels on the screen, making images sharper yet smaller on the screen.

Restore point A snapshot of your computer system settings taken by Windows at a scheduled time as well as before any major change, such as installing an app or updating system files. If you experience problems with your system, you can restore it to any saved restore point without undoing changes to your personal files. You use System Restore to do this.

Ribbon A feature that appeared in Microsoft Office apps a few years ago and is now part of the Windows 8.1 graphical user interface. The ribbon is made up of tabs that, when selected, present a related set of tools and features. The ribbon replaces the older menu bar, menus, and drop-down menu lists.

Right-click To point to an interface element and press the secondary (right) mouse button one time.

Rip A term that describes the process of copying files from a physical CD to your hard disk. Generally, the term is used to describe the process of copying music CDs to the music library on your computer.

Router A piece of equipment that connects two dissimilar networks and sends data from computer to computer on a LAN. A router directs the data to the correct computer and rejects data that is deemed harmful.

Screen resolution The fineness or coarseness of detail attained by a monitor in producing an image, measured in pixels, expressed as the number of pixels wide by the number of pixels high; for example, 1024 × 768.

ScreenTip Information that appears when you point to an item.

Scroll bar A scroll bar appears when the content that is available to show on the screen is more than can be viewed on it. You'll see a scroll bar on the Start screen, on webpages, in long documents, and in other places.

Scroll up and scroll down A process of using the mouse, the arrow keys on a keyboard, or a flick of your finger to scroll when a scroll bar is available.

Search A Windows 8.1 feature that that you can use to look for apps, settings, files, emails, and more. You can access Search by clicking its charm (swipe inward from the right edge of the screen or press Windows key+C), or, on the Start screen, you can simply type a description of the item for which you're searching.

Search provider A company that provides a search engine, which you can use to find information on the Internet.

Search term The term you type in the Search box of the Start menu or any folder window. Windows then filters the contents of the available storage locations or of the folder window's Content pane to include only the items that contain the search term.

Secondary display In a multimonitor system, the monitor onto which you can expand apps so that you can increase your work area. See also **primary display**.

Secondary tile A special kind of Start screen tile that is created from within an app that is capable of producing one. For example, a contacts app can have its own tile, but you can also create a tile for your favorite contact on the Start screen.

Semantic zoom The technical term for the technology by which you can pinch with two fingers to zoom in and out of the screen.

Shared component A component, such as a DLL file, that is used by multiple apps. When uninstalling an app that uses a shared component, Windows requests confirmation before removing the component.

Shared drive A storage device that has been made available for other people on a network to access.

Shared folder A folder that has been made available for other people on a network to access.

Shared printer A printer connected to a computer and made available from that computer for use by other computers on a network.

Share A charm with which you can share information in one app with another app and, possibly, with other people (by Mail, for instance). This charm can also make local files or resources available to other users of the same computer or other computers on a network. You can also share items manually, such as printers and folders.

Shortcut An icon with an arrow on it that offers access to a particular item on the hard disk. You can put shortcuts on your desktop, for instance, that when double-clicked open apps, files, and folders stored in places other than the desktop.

Shortcut menu A menu displayed when you right-click an object, showing a list of commands relevant to that object.

Shut down To initiate the process that closes all your open apps and files, ends your computing session, closes network connections, stops system processes, stops the hard disk, and turns off the computer.

Shut down options Ways in which you can disconnect from the current computing session. You can shut down the computer, switch to a different user account, log off from the computer, lock the computer, restart the computer, or put the computer into Sleep mode or Hibernate mode.

Simple Mail Transfer Protocol (SMTP) A protocol for sending messages from one computer to another on a network. This protocol is used on the Internet to route email.

SkyDrive A location in the cloud offered by Microsoft where you can store data, including documents and pictures, among other things. Data is saved on Internet servers, and you can access the data from any Internet-enabled, compatible device.

SmartScreen A Windows 8.1 security technology that prevents malware from infecting your system.

Snap The process by which you can display two to four apps side by side in Windows 8.1. This makes it possible for you to work with multiple apps at one time.

Snipping tool A feature in Windows 8.1 by which you can drag your pointer around any area on the screen to copy and capture it. You can then save the captured data to edit it or attach it to an email or embed it in a Word document. The Snipping Tool is a desktop app.

Software Apps that you use to do things with hardware, such as print to a printer. Software also refers to operating systems, desktop applications, apps, device drivers, and other computer programs that enable communications between the user and the computer hardware, most often to perform tasks.

Software piracy The illegal reproduction and distribution of software apps.

Sound recorder A tool included with Windows 8.1 that offers three options: Start Recording, Stop Recording, and Resume Recording. You can save recorded clips for use with other apps.

Spam Unwanted email; junk email.

Speech Recognition An app included with Windows 8.1 by which you control your computer with your voice. Speech Recognition provides a wizard to help you set up your microphone and use the app.

Spyware Software that can display advertisements (such as pop-up ads), collect information about you, or change settings on your computer, generally without appropriately obtaining your consent.

Standard toolbar A toolbar that is often underneath a menu bar in apps that do not offer a ribbon, which contains icons or pictures of common commands. You might already be familiar with the graphic icons for Save, Print, Cut, Copy, Paste, Undo, and others. These toolbars are being phased out and are being replaced by the ribbon.

Standard user account A type of Windows user account that allows the user to install software and change system settings that do not affect other users or the security of the computer. This account type is recommended for daily use.

Start button A button now available in the lower-right corner that, when clicked, takes you to the Start screen. You can right-click this button to access a shortcut menu that offers shut down options, access to Control Panel, and more.

Start screen The Windows 8.1 graphical user experience that offers access to Windows Store–style and desktop apps, the desktop itself, and more. You can type while on the Start screen to locate something on it or elsewhere on your computer.

Status bar A toolbar that often appears at the bottom of an app window (such as the desktop version of Internet Explorer 11) and offers information about what is happening at the moment.

Sticky Keys A setting by which you can configure the keyboard so that you never have to press three keys at once (such as when you must press the Ctrl, Alt, and Delete keys together to access Task Manager).

Store See **Windows Store**.

Subfolder A folder within another folder. You often create subfolders to further organize data that is stored in folders.

Sync To compare data in one location to the data in another. Synchronizing is the act of performing the tasks required to match up the data. When data is synchronized, the data in both places matches.

System cache An area in the computer memory where Windows stores information it might need to access quickly for the duration of the current computing session.

System disk The hard disk on which the operating system is installed.

System folder A folder created on the system hard disk that contains files required by the Windows operating system.

System Restore If turned on, this features creates and stores restore points on your computer or device's hard disk. If something goes wrong, you can run System Restore and revert to a pre-problem date by selecting the desired point in time. System Restore deals with system data only, so none of your personal data will be changed when you run it.

Tab In a dialog box, tabs indicate separate pages of settings within the dialog box window; the tab title indicates the nature of the group. You can display the settings by clicking the tab. In Internet Explorer, when tabbed browsing is turned on, tabs indicate separate webpages displayed within one browser window. You can display a page by clicking its tab or display a shortcut menu of options for working with a page by right-clicking its tab.

Tabbed browsing An Internet Explorer feature with which you can open and view multiple webpages or files by displaying them on different tabs. You can easily switch among pages or files by clicking the tabs.

Tags Metadata included with a file, such as the date a photo was taken or the artist who sang a particular song. You can create your own tags in compatible apps and then sort data by using those tags.

Tap (Touch) A gesture you perform with your finger or a pen or stylus. A tap or touch is often the equivalent of a single click with a mouse.

Taskbar The bar that runs horizontally across the bottom of the Windows 8.1 desktop. It contains icons for running apps, File Explorer, and Internet Explorer, and offers the Notification area, among other things. You can access open files, folders, and apps from the taskbar, too.

Taskbar button A button on the taskbar representing an open window, file, or app. See also **pinned taskbar button**.

Task Manager A way to access, manage, stop, or start running apps, processes, and services. You often use Task Manager to close something that has stopped working and is unresponsive, such as an app or process.

Theme A set of visual elements and sounds that applies a unified look to the computer user interface. A theme can include a desktop background, screen saver, window colors, and sounds. Some themes might also include icons and mouse pointers.

This PC An entry in the Navigation pane of File Explorer that offers access to installed hard disks, CD and DVD drives, connected external drives, network locations (drives), network media servers, and similar connected media and locations.

Tiles Graphical user interface elements on the Windows 8.1 Start screen. Some can offer live information, such as the news headlines or the number of unread emails. Tiles are said to be pinned to the Start screen.

Title bar The horizontal area at the top of a window that displays the title of the app or file displayed in the window as well as buttons for controlling the display of the window.

Toolbar A horizontal or vertical bar that displays buttons representing commands that you can use with the content of the current window. When more commands are available than can fit on the toolbar, a chevron (>>) appears at the right end of the toolbar; clicking the chevron displays the additional commands.

Transition A segue you can configure to appear when moving from one picture to another in a slide show, such as fading in or out. Transitions can be applied in other places, too, such as in Microsoft PowerPoint presentations.

Uniform Resource Locator (URL) An address that uniquely identifies the location of a website or webpage. A URL is usually preceded by http://, as in http://www.microsoft.com. URLs are used by web browsers to locate Internet resources.

Universal Naming Convention (UNC) A system for identifying the location on a network of shared resources such as computers, drives, and folders. A UNC address is in the form of \\ComputerName\SharedFolder.

Universal Serial Bus (USB) A connection that provides data transfer capabilities and power to a peripheral device. See also **USB hub** and **USB port**.

Upgrade To replace older hardware with newer hardware or an earlier version of an app with the current version.

USB flash drive A portable flash memory device that plugs into a computer's USB port. You can store data on a USB flash drive or, if the USB flash drive supports ReadyBoost, use all or part of the available drive space to increase the operating system speed. See also **ReadyBoost**.

USB hub A device used to connect multiple USB devices to a single USB port or to connect one or more USB devices to USB ports on multiple computers. The latter type of USB hub, called a sharing hub, operates as a switch box to give control of the hub-connected devices to one computer at a time.

USB port A connection that provides both power and data transfer capabilities to a hardware device.

User account On a Windows computer, a uniquely named account that allows an individual to gain access to the system and to specific resources and settings. Each user account includes a collection of information that describes the way the computer environment looks and operates for that particular user as well as a private folder not accessible by other people using the computer, in which you can store personal documents, pictures, media, and other files. See also **administrator account** and **standard user account**.

User Account Control (UAC) A Windows security feature that allows or restricts actions by the user and the system to prevent malicious apps from damaging the computer.

User account name A unique name identifying a user account to Windows.

User account picture An image representing a user account. You'll see this picture on the log in screen and at the top of the Start screen, among other places.

User interface (UI) The portion of an app with which a user interacts. Types of user interfaces include command-line interfaces, menu-driven interfaces, and graphical user interfaces.

Virtual A software system that acts as if it were a hardware system. Examples are virtual folders (called libraries) and virtual printers.

Virtual printer An app that "prints" content to a file rather than on paper. When viewed in the file, the content looks as it would if it were printed.

Virus A self-replicating app that infects computers with intent to do harm. Viruses can come as an attachment in an email, from a USB stick, from a macro in an Office app, through a network connection, and even in instant messages, among other places.

Wallpaper The picture that appears on the desktop. Windows 8.1 comes with several options, but you can use your own picture(s) or graphics if desired.

Web An abbreviated way to say *World Wide Web*. A worldwide network consisting of millions of smaller networks that exchange data.

Web browser An app that displays webpage content and makes it possible for you to interact with webpage content and navigate the Internet. Internet Explorer is a web browser.

Webcam A camera that can send live images over the Internet. Windows 8.1 comes with a camera app that should be able to find and use your camera without any setup.

Website A webpage or a group of webpages that contain related information. The Microsoft website contains information about Microsoft products, for instance.

Wi-Fi A technology by which an electronic device can exchange data or connect to the Internet wirelessly using radio waves. Public hotspots often offer free Wi-Fi connections to the Internet.

Window Desktop apps open a window of their own. Window, as it is used here, has nothing to do with the name of the operating system Windows 8.1; it is a generic term. Windows have minimize, restore, and maximize buttons so that you can resize them.

Windows Defender A built-in tool that provides antivirus and antimalware functionality.

Windows Live ID An older term for an email address, registered with the Windows Live ID authentication service, that identifies you to sites and services that use Windows Live ID authentication. This has been replaced with the Microsoft account.

Windows Firewall If turned on, the firewall should lessen the ability of unauthorized users to access your computer or device and its data. The firewall blocks the apps that can be a threat. You can allow apps through the firewall or create exceptions if the need arises.

Windows Media Center A full-fledged media and media management desktop app. You can view and manage photos, music, videos, and even television here. This is not included with Windows 8.1 by default; it is an add-on.

Windows Store The Microsoft online store for Windows 8.1 apps. There is also an XBox Music store and an XBox Video store.

Windows To Go A way to run Windows 8.1 from a USB key rather than from a traditional hard disk. This makes it possible for you to take Windows anywhere.

Windows Update When set to use the recommended settings, Windows 8.1 checks for security updates automatically and installs them. You can choose which optional updates to install.

Wizard A tool that walks you through the steps necessary to accomplish a particular task.

Workgroup A peer-to-peer computer network through which computers can share resources, such as files, printers, and Internet connections.

XML Paper Specification (XPS) A digital file format for saving documents. XPS is based on XML, preserves document formatting, and enables file sharing. XPS was developed by Microsoft but is platform-independent and royalty-free.

Index

Symbols

+ (plus) sign
  adjacent to songs, 101
  with wrench icon, 167

A

.aac file extension, 130
accessible, making computer
  about, 499
  locating Ease of Access options, 500–501
  logging on to Windows without password, 516–517
  on touch-enabled devices, 558
  using Magnifier, 504–507
  using Narrator, 507–509
  using On-Screen Keyboard, 509–513
  using Windows Speech Recognition, 513–514
  Windows suggesting Ease of Access options, 502–504
accessories and tools
  Control Panel, 117
  exploring from Start screen, 116–117
  paint tools, 116
  snipping tool, 116
Access Performance Monitor, troubleshooting using, 642
Access Resource Monitor, troubleshooting using, 643
access to current location, app asking for, 258
Account picture section, 362
Accounts category option, in PC Settings, 49
Action Center
  checking for solutions from, 621
  color coding of messages, 471
  configuring messages, 471–472
  definition of, 735

  flag icon, 30, 468
  using, 467–470
activating Windows 8.1, 690
activation code (product key), for installing Windows 8.1, 671, 675
activation, definition of, 735
active window, definition of, 735
ActiveX control, definition of, 735
ad blockers, considering commercial solutions for, 441–442
Add A Message event field, in Calendar app, 236
Add an account option, 226
Add A Title event field, in Calendar app, 236
Add A User page, 342–343
Add Favorite icon, in Map app, 108
Add files button, in SkyDrive app, 193
Address bar
  accessing Paste And Go option, 168
  definition of, 735
  on toolbar desktop Internet Explorer app, 170
  on toolbar Internet Explorer app, 163–166
Add to favorites button, 172
Add Your Outlook Account window, 215
administrative tools, troubleshooting difficult-to-diagnose problems using, 640, 643
Administrator account
  about, 334–335
  changing from standard to, 367–368
  definition of, 735
administrator permissions
  removing quarantined files in Windows Defender, 437
  setting firewall exceptions, 419
  UAC and, 412–414
administrator privileges, running apps with, 116
Administrator, running desktop apps as, 574–575
Adobe Flash Player, in Internet Explorer 8.1, 158

N

R

S

About the authors

CIPRIAN ADRIAN RUSEN is a technology aficionado and former IT project manager for a major consumer goods corporation. In his spare time, he likes to experiment with the latest technologies, learning how to use them and sharing his knowledge with others. He coordinates the team of bloggers at 7 Tutorials, writing tutorials for Windows users and helping them achieve the best possible computing experience. He is the author or co-author for several Microsoft Press books, including *Microsoft Office Professional 2013 Step by Step* and *Network Your Computers and Devices Step by Step*.

JOLI BALLEW is a Microsoft MVP for Windows and holds many Microsoft certifications, including MCSE, MCTS, MCDST, and MCT. She is an award-winning, best-selling technical author of over 50 books. Joli has been working with computers, gadgets, and all things media since her freshman year in college in 1982, where, even then, she was aware of her interests and strengths and majored in computer science and systems analysis. Joli is the Microsoft IT Academic Coordinator at Brookhaven College in Dallas, Texas, where she also teaches. Among the many titles Joli has written for Microsoft Press, she is the co-author of *MCTS Self-Paced Training Kit (Exam 70-632): Managing Projects with Microsoft Office Project 2007* and *Windows 8.1 Plain & Simple*.

Now that you've read the book...

Tell us what you think!

Was it useful?
Did it teach you what you wanted to learn?
Was there room for improvement?

Let us know at http://aka.ms/tellpress

Your feedback goes directly to the staff at Microsoft Press,
and we read every one of your responses. Thanks in advance!

Microsoft

How to download your ebook

To download your eBook, go to http://aka.ms/PressEbook and follow the instructions.

Please note: You will be asked to create a free online account and enter the access code below.

ACCESS CODE:

> ## MGNXPNM

Windows 8.1 Step by Step

Your PDF eBook allows you to:

- search the full text
- print
- copy and paste

Best yet, you will be notified about free updates to your eBook.

If you ever lose your eBook file, you can download it again just by logging in to your account.

Need help? Please contact:
mspinput@microsoft.com